Critical Essays on
Stephen Crane's
The Red Badge of Courage

Critical Essays on
Stephen Crane's
The Red Badge of Courage

Donald Pizer

G. K. Hall & Co. • Boston, Massachusetts

First published 1990.
10 9 8 7 6 5 4 3 2 1

Library of Congress Cataloging-in-Publication Data

Critical essays on Stephen Crane's The Red Badge of Courage /
    [edited by] Donald Pizer.
        p.   cm.—(Critical essays on American literature)
    ISBN 0-8161-8898-X (alk. paper)
    1. Crane, Stephen, 1871-1900. Red badge of courage. 2. United
States—History—Civil War, 1861-1865—Literature and the war.
I. Pizer, Donald. II. Series.
    PS1449.C85R3924 1990
813'.4—dc20   90-30087
                                                                    CIP

The paper used in this publication meets the minimum requirements
of American National Standard for Information Sciences—
Permanence of Paper for Printed Library Materials, ANSI
Z39.48-1984. ∞™

Printed and bound in the United States of America

CRITICAL ESSAYS ON AMERICAN LITERATURE

This series seeks to anthologize the most important criticism on a wide variety of topics and writers in American literature. Our readers will find in various volumes not only a generous selection of reprinted articles and reviews but original essays, bibliographies, manuscript sections, and other materials brought to public attention for the first time. This volume, *Critical Essays on Stephen Crane's "The Red Badge of Courage,"* is the most comprehensive collection of essays available on Crane's most famous novel. It contains both a sizable gathering of early reviews and a broad selection of more modern scholarship as well. Among the authors of reprinted articles and reviews are William Dean Howells, Harold Frederic, R. W. Stallman, J. C. Levenson, James Nagel, and Jean Cazemajou. In addition to a substantial introduction by Donald Pizer, there are also two original essays commissioned specifically for publication in this volume, new studies by Alfred Habegger and James Colvert. We are confident that this book will make a permanent and significant contribution to the study of American literature.

James Nagel, GENERAL EDITOR

Northeastern University

CONTENTS

INTRODUCTION

Stephen Crane's *The Red Badge of Courage* is one of the most widely known and deeply influential novels in the history of American fiction. The work was almost immediately popular on its appearance in late 1895, and it later played a major role in instructing a generation of great post–World War I writers, led by Ernest Hemingway, in the possibilities of a new American fiction. *The Red Badge* has continued throughout the twentieth century to attract a large general audience. It has also stimulated in each age a body of literary criticism that has contributed to an understanding both of the work itself and of the critical preoccupations of that age.

Despite this widespread and continuing interest in Crane and his work, we know remarkably little about the facts of the origin of *The Red Badge of Courage*. Crane was an obscure figure, living on the fringes of the New York artistic and journalistic world of the mid-1890s, when he conceived and wrote the novel. In addition, somewhat like William Faulkner, he was by nature often either evasive or misleading about his literary ideals and methods and seldom replied in any useful way to direct questions about the impulses that led him to *The Red Badge*. Crane's death in 1900 at the age of twenty-eight was much lamented, but in fact it was to be 1923 before Thomas Beer published the first biography of Crane. By this time memories had become unreliable and documents had been lost. And Beer, himself very much a free artistic spirit of the 1920s, cast a seemingly permanent haze over Crane biography by his cavalier use of his sources, many of which have proven to be unverifiable. Nevertheless, more recent biographers and scholars such as John Berryman, R. W. Stallman, J. C. Levenson, and Fredson Bowers have pieced together an account of the genesis of *The Red Badge,* and amid much obscurity a reliable rough outline has emerged.[1]

Stephen Crane was born in Newark, New Jersey, in November 1871, the fourteenth child of a clerical family with deep roots in New Jersey and New York history. The Reverend Jonathan Townley Crane died in 1880, and in 1883 the Crane family settled in Asbury Park on the New Jersey coast. Stephen attended boarding schools and then, after a half year at Lafayette College and a half year at Syracuse University in 1890–91, decided to leave college and become a writer. There followed some four years of hand-to-mouth existence

1

as Crane, while writing poorly paid sketches and stories for New York newspapers and magazines, also sought to write longer fiction that was more innovative in theme and form. (During these years he often alternated between living with artist friends in New York and periods of "recuperation" at the homes of his older brothers not far from the city.) The first such ground-breaking longer work was *Maggie: A Girl of the Streets*, which Crane wrote in late 1892 and then— after several futile attempts at publication—issued at his own expense in early 1893. This brilliantly ironic and expressionistic account of the life of a New York slum girl from childhood to death as a prostitute attracted almost no attention, though it was eventually to be regarded as Crane's most significant longer work of fiction after *The Red Badge*.

Crane had in part written *Maggie* in reaction against the often morally flabby and sentimental slum fiction of his day. Something of a similar intent was no doubt a principal motive in his undertaking, in April 1893, a novel about the Civil War. The typical Civil War novel of Crane's time concentrated on a Southern belle and a Northern officer whose initial antagonism and final love symbolized the theme of national discord followed by permanent union. The minimally portrayed battle scenes in fiction of this kind were primarily the occasion for self-sacrificial heroic posturing.[2] Crane, however, had heard (and probably read) differing accounts of the war by the veterans who were an inseparable part of a boy's world during the 1870s and 1880s, accounts that stressed the loneliness, terror, and bewilderment of men in battle. And he discovered in Tolstoy's *Sebastopol*—as J. C. Levenson demonstrates in his "Introduction: *The Red Badge of Courage*" (1975)—an apt fictional structure for the study of battle psychology, that of the initiation of a youthful soldier into the realities of combat. And, finally, he found in the large volumes of *Battles and Leaders of the Civil War*, a popular but reliable history of the war published initially in the *Century* magazine, a specific battle that could serve—as Harold Hungerford reveals in his " 'That Was at Chancellorsville' " (1963)—as the documentary base for his dramatization of the interplay between emotion and event in combat.

After an initial false start, Crane brooded over *The Red Badge* for some six months. When he took up the novel again in the fall of 1893 he worked steadily on it, and by March 1894 he was able to show Hamlin Garland a completed draft. Garland, a somewhat older Midwestern writer who was then living in New York, had earlier offered Crane aid and encouragement. He now suggested to Crane that the dialect of the novel was overdone. Crane, who even before he brought *The Red Badge* to Garland had begun a process of revision that included the frequent changing of proper names to descriptive epithets ("Fleming" to "the youth," for example), may have seized upon the need to revise the dialect to make other changes as well.

The most important of these involved the cutting of a series of passages at the end of chapters, as well as an entire chapter (the original Chapter XII of the manuscript), most of which were given over to Henry's ruminations about his behavior. It was probably this considerably revised version of *The Red Badge* that Crane submitted to the publisher S. S. McClure in the spring of 1894. McClure held the book for almost half a year without reaching a decision until Crane retrieved it and offered it to a newspaper syndicate. The heavily truncated version of *The Red Badge* that appeared in newspapers throughout the country in December 1894 brought Crane some attention, and in February 1895 the firm of D. Appleton and Company accepted the full version of the novel. Crane undertook one further revision in the spring of 1895 while traveling in the West, a revision that included some significant cuts and additions to the last chapter. *The Red Badge* was finally published—after two-and-a-half years of a complex and still often hazy history—in October 1895.

The Red Badge of Courage was widely and on the whole positively reviewed in America, with many reviewers devoting much of their attention to the seeming impossibility that Crane could write so realistically about war without ever having experienced combat.[3] Almost all of these early American reviews appeared in newspapers; the major magazines either ignored the novel or mentioned it briefly. When *The Red Badge* appeared in England in late November, however, its London publisher, William Heinemann, succeeded in gaining for it a number of substantial reviews in important magazines. With a fuller appreciation of the relationship of Crane's story to the modern continental tradition of war fiction stemming from Tolstoy and Émile Zola, English reviewers were in general both more perceptive and more laudatory. In January 1896, George Wyndham's long review, "A Remarkable Book," appeared in the influential *New Review*, and Harold Frederic, the London correspondent of the *New York Times*, also praised the novel lavishly and noted the stir it had created among British readers.[4] This praise from abroad quickly revived American interest in *The Red Badge*, an interest further stimulated in April when a vitriolic attack on the novel by the well-known publisher and Civil War veteran Alexander C. McClurg appeared in the *Dial*.[5] McClurg's charge—that the novel had initially been ignored in America and had then been praised by English critics because of the work's contempt for the American soldier—was quickly refuted by Ripley Hitchcock and Sydney Brooks in the *Dial*, with Hitchcock in particular at pains to note the positive reception of the work in America before its British publication.[6] But the controversy was much commented upon on both sides of the Atlantic, and by the spring of 1896 Crane found himself as much talked about in New York as in London. At twenty-four he had achieved fame.

A large number of the reviews of *The Red Badge* of course merely recounted the story of the novel. But in the more substantial reviews, many critics—after making the almost obligatory comment on Crane's lack of firsthand experience of warfare—did recognize the striking originality and power of Crane's portrayal of combat through the thoughts and feelings of a young recruit. As was to be true of criticism of the novel from its appearance onward, these early commentators also often differed widely in their interpretation of Fleming's initiation. While one reviewer, for example, stressed the "animalistic" in Henry's nature,[7] another found that the novel depicted his "redemption" within "a baptism of fire."[8] And many reviewers were of course impressed by Crane's strikingly original prose style, though in this instance as in others they frequently varied in estimating its success.[9]

Of these early responses to *The Red Badge*, George Wyndham's brilliant review has best stood the test of time. Himself a veteran of British military action in Egypt, Wyndham fully realized that Crane's subject was not the depiction of battle but rather the portrayal of the response to battle by an untried youthful soldier. He also recognized that one of Crane's major themes was that war is not an opportunity for personal achievement but rather a mechanical, anonymous force that reflects the truth that "all life is a battle." In one stroke, therefore, Wyndham opened up two large-scale and permanent critical approaches to *The Red Badge*—that the novel was both a study of human psychology and a social and moral allegory. It is not surprising that Crane was deeply moved by Wyndham's review and praised it as "fine and generous."[10] "I have just read Mr. George Wyndham's review," he wrote his English publisher, "and I feel glad to be able to write you that I think it a wonderful thing. . . ."[11]

Crane's remaining four years, between the recognition brought him by *The Red Badge* and his death from tuberculosis in June 1900, were crowded with much varied experience and writing, but only some of his shorter work of this period is of the highest caliber. His notoriety as a war writer brought him assignments as a newspaper correspondent reporting on the Cuban revolution in 1896–97, the Greco-Turkish War in 1897, and the Spanish-American War in 1898. From mid-1897 he lived principally in England with Cora Crane, the former proprietor of a Jacksonville brothel whom he had met in late 1896. Their increasingly extravagant way of life forced Crane into much hack work, and his novels of this period are weak and derivative. But in such shorter works of fiction of 1896–98 as "The Open Boat," "The Blue Hotel," "The Bride Comes to Yellow Sky," and "The Monster" he revealed again the combination of thematic depth and complex fictional technique that he had exhibited for the first time in *The Red Badge*.

Crane's work was for the most part neglected in the decade and a half after his death. The outbreak of World War I, however, renewed interest in Crane, an interest kept alive in the 1920s by Thomas Beer's image of Crane as a self-tormented bohemian rebel. The second world war again stimulated an absorption in *The Red Badge*. (Ernest Hemingway, for example, included it in his 1942 anthology *Men at War*.) But more significant for Crane's long-term reputation, his work in the years following World War II began, for a number of reasons, to attract a large body of academic criticism, a flow of research and critical readings that continues unabated to this day. One obvious reason for Crane's popularity among academic critics during the 1940s and 1950s was the adaptability of his work to the strategies and emphases of the New Criticism. Crane's compressed blend of irony and symbolism brought his best fiction close to the kind of poetry the New Criticism had initially engaged. Within a short time after the war, such Crane works as *The Red Badge* and "The Blue Hotel" were frequently targeted for elaborate readings of patterns of symbolic imagery.[12] In addition, Crane's mix in his fiction of various turn-of-the-century "isms"—impressionism, symbolism, naturalism, expressionism, and so on—as well as his often jaundiced view of human nature marked him as one of the most significant early exponents of literary modernism in America and therefore as a figure of great interest to the literary historian. And finally, the relationship between Crane's unusual and troubled life and his work provided a rich basis for psychoanalytical criticism of various kinds.[13]

The modern critical revival of Crane thus began in the early 1950s with a burst of major work. John Berryman's psychoanalytical biography in 1950 (the first biography since Beer's in 1923) was followed by R. W. Stallman's edition of *The Red Badge* (with an important introduction) in the Modern Library series (1950), by Stallman's lengthy discussion of Crane as an impressionist and religious symbolist in his "Stephen Crane: A Revaluation" (1951), and most of all by his ground-breaking *Stephen Crane: An Omnibus* (1952), a volume that combined a collection of Crane's best work in all forms and Stallman's interpretive introductions to this work. (This early body of criticism represents Stallman at his most influential in Crane studies, though he continued to produce major scholarship devoted to Crane for over twenty years, culminating in his efforts at a definitive biography and bibliography in *Stephen Crane: A Biography* [1968] and *Stephen Crane: A Critical Bibliography* [1972].)

Stallman's interpretations of Crane's fiction—and especially of *The Red Badge*—were deeply conditioned by the attitudes and methods of the New Criticism in that he stressed in Crane the role of symbolic patterns in expressing an essentially religious theme. He therefore believed that *The Red Badge* was at its center a study of Henry Fleming's spiritual redemption, with Jim Conklin serving as a sacrificial Christ figure in Fleming's salvation. The persuasiveness of Stallman's reading of *The Red Badge* is suggested by its impact on John E. Hart in his "*The Red Badge of Courage* as Myth and Symbol" (1953) and on Daniel Hoffman in his *The Poetry of Stephen Crane* (1957), both of whom read the novel as basically a redemption narrative. This approach to Crane and to *The Red Badge* was immediately challenged, however, by a body of criticism that located the center of Crane's ethical sensibility not in Christian myth but in the late nineteenth-century Darwinian stress on the instinctive animality of man's underlying nature. Such critics, therefore, as Charles C. Walcutt in his long-influential *American Literary Naturalism, A Divided Stream* (1956) or William Dillingham in his "Insensibility in *The Red Badge*" (1963) interpret the novel largely in naturalistic terms. Henry may fatuously believe that he has matured into manhood at the conclusion of the novel, but his nature and actions throughout the work demonstrate that it is only his self-conception and the beliefs of his comrades about him that have changed. At the center of his being he remains as he was, a confused youth whose actions have been determined by a mix of external stimulus and internal instinct.[14]

The outlines of the modern academic debate over the meaning of *The Red Badge* were thus clearly drawn by the late 1950s, with controversy over the narrative tone of the last chapter of the novel the center of much of the argument. Was Crane ironic in his depiction of Henry's final self-estimation, or did he accept as valid Henry's judgment? An ironic reading led in the direction of a naturalistic interpretation of the novel; a reading of Henry's final self-examination as apt led toward an acceptance of the themes of growth, development, and spiritual rebirth. Both positions could find support in the passages Crane cut from the manuscript version of *The Red Badge*, passages that Stallman had made accessible in his 1952 *Omnibus* volume.[15] While these passages, because they blatantly accentuate Henry's capacity for rationalization of his motives and actions, would seem to endorse an ironic reading of the conclusion, it could also be argued that Crane's omission of them reveals his effort to present a less negative image of Henry than he had originally intended.

Crane's rediscovery in the 1950s also occasioned a new interest in the sources of his work—both in the general influences on his literary imagination and in the specific sources of specific works. This traditional scholarly activity was rendered even more problematical than usual in the instance of Crane because of the paucity of knowledge about his reading or literary enthusiasms. Initially, French naturalism, and for *The Red Badge* in particular Zola's *La Débâcle*, was offered as a major influence, though often with an unconvincing stress on the significance of parallel incidents, as in Lars Ahnebrink's long-standard *The Beginnings of Naturalism in American Fiction, 1891–1902*

(1950). This emphasis on foreign sources was followed by an effort to locate Crane's knowledge of the Civil War and of battlefield psychology in specific Civil War novels, memoirs, and histories.[16] Of these, Harold Hungerford's definitive pinpointing of Crane's use of the Battle of Chancellorsville remains the most informative study of Crane's Civil War sources for *The Red Badge.* Another major kind of source study of long standing in *Red Badge* scholarship is that which seeks to discover a specific source—and thus Crane's intent—in the famous image "The red sun was pasted in the sky like a wafer," which closes Chapter IX. Stimulated by Stallman's claim that the wafer is a communion symbol, other scholars have located the source of the image variously in a sealing wax wafer, in an artillery primer, and in an analogous image in Kipling.[17]

Both the inherent weaknesses in Stallman's almost obsessive emphasis on religious symbols in Crane and a general turn against the often ingenious readings of the New Criticism led in the late 1950s and early 1960s to a severe critique of the interpretation of *The Red Badge* as a redemption story and to a demand for a more balanced view of all of Crane's work. Two of the more significant examples of this demand were Stanley Greenfield's influential *PMLA* essay "The Unmistakable Stephen Crane" (1958),[18] which convincingly refuted Stallman's critical method and findings, and Edwin Cady's *Stephen Crane* (1962) in the Twayne United States Authors series. Both critics rejected a single-dimensional interpretation of Crane in favor of a recognition of the many complex and often antiphonal voices that comprise Crane's literary themes and techniques. In particular, Greenfield's conclusion that Crane's work exhibited an often ineluctable "balance between the deterministic and volitional views of life" was echoed in a series of major essays by, among others, James Colvert and Max Westbrook, two of the leading Crane scholars of the period.[19]

In the almost three decades since the dust settled on the critical storm raised by Stallman's religious reading of Crane's major work, the issues raised by Stallman in his interpretation of *The Red Badge* continue nevertheless to be central to much discussion of the novel. For example, such interrelated problematical matters as the nature and role of the ironic narrative voice, the degree of authorial distance in Henry's final self-estimation, and the relation of certain pivotal scenes and symbols to the work as a whole persist as major critical concerns. But these seemingly permanent centers of critical interest in the novel in fact have seldom been addressed directly in criticism since the early 1960s. Rather, they are present as interpretive touch points within a variety of critical strategies, strategies that have often succeeded in casting much new light on the novel without necessarily "solving" the issues raised by Stallman.

So, for example, America's engagement in Vietnam occasioned a revival of George Wyndham's early position that *The Red Badge* is above all a story of a young man's initial experience of combat and that all judgmental criticism of Henry's weaknesses should be weighed against this elemental truth. Thus John Fraser's attempt, in his "Crime and Forgiveness: *The Red Badge* in Time of War" (1967), to remind readers of the psychological and social realism at the heart of the novel is similar in intent to efforts by a number of critics to stress that *The Red Badge*, though ostensibly an historical novel, is closely related to the social reality of Crane's own day as he and others of his generation viewed their world. Violence is the key trope in *The Red Badge* to interpreters of the work who find it powerfully reflective of the class, ethnic, and racial conflicts of late nineteenth-century American life. Robert Rechnitz, in his "Depersonalization and the Dream in *The Red Badge of Courage*" (1974), notes that Henry's reaction to the violence that threatens his sense of self is to seek the traditional American response of a recuperative escape, but that for Henry—as for Crane's generation—escape is possible only through the imagination. Robert Shulman, in his "*The Red Badge of Courage* and Social Violence: Crane's Myth of His America" (1981), and Harold Kaplan, in his "Violence as Ritual and Apocalypse" (1981), also stress that Henry's world of struggle is a mirror image of the social violence and loss of individuality of late nineteenth-century America, with Kaplan in particular finding a sinister implication for modern political history in Henry's regeneration through violence.

But while a number of recent critics have dealt with *The Red Badge* principally in relation to its social themes, other readers have found that the most productive approach to the novel, given its complexity of expression, is through its form and techniques. Because of Crane's extraordinary color sense and because his fiction was associated, even in his own time, with Joseph Conrad's impressionistic narrative style, Crane's fictional method has long been identified with various impressionistic devices. R. W. Stallman revived this approach to Crane's style in the early 1950s when he claimed that Crane wrote a form of "prose pointillism," thereby linking Crane's technique with that of the French impressionist Georges Seurat. But it was not until the major essays by Orm Overland, Sergio Perosa, and Rodney Rogers in the late 1960s that the nature and role of Crane's impressionism were fully charted and clarified.[20] In these essays, as in James Nagel's "Impressionism in *The Red Badge of Courage*" (1980), Crane's obvious indebtedness to the vivid color sense of late nineteenth-century painting is emphasized far less than his impressionistic narrative aesthetic in which his effort is above all to render dramatically the impact of event on a distinctive consciousness.

This belief that *The Red Badge* is in the great twentieth-century fictional tradition of a drama of consciousness is also reflected in a body of significant recent criticism that seeks to describe both the various ways in which Crane achieves a representation of the inner life and the relationship of these methods to his themes. Marston LaFrance, in his "Private Fleming: His Various Battles" (1971), closely examines Crane's ironic strategies for rendering the distinction between Henry's perception of himself and his world on the one hand and their actual nature on the other, while Jean Cazemajou, in *"The Red Badge of Courage:* The 'Religion of Peace' and the War Archetype" (1972), interprets Henry's mental processes in relation to a powerful archetypal conflict in all human experience. And Alfred Habegger, in his original essay "Fighting Words: The Talk of Men at War in *The Red Badge,"* pursues the implications of Henry's language for an understanding of his underlying moral nature. This pervasive stance of many Crane critics of recent years—that Crane in *The Red Badge* wishes not to state a thesis but rather to represent dramatically the complexities and ambiguities inherent in the acts of perceiving and knowing—is well summed-up in two of the most important studies of Crane in the last several decades, Frank Bergon's *Stephen Crane's Artistry* (1975) and James Nagel's *Stephen Crane and Impressionism* (1980).

The immense stimulus given bibliographical and textual scholarship by the decision of the National Endowment for the Humanities to sponsor (through the Center for Editions of American Authors) a series of scholarly editions of the major American writers has had the indirect effect of reviving and making central to much recent Crane criticism the issue of the text of *The Red Badge.* Stallman had given the manuscript revision of the novel prominence by publishing Crane's omissions in his *Omnibus,* but almost all scholars after Stallman—including Fredson Bowers in his editing of *Stephen Crane: The Red Badge of Courage: A Facsimile of the Manuscript* (1972) and Bowers and J. C. Levenson in their CEAA-approved edition of the novel as Volume II (1975) in *The Works of Stephen Crane*—had accepted the premise that Crane willingly cut the novel in an effort to improve it. In the late 1970s, however, Henry Binder, a student of Hershel Parker, claimed that Crane had been forced to cut *The Red Badge* by his D. Appleton editor Ripley Hitchcock and that the cuts adversely affected the more naturalistic thrust of Crane's original conception of the novel.[21] This claim was rejected by the editor of this volume in his *"The Red Badge of Courage:* Text, Theme, and Form" (1985) and by James Colvert in his original essay "Crane, Hitchcock, and the Binder Edition of *The Red Badge of Courage"* as well as by others, and it was defended by Parker and others.[22] Many textual controversies appear to be much ado about very little. The question of the intent and effect of Crane's cutting of *The Red Badge,* however, is also the question of the very nature of the novel. Although it now appears that few editors or critics wish to consider Crane's unrevised draft of *The Red Badge* as the "true" novel, all informed readers of the work have been made more sensitive to a number of basic issues in its interpretation by the need to reconsider Crane's editing.

Another tendency in criticism of *The Red Badge* of the last decade has been the application of various post-structuralist theoretical approaches to an interpretation of the novel. Most of this commentary has displayed the conventional weaknesses of a good deal of theoretical criticism, including a density of expression bordering on incomprehensibility, a propensity for jargon, and an often perverse revisionism. *The Red Badge* is no doubt a novel capable of responding to criticism with a theoretical bent—one thinks especially of studies with a semiotic or phenomenological emphasis—but no significant work of this kind has as yet been forthcoming.

DONALD PIZER

Tulane University

Notes

1. Thomas Beer, *Stephen Crane: A Study in American Letters* (New York: Knopf, 1923); John Berryman, *Stephen Crane* (New York: Sloane, 1950); R. W. Stallman, *Stephen Crane: A Biography* (New York: Braziller, 1968); Stephen Crane, *The Red Badge of Courage*, Vol. II in *The Works of Stephen Crane*, ed. Fredson Bowers, introduction by J. C. Levenson (Charlottesville: University Press of Virginia, 1975). The best recent short life of Crane is James Colvert, *Stephen Crane* (New York: Harcourt, Brace, Jovanovich, 1984).

2. See Eric Solomon, *Stephen Crane: From Parody to Realism* (Cambridge: Harvard University Press, 1966), 66–77.

3. See Richard M. Weatherford, ed., *Stephen Crane: The Critical Heritage* (London: Routledge & Kegan Paul, 1973).

4. *New Review* 14 (January 1896): 30–40 and "Stephen Crane's Triumph," *New York Times*, 26 January 1896, p. 22; both reviews are reprinted in this volume.

5. "The Red Badge of Hysteria," *Dial* 20 (16 April 1896): 227–28; reprinted in this volume.

6. Hitchcock, "*The Red Badge of Courage*—A Correction," *Dial* 20 (1 May 1896): 263 and Brooks, "Mr. Stephen Crane and His Critics," *Dial* 20 (16 May 1896): 297–98; Brooks's reply is reprinted in this volume.

7. [A. G. Sedgwick], "*The Red Badge of Courage*," *Nation* 63 (2 July 1896): 15; reprinted in this volume.

8. [H. B. Marriott-Watson], "The Heart of a Soldier," *Pall Mall Gazette* 61 (26 November 1895): 4.

9. The *New York Times*, for example, in "A Green Private Under Fire," 19 October 1895, p. 3 (reprinted in this volume), commented in an otherwise favorable review on Crane's "unpleasant affectations of style," while the *Bookman* 3 (March 1896): 17, praised Crane's color sense as "wonderfully effective."

10. Crane to William Heinemann, 17 February 1896, in *The Correspondence of Stephen Crane*, ed. Stanley Wertheim and Paul Sorrentino (New York: Columbia University Press, 1988), I, 207.

11. Crane to William Heinemann, 27 January 1896; *Correspondence*, I, 190.

12. See, for example, James T. Cox, "The Imagery of *The Red Badge of Courage*," *Modern Fiction Studies* 5 (1959): 209–19.

13. See, in particular, Daniel Weiss, *"The Red Badge of Courage,"* *Psychoanalytic Review* 52 (1965): 176–96, 460–84 and Maxwell Geismar, *Rebels and Ancestors: The American Novel, 1890–1915* (Boston: Houghton Mifflin, 1953), 69–136.

14. For a suggestive recent effort to revive this approach to the novel, see Lee Clark Mitchell, "The Spectacle of Character in Crane's *The Red Badge of Courage*," *Determined Fictions: American Literary Naturalism* (New York: Columbia University Press, 1989), 96–116.

15. R. W. Stallman, ed., *Stephen Crane: An Omnibus* (New York: Knopf, 1952). See also Stallman's 1960 Signet paperback edition of *The Red Badge*.

16. These studies are described by Donald Pizer in his essay on Crane scholarship in *Fifteen American Authors Before 1900: Bibliographical Essays on Research and Criticism*, ed. Earl N. Harbert and Robert A. Rees (Madison: University of Wisconsin Press, 1984), 160–63.

17. Besides passages in the essays in this volume by R. W. Stallman, Edwin H. Cady, and Robert Rechnitz, major commentary on the wafer image includes Scott C. Osborn, "Stephen Crane's Imagery: 'Pasted Like a Wafer,' " *American Literature* 23 (1951): 362; Edward Stone, "The Many Suns of *The Red Badge of Courage*," *American Literature* 29 (1957): 322–26; and Jean Marlowe, "Crane's Wafer Image: Reference to an Artillery Primer?" *American Literature* 43 (1972): 645–47.

18. Stanley B. Greenfield, "The Unmistakable Stephen Crane," *PMLA* 73 (1958): 562–72.

19. James Colvert, "Structure and Theme in Stephen Crane's Fiction," *Modern Fiction Studies* 5 (1959): 199–208 and "Stephen Crane: Style as Invention," in *Stephen Crane in Transition: Centenary Essays*, ed. Joseph Katz (Dekalb: Northern Illinois University Press, 1972), 127–52; Max Westbrook, "Stephen Crane: The Pattern of Affirmation," *Nineteenth Century Fiction* 14 (1959): 219–30 and "Stephen Crane and the Personal Universal," *Modern Fiction Studies* 8 (1962–63): 351–60.

20. Orm Overland, "The Impressionism of Stephen Crane," in *Americana Norvegica*, ed. Sigmund Skard and Henry Wasser (Philadelphia: University of Pennsylvania Press, 1966), 239–85; Sergio Perosa, "Naturalism and Impressionism in Stephen Crane's Fiction," in *Stephen Crane: A Collection of Critical Essays*, ed. Maurice Bassan (Englewood Cliffs, N.J.: Prentice-Hall, 1967), 90–94; and Rodney O. Rogers, "Stephen Crane and Impressionism," *Nineteenth Century Fiction* 24 (1969): 292–304.

21. See Binder's *"The Red Badge of Courage* Nobody Knows," *Studies in the Novel* 10 (1978): 9–47 and his edition of *The Red Badge of Courage* (New York: Norton, 1982).

22. See, in particular, Hershel Parker, *Flawed Texts and Verbal Icons: Literary Authority in American Fiction* (Evanston, Ill.: Northwestern University Press, 1984), 147–97.

REVIEWS

A Green Private Under Fire Anonymous*

Stephen Crane is very young—not yet twenty-five, it is said—and this picture he presents of war is therefore a purely imaginative work. The very best thing that can be said about it, though, is that it strikes the reader as a statement of facts by a veteran. The purpose of the book is to set forth the experiences of a volunteer soldier in his first battle. The poetical idea of the hero and the coward in war was long since abandoned by well-informed writers. A recent autobiographical account of actual experiences in our civil war bears testimony that every soldier is frightened at the moment of entering battle, and his fright increases rather than diminishes as he grows old in service and more familiar with the dangers he has to encounter. It is true, also, that once in battle all men are much alike. They fight like beasts. Cowards and skulkers are the exception, and cowardice is often the result of some sudden physical disability.

The young private soldier who is the central personage in this remarkable work was a farm boy in one of the Middle States, probably Ohio, though certain peculiarities of the dialect in which Mr. Crane chooses to clothe the speech of all his persons, belong also to Western Pennsylvania and the Hoosier country. Except for those few expressions, such as "Watch out" for "Look out," the talk is a very fair phonetic equivalent for the common speech in parts of this State and Connecticut. The boy does not enlist at the beginning of the war, but his duty to go to the front weighs upon him day and night. He is the only son of his mother, and she a widow and a typical American woman of the old New-England stock, who ever conceals her emotions, and seems to possess no imaginative faculty whatever. She is peeling potatoes when her boy, in his new blue clothes, says "Goodbye," and the exhortation she then delivers is perfectly practical and devoid of all sentiment. There is a black-eyed girl, nameless in the story, who looks after the youth as he trudges down the road, but when he looks back pretends to be gazing at the sky.

* Reprinted from *New York Times*, 19 October 1895, 3.

In other words, the early environment of Mr. Crane's hero is absolutely typical, differing in no particular from that of tens of thousands of young men who went to the front in the interval between the Sumter episode and the fall of Richmond. But as to his temperament and the quality of his mind, we cannot speak so positively. He is certainly of a more emotional type than any one of his comrades. His aspirations, perhaps, are no higher than theirs, his mental capacity no larger, his will, certainly, no stronger. But there is a touch of poetry in his nature which most men lack.

Probably Mr. Crane has put some of his own mental traits into the composition of his otherwise commonplace hero. Therefore, it is not possible to accept this graphic study of his mind under the stress of new and frightful experiences as an exact picture of the mental states of every green soldier under his first fire. All its complexities are surely not typical.

Yet it is as a picture which seems to be extraordinarily true, free from any suspicion of ideality, defying every accepted tradition of martial glory, that the book commends itself to the reader. The majesty, the pomp and circumstance of glorious war, Mr. Crane rejects altogether. War, as he depicts it, is a mean, nasty, horrible thing; its seeming glories are the results of accident or that blind courage when driven to bay and fighting for life that the meanest animal would show as strongly as man. For it must be remembered that the point of view is consistently that of the humblest soldier in the ranks, who never knows where he is going or what is expected of him until the order comes, who never comprehends the whole scheme, but only his small share of it, who is frequently put forward as an intentional sacrifice, but yet is a sentient human being, who is bound to have his own opinions founded on the scanty knowledge he possesses, his own hopes and fears and doubts and prejudices.

Private Henry Fleming goes to the war a hot-headed young patriot with his mind brimful of crude ideas of glory, and a settled conviction that his capacity for heroism is quite out of the common. Weary months of drill in camp reduce him seemingly to the proper machinelike condition. He learns many things, among them that the glories of war have been greatly exaggerated in books, that the enemy is not composed chiefly of bragging cowards, that victory is rare and dear, and that the lot of a private soldier is very hard. On the eve of his first battle he has about abandoned all hope of ever getting a chance to distinguish himself. Yet when the hour comes it brings depression instead of exhilaration. He communes with himself, and fears that he is a coward.

The battle Mr. Crane describes is one of those long and bloody conflicts of our civil war that we now freely admit were badly mismanaged through lack of good generalship, which had no particular result except the destruction of human life, and were claimed as prodigious victories by both sides. The green regiment is part of a brigade which is in the centre at first, and for a long while it has nothing to do. Then it has to stand on the edge of a piece of woods and receive the enemy's fire, and return it. This is a short and sharp proceeding, and while it lasts Private Henry Fleming acquits himself creditably. When the enemy's fire stops, he feels himself a hero and feels also that he has done the greatest day's work of his life. The nervous tension has been awful, the revulsion of feeling is correspondingly great. When the enemy's fire is resumed, a few minutes later, he is entirely unprepared. Panic seizes him, he drops his musket and runs for his life.

All that day he is a skulker in the rear of a great battle. His emotions, his mental vagaries, his experiences with the dead and dying, and the terrible nervous ordeal be undergoes are depicted by Mr. Crane with a degree of vividness and original power almost unique in our fiction. The night of the first day finds him back in the camp of his own regiment, lauded by his surviving comrades as a wounded hero. His scalp was cut by a blow of a musket by a retreating soldier, whose flight he tried to stop, for no reason, and he has tied his handkerchief over the wound. He is physically exhausted, and his conscience troubles him sorely.

In the next day's conflict he remains with his regiment. His nervous excitement has increased, but he is no longer so greatly shocked by the spectacle of the dead and dying. He has lost all control of his tongue, and he jabbers oaths incessantly. When his regiment is called upon to repel an advance of the enemy, he excels all his comrades in the ferocious rapidity of his fire. He is again extolled as a hero, but scarcely comprehends the praise. His regiment, esteemed by the division officers, apparently with good reason, as nearly worthless is selected to make a charge which is intended merely to check a contemplated attack of the enemy on the left until reinforcements can be forwarded to that point. It is not expected that any member of the regiment will return alive, and some rude remarks of a staff officer to this effect reach the ears of the men and transform them into demons, but very impotent and purposeless demons. The order is only half carried out. A file of soldiers in gray, behind a rail fence, keeps the blue fellows at bay. They stand like lost sheep, and scarcely return the fire which is destroying them. Yet, on their retreat, they combat bravely enough with a small Confederate body which tries to cut them off. Returning to their own lines, they are received with derision, while their Colonel is roundly abused by his superior. The charge has been a failure, yet it has transformed Private Henry Fleming. He has saved the colors, and he has sounded his own depths. He feels that he will never run away again.

> At last his eyes seem to open to some new ways. He found that he could look back upon the brass and bombast of his earlier gospels and see them truly. He was gleeful when he discovered that he now despised them. With this conviction came a store of assurance. He felt a quiet manhood, non-assertive, but of sturdy and strong blood. He knew that he would no more quail before his guides wherever they should point. He had been in touch with the great death, and found that, after all, it was but the great death. He was a man.

The book is written in terse and vigorous sentences, but not without some unpleasant affectations of style which the author would do well to correct. His natural talent is so strong that it is a pity its expression should be marred by petty tricks. When he begins a sentence with "too," for instance, he makes a sensitive reader squirm. But he is certainly a young man of remarkable promise.

Life and Letters   William Dean Howells[1]

Of our own smaller fiction I have been reading several books without finding a very fresh note except in *The Red Badge of Courage*, by Mr. Stephen Crane. He is the author of that story of New York tough life, *Maggie*, which I mentioned some time ago as so good but so impossible of general acceptance because of our conventional limitations in respect of swearing, and some other traits of the common parlance. He has now attempted to give a close-at-hand impression of battle as seen by a young volunteer in the civil war, and I cannot say that to my inexperience of battle he has given such a vivid sense of it as one gets from some other authors. The sense of deaf and blind turmoil he does indeed give, but we might get that from fewer pages than Mr. Crane employs to impart it. The more valuable effect of the book is subjective: the conception of character in the tawdry-minded youth whom the slight story gathers itself about, and in his comrades and superiors of all sorts. The human commonness (which we cannot shrink from without vulgarity) is potently illustrated throughout in their speech and action and motive; and the cloud of bewilderment in which they all have their being after the fighting begins, the frenzy, the insensate resentment, are graphically and probably suggested. The dialect employed does not so much convince

* Reprinted from *Harper's Weekly* 39 (26 October 1895): 1013.

me; I have not heard people speak with those contractions, though perhaps they do it; and in commending the book I should dwell rather upon the skill shown in evolving from the youth's crude expectations and ambitions a quiet honesty and self-possession manlier and nobler than any heroism he had imagined. There are divinations of motive and experience which cannot fail to strike the critical reader, from time to time; and decidedly on the psychological side the book is worth while as an earnest of the greater things that we may hope from a new talent working upon a high level, not quite clearly as yet, but strenuously.

Note

1. [Ed. note: Howells, whom Crane considered one of his literary mentors, was the most influential American man of letters of this period. His review, though brief, thus attracted considerable notice.]

The Red Badge of Courage   Anonymous*

Having recently startled part of the world and amused another part by the unconventional thought and expression of *The Black Riders,* Mr. Crane has now given us, in his latest prose work, something which can more easily be appreciated by "the general," but which, we think, will none the less be valued by the more discriminating. The first and simplest impression made by its perusal is one of power— power perhaps a thought undisciplined, perhaps a little youthful in the exuberance of its expression, but very real. A strong book, then, is *The Red Badge of Courage,* and it is a true book; true to life, whether it be taken as a literal transcript of a soldier's experiences in his first battle, or (as some have fancied) a great parable of the inner battle which every man must fight. Taking it in the obvious sense, we are struck, also, by the vivid power of realization which Mr. Crane shows at an age when he can hardly have seen real fighting, born as he was some years after the close of the Civil War, of which the story is an episode. In assembling the good qualities of the book, we must name also the quick eye for color which is shown on every page, and not for the mere externals of color alone, but for the inner significance of its relation to the events and emotions under hand. Metaphors and similes, too, abound in rich profusion, not strung on for effect, but living and actual as Homer's.

* Reprinted from *Critic* n.s. 24 (30 November 1895); 363.

The whole book, in fact, is full of primitive elements; it differs from the type of an Augustan age, with its artificial restraints and its faint perfumes, as a virgin forest from a trim Italian garden. We do not say this wholly to commend; there are certain roughnesses of phrase—the recurrence of "too" as a conjunction at the beginning of a sentence, or such expressions as "were being rended," "a little ways," "the clangoring of the church-bell,"—which suggest improvement; and in the writing of dialect (always a delicate matter), the incessant representation of "you" by "yeh" becomes irritating. We question, moreover, whether certain expletives current among soldiers at least since the days of memorable campaigns in Flanders do not lose force, without gaining propriety, when they are written "dum" or "dumb," or, with still more cryptic reserve, "a heluva row." But all these are small matters compared with the genuine force which must set Mr. Crane, as was said of him when he was even younger, among those who are henceforth to be reckoned with.

A Remarkable Book   George Wyndham*

All men are aware of antagonism and desire, or at the least are conscious, even in the nursery, that their hearts are the destined theatres of these emotions; all have felt or heard of their violence; all know that, unlike other emotions, these must often be translated into the glittering drama of decisive speech and deed; all, in short, expect to be lovers, and peer at the possibility of fighting. And yet how hard it is for the tried to compare notes, for the untried to anticipate experience! Love and war have been the themes of song and story in every language since the beginning of the world, love-making and fighting the supreme romances of most men and most nations; but any one man knows little enough of either beyond the remembered record of his own chances and achievements, and knows still less whither to turn in order to learn more. We resent this ignorance as a slur on our manhood, and snatch at every chance of dispelling it. And at first, in the scientific "climate" of our time, we are disposed to ask for documents: for love-letters, and letters written from the field of battle. These we imagine, if collected and classified, might supply the evidence for an induction. But, on second thoughts, we remember that such love-letters as have been published are, for the most part, not nearer to life than romantic literature, but further removed from it by many stages: that they are feeble echoes of

* Reprinted from New Review 14 (January 1896): 30–40.

conventional art—not immediate reflections, but blurred impressions of used plates carelessly copied from meretricious paintings. And so it is with the evidence at first hand upon war. The letters and journals of soldiers and subordinate officers in the field are often of a more pathetic interest than most love-letters; but to the searcher after truth they are still disappointing, for they deal almost exclusively with matters beyond the possibilities of the writer's acquaintance. They are all of surmises—of what dear ones are doing at home, or of the enemy's intentions and the general's plans for outwitting him: they reflect the writer's love and professional ambition, but hardly ever the new things he has heard and seen and felt. And when they attempt these things they sink to the level of the love-letters, and become mere repetitions of accepted forms.

I can remember one letter from an English private, describing an engagement in which some eighty men were killed and wounded out of a force of eight thousand: he wrote of comrades in his own battalion "falling like sheep," and gave no clue to the country in which he served. It might have been in Siberia or the Sahara, against savages or civilised troops; you could glean nothing except that he had listened to patriotic songs in music halls at home. Perhaps the most intimate love-letters and battle-letters never get printed at all. But, as it is, you cannot generalise from collections of documents as you can from collections of ferns and beetles: there is not, and there never can be, a science of the perceptions and emotions which thrill young lovers and recruits. The modern soldier is a little less laconic than his mediæval forbear. Indeed he could hardly surpass the tantalising reserve of, say, Thomas Denyes, a gentleman who fights at Towton, and sums up the carnage of thirty-eight thousand men in a single sentence:—"Oure Soveraign Lord hath wonne the feld."[1] But it is astonishing to note how little even the modern soldier manages to say. He receives rude and swift answers in the field to the questions that haunted his boyish dreams, but he keeps the secret with masonic self-possession.

Marbot's *Memoirs* and, in a lesser degree, Tomkinson's *Diary of a Cavalry Officer* are both admirable as personal accounts of the Peninsular Campaign, but the warfare they describe is almost as obsolete as that of the Roses, and, even if it were not so, they scarcely attempt the recreation of intense moments by the revelation of their imprint on the minds that endured them. And, on the score of art and of reticence, one is glad that they do not. Their authors were gallant soldiers waging war in fact, and not artists reproducing it in fiction. They satisfy the special curiosity of men interested in strategy and tactics, not the universal curiosity of Man the potential Combatant. He is fascinated by the picturesque and emotional aspects of battle, and the experts tell him little of either. To gratify that curiosity you must turn from the Soldier to the Artist, who is trained both to see and tell, or inspired, even without seeing, to divine what things have been and must be. Some may rebel against accepting his evidence, since it is impossible to prove the truth of his report. But it is equally impossible to prove the beauty of his accomplishment. Yet both are patent to every one capable of accepting truth or beauty, and by a surer warrant than any chance coincidence of individual experience and taste.

Mr. Stephen Crane, the author of *The Red Badge of Courage* (London: Heinemann), is a great artist, with something new to say, and consequently, with a new way of saying it. His theme, indeed, is an old one, but old themes re-handled anew in the light of novel experience are the stuff out of which masterpieces are made, and in *The Red Badge of Courage* Mr. Crane has surely contrived a masterpiece. He writes of war—the ominous and alluring possibility for every man, since the heir of all the ages has won and must keep his inheritance by secular combat. The conditions of the age-long contention have changed and will change, but its certainty is coeval with progress: so long as there are things worth fighting for fighting will last, and the fashion of fighting will change under the reciprocal stresses of rival inventions. Hence its double interest of abiding necessity and ceaseless variation. Of all these variations the most marked has followed, within the memory of most of us, upon the adoption of long-range weapons of precision, and continues to develop, under our eyes, with the development of rapidity in firing. And yet, with the exception of Zola's *la Débâcle,* no considerable attempt has been made to portray war under its new conditions. The old stories are less trustworthy than ever as guides to the experiences which a man may expect in battle and to the emotions which those experiences are likely to arouse. No doubt the prime factors in the personal problem—the chances of death and mutilation—continue to be about the same. In these respects it matters little whether you are pierced by a bullet at two thousand yards or stabbed at hands' play with a dagger. We know that the most appalling death-rolls of recent campaigns have been more than equalled in ancient warfare; and, apart from history, it is clear that, unless one side runs away, neither can win save by the infliction of decisive losses. But although these personal risks continue to be essentially the same, the picturesque and emotional aspects of war are completely altered by every change in the shape and circumstance of imminent death. And these are the fit materials for literature—the things which even dull men remember with the undying imagination of poets, but which, for lack of the writer's art, they cannot communicate. The sights flashed indelibly on the retina of the eye; the sounds that after long silences suddenly cypher; the stenches that sicken in after-life at any chance allusion to decay; or, stirred by these, the storms of passions that force yells of defiance out of inarticulate clowns; the winds of fear that sweep by night along prostrate ranks, with the acceleration of trains and the noise as of a whole town waking from nightmare with stertorous, indrawn gasps—these colossal facts of the senses and the soul are the only colours in which the very image of war can be painted. Mr. Crane has composed his palette with these colours, and has painted a picture that challenges comparison with the most vivid scenes of Tolstoï's *la Guerre et la Paix* or of Zola's *la Débâcle*. This is unstinted praise, but I feel bound to give it after reading the book twice and comparing it with Zola's *Sédan* and Tolstoï's account of Rostow's squadron for the first time under fire. Indeed, I think that Mr. Crane's picture of war is more complete than Tolstoï's, more true than Zola's. Rostow's sensations are conveyed by Tolstoï with touches more subtile than any to be found even in his *Sébastopol*, but they make but a brief passage in a long book, much else of which is devoted to the theory that Napoleon and his marshals were mere waifs on a tide of humanity or to the analysis of divers characters exposed to civilian experiences. Zola, on the other hand, compiles an accurate catalogue of almost all that is terrible and nauseating in war; but it is his own catalogue of facts made in cold blood, and not the procession of flashing images shot through the senses into one brain and fluctuating there with its rhythm of exaltation and fatigue. *La Débâcle* gives the whole truth, the truth of science, as it is observed by a shrewd intellect, but not the truth of experience as it is felt in fragments magnified or diminished in accordance with the patient's mood. The terrible things in war are not always terrible; the nauseating things do not always sicken. On the contrary, it is even these which sometimes lift the soul to heights from which they become invisible. And, again, at other times, it is the little miseries of most ignoble insignificance which fret through the last fibres of endurance.

Mr. Crane, for his distinction, has hit on a new device, or at least on one which has never been used before with such consistency and effect. In order to show the features of modern war, he takes a subject—a youth with a peculiar temperament, capable of exaltation and yet morbidly sensitive. Then he traces the successive impressions made on such a temperament, from minute to minute, during two days of heavy fighting. He stages the drama of war, so to speak, within the mind of one man, and then admits you as to a theatre. You may, if you please, object that this youth is unlike most other young men who serve in the ranks, and that the same events would have impressed the average man differently; but you are convinced that this man's soul is truly drawn, and that the impressions made in it are faithfully rendered. The youth's temperament is merely the medium which the artist has chosen: that it is exceptionally plastic makes but for the deeper incision of his work. It follows from Mr. Crane's method that he creates by his art even such a first-hand report of war as we seek in vain among the journals and letters of soldiers. But the book is not written in the form of an autobiography: the author narrates. He is therefore at liberty to give scenery and action, down to the slightest gestures and outward signs of inward elation or suffering, and he does this with the vigour and terseness of a master. Had he put his descriptions of scenery and his atmospheric effects, or his reports of overheard conversations, into the mouth of his youth, their very excellence would have belied all likelihood. Yet in all his descriptions and all his reports he confines himself only to such things as that youth heard and saw, and, of these, only to such as influenced his emotions. By this compromise he combines the strength and truth of a monodrama with the directness and colour of the best narrative prose. The monodrama suffices for the lyrical emotion of Tennyson's *Maud;* but in Browning's *Martin Relf* you feel the constraint of a form which in his *Ring and the Book* entails repetition often intolerable.

Mr. Crane discovers his youth, Henry Fleming, in a phase of disillusion. It is some monotonous months since boyish "visions of broken-bladed glory" impelled him to enlist in the Northern Army towards the middle of the American war. That impulse is admirably given:—"One night as he lay in bed, the winds had carried to him the clangouring of the church bells, as some enthusiast jerked the rope frantically to tell the twisted news of a great battle. This voice of the people rejoicing in the night had made him shiver in a prolonged ecstasy of excitement. Later he had gone down to his mother's room, and had spoken thus: 'Ma, I'm going to enlist.' 'Henry, don't you be a fool,' his mother had replied. She had then covered her face with the quilt. There was an end to the matter for that night." But the next morning he enlists. He is impatient of the homely injunctions given him in place of the heroic speech he expects in accordance with a tawdry convention, and so departs, with a "vague feeling of relief." But, looking back from the gate, he sees his mother "kneeling among the potato parings. Her brown face upraised and stained with tears, her spare form quivering." Since then the army has done "little but sit still and try to keep warm" till he has "grown to regard himself merely as a part of a vast blue demonstration." In the sick langour of this waiting, he begins to suspect his courage and lies awake by night through hours of morbid introspection. He tries "to prove to himself mathematically that he would not run from a battle"; he constantly leads the conversation round to the problem of courage in order to gauge the confidence of his messmates.

"How do you know you won't run when the time comes?" asked the youth. "Run?" said the loud one, "run?—of course not!" He laughed. "Well," continued the youth, "lots of good-a-'nough men have thought they was going to do great things before the fight, but when the time come they skedaddled." "Oh, that's all true, I s'pose," replied the other, "but I'm not going to skedaddle. The man that bets on my running will lose his money, that's all." He nodded confidently.

The youth is a "mental outcast" among his comrades, "wrestling with his personal problem," and sweating as he listens to the muttered scoring of a card game, his eyes fixed on the "red, shivering reflection of a fire." Every day they drill; every night they watch the red campfires of the enemy on the far shore of a river, eating their hearts out. At last they march:—"In the gloom before the break of the day their uniforms glowed a deep purple blue. From across the river the red eyes were still peering. In the eastern sky there was a yellow patch, like a rug laid for the feet of the coming sun; and against it, black and pattern-like, loomed the gigantic figure of the colonel on a gigantic horse." The book is full of such vivid impressions, half of sense and half of imagination:—The columns as they marched "were like two serpents crawling from the cavern of night." But the march, which, in his boyish imagination, should have led forthwith into melodramatic action is but the precursor of other marches. After days of weariness and nights of discomfort, at last, as in life, without preface, and in a lull of the mind's anxiety, the long-dreaded and long-expected is suddenly and smoothly in process of accomplishment:—"One grey morning he was kicked on the leg by the tall soldier, and then, before he was entirely awake, he found himself running down a wood road in the midst of men who were panting with the first effects of speed. His canteen banged rhythmically upon his thigh, and his haversack bobbed softly. His musket bounced a trifle from his shoulder at each stride and made his cap feel uncertain upon his head." From this moment, reached on the thirtieth page, the drama races through another hundred and sixty pages to the end of the book, and to read those pages is in itself an experience of breathless, lambent, detonating life. So brilliant and detached are the images evoked that, like illuminated bodies actually seen, they leave their fever-bright phantasms floating before the brain. You may shut the book, but you still see the battle-flags "jerked about madly in the smoke," or sinking with "dying gestures of despair," the men "dropping here and there like bundles"; the captain shot dead with "an astonished and sorrowful look as if he thought some friend had done him an ill-turn"; and the litter of corpses, "twisted in fantastic contortions," as if "they had fallen from some great height, dumped out upon the ground from the sky." The book is full of sensuous impressions that leap out from the picture: of gestures, attitudes, grimaces, that flash into portentous definition, like faces from the climbing clouds of nightmare. It leaves the imagination bounded with a "dense wall of smoke, furiously slit and slashed by the knife-like fire from the rifles." It leaves, in short, such indelible traces as are left by the actual experience of war. The picture shows grisly shadows and vermilion splashes, but, as in the vast drama it reflects so truly, these features, though insistent, are small in size, and are lost in the immensity of the theatre. The tranquil forest stands around; the "fairy-blue of the sky" is over it all. And, as in the actual experience of war, the impressions which these startling features inflict, though acute, are localised and not too deep: are as it were mere pin-pricks, or, at worst, clean cuts from a lancet in a body thrilled with currents of physical excitement and sopped with anæsthetics of emotion. Here is the author's description of a forlorn hope:

> As the regiment swung from its position out into a cleared space the woods and thickets before it awakened. Yellow flames leaped toward it from many directions. The line swung straight for a moment. Then the right wing swung forward; it in turn was surpassed by the left. Afterward the centre careered to the front until the regiment was a wedge-shaped mass . . . the men, pitching forward insanely, had burst into cheerings, mob-like and barbaric, but tuned in strange keys that can arouse the dullard and the stoic. . . . There was the delirium that encounters despair and death, and is heedless and blind to odds. . . . Presently the straining pace ate up the energies of the men. As if by agreement, the leaders began to slacken their speed. The volleys directed against them had a seeming wind-like effect. The regiment snorted and blew. Among some stolid trees it began to falter and hesitate. . . . The youth had a vague belief that he had run miles, and he thought, in a way, that he was now in some new and unknown land. . . .

The charge withers away, and the lieutenant, the youth, and his friend run forward to rally the regiment.

> In front of the colours three men began to bawl, "Come on! Come on!" They danced and gyrated like tortured savages. The flag, obedient to these appeals, bended its glittering form and swept toward them. The men wavered in indecision for a moment, and then with a long wailful cry the dilapidated regiment surged forward and began its new journey. Over the field went the scurrying mass. It was a handful of men splattered into the faces of the enemy. Toward it instantly sprang the yellow tongues. A vast quantity of blue smoke hung before them. A mighty banging made ears valueless. The youth ran like a madman to reach the woods before a bullet could discover him. He ducked his head low, like a football

player. In his haste his eyes almost closed, and the scene was a
wild blur. Pulsating saliva stood at the corner of his mouth. Within
him, as he hurled forward, was born a love, a despairing fondness
for this flag that was near him. It was a creation of beauty and
invulnerability. It was a goddess radiant, that bended its form with
an imperious gesture to him. It was a woman, red and white, hating
and loving, that called him with the voice of his hopes. Because
no harm could come to it he endowed it with power. He kept near,
as if it could be a saver of lives, and an imploring cry went from
his mind.

This passage directly challenges comparison with Zola's scene, in
which the lieutenant and the old tradition, of an invincible Frenchman
over-running the world "between his bottle and his girl," expire
together among the morsels of a bullet-eaten flag. Mr. Crane has
probably read *la Débâcle*, and wittingly threw down his glove. One
can only say that he is justified of his courage.

Mr. Crane's method, when dealing with things seen and heard,
is akin to Zola's: he omits nothing and extenuates nothing, save the
actual blasphemy and obscenity of a soldier's oaths. These he indicates,
sufficiently for any purpose of art, by brief allusions to their vigour
and variety. Even Zola has rarely surpassed the appalling realism of
Jim Conklin's death in Chapter X. Indeed, there is little to criticise
in Mr. Crane's observation, except an undue subordination of the
shrill cry of bullets to the sharp crashing of rifles. He omits the long
chromatic whine defining its invisible arc in the air, and the fretful
snatch a few feet from the listener's head. In addition to this gift of
observation, Mr. Crane has at command the imaginative phrase. The
firing follows a retreat as with "yellings of eager metallic hounds";
the men at their mechanic loading and firing are like "fiends jigging
heavily in the smoke"; in a lull before the attack "there passed slowly
the intense moments that precede the tempest"; then, after single
shots, "the battle roar settled to a rolling thunder, which was a single
long explosion." And, as I have said, when Mr. Crane deals with
things felt he gives a truer report than Zola. He postulates his hero's
temperament—a day-dreamer given over to morbid self-analysis who
enlists, not from any deep-seated belief in the holiness of fighting
for his country, but in hasty pursuit of a vanishing ambition. This
choice enables Mr. Crane to double his picturesque advantage with
an ethical advantage equally great. Not only is his youth, like the
sufferer in *The Fall of the House of Usher*, super-sensitive to every
pin-prick of sensation: he is also a delicate meter of emotion and
fancy. In such a nature the waves of feeling take exaggerated curves,
and hallucination haunts the brain. Thus, when awaiting the first
attack, his mind is thronged with vivid images of a circus he had
seen as a boy: it is there in definite detail, even as the Apothecary's

shop usurps Romeo's mind at the crisis of his fate. And thus also, like Herodotus' Aristodemus, he vacillates between cowardice and heroism. Nothing could well be more subtle than his self-deception and that sudden enlightenment which leads him to "throw aside his mental pamphlets on the philosophy of the retreated and rules for the guidance of the damned." His soul is of that kind which, "sick with self-love," can only be saved "so as by fire"; and it is saved when the battle-bond of brotherhood is born within it, and is found plainly of deeper import than the cause for which he and his comrades fight, even as that cause is loftier than his personal ambition. By his choice of a hero Mr. Crane displays in the same work a pageant of the senses and a tragedy of the soul.

But he does not obtrude his moral. The "tall soldier" and the lieutenant are brave and content throughout, the one by custom as a veteran, the other by constitution as a hero. But the two boys, the youth and his friend, "the loud soldier," are at first querulous brag-garts, but at the last they are transmuted by danger until either might truly say:

> We have proved we have hearts in a cause, we are noble still,
> And myself have awaked, as it seems, to the better mind;
> It is better to fight for the good than to rail at the ill;
> I have felt with my native land, I am one with my kind,
> I embrace the purpose of God, and the doom assigned.

Let no man cast a stone of contempt at these two lads during their earlier weakness until he has fully gauged the jarring discordance of battle. To be jostled on a platform when you have lost your luggage and missed your train on an errand of vital importance gives a truer pre-taste of war than any field-day; yet many a well-disciplined man will denounce the universe upon slighter provocation. It is enough that these two were boys and that they became men.

Yet must it be said that this youth's emotional experience was singular. In a battle there are a few physical cowards, abjects born with defective circulations, who literally turn blue at the approach of danger, and a few on whom danger acts like the keen, rare atmosphere of snow-clad peaks. But between these extremes come many to whom danger is as strong wine, with the multitude which gladly accepts the "iron laws of tradition" and finds welcome support in "a moving box." To this youth, as the cool dawn of his first day's fighting changed by infinitesimal gradations to a feverish noon, the whole evolution pointed to "a trap"; but I have seen another youth under like circumstances toss a pumpkin into the air and spit it on his sword. To this youth the very landscape was filled with "the stealthy approach of death." You are convinced by the author's art that it was so to this man. But to others, as the clamour increases, it is as if the serenity of the morning had taken refuge in their brains. This man "stumbles over the stones as he runs breathlessly forward"; another realises for the first time how right it is to be adroit even in running. The movement of his body becomes an art, which is not self-conscious, since its whole intention is to impress others within the limits of a modest decorum. We know that both love and courage teach this mastery over the details of living. You can tell from the way one woman, out of all the myriads, walks down Piccadilly, that she is at last aware of love. And you can tell from the way a man enters a surgery or runs toward a firing-line that he, too, realises how wholly the justification of any one life lies in its perfect adjustment to others. The woman in love, the man in battle, may each say, for their moment, with the artist, "I was made perfect too." They also are of the few to whom "God whispers in the ear."

But had Mr. Crane taken an average man he would have written an ordinary story, whereas he has written one which is certain to last. It is glorious to see his youth discover courage in the bed-rock of primeval antagonism after the collapse of his tinsel bravado; it is something higher to see him raise upon that rock the temple of resignation. Mr. Crane, as an artist, achieves by his singleness of purpose a truer and completer picture of war than either Tolstoï, bent also upon proving the insignificance of heroes, or Zola, bent also upon prophesying the regeneration of France. That is much; but it is more that his work of art, when completed, chimes with the universal experience of mankind; that his heroes find in their extreme danger, if not confidence in their leaders and conviction in their cause, at least the conviction that most men do what they can or, at most, what they must. We have few good accounts of battles—many of shipwrecks; and we know that, just as the storm rises, so does the commonplace captain show as a god, and the hysterical passenger as a cheerful heroine.

It is but a further step to recognise all life for a battle and this earth for a vessel lost in space. We may then infer that virtues easy in moments of distress may be useful also in everyday experience.

Note

1. Review of the Paston Letters, *Saturday Review*, November 30th, 1895.

In the School of Battle:
The Making of a Soldier   [Sydney Brooks*]

At a time like the present, when England, isolated by the jealousy and assailed by the threats of powerful rivals, is rising to the situation, and showing that the heart of the nation is as sound after the long Victorian peace as it was in the days of the Armada, that the desperate if lawless enterprise of Jameson and Willoughby[1] is as near to the general heart of the people as were the not very dissimilar enterprises of the old Elizabethan captains, a want, which has long existed, makes itself felt with increased intensity—the want of some book that shall satisfy the well-nigh universal desire to know the inmost truths of the experiences which actual battle alone bestows on the men engaged in it.

The want finds the book as the opportunity finds the man: Mr. Stephen Crane's *Red Badge of Courage* really supplies the want more completely, and therefore more satisfactorily, than any other book with which we are acquainted. Tolstoï, in his *War and Peace* and his sketches of Sebastopol, has given, with extraordinary depth of insight and extraordinary artistic skill, the effect of battle on the ordinary man, whether cultured officer or simple and rough soldier; but he takes no one man through the long series of experiences and impressions which Mr. Crane describes in its effects on young Henry Fleming, a raw recruit who first saw service in the last American Civil War. While the impressions of fighting, and especially of wounds and death, on an individual soldier have been painted with marvellously vivid touches by Tolstoï, the impressions of battle on a body of men, a regiment, have been also realized and represented with characteristic vigour by Mr. Rudyard Kipling in such admirable work as *The Drums of the Fore and Aft*. With less imagination, but with an accumulated mass of studied knowledge altogether too laboured, M. Zola in *La Débâcle* has done some excellent literary work, but work not so convincing as Kipling's, and work certainly far inferior to Mr. Stephen Crane's, whose picture of the effect of actual fighting on a raw regiment is simply unapproached in intimate knowledge and sustained imaginative strength. This we say without forgetting Mérimée's celebrated account of the taking of the redoubt. The writing of the French stylist is, no doubt, much superior in its uniform excellence; but Mr. Crane, in the supreme moments of the fight, is possessed by the fiery breath of battle, as a Pythian priestess by the breath of the God, and finds an inspired utterance that will reach the universal heart of man. Courage in facing wounds and death is the special

* Reprinted from *Saturday Review* 81 (11 January 1896): 44–45.

characteristic of man among the animals, of man who sees into the future, and has therefore much to deter him that affects him alone. Indeed, man, looking at the past, might almost be described as the fighting animal; and Mr. Crane's extraordinary book will appeal strongly to the insatiable desire, latent or developed, to know the psychology of war—how the sights and sounds, the terrible details of the drama of battle, affect the senses and the soul of man. Whether Mr. Crane has had personal experience of the scenes he depicts we cannot say from external evidence; but the extremely vivid touches of detail convince us that he has. Certainly, if his book were altogether a work of the imagination, unbased on personal experience, his realism would be nothing short of a miracle. Unquestionably his knowledge, as we believe acquired in war, has been assimilated and has become a part of himself. At the heated crises of the battle he has the war fever—the Berserk fury in his veins, he lives in the scenes he depicts, he drinks to the dregs the bitter cup of defeat and the bitter cup of fear and shame with his characters no less completely than he thrills with their frantic rage when repulsed by the enemy, and their frantic joy when they charge home.

The Red Badge of Courage—a name which means, we may perhaps explain, a wound received in open fight with the enemy—is the narrative of two processes: the process by which a raw youth develops into a tried and trustworthy soldier, and the process by which a regiment that has never been under fire develops into a finished and formidable fighting machine. Henry Fleming, the youth who is the protagonist of this thrillingly realistic drama of war, has for deuter-agonist Wilson, the loud young boaster. Wilson, however, comes only occasionally into the series of pictures of fighting, and of the impressions that fighting produces on the hypersensitive nerves of the chief character. Fleming, a neurotic lad, constitutionally weak and intensely egotistic, fanciful and easily excited, enlists in the Northern Army, and finds himself a raw recruit in a new regiment, derisively greeted by veteran regiments as "fresh fish." Nights of morbid introspection afflict the youth with the intolerable question, Will he funk when the fighting comes? Thus he continues to question and torture himself till his feelings are raised to the nth power of sensitiveness. At last, after many false alarms and fruitless preparations, the real battle approaches, and whatever confidence in himself remained oozes away from the lonely lad. "He lay down in the grass. The blades pressed tenderly against his cheek. The liquid stillness of the night enveloping him made him feel vast pity for himself. . . . He wished without reserve that he was at home again." He talked with his comrades, but found no sign of similar weakness. He felt himself inferior to them: an outcast. Then, in the grey dawn, after such a night of fear, they start hastily for the front. "He felt carried along by a mob. The sun spread disclosing rays, and one by one regiments burst into view like armed men just born from the earth. The youth perceived that the time had come. He was about to be measured. For a moment he felt in the face of his great trial like a babe, and the flesh over his heart seemed very thin." He looked round him, but there was no escape from the regiment. "He was in a moving box." The experiences of the battle are led up to with masterly skill. First he is fascinated by the skirmishers, whom he sees running hither and thither, "firing at the landscape." Then comes one of Mr. Crane's vivid poetical conceptions: the advancing line encounters a dead soldier.

> He lay upon his back staring at the sky. He was dressed in an awkward suit of yellowish brown. The youth could see that the soles of his shoes had been worn to the thinness of writing paper, and from a great rent in one the dead foot projected piteously. And it was as if death had betrayed the soldier. In death it exposed to his enemies that poverty which in life he had perhaps concealed from his friends. The ranks opened covertly to avoid the corpse. The invulnerable dead man forced a way for himself. The youth looked keenly at the ashen face. The wind raised the tawny beard. It moved as if a hand were stroking it.

An unreasoning dread swept over the young recruit; the forest everywhere seemed to hide the enemy, and might any moment bristle with rifle-barrels. He lagged at last, with tragic glances at the sky; only to bring down on himself the young lieutenant of his company with loud reproaches for skulking. The new regiment took its ground in a fringe of wood. Shells came screaming over. "Bullets began to whistle among the branches and hiss at the trees. Twigs and leaves came sailing down. It was as if a thousand axes, wee and invisible, were being wielded." Then the tide of battle moved toward them, and out of the grey smoke came the yells of the combatants, and then a mob of beaten men rushed past, careless of the grim jokes hurled at them. "The battle reflection that shone for an instant on their faces on the mad current made the youth feel" that he would have gladly escaped if he could. "The sight of this stampede exercised a flood-like force that seemed able to drag sticks and stones and men from the ground." At last, "Here they come! Here they come! Gun-locks clicked. Across the smoke-infested fields came a brown swarm of running men who were giving shrill yells. A flag tilted forward sped near the front."

The man at the youth's elbow was mumbling, as if to himself, "Oh! we're in for it now; oh! we're in for it now." The youth fired a wild first shot, and immediately began to work at his weapon automatically. He lost concern for himself, and felt that something of which he was a part was in a crisis. "He felt the subtle battle-brotherhood more potent even than the cause for which they were fighting." "Following this came a red rage. He had a mad feeling against his rifle, which could only be used against one life at a time." The description goes on, full of vivid realistic touches, of which we can only give a fragment or two. "The steel ramrods clanked and clanged with incessant din as the men pounded them furiously into the hot rifle barrels." The "men dropped here and there like bundles." One man "grunted suddenly as if he had been struck by a club in the stomach. He sat down and gazed ruefully. In his eyes there was mute indefinite reproach." The first attack was repulsed. The youth had stood his ground and was in an ecstasy of self-satisfaction. The supreme trial, he thought, was over. Suddenly from the ranks rose the astonished cry, "Here they come again!" and a fresh attack developed. The men groaned and began to grumble. On came the rebel attack. "Reeling with exhaustion, the youth began to overestimate the strength of the assailants. They must be machines of steel." "He seemed to shut his eyes and wait to be gobbled." Then "a man near him ran with howls—a lad whose face had borne an expression of exalted courage—was in an instant smitten abject. He, too, threw down his gun and fled. There was no shame in his face. He ran like a rabbit." The youth saw their flight—yelled—swung about—and sped to the rear in great leaps. "He ran like a blind man. Two or three times he fell down. Once he knocked his shoulder so heavily against a tree that he went headlong."

The fugitive, after a time, comes upon a procession of wounded men, limping and staggering to the rear. The wounded men fraternize with him, supposing him to be wounded also. The growth of shame that begins with a brotherly question, "Where yeh hit, ol' boy?" is as good as any part of this long psychological study. "At times he regarded the wounded soldiers in an envious way. He wished he too had a wound, a red badge of courage." There was a spectral soldier at his side, whose eyes were fixed in a stare into the unknown; he suddenly recognized his old comrade, Jim Conklin, the tall soldier. The gradual dying on his legs of the tall soldier is described with extraordinary vividness. The soldier, with the instinct of the animal wounded unto death, wishes to creep off and be alone. His comrades, anxious to help him, insist on following him. He suddenly slips away and leaves them. "Leave me be, can't ye? Leave me be for a moment," is his entreaty, and they follow at a distance. They watch his death, as wonderfully described as a death in Tolstoï. "Well, he was reg'lar jim-dandy fer nerve, wa'nt he?" says the tattered soldier in a little awestruck voice. "I never seen a man do like that before." Presently, the incoherent talk of the wounded man is made to reflect with a Sophoclean irony on the runaway youth. The night bivouac in the

forest after the battle is finely described. The weary men lying round
the fires, under the forest roof; the break in the trees, through which
a space of starry sky is seen. At dawn the motionless mass of bodies,
thick spread on the ground, look in the grey light as if the place
were a charnel-house.

The fighting of the new regiment, a forlorn hope, proceeds with
a breathless speed of narrative that emulates the actual rush of the
battle-worn and desperate men, among whom there is no flinching
or fear now, any more than there is in the sensitive youth, who,
having had his battle baptism, is soon to bear the colours, wrenched
from the iron grip of the dead colour-sergeant. "As the regiment
swung from its position out into a cleared space, the woods and
thickets before it awakened. Yellow flames leaped towards it from
many directions. . . . The song of the bullets was in the air, and
shells snarled in the tree-tops. One tumbled directly in the middle
of a hurrying group and exploded in crimson fury. There was an
instant's spectacle of a man, almost over it, throwing up his hands
to shield his eyes. Other men, punctured by bullets, fell in grotesque
agonies." The regiment stopped for breath, and as it saw the gaps
the bullets were making in the ranks, faltered and hesitated. The
lieutenant worked them forward painfully with volleys of oaths. They
halted behind some trees. Then the lieutenant, with the two young
soldiers, made a last effort. They led the regiment, bawling "Come
on! come on!"

> The flag, obedient to these appeals, bended its glittering form and
> swept toward them. The men wavered in indecision for a moment,
> and then, with a long wailful cry, the dilapidated regiment surged
> forward and began its new journey. Over the field went the scurrying
> mass. It was a handful of men splattered into the faces of the enemy.
> Towards it instantly sprang the yellow tongues. A vast quantity of
> blue smoke hung before them. A mighty banging made ears val-
> ueless. The youth ran like a madman to reach the woods before a
> bullet could discover him. He ducked his head low like a football-
> player. In his haste his eyes almost closed, and the scene was a
> wild blur. Pulsating saliva stood at the corners of his mouth.

At last the men began to trickle back. In vain the youth carrying
the colours aided the lieutenant to rally them. The battered and
bruised regiment slowly makes its way back, only to be condemned
by the general who had ordered the charge.

Then comes a capital account of the young soldier's reward.
Several men hurry up with good news to the hero of the book:—
"Th' colonel met your lieutenant right by us. 'Who was the lad that
carried the flag?' he ses; an' th' lieutenant he speaks up right away:
'That's Flemin', an' he's a jimhickey,' he ses right away. 'He's a good

un',' ses th' colonel. 'You bet!' ses th' lieutenant. 'He and a feller named Wilson was at th' head 'a th' charge, an' howlin' like Injins all the time,' he ses. 'My sakes!' ses th' colonel. 'Well, well, well, those two babies' "—and the heart of the young soldier swelled with happiness and with affection for the colonel and the youthful lieutenant.

And then, after other desperate charges, the army is withdrawn across the river—nothing apparently accomplished by all their struggles and all their sufferings, and the book closes with a few words on the moral effect of the heavy fighting on the youth. "He found that he could look backward on the brass and bombast of his earlier gospels and see them. He was gleeful when he discovered that he now despised them. With this conviction came a store of assurance. He felt a quiet manhood, non-assertive, but of steady and strong blood. . . . He had been to touch the great death, and found that after all it was but the great death. He was a man." The book is crowded with vivid passages and striking descriptions, often expressed in original and picturesque diction. "A mass of wet grass marched upon rustled like silk"; "A dense wall of smoke settled slowly down. It was furiously slit and slashed by the knife-like fire from the rifles"; Bullets "spanged"; "Bullets buffed into men"; "His dead body lying torn and gluttering upon the field." One is not inclined to criticize the giver of such a book; but it will be observed that when the Berserk inspiration is not upon him, Mr. Crane writes as badly as, when his imagination is heated, he writes well—*e.g.* "Too, the clothes seemed new."

Note

1. [Ed. note: Leander Starr Jameson was the leader of Jameson's Raid, an abortive effort in late 1895 by British settlers to overthrow the Afrikaans government of the Transvaal in South Africa. John Willoughy was Jameson's chief-of-staff.]

Stephen Crane's Triumph   Harold Frederic[*]

London, Jan. 15—Who in London knows about Stephen Crane? The question is one of genuine interest here. It happens, annoyingly enough, that the one publishing person who might throw some light on the answer is for the moment absent from town. Other sources yield only the meagre information that the name is believed to be a

[*] Reprinted from *New York Times*, 26 January 1896, 22.

real, and not an assumed, one, and that its owner is understood to be a very young man, indeed. That he is an American, or, at least, learned to read and write in America, is obvious enough. The mere presence in his vocabulary of the verb "loan" would settle that, if the proof were not otherwise blazoned on every page of his extraordinary book. For this mysteriously unknown youth has really written an extraordinary book.

The Red Badge of Courage appeared a couple of months ago, unheralded and unnoticed, in a series which, under the distinctive label of "Pioneer," is popularly supposed to present fiction more or less after the order of The Green Carnation,[1] which was also of that lot. The first one who mentioned in my hearing that this Red Badge was well worth reading happened to be a person whose literary admirations serve me generally as warnings what to avoid, and I remembered the title languidly from that standpoint of self-protection. A little later others began to speak of it. All at once, every bookish person had it at his tongue's end. It was clearly a book to read, and I read it. Even as I did so, reviews burst forth in a dozen different quarters, hailing it as extraordinary. Some were naturally more excited and voluble than others, but all the critics showed, and continue to show, their sense of being in the presence of something not like other things. George Wyndham, M. P., has already written of it in The New Review as "a remarkable book." Other magazine editors have articles about it in preparation, and it is evident that for the next few months it is to be more talked about than anything else in current literature. It seems almost equally certain that it will be kept alive, as one of the deathless books which must be read by everybody who desires to be, or to seem, a connoisseur of modern fiction.

If there were in existence any books of a similar character, one could start confidently by saying that it was the best of its kind. But it has no fellows. It is a book outside of all classification. So unlike anything else is it, that the temptation rises to deny that it is a book at all. When one searches for comparisons, they can only be found by culling out selected portions from the trunks of masterpieces, and considering these detached fragments, one by one, with reference to the Red Badge, which is itself a fragment, and yet is complete. Thus one lifts the best battle pictures from Tolstoï's great War and Peace, from Balzac's Chouans, from Hugo's Les Misérables, and the forest fight in '93, from Prosper Mérimée's assault of the redoubt, from Zola's La Débâcle and Attack on the Mill, (it is strange enough that equivalents in the literature of our own language do not suggest themselves,) and studies them side by side with this tremendously effective battle painting by the unknown youngster. Positively they are cold and ineffectual beside it. The praise may sound exaggerated, but really it is inadequate. These renowned battle descriptions of the

big men are made to seem all wrong. The *Red Badge* impels the
feeling that the actual truth about a battle has never been guessed
before.

In construction the book is as original as in its unique grasp of
a new grouping of old materials. All the historic and prescribed
machinery of the romance is thrust aside. One barely knows the name
of the hero; it is only dimly sketched in that he was a farm boy and
had a mother when he enlisted. These facts recur to him once or
twice; they play no larger part in the reader's mind. Only two other
characters are mentioned by name—Jim Conklin and Wilson; more
often even they are spoken of as the tall soldier and the loud soldier.
Not a word is expended on telling where they come from, or who
they are. They pass across the picture, or shift from one posture to
another in its moving composition, with the impersonality of one's
chance fellow-passengers in a railroad car. There is a lieutenant who
swears new oaths all the while, another officer with a red beard, and
two or three still vaguer figures, revealed here and there through
the smoke. We do not know, or seek to know, their names, or anything
about them except what, staring through the eyes of Henry Fleming,
we are permitted to see. The regiment itself, the refugees from other
regiments in the crowded flight, and the enemy on the other side of
the fence, are differentiated only as they wear blue or gray. We
never get their color out of our mind's eye. This exhausts the dramatis
personae of the book, and yet it is more vehemently alive and heaving
with dramatic human action than any other book of our time. The
people are all strangers to us, but the sight of them stirs the pro-
foundest emotions of interest in our breasts. What they do appeals
as vividly to our consciousness as if we had known them all our life.

The central idea of the book is of less importance than the
magnificent graft of externals upon it. We begin with the young raw
recruit, hearing that at last his regiment is going to see some fighting,
and brooding over the problem of his own behavior under fire. We
follow his perturbed meditations through thirty pages, which cover
a week or so of this menace of action. Then suddenly, with one gray
morning, the ordeal breaks abruptly over the youngster's head. We
go with him, so close that he is never out of sight, for two terribly
crowded days, and then the book is at an end. This cross-section of
his experience is made a part of our own. We see with his eyes,
think with his mind, quail or thrill with his nerves. He strives to
argue himself into the conventional soldier's bravery; he runs inglo-
riously away; he excuses, defends, and abhors himself in turn; he
tremblingly yields to the sinister fascination of creeping near the
battle; he basely allows his comrades to ascribe to heroism the wound
he received in the frenzied "sauve qui peut" of the fight, he gets
at last the fire of combat in his veins, and blindly rushing in, deports

himself with such hardy and temerarious valor that even the Colonel notes him, and admits that he is a "jimhickey." These sequent processes, observed with relentless minutiae, are so powerfully and speakingly portrayed that they seem the veritable actions of our own minds. To produce this effect is a notable triumph, but it is commonplace by comparison with the other triumph of making us realize what Henry saw and heard as well as what he felt. The value of the former feat has the limitations of the individual. No two people are absolutely alike; any other young farm boy would have passed through the trial with something different somewhere. Where Henry fluttered, he might have been obtuse; neither the early panic nor the later irrational ferocity would necessarily have been just the same. But the picture of the trial itself seems to me never to have been painted as well before.

Oddly enough, *The Saturday Review* and some other of the commentators take it for granted that the writer of the *Red Badge* must have seen real warfare. "The extremely vivid touches of detail convince us," says *The Review*, "that he has had personal experience of the scenes he depicts. Certainly, if his book were altogether a work of imagination, unbased on personal experience, his realism would be nothing short of a miracle." This may strike the reader who has not thought much about it as reasonable, but I believe it to be wholly fallacious. Some years ago I had before me the task of writing some battle chapters in a book I was at work upon. The novel naturally led up to the climax of a battle, and I was excusably anxious that when I finally got to this battle, I should be as fit to handle it as it was possible to make myself. A very considerable literature existed about the actual struggle, which was the Revolutionary battle of Oriskany, fought only a few miles from where I was born.[2] This literature was in part the narratives of survivors of the fight, in part imaginative accounts based on these by later writers. I found to my surprise that the people who were really in the fight gave one much less of an idea of a desperate forest combat than did those who pictured it in fancy. Of course, here it might be that the veterans were inferior in powers of narration to the professional writer. Then I extended the test to writers themselves. I compared the best accounts of Franco-German battles, written for the London newspapers by trained correspondents of distinction who were on the spot, with the choicest imaginative work of novelists, some of them mentioned above, who had never seen a gun fired in anger. There was literally no comparison between the two. The line between journalism and literature obtruded itself steadily. Nor were cases lacking in which some of these war correspondents had in other departments of work showed themselves capable of true literature. I have the instance of David Christie Murray in mind. He saw some of the stiffest fighting that was done in his time, and that, too, at an early stage of his career, but he never tried to put a great battle chapter into one of his subsequent novels, and if he had I don't believe it would have been great.[3]

Our own writers of the elder generation illustrate this same truth. Gen. Lew Wallace, Judge Tourgée, Dr. Weir Mitchell, and numbers of others saw tremendous struggles on the battlefield, but to put the reality into type baffles them. The four huge volumes of *The Century*'s *Battles and Leaders of the Civil War* are written almost exclusively by men who took an active part in the war, and many of them were in addition men of high education and considerable literary talent, but there is not a really moving story of a fight in the whole work. When Warren Lee Goss began his *Personal Recollections of a Private*, his study of the enlistment, the early marching and drilling, and the new experiences of camp life was so piquant and fresh that I grew quite excited in anticipation. But when he came to the fighting, he fell flat. The same may be said, with more reservations, about the first parts of Judge Tourgée's more recent *Story of a Thousand.* It seems as if the actual sight of a battle has some dynamic quality in it which overwhelms and crushes the literary faculty in the observer. At best, he gives us a conventional account of what happened; but on analysis you find that this is not what he really saw, but what all his reading has taught him that he must have seen. In the same way battle painters depict horses in motion, not as they actually move, but as it has been agreed by numberless generations of draughtsmen to say that they move. At last, along comes a Muybridge, with his instantaneous camera, and shows that the real motion is entirely different.[4]

It is this effect of a photographic revelation which startles and fascinates one in *The Red Badge of Courage.* The product is breathlessly interesting, but still more so is the suggestion behind it that a novel force has been disclosed, which may do all sorts of other remarkable things. Prophecy is known of old as a tricky and thankless hag, but all the same I cannot close my ears to her hint that a young man who can write such a first book as that will make us all sit up in good time.

Notes

1. [Ed. note: Robert Hichens's *The Green Carnation* (1894), a popular novel of fashionable London life.]

2. [Ed. note: Frederic, the London correspondent of the *New York Times*, was himself a major novelist, with a number of his works set in the upstate New York area where he was born and raised. He refers here to his Revolutionary War novel *In the Valley* (1890).]

3. [Ed. note: Murray was a popular British novelist and travel writer. Early in his career he had reported on the Russian-Turkish War of 1877–78.]

4. [Ed. note: Earweard Muybridge, a photographer and naturalist, had in the 1870s demonstrated through photography that all four of a running horse's hooves are at times simultaneously off the ground.]

The Red Badge of Hysteria   [Alexander C. McClurg*]

Must we come to judge of books only by what the newspapers have said of them, and must we abandon all the old standards of criticism?[1] Can a book and an author, utterly without merit, be puffed into success by entirely undeserved praise, even if that praise come from English periodicals?

One must ask these questions after he has been seduced into reading a book recently reprinted in this country entitled *The Red Badge of Courage, an Episode of the American Civil War.* The chorus of praise in the English papers has been very extravagant, but it is noticeable that so far, at least, the American papers have said very little about the merits or demerits of the book itself. They simply allude to the noise made over it abroad, and therefore treat its author as a coming factor in our literature. Even *The Dial*'s very acute and usually very discerning critic of contemporary fiction (Mr. Payne) treats the book and the author (in your issue of Feb. 1) in very much this way—that is, as a book and an author to be reckoned with, not because of any good which he himself finds in them, but because they have been so much talked about.

The book has very recently been reprinted in America, and would seem to be an American book, on an American theme, and by an American author, yet originally issued in England. If it is really an American production one must suppose it to have been promptly and properly rejected by any American publishers to whom it may have been submitted, and afterward more naturally taken up by an English publisher.

It is only too well known that English writers have had a very low opinion of American soldiers, and have always, as a rule, assumed to ridicule them. *Blackwood's Magazine* is quoted by a recent writer as saying during the War: "We cannot even pretend to keep our countenance when the exploits of the Grand Army of the Potomac are filling all Europe with inextinguishable laughter," and adds "we know not whether to pity most the officers who lead such men, or the men who are led by such officers" (Vol. 90, pp. 395–6). And

* Reprinted from *Dial* 20 (16 April 1896): 227–28.

again, in January, 1862: "Englishmen are unable to see anything peculiarly tragical in the fact that half a million of men have been brought together in arms to hurl big words at each other across a river" (Vol. 91, p. 118). Again, in April, 1862, *Blackwood* tells us that Americans "do not demand our respect because of their achievements in art, or in literature, or in science, or philosophy. They can make no pretence to the no less real, though less beneficent, reputation of having proved themselves a great military power" (Vol. 91, p. 534). And in October, 1861, *Blackwood* said exultantly: "The venerable Lincoln, the respectable Seward, the raving editors, the gibbering mob, and the swift-footed warriors of Bull's Run, are no malicious tricks of fortune, played off on an unwary nation, but are all of them the legitimate offspring of the Great Republic," and is "glad that the end of the Union seems more likely to be ridiculous than terrible" (Vol. 90, p. 396).

We all know with what bitterness and spitefulness the *Saturday Review* always treats Americans; and with what special vindictiveness it reviews any book upon our late struggle written from the Northern standpoint. And so it is with all British periodicals and all British writers. They are so puffed up with vain-glory over their own soldiers who seldom meet men of their own strength, but are used in every part of the world for attacking and butchering defenseless savages, who happen to possess some property that Englishmen covet, that they cannot believe that there can be among any peoples well-disciplined soldiers as gallant and courageous as their own.

Under such circumstances we cannot doubt that *The Red Badge of Courage* would be just such a book as the English would grow enthusiastic over, and we cannot wonder that the redoubtable *Saturday Review* greeted it with the highest encomiums, and declared it the actual experiences of a veteran of our War, when it was really the vain imaginings of a young man born long since that war, a piece of intended realism based entirely on unreality. The book is a vicious satire upon American soldiers and American armies. The hero of the book (if such he can be called—"the youth" the author styles him) is an ignorant and stupid country lad, who, without a spark of patriotic feeling, or even of soldierly ambition, has enlisted in the army from no definite motive that the reader can discover, unless it be because other boys are doing so; and the whole book, in which there is absolutely no story, is occupied with giving what are supposed to be his emotions and his actions in the first two days of battle. His poor weak intellect, if indeed he has any, seems to be at once and entirely overthrown by the din and movement of the field, and he acts throughout like a madman. Under the influence of mere excitement, for he does not even appear to be frightened, he first rushes madly to the rear in a crazy panic, and afterward plunges forward to the rescue of the colors under exactly the same influences. In neither case has reason or any intelligent motive any influence on his action. He is throughout an idiot or a maniac, and betrays no trace of the reasoning being. No thrill of patriotic devotion to cause or country ever moves his breast, and not even an emotion of manly courage. Even a wound which he finally gets comes from a comrade who strikes him on the head with his musket to get rid of him; and this is the only *Red Badge of Courage* (!) which we discover in the book. A number of other characters come in to fill out the two hundred and thirty-three pages of the book,—such as "the loud soldier," "the tall soldier," "the tattered soldier," etc., but not one of them betrays any more sense, self-possession, or courage than does "the youth." On the field all is chaos and confusion. "The young lieutenant," "the mounted officer," even "the general," are all utterly demented beings, raving and talking alike in an unintelligible and hitherto unheard-of jargon, rushing about in a very delirium of madness. No intelligent orders are given; no intelligent movements are made. There is no evidence of drill, none of discipline. There is a constant, senseless, and profane babbling going on, such as one could hear nowhere but in a madhouse. Nowhere are seen the quiet, manly, self-respecting, and patriotic men, influenced by the highest sense of duty, who in reality fought our battles.

It can be said most confidently that no soldier who fought in our recent War ever saw any approach to the battle scenes in this book— but what wonder? We are told that it is the work of a young man of twenty-three or twenty-four years of age, and so of course must be a mere work of diseased imagination. And yet it constantly strains after so-called realism. The result is a mere riot of words.

Although its burlesques and caricatures are quite enough to dismiss it from attention, it is worth while to give some samples of its diction to show that there is in it an entire lack of any literary quality. Notice the violent straining after effect in the mere unusual association of words, in the forced and distorted use of adjectives. Notice, too, the absurb similes, and even the bad grammar. Startling sentences are so frequent they might be quoted indefinitely; but here are a few:

> "A brigade ahead of them and on the right went into action *with a rending roar. It was as if it had exploded*" (p. 45).
> "The lieutenant of the youth's company was shot in the hand. He began to swear so wondrously that a nervous laugh went along the regimental line. The officer's profanity sounded conventional. It relieved the tightened senses of the new men. *It was as if he had hit his fingers with a tack hammer at home*" (p. 49).
> "Another [mounted officer] was galloping about *bawling*. His hat was gone, and his clothes were awry. *He resembled a man who*

has come from bed to go to a fire. The hoofs of his horse often threatened the heads of the running men, but they scampered with singular fortune. In this rush they were apparently all deaf and blind. They heeded not the largest and longest of oaths which were thrown at them from all directions" (p. 51).

"The battle reflection that shone for an instant in the faces on the mad current made the youth feel that forceful hands from heaven would not have been able to have held him in place if he could have got intelligent control of his legs" (p. 52).

"*A small thrillful boy*" (p. 53).

"The cartridge-boxes were pulled around into various positions, and adjusted with great care. *It was as if seven hundred new bonnets were being tried on*" (p. 53).

"Buried in the smoke of many rifles, his anger was directed not so much against the men *whom he knew were rushing* toward him as against the swishing battle phantoms which were choking him, stuffing their smoke robes down his parched throat" (p. 57).

"There was a *blare of heated rage*" (p. 58).

"The officers at their intervals rearward . . . were bobbing to and fro roaring directions. *The dimensions of their howls were extraordinary*" (p. 59).

"To the youth it was like an onslaught of redoubtable dragons. He became like the man who lost his legs at the approach of the red and green monster. He waited in a sort of horrified, listening attitude. He seemed to shut his eyes, and wait to be gobbled" (p. 68).

"*A crimson roar* came from a distance" (p. 82).

"With the courageous words of the artillery and the spiteful sentences of the musketry mingled *red cheers*" (p. 85).

"The youth had reached an anguish when *the sobs scorched him*" (p. 94).

"*They were ever up-raising the ghost of shame on the stick of their curiosity*" (p. 104).

"The *new silence of his wound* made much worryment" (p. 124).

"The distance *was splintering* and blaring with the noise of fighting" (p. 139).

". . . began *to mutter softly in black curses*" (p. 201).

"His corpse would be for those eyes *a great and salt reproach*" (p. 215).

It is extraordinary that even a prejudiced animus could have led English writers to lavish extravagant praise on such a book; it is still more extraordinary that an attempt should be made to foist it upon the long-suffering American public, and to push it into popularity here. Respect for our own people should have prevented its issue in this country.

There may have been a moderate number of men in our service

who felt and acted in battle like those in this book; but of such deserters were made. They did not stay when they could get away: why should they? The army was no healthy place for them, and they had no reason to stay; there was no moral motive. After they had deserted, however, they remained "loud soldiers," energetic, and blatant,—and they are possibly now enjoying good pensions. It must have been some of these fellows who got the ear of Mr. Crane and told him how they felt and acted in battle.

A. C. McC.

Chicago, April 11, 1896.

Note

1. [Ed. note: McClurg, the owner of the *Dial*, a Chicago literary journal, had served with distinction in the Union army during the Civil War, rising from private to colonel.]

Mr. Stephen Crane and His Critics
Sydney Brooks*

It really requires some courage to confess it, but I was one of the first English reviewers to whose lot fell the reviewing of Mr. Stephen Crane's book, *The Red Badge of Courage*. Worse still—a quite damning fact, I fear—I even ventured to praise it. Mr. Crane I had never heard of when his book came to me in the ordinary course of business, but I read the volume with the greatest interest; I thought it in many ways a remarkable performance, and I did my best to give reasons for the faith that was in me. But apparently it is a subtle insult for an Englishman to praise an American book. I used to think that a good book was a good book the whole world over. It is only since landing in this country and picking up *The Dial* of April 16 that I have learned better. Your correspondent, "A. C. McC.," is my authority. Now, I am truly sorry that any criticisms of mine or of my brother reviewers in London should have so annoyed your correspondent, for he evidently was very much annoyed. He came out on the warpath, arrested Mr. Crane as a literary spy, court-martialled him, and shot the poor fellow off-hand.

This book, says "A. C. McC." in effect, cannot be a good one for Americans to read because the English have praised it. He puts the whole thing in a nutshell, you see. This English praise, he is

* Reprinted from *Dial* 20 (16 May 1896): 297–98.

convinced, is a Grecian gift. I personally thought I was merely pointing out the merits of what seemed to me a book that deserved some notice. But he saw the ambush we English reviewers were laying. Deep under our affected enthusiasm for this young writer was an intense desire to insult America. It sounds oddly, doesn't it? But he has chapter and verse to prove it. He comes across some cruel, senseless gibes at the Union soldiers in *Blackwood's Magazine.* They are over thirty years old, and to-day, from one end of England to the other, you could not find a man to express anything but the bitterest shame of them. But what of that? "There," exclaims "A. C. McC." exultantly, "that is why these English are praising Stephen Crane. The hero of his book is a coward. Thirty years ago an ignorant British magazine talked of 'the swift-footed warriors of Bull's Run.' Don't you see the connection? It is all a deep-laid plot to throw mud at American soldiers." To be sure! And so when I sat, pipe in mouth, a peaceable, jaded reviewer, happy to have come across a book above the dull dead level, my mind was really full of schemes for avenging Bunker's Hill!

Your correspondent's letter is a compound of misjudged patriotism and bad criticism. Take only these two sentences. "The book," he says, "is a vicious satire upon American soldiers and American armies." "Respect for our own people should have prevented its issue in this country." A curious attitude to take up towards a book, unworthy of an American, as it seems to me, and peculiarly unworthy of an American who, as I hear, fought through the war with distinction. I will say at once that no such idea ever presented itself to a single Englishman into whose hands the book fell. The most insignificant thing about the book, the one point which every sensible reviewer would at once dismiss form his mind as quite immaterial, is the fact that the hero fought for the North. If he had been an Englishman in the ditches before Sebastopol, or a Frenchman at Sedan, the book would have been just as remarkable, and the praise of the English journals no less warm. But to "A. C. McC." Mr. Crane's one unforgivable crime lies in portraying a Northerner who fled from the field.

Scarcely less wrong-headed is your correspondent's criticism of the book as a piece of literature. He has missed the whole point of the tale. Part of Mr. Crane's plan, I take it, was to give an idea of the impressions made on a raw recruit by the movements of a regiment in battle. Who can doubt that to a man who but yesterday was working at the plough the whole thing appears one intolerable confusion? As for the style in which the book is written, "A. C. McC." finds in it "an entire lack of any literary quality." Mr. Crane, once more, is an author "utterly without merit." No half-measures with "A. C. McC." Again quotations are at hand. Detached sentences are given, and anything disapproved of is italicised. The odd part about it is that most of the expressions thus crucified seem to me admirable and picturesque. That there is a youthful and occasionally reckless daring about some, is true enough. But on the whole I am prepared to back Mr. Crane's sense of language against "A. C. McC.'s."

However, I am concerned little here with the merits of Mr. Crane's work. The book can take care of itself quite well. I was surprised at "A. C. McC.'s" singular criticisms, and thought that a few words from "the other side" might be fairly called for.

SYDNEY BROOKS.

Chicago, May 9, 1896.

Book and Heart: A Bit
of War Photography   Thomas Wentworth Higginson°

After the applause won by Mr. Stephen Crane's *Red Badge of Courage,* a little reaction is not strange; and this has already taken, in some quarters, a form quite unjust and unfair.[1] Certainly any one who spent so much as a week or two in camp, thirty years ago, must be struck with the extraordinary freshness and vigor of the book. No one except Tolstoi, within my knowledge, has brought out the daily life of war so well; it may be said of these sentences, in Emerson's phrase, "Cut these and they bleed." The breathlessness, the hurry, the confusion, the seeming aimlessness, as of a whole family of disturbed ants, running to and fro, yet somehow accomplishing something at last; all these aspects, which might seem the most elementary and the easiest to depict, are yet those surest to be omitted, not merely by the novelists, but by the regimental histories themselves.

I know that when I first read Tolstoi's *War and Peace, The Cossacks* and *Sevastopol,* it seemed as if all other so-called military novels must become at once superannuated and go out of print. All others assumed, in comparison, that bandbox aspect which may be seen in most military or naval pictures; as in the well known engraving of the death of Nelson, where the hero is sinking on the deck in perfect toilette, at the height of a bloody conflict, while every soldier or sailor is grouped around him, each in spotless garments and heroic attitude. It is this Tolstoi quality—the real tumult and tatters of the thing itself—which amazes the reader of Crane's novel. Moreover, Tolstoi had been through it all in person; whereas this author is a youth of twenty-four, it seems, born since the very last shot fired in the Civil War. How did he hit upon his point of view?

° Reprinted from *Philistine* 3 (July 1896): 33–38.

Yet this very point of view, strange to say, has been called a defect. Remember that he is telling the tale, not of a commanding general, but of a common soldier—a pawn in the game; a man who sees only what is going on immediately around him, and, for the most part, has the key to nothing beyond. This he himself knows well at the time. Afterward, perhaps, when the affair is discussed at the campfire, and his view compared with what others say, it begins to take shape, often mixed with all sorts of errors; and when it has reached the Grand Army Post and been talked over afterward for thirty years, the narrator has not a doubt of it all. It is now a perfectly ordered affair, a neat and well arranged game of chess, often with himself as a leading figure. That is the result of too much perspective. The wonder is that this young writer, who had no way of getting at it all except the gossip—printed or written—of these very old soldiers, should be able to go behind them all, and give an account of their life, not only more vivid than they themselves have ever given, but more accurate. It really seems a touch of that marvelous intuitive quality which for want of a better name we call genius.

Now it is a correct criticism of the book to complain, as one writer has done, that it does not dwell studiously on the higher aspects of the war? Let the picture only be well drawn, and the moral will take care of itself; never fear. The book is not a patriotic tract, but a delineation; a cross section of the daily existence of the raw enlisted-man. In other respects it is reticent, because it is truthful. Does any one suppose that in the daily routine of the camp there was room for much fine talk about motives and results—that men were constantly appealing, like Carlyle's Frenchman, "to posterity and the immortal Gods?" Fortunately or unfortunately, the Anglo Saxon is not built that way; he errs on the other side; habitually understates instead of overstating his emotions; and while he is making the most heroic sacrifices of his life, usually prefers to scold about rations or grumble at orders. He is to be judged by results; not by what he says, which is often ungracious and unornamental, but by what he does.

The very merit of this book is that in dealing with his men the author offers, within this general range, all the essential types of character—the man who boasts and the man who is humble—the man who thinks he may be frightened and is not, and the man who does not expect to be, but is. For his main character he selects a type to be found in every regiment—the young man who does not know himself, who first stumbles into cowardice, to his own amazement, and then is equally amazed at stumbling into courage; who begins with skulking, and ends by taking a flag. In Doyle's *Micah Clarke* the old Roundhead soldier tells his grandchildren how he felt inclined to bob his head when he first heard bullets whistle, and adds

"If any soldier ever told you that he did not, the first time that he was under fire, then that soldier is not a man to trust." This is putting it too strongly, for some men are born more stolid, other more nervous; but the nervous man is quite as likely to have the firmer grain, and to come out the more heroic in the end. In my own limited experience, the only young officer whom I ever saw thoroughly and confessedly frightened, when first under fire, was the only one of his regiment who afterwards chose the regular army for his profession, and fought Indians for the rest of his life.

As for *The Red Badge of Courage*, the test of the book is in the way it holds you. I only know that whenever I take it up I find myself reading it over and over, as I do Tolstoi's *Cossacks*, and find it as hard to put down. None of Doyle's or Weyman's books bear re-reading, in the same way; you must wait till you have forgotten their plots. Even the slipshod grammar seems a part of the breathless life and action. How much promise it gives, it is hard to say. Goethe says that as soon as a man has done one good thing, the world conspires against him to keep him from doing another. Mr. Crane has done one good thing, not to say two; but the conspiracy of admiration may yet be too much for him. It is earnestly to be hoped, at least, that he may have the wisdom to stay in his own country and resist the temptation to test his newly-found English reputation by migrating—an experiment by which Bret Harte has been visibly dwarfed and Henry James hopelessly diluted.

Note

1. [Ed. note: Higginson was a New England reformer who commanded a regiment of freed slaves during the Civil War. He later became a popular lecturer and literary critic.]

The Red Badge of Courage   [A. G. Sedgwick°]

Mr. Stephen Crane is said never to have seen a battle; but his first book, *The Red Badge of Courage*, is made up of the account of one. The success of the story, however, is due, not merely to what Mr. Crane knows of battle-fields, but to what he knows of the human heart. He describes the adventures of a private—a raw recruit—in one of those long engagements, so common in our civil war, and indeed in all modern wars, in which the field of battle is too extensive

° Reprinted from *Nation* 63 (2 July 1896): 15.

for those in one part of it to know what is going on elsewhere, and where often a regiment remains in ignorance for some time whether it is victorious or defeated, where the nature of the country prevents hand-to-hand fighting, and a *coup d'œil* of the whole scene is out of the question. In such an action Mr. Crane's hero plays an active part. It is what goes on in his mind that we hear of, and his experience is in part so exactly what old soldiers tell young soldiers to expect that Mr. Crane might easily have got it at second-hand. The hero is at first mortally afraid that he is going to be afraid, he then does his duty well enough, but later is seized with a panic and runs away, only to come out a hero again in the end. His panic and flight are managed well; the accidental wound which he luckily gets in running, helps him to a reputation for bravery before he has earned it. When he fights in the end, he fights like a devil, he saves the regimental flag, he is insane with the passion of battle; he is baptized into the brotherhood of those who have been to hell and returned alive. The book is undeniably clever; its vice is over-emphasis. Mr. Crane has not learnt the secret that carnage is itself eloquent, and does not need epithets to make it so. What is a "crimson roar"? Do soldiers hear crimson roars, or do they hear simply roars? If this way of getting expression out of language is allowable, why not extend it to the other senses, and have not only crimson sounds, but purple smells, prehensile views, adhesive music? Color in language is just now a fashionable affectation; Mr. Crane's originality does not lie in falling into it. *George's Mother* is the story of a degenerate drunkard who breaks his mother's heart; *Maggie* is a story of the Bowery, in the "dialect" of "Chimmie Fadden."[1]

Taking all three stories together, we should classify Mr. Crane as a rather promising writer of the animalistic school. His types are mainly human beings of the order which makes us regret the power of literature to portray them. Not merely are they low, but there is little that is interesting in them. We resent the sense that we must at certain points resemble them. Even the old mother is not made pathetic in a human way; her son disgusts us so that we have small power of sympathy with her left. Maggie it is impossible to weep over. We can feel only that it is a pity that the gutter is so dirty, and turn in another direction. In short, Mr. Crane's art is to us very depressing. Of course, there is always the crushing reply that one who does not love art for the sake of art is a poor devil, not worth writing for. But we do not; we do not even love literature for its own sake.

It is only fair to say that what we have called animalism others pronounce wonderful realism. We use the word animalism for the sake of clearness, to denote a species of realism which deals with man considered as an animal, capable of hunger, thirst, lust, cruelty, vanity, fear, sloth, predacity, greed, and other passions and appetites that make him kin to the brutes, but which neglects, so far as possible, any higher qualities which distinguish him from his four-footed relatives, such as humor, thought, reason, aspiration, affection, morality, and religion. Real life is full of the contrasts between these conflicting tendencies, but the object of the animalistic school seems always to make a study of the *genus homo* which shall recall the menagerie at feeding-time rather than human society.

Note

1. [Ed. note: The Bowery protagonist in a series of stories by Edward W. Townsend, collected in *Chimmie Fadden, Major Max and Other Stories* (1895).]

ARTICLES AND ESSAYS

Stephen Crane: A Revaluation   R. W. Stallman[*]

That Crane is incapable of architectonics has been the critical consensus that has prevailed for over half a century: "his work is a mass of fragments"; "he can only string together a series of loosely cohering incidents"; *The Red Badge of Courage* is not constructed. Edward Garnett, the first English critic to appraise Crane's work, aptly pointed out that Crane lacks the great artist's arrangement of complex effects, which is certainly true. We look to Conrad and Henry James for "exquisite grouping of devices"; Crane's figure in the carpet is a much simpler one. What it consists of is the very thing Garnett failed to detect—a schemework of striking contrasts, alternations of contradictory moods. Crane once defined a novel as a "succession of . . . sharply-outlined pictures, which pass before the reader like a panorama, leaving each its definite impression." His own novel, nonetheless, is not simply a succession of pictures. It is a sustained structural whole. Every Crane critic concurs in this mistaken notion that *The Red Badge of Courage* is nothing more than "a series of episodic scenes," but not one critic has yet undertaken an analysis of Crane's work to see *how* the sequence of tableaux is constructed. Critical analysis of Crane's unique art is practically nonexistent. Probably no American author, unless it is Mark Twain, stands today in more imperative need of critical revaluation.

The Red Badge of Courage begins with the army immobilized—with restless men waiting for orders to move—and with Henry, because the army has done nothing, disillusioned by his first days as a recruit. In the first picture we get of Henry, he is lying on his army cot—resting on an idea. Or rather, he is wrestling with the personal problem it poses. The idea is a thirdhand rumor that tomorrow, at last, the army goes into action. When the tall soldier first announced it, he waved a shirt which he had just washed in a muddy

* From *Critiques and Essays on Modern Fiction, 1920–1951*, ed. John W. Aldridge (New York: Ronald Press, 1952), 262–69. Reprinted by permission of Scott, Foresman and Co. and Random House, Inc.

brook, waved it in banner-like fashion to summon the men around the flag of his colorful rumor. It was a call to the colors—he shook it out and spread it about for the men to admire. But Jim Conklin's prophecy of hope meets with disbelief. "It's a lie!" shouts the loud soldier. "I don't believe the derned old army's ever going to move." No disciples rally around the red and gold flag of the herald. The skeptical soldiers think the tall soldier is telling just a tall tale; a furious altercation ensues. Meanwhile Henry in his hut engages in a spiritual debate with himself; whether to believe or disbelieve the word of his friend, whom he has known since childhood. It is the gospel truth, but Henry is one of the doubting apostles.

The opening scene thus sets going the structural pattern of the whole book. Hope and faith (paragraphs 1–3) shift to despair or disbelief (4–7). The counter-movement of opposition begins in paragraph 4, in the small detail of the Negro teamster who stops his dancing, when the men desert him to wrangle over Jim Conklin's rumor. "He sat mournfully down." This image of motion and change (the motion ceasing and the joy turning to gloom) presents the dominant leitmotiv and the form of the whole book in miniature. (Another striking instance of emblematic form occurs in Chapter VI, where Crane pictures a terror-stricken lad who throws down his gun and runs: "A lad whose face had borne an expression of exalted courage, the majesty of he who dares give his life, was, at an instant, smitten abject.") In Chapter I the opening prologue ends in a coda (paragraph 7) with theme and anti-theme here interjoined. It is the picture of the corporal—his uncertainties (whether to repair his house) and his shifting attitudes of trust and distrust (whether the army is going to move) parallel the skeptical outlook of the wrangling men. The same anti-theme of distrust is dramatized in the episode which follows this coda, and every subsequent episode in the sequence is designed similarly by one contrast pattern or another.

Change and motion begin the book. The army, which lies resting upon the hills, is first revealed to us by "the retiring fogs," and as the weather changes so the landscape changes, the brown hills turning into a new green. Now as nature stirs so the army stirs too. Nature and man are in psychic affinity; even the weather changes as though in sympathetic accord with man's plight. In the final scene it is raining but the leaden rain clouds shine with "a golden ray" as though to reflect Henry's own bright serenity, his own tranquility of mind. But now at the beginning, and throughout the book, Henry's mind is in a "tumult of agony and despair." This psychological tumult began when Henry heard the church bell announce the gospel truth that a great battle had been fought. Noise begins the whole mental melee. The clanging church bell and then the noise of rumors disorder his mind by stirring up legendary visions of heroic selfhood. The noisy world that first colored his mind with myths now clamors to Henry to become absorbed into the solidarity of self-forgetful comradeship, but Henry resists this challenge of the "mysterious fraternity born of the smoke and danger of death," and withdraws again and again from the din of the affray to indulge in self-contemplative moods and magic reveries. The walls of the forest insulate him from the noise of battle. In seeking retreat there to absolve his shame and guilt, Henry, renouncing manhood, is "seeking dark and intricate places." It is as though he were seeking return to the womb. Nature, that "woman with a deep aversion to tragedy," is Mother Nature, and the human equation for the forest is of course Henry's own mother. Henry's flight from the forest-sanctuary represents his momentary rejection of womb-like innocence; periodically he rejects Mother Nature with her sheltering arms and her "religion of peace," and his flight from Mother Nature is symbolic of his initiation into the truth of the world he must measure up to. He is the deceived youth, for death lurks even in the forest-sanctuary. In the pond a gleaming fish is killed by one of the forest creatures, and in the forest Henry meets a rotted corpse, a man whose eyes stare like a dead fish, with ants scurrying over the face. The treachery of this forest retreat, where nothing is as it seems, symbolizes the treachery of ideals— the illusions by which we are all betrayed.

Henry's mind is in constant flux. Henry's self-combat is symbolized by the conflict among the men and between the armies, their altercation being a duplication of his own. Like the regiment that marches and countermarches over the same ground, so Henry's mind traverses the same ideas over and over again. As the cheery-voiced soldier says about the battle, "It's th' most mixed up dern thing I ever see." Mental commotion, confusion, and change are externalized in the "mighty altercation" of men and guns and nature herself. Everything becomes activated, even the dead. That corpse Henry meets on the battlefield, "the *invulnerable* dead man," cannot stay still—he "*forced* a way for himself" through the ranks. And guns throb too, "restless guns." Back and forth the stage-scenery shifts from dreams to "jolted dreams" and grim fact. Henry's illusions collapse, dreams pinpricked by reality.

Throughout the whole book *withdrawals* alternate with *engagements,* with scenes of entanglement and tumult, but the same nightmarish atmosphere of upheaval and disorder pervades both the inner and the outer realms. The paradox is that when Henry becomes activated in the "vast blue demonstration" and is thereby reduced to anonymity he is then most a man, and conversely, when he affects self-dramatizing picture-postcard poses of himself as hero he is then least a man and not at all heroic. He is then innocent as a child. When disengaged from the external tumult, Henry's mind recollects former domestic scenes. Pictures of childhood and nursery imagery of babes recur at almost every interval of withdrawal. Childhood innocence and withdrawal are thus equated. The nursery limerick which the wounded soldiers sing as they retreat from the battlefront is at once a travesty of their own plight and a mockery of Henry's mythical innocence.

> Sing a song 'a vic'try
> A pocketful 'a bullets,
> Five an' twenty dead men
> Baked in a—pie.

Everything goes awry; nothing turns out as Henry had expected. Battles turn out to be "an immense and terrible machine to him" (the awful machinery of his own mind). At his battle task Henry, we are told, "was like a carpenter who has made many boxes, making still another box, only there was furious haste in his movements." Henry, "frustrated by hateful circumstances," pictures himself as boxed in by fate, by the regiment, and by the "iron laws of tradition and law on four sides. He was in a moving box." And furthermore there are those purely theoretical boxes by which he is shut in from reality—his romantic dreams, legendary visions of heroic selfhood, illusions which the vainglorious machinery of his own mind has manufactured.

The youth who had envisioned himself in Homeric poses, the legendary hero of a Greeklike struggle, has his pretty illusion shattered as soon as he announces his enlistment to his mother. "I've knet yeh eight pair of socks, Henry. . . ." His mother is busy peeling potatoes, and, madonna-like, she kneels among the parings. They are the scraps of his romantic dreams. The youthful private imagines armies to be monsters, "redoubtable dragons," but then he sees the real thing— the colonel who strokes his mustache and shouts over his shoulder, "Don't forget that box of cigars!"

The Red Badge of Courage probes a state of mind under the incessant pinpricks and bombardments of life. The theme is that man's salvation lies in change, in spiritual growth. It is only by immersion in the flux of experience that man becomes disciplined and develops in character, conscience, or soul. Potentialities for change are at their greatest in battle—a battle represents life at its most intense flux. Crane's book is not about the combat of armies; it is about the self-combat of a youth who fears and stubbornly resists change, and the actual battle is symbolic of this spiritual warfare against change and growth. To say that the book is a study in fear is as shallow an interpretation as to say that it is a narrative of the Civil War. It is the standard reading of all Crane's writings, the reading of fear into everything he wrote, and for this misleading diagnosis Thomas Beer's biography of 1923 is almost solely responsible.[1] It is this Handbook of Fear that accounts for the neglect of all critics to attempt any other reading. Beer's thesis is that all the works from the first story to the last dissect fear and that *as* they deal exclusively with fear *so* fear was the motivating passion of Crane's life. "That newspaper feller was a nervy man," said the cook of the ill-fated *Commodore*. "*He didn't seem to know what fear was.*" Yet in his art there is fear, little more than that, and in "The Blue Hotel"—so the *Literary History of the United States* tells us—the premonition of the Swede is nothing "but the manifestation of Crane's own intense fear." This equation of Crane's works with his life, however seemingly plausible, is critically fallacious, and the resultant reading is a grossly oversimplified one. Fear is only one of the many passions that comprise *The Red Badge of Courage*; they include not alone fear but rage, elation, and the equally telltale passions of pride and shame. What was Crane afraid of? If Crane was at all afraid, he was afraid of time and change. Throughout Crane's works, as in his life, there is the conflict between ideals and reality.

Our critical concern is with the plight of his hero: Henry Fleming recognizes the necessity for change and development, but he wars against it. The youth develops into the veteran—"*So it came to pass . . . his soul changed.*" Significantly enough, in thus stating what his book is about Crane intones Biblical phrasing.

Spiritual change, *that* is Henry Fleming's red badge. *His red badge is his conscience reborn and purified.* Whereas Jim Conklin's red badge of courage is the literal one, the wound of which he dies, Henry's is the psychological badge, the wound of conscience. Internal wounds are more painful than external ones. It is fitting that Henry should receive a head wound, a bump that jolts him with a severe headache! But what "salve" is there to ease the pain of his internal wound of dishonor? That is Henry's "headache"! It is the ache of his conscience that he has been honored by the regiment he has dishonored. Just as Jim runs into the fields to hide his true wound from Henry, so Henry runs into the fields to hide his false wound, his false badge of courage, from the tattered man who asks him where he is wounded. "It might be inside mostly, an' them plays thunder. Where is it located?" The men, so Henry feels, are perpetually probing his guilt-wound, "ever upraising the ghost of shame on the stick of their curiosity." The unmistakable implication here is of a flag, and the actual flag which Henry carries in battle is the symbol of his conscience. Conscience is also symbolized by the forest, the cathedral-forest where Henry retreats to nurse his guilt-wound and be consoled by the benedictions which nature sympathetically bestows upon him. Here in this forest-chapel there is a churchlike silence as insects "bow their beaks" while Henry bows his head in shame; they make a "devotional pause" while the trees chant a soft hymn to comfort him. But Henry is troubled; he cannot "conciliate the forest." Nor can he conciliate the flag. The flag registers the commotion of his mind, and it registers the restless movements of the nervous regiment—it flutters when the men expect battle. And when the regiment runs from the battle, the flag sinks down "as if dying. Its motion as it fell was a gesture of despair." Henry dishonors the flag not when he flees from battle but when he flees from himself, and he redeems it when he redeems his conscience.[2]

Redemption begins in confession, in absolution—in change of heart. Henry's wounded conscience is not healed until he confesses to himself the truth and opens his eyes to new ways; not until he strips his enemy heart of "the brass and bombast of his earlier gospels," the vainglorious illusions he had fabricated into a cloak of pride and self-vindication; not until he puts on new garments of humility and loving kindness for his fellow-men. Redemption begins in humility—Henry's example is the loud soldier who becomes the humble soldier. The loud soldier admits the folly of his former ways. Henry's spiritual change is a prolonged process, but it is signalized in moments when he loses his soul in the flux of things; *then* he courageously deserts himself instead of his fellow-men; then fearlessly plunging into battle, charging the enemy like "a pagan who defends his religion," he becomes swept up in a delirium of selflessness and feels himself "capable of profound sacrifices." The brave new Henry, "new bearer of the colors," triumphs over the former one. The enemy flag is wrenched from the hands of "the rival color bearer," the symbol of Henry's own other self, and as this rival color bearer dies Henry is reborn.

Henry's regeneration is brought about by the death of Jim Conklin, the friend whom Henry had known since childhood. He goes under various names. He is sometimes called the spectral soldier (his face is a pasty gray) and sometimes the tall soldier (he is taller than all other men), but there are unmistakable hints—in such descriptive details about him as his wound in the side, his torn body and his gory hand, and even in the initials of his name, Jim Conklin—that he is intended to represent Jesus Christ. We are told that there is "a resemblance in him to a devotee of a mad religion," and among his followers the doomed man stirs up "thoughts of a solemn ceremony." When he dies, the heavens signify his death—the red sun bleeds with the passion of his wounds:

The red sun was pasted in the sky like a wafer.

This grotesque image, the most notorious metaphor in American literature, has been much debated and roundly damned by Crane's critics (e.g., Pattee, Quinn, Cargill, and a dozen others) as downright bad writing, a false, melodramatic and nonfunctional figure. Joseph Hergesheimer, Willa Cather, and Conrad admired it, but no one ventured to explain it. The other camp took potshots at it without attempting to understand what it is really all about. It is, in fact, the key to the symbolism of the whole novel, particularly the religious symbolism which radiates outwards from Jim Conklin. Like any image, it has to be related to the structure of meaning in which it functions; when lifted out of its context it is bound to seem artificial and irrelevant or, on the other hand, merely "a superb piece of imagery." I do not think it can be doubted that Crane intended to suggest here the sacrificial death celebrated in communion.

Henry and the tattered soldier consecrate the death of the spectral soldier in "a solemn ceremony." Henry partakes of the sacramental blood and body of Christ, and the process of his spiritual rebirth begins at this moment when the wafer-like sun appears in the sky. It is a symbol of salvation through death. Henry, we are made to feel, recognizes in the lifeless sun his own lifeless conscience, his dead and as yet unregenerated selfhood or conscience, and that is why he blasphemes against it. His moral salvation and triumph are prepared for (1) by this ritual of purification and religious devotion and, at the very start of the book (2), by the ritual of absolution which Jim Conklin performs in the opening scene. It was the tall soldier who first "developed virtues" and showed the boys how to cleanse a flag. The way is to wash it in the muddy river. Only by experiencing life, the muddy river, can the soul be cleansed. In "The Open Boat" it is the black sea, and the whiteness of the waves as they pace to and fro in the moonlight, signifies the spiritual purification which the men win from their contest against the terrible water. The ritual of domestic comforts bestowed upon the saved men by the people on the shore, "all the remedies sacred to their minds," is a shallow thing, devoid of spiritual value. The sea offers the only true remedy, though it costs a "terrible grace." The way is to immerse oneself in the destructive element!

Kurtz, in Conrad's *Heart of Darkness*, washed his soul in the Congo, and Marlow, because he had become a part of Kurtz, redeemed the heart of darkness by the same token. Conrad, like Crane, had himself experienced his own theme, but Crane was the first to produce a work based upon it. Crane's influence on Conrad is apparent in *Lord Jim*, which makes use of the same religious symbolism as *The Red Badge of Courage*. When Lord Jim goes to his death, you recall, there is an awful sunset. Conrad's "enormous sun" was suggested by Crane's grotesque symbol and paradox image of the red sun that was pasted wafer-like in the sky when Jim Conklin died. For the other Jim, "The sky over Patusan was blood-red, immense, streaming like an open vein."

Notes

1. "Let it be stated," says Beer, "that the mistress of this boy's mind was fear. His search in aesthetic was governed by terror as that of tamer men is governed by the desire of women." A very pretty analogy!

2. Henry's plight is identical with the Reverend Dimmesdale's plight in Hawthorne's psychological novel, *The Scarlet Letter*, with which *The Red Badge of Courage* has bondship by the similitude of the theme of redemption through self-confession and, even more strikingly, by the symbol of the forest to signify conscience. The mythology of the scarlet letter is much the same as the mythology of the red badge: each is the emblem of moral guilt and salvation. The red badge is the scarlet letter of dishonor transferred from the bosom of Hester, the social outcast, to the mind of Henry Fleming, the "mental outcast."

The Red Badge of Courage as Myth and Symbol

John E. Hart*

When Stephen Crane published *The Red Badge of Courage* in 1895, the book created an almost immediate sensation. Crane had had no experience in war, but in portraying the reactions of a young soldier in battle, he had written with amazing accuracy. As one way of re-examining *The Red Badge of Courage*, we would want to read it as myth and symbolic action. Clearly, the construction of the story, its moral and meaning, its reliance on symbol follow in detail the traditional formula of myth.[1] Crane's main theme is the discovery of self, that unconscious self, which, when identified with the inexhaustible energies of the group, enables man to understand the "deep forces that have shaped man's destiny."[2] The progressive movement of the hero, as in all myth, is that of separation, initiation, and return.[3] Within this general framework, Crane plots his story with individual variation. Henry Fleming, a Youth, ventures forth from his known environment into a region of naturalistic, if not super-naturalistic wonder; he encounters the monstrous forces of war and death; he is transformed through a series of rites and revelations into a hero; he returns to identify his new self with the deeper communal forces of the group and to bestow the blessings of his findings on his fellow comrades.

Whatever its "realistic" style, much of the novel's meaning is revealed through the use of metaphor and symbol. The names of characters, for example, suggest both particular attributes and general

*From *University of Kansas City Review* 19 (Summer 1953): 249–56. Reprinted by permission of *New Letters*, John E. Hart, and the Curators of the University of Missouri-Kansas City.

qualities: the Tall Soldier, whose courage and confidence enable him to measure up to the vicissitudes of war and life; the Loud Soldier, the braggart, the over-confident, whose personality is, like Henry's, transformed in war; the Tattered Soldier, whose clothes signify his lowly and exhausted plight; the Cheery Man, whose keenness and valor prevent his falling into despair. Likewise, the use of color helps to clarify and extend the meaning. Red, traditionally associated with blood and fire, suggests courage, flag, life-energy, desire, ambition. Black, traditionally associated with death, implies "great unknown," darkness, forests, and, by extension, entombment and psychological death. The whole paraphernalia of myth-religious and sacrificial rites— the ceremonial dancing, the dragons with fiery eyes, the menacing landscape, the entombment, the sudden appearance of a guide, those symbols so profoundly familiar to the unconscious and so frightening to the conscious personality—give new dimensions of meaning to the novel.

What prompts Henry to leave his known environment is his unconscious longing to become a hero. In a state of conscious re-flection, he looks on war with distrust. Battles belonged to the past. Had not "secular and religious education" effaced the "throat grap-pling instinct" and "firm finance" "held in check the passions"? But in dreams, he has thrilled to the "sweep and fire" of "vague and bloody conflicts"; he has "imagined people secure in the shadow of his eagle-eyed prowess." As the wind brings the noise of the ringing church bells, he listens to their summons as a proclamation from the "voice of the people." Shivering in his bed in a "prolonged ecstasy of excitement," he determines to enlist. If the call has come in an unconscious dream-like state where the associations of wind, church bells, ecstasy, heroism, glory are identied with the "voice" of the "group," Henry, fully "awake," insists on his decision. Although his mother, motivated apparently by "deep conviction" and impregnable ethical motives, tries to dissuade his ardor, she actually helps him in the initial step of his journey. She prepares his equipment: "eight pairs of socks," "yer best shirts," "a cup of blackberry jam." She advises him to watch the company he keeps and to do as he is told. Underlining the very nature of the problem, she warns that he will be "jest one little fellow amongst a hull lot of others."

It is this conflict between unconscious desire and conscious fear that prevents Henry from coming to terms with his new environments. Consciously concerned with thoughts of rumored battle, he crawls into his hut "through an intricate hole that served it as a door," where he can be "alone with some new thoughts that had lately come to him." Although his apparent concern is over fear of battle, his real anxiety is that of his individuation. As far as his relationship to war is concerned, he knows "nothing of himself." He has always "taken certain things for granted, never challenging his belief in ultimate success, and bothering little about means and roads." Now, he is an "unknown quantity." If his problems merge into that of whether he will or will not run from an "environment" that threatens to "swallow" his very identity, he sees that it cannot be solved by "mental slate and pencil." Action—"blaze, blood, and danger"—is the only test.

In giving artistic conception to Henry's conflict, Crane relies on a pattern of darkness and light, but adapts such traditional machinery to his particular purpose. As we have seen, Henry achieves courage and strength in the "darkness" of his tent, where his unconscious mind faces the problems of his new surroundings openly and bravely. As he peers into the "ominous distance" and ponders "upon the mystic gloom" in the morning twilight, he is eager to settle his "great problem" with the "red eyes across the river"—eyes like "orbs of a row of dragons advancing." Coming from the darkness towards the dawn, he watches "the gigantic figure of the colonel on a gigantic horse." They loom "black and pattern like" against the yellow sky. As the "black rider," the messenger of death lifts "his gigantic arm and calmly stroke[s] his mustache," Henry can hardly breathe. Then, with the hazy light of day, he feels the consciousness of growing fear. It seems ironic that his comrades, especially the Tall Soldier, should be filled with ardor, even song—just as he was in the darkness of his room at home. With the "developing day," the "two long, thin, black columns" have become "two serpents crawling from the cavern of night." These columns, monsters themselves, move from darkness to light with little fear, for they move, not as so many individuals, but as group units. Clearly, if Henry is to achieve his ambitions, he must "see" and "face" the enemy in the light of day without fear, as well as "perceive" his relationship to the group, which is, in a sense, a "monster" itself.

Henry's growing concern is not for his comrades, but for himself. Although he must march along with them, he feels caught "by the iron laws of tradition." He considers himself "separated from the others." At night, when the campfires dot the landscape "like red peculiar blossoms (as communal fires which impregnate the landscape with "life" and "vitality," they suggest the life energy of the group), Henry remains a "few paces in the gloom," a "mental outcast." He is "alone in space," where only the "mood of darkness" seems to sympathize with him. He concludes that no other person is "wrestling with such a terrific personal problem." But even in the darkness of his tent he cannot escape: the "red, shivering reflection of a fire" shines through the canvas. He sees "visions of a thousand-tongued fear that would babble at his back and cause him to flee." His "fine mind" can no more face the monster war than it can cope with the "brute minds" of his comrades.

Next day as Henry, with sudden "impulse of curiosity," stares at the "woven red" against the "soft greens and browns," the harmony of landscape is broken when the line of men stumble onto a dead soldier in their path. Henry pauses and tries to "read in the dead eyes the answer to the Question." What irony it is that the ranks open "to avoid the corpse," as if, invulnerable, death forces a way itself. He notes that the wind strokes the dead man's beard, just as the black rider had stroked his mustache. Probing his sensations, he feels no ardor for battle. His soldier's clothes do not fit, for he is not a "real" soldier. His "fine mind" enables him to see what the "brute minds" of his comrades do not: the landscape threatens to engulf them. Their ardor is not heroism. They are merely going to a sacrifice, going "to look at war, the red animal—war the blood-swollen god." Even if he warned them, they would not listen. Misunderstood, he can only "look to the grave for comprehension." His feeling is prophetic, for it anticipates the death and transformation of personality that is about to occur.

Before he actually runs from battle, Henry experiences a moment of true realization. Impatient to know whether he is a "man of traditional courage," he suddenly loses "concern for himself," and becomes "not a man but a member." "Welded into a common personality" and "dominated by a single desire," he feels the "red rage" and "battle brotherhood"—that "mysterious fraternity born of the smoke and danger of death." He is carried along in a kind of "battle sleep." He rushes at the "black phantoms" like a "pestered animal." Then, awakening to the awareness of a second attack, he feels weak and bloodless. "Like the man who lost his legs at the approach of the red and green monster," he seems "to shut his eyes and wait to be gobbled." He has a revelation. Throwing down his gun, he flees like a "blind man." His vision of "selflessness" disappears; in this "blindness" his fears are magnified. "Death about to thrust him between the shoulder blades [is] far more dreadful than death about to smite him between the eyes." Impotent and blind (without gun and "vision"), he runs into the forest "as if resolved to bury himself." He is both physically and psychologically isolated from the group and hence from the very source of food and energy, both material and spiritual, that impels heroic achievement.

In the language of myth Henry's inability to face the monsters of battle in the "light," to identify himself with his comrades (both acts are, in a sense, identical), and thus to give up his individual self, which is sustained only in "darkness" and in isolation, so that his full self can be realized in the light of communal identification symbolize a loss of spiritual, moral, and physical power, which only a rebirth of identity can solve. Only by being reborn can he come to understand that man's courage springs from the self-realization that he must participate harmoniously as a member of the group. Only then can he understand the "deep forces" from which his individual energy and vitality spring. Thus, Henry's entombment in the forest is only preliminary to the resurrection that will follow. Without his full powers, his transformation cannot be effected by himself, but requires the necessity of ritualistic lessons and the aid of outside forces or agents. His own attempts to expiate his feeling of guilt by logic only leave him lost and confused in the labyrinth of his limitations.

After the burial of himself in the forest, it is his unconscious awareness of the nature of death that restores the strength and energy he had felt in his dreams at home. As he pushes on, going from "obscurity into promises of a greater obscurity," he comes face to face with the very "act" from which he is running. It is a dead soldier covered with "black" ants. As he recoils in terror, the branches of the forest hold him firm. In a moment of blind fear, he imagines that "some strange voice . . . from the dead throat" will squawk after him in "horrible menaces," but he hears, almost unconsciously, only a soft wind, which sings a "hymn of twilight." This aura of tranquility, produced in a "religious half light"—the boughs are arched like a chapel—transfixes Henry. He hears a "terrific medley of all noises." It is ironic that he should be fleeing from the black rider only to encounter death and "black ants." His ego is deflated. Did he ever imagine that he and his comrades could decide the war as if they were "cutting the letters of their names deep into everlasting tablets of brass?" Actually, the "affair" would receive only a "meek and immaterial title." With this thought and the song of the wind comes a certain faith. "Pictures of stupendous conflicts" pass through his mind. As he hears the "red cheers" of marching men, he is determined: he runs in the direction of the "crimson roar" of battle.

Although Henry's old fears have not been completely overcome, his meeting with the Tattered Man clarifies the need and method of atoning for his guilt. Having joined the marching soldiers, Henry is envious of this mob of "bleeding men." He walks beside the twice-wounded Tattered Man, whose face is "suffused with a light of love for the army which [is] to him all things beautiful and powerful." Moving in the "light of love," the Man speaks in a voice as "gentle as a girl's." "Where yeh hit?" he repeatedly asks Henry. "Letters of guilt" burn on the Youth's brow. How can he defend himself against an agency which so pitilessly reveals man's secrets? How can he atone for his guilt? His wish that "he, too, had a wound, a red badge of courage" is only preliminary to the fulfillment of atonement, just as in the rites of some primitive tribes or as in Christ's crucifixion on the cross, "blood" plays an essential part in the act of atonement and in the process of transformation.

If the Tattered Man's questioning reveals the need and nature of atonement, meeting the Tall Soldier shows the quality of character needed to make the sacrifice. Justifying the "tall" of his name by his "supreme unconcern" for battle, Conklin accepts his role as part of the group with coolness and humility. Because he realizes the insignificance of self, he has no fear of a threatening landscape. Sleeping, eating, and drinking afford him greatest satisfaction. During meal time, he is "quiet and contented," as if his spirit were "communing with viands." Now, fatally wounded, he is at his rendezvous with death; his actions are ceremonial, "rite-like." He moves with "mysterious purpose," like "the devotee of a mad religion, blood-sucking, muscle-wrenching, bone-crushing." His chest heaves "as if an animal was within," his "arms beat wildly," "his tall figure [stretches] itself to its full height" and falls to the ground—dead. His side looks "as if it had been chewed by wolves," as if the monster war had eaten him and then swallowed his life. This "ceremony at the place of meeting," this sacrificial ritual of placating the monster has enabled him to find the ultimate answer to the Question, but it has consumed its victim in the process.

It is the receiving of the wound, a kind of "magic" touch, whatever its irony of being false, that actually enables Henry to effect atonement. As the army itself retreats, he is truly "at one" with the group ("at one" and atone have similar functions as the very words imply), for both are running from battle. Actually, Henry is not "conscious" of what has happened. Clutching boldly at a retreating man's arm, he begs for an answer. Desperate at being restrained, the man strikes the Youth with his rifle. Henry falls. His legs seem "to die." In a ritual not unlike that of Conklin's dying (it is Henry's "youth," his immature self dying), he grabs at the grass, he twists and lurches, he fights "an intense battle with his body." Then, he goes "tall soldier fashion." In his exaltation, he is afraid to touch his head lest he disturb his "red badge of courage." He relishes "the cool, liquid feeling," which evokes the memory of "certain meals his mother had cooked," "the bank of a shaded pool," "the melody in the wind of youthful summer." The association of blood with that of food suggests the identical function of each. Just as food is nourishment to the body, so blood is nourishment to his spiritual and moral self. Because the monster has "eaten" of him and thus destroyed his fears, he has achieved a moral and spiritual maturity, even, as his going "tall" implies, sexual potency. He feels the tranquility and harmony that has always characterized his dream state. But his wound is an actual fact, and the achieved atonement is not quite the same as in a "pure" dream state. Yet it is still achieved under the ægis of "dusk," and can only be fully realized in the full "light" of group identification.

Henry is further assisted in his transformation by an "unseen guide." Wandering in the darkness, he is overtaken by the Cheery Man, whose voice, possessing a "wand of a magic kind," guides him to his regiment. Thinking of him later, Henry recalls that "he had not once seen his face."

It is important to note here what part food and eating play in Henry's atonement and rebirth. As we have seen, food has both physical and spiritual significance. From the first, Henry has observed that "eating" was of greatest importance to the soldiers. After the Tall Soldier's death, he has speculated on "what those men had eaten that they could be in such haste to force their way to grim chances of death." Now, he discovers that he has "a scorching thirst," a hunger that is "more powerful than a direct hunger." He is desperately tired. He cannot see distinctly. He feels the need "of food and rest, at whatever cost." On seeing his comrades again, he goes directly towards the "red light"—symbol of group energy. They fuss over his wound and give him a canteen of coffee. As he swallows the "delicious draught," the mixture feels as cool to him as did the wound. He feels like an "exhausted soldier after a feast of war." He has tasted of and been eaten by the great monster. By the wound (the being eaten), he has atoned for his guilt with blood. In eating and drinking with his comrades (the communal feasting), he has achieved both literal and spiritual identification with the group. Through his initiation, he has returned as a "member," not an isolated individual. By "swallowing or being swallowed," he has, through atonement and rebirth, come to be master of himself and, henceforth, to be master of others. The Loud Soldier gives up his blankets, and Henry is, in sleep, soon "like his comrades."

In the language of myth, Henry has become a hero. When he awakes next morning from a "thousand years'" sleep, he finds, like Rip Van Winkle, a new "unexpected world." What he discovers has happened to the Loud Soldier is actually the same change that has come over him. For the first time Henry is aware that others have been wrestling with problems not unlike his own. If the Loud Soldier is now a man of reliance, a man of "purpose and abilities," Henry perceives in imagery that recalls the "blossoming campfires" of his comrades that

> a faith in himself had secretly blossomed. There was a little flower of confidence growing within him. He was a man of experience.

Again like the Loud Soldier, he has at last

> overcome obstacles which he admitted to be mountainous. They had fallen like paper peaks, and he was now what he called a hero.

He had not been aware of the process. He had slept and, awakening, found himself a knight.

Having overcome the obstacle of self, Henry has at last discovered that the dragon war is, after all, only a gigantic guard of the great death.

If the hero is to fulfill the total requirements of his role, he must bring back into the normal world of day the wisdom that he has acquired during his transformation. Like the "knight" that he is, Henry is now able to face the red and black dragons on the "clear" field of battle. He performs like a "pagan who defends his religion," a "barbarian," "a beast." As the regiment moves forward, Henry is "unconsciously in advance." Although many men shield their eyes, he looks squarely ahead. What he sees "in the new appearance of the landscape" is like "a revelation." There is both a clarity of vision and of perception: the darkness of the landscape has vanished; the blindness of his mental insight has passed. As with the wound and the coffee, he feels the "delirium that encounters despair and death." He has, perhaps, in this "temporary but sublime absence of selfishness," found the reason for being there after all. As the pace quickly "eats up the energies of the men," they dance and gyrate "like savages." Without regard for self, Henry spurs them forward towards the colors.

In the language of myth, it is woman who represents the totality of what can be known. As "life," she embodies both love and hate. To accept her is to be king, the incarnate god, of her created world. As knower (one who recognizes her), the hero is master. Meeting the goddess and winning her is the final test of the hero's talent. Curiously, it is the flag that occupies the position of goddess in the story. The flag is the lure, the beautiful maiden of the configuration, whose capture is necessary if Henry is to fulfill his role as hero. Crane writes:

> With [Henry], as he hurled himself forward, was born a love, a despairing fondness of this flag which was near him. It was a creation of beauty and invulnerability. It was a goddess, radiant, that bended its form with an imperious gesture to him. It was a woman, red and white, hating and loving, that called him with the voice of his hope. Because no harm could come to it he endowed it with power. He kept near, as if it could be a saver of lives, and an imploring cry went from his mind.

As Henry and his comrade wrench the pole from the dead bearer, they both acquire an invincible wand of hope and power. Taking it roughly from his friend, Henry has, indeed, reached heroic proportions.

In his role as hero, Henry stands "erect and tranquil" in face of the great monster. Having "rid himself of the red sickness of battle," having overcome his fear of losing individual identity, he now despises the "brass and bombast of his earlier gospels." Because he is at-one with his comrades, he has acquired their "daring spirit of a savage religion-mad," their "brute" strength to endure the violence of a violent world, the "red of blood and black of passion." His individual strength is their collective strength, that strength of the totality which the flag symbolizes. As Crane says:

> He felt a quiet manhood, nonassertive but of sturdy and strong blood. He knew that he would no more quail before his guides wherever they should point. He had been to touch the great death, and found that, after all, it was but the great death. He was a man.

At last he has put the "somber phantom" of his desertion at a distance. Having emerged into the "golden ray of sun," Henry feels a "store of assurance."

Following the general pattern of myth with peculiar individual variations, Crane has shown how the moral and spiritual strength of the individual springs from the group, and how, through the identification of self with group, the individual can be "reborn in identity with the whole meaning of the universe." Just as his would-be hero was able to overcome his fears and achieve a new moral and spiritual existence, so all men can come to face life, face it as calmly and as coolly as one faces the terrors, the odd beings, the deluding images of dreams. If it is, as Campbell points out, the "unconscious" which supplies the "keys that open the whole realm of the desired and feared adventures of the discovery of self," then man, to discover self, must translate his dreams into actuality. To say that Henry accomplishes his purpose is not to imply that Crane himself achieved the same kind of integration. Whatever the final irony implied, he certainly saw that the discovery of self was essential to building the "bolder, cleaner, more spacious, and fully human life."

Notes

1. See Joseph Campbell, *The Hero with a Thousand Faces* (New York, 1949), p. 3. Campbell defines myth as "the secret opening through which the inexhaustible energies of the cosmos pour into human cultural manifestation."

2. Ibid., p. 256.

3. Ibid., p. 30.

Stephen Crane: Naturalist   Charles C. Walcutt*

My thesis is that naturalism is the offspring cf transcendentalism. American transcendentalism asserts the unity of Spirit and Nature and affirms that intuition (by which the mind discovers its affiliation with Spirit) and scientific investigation (by which it masters Nature, the symbol of Spirit) are equally rewarding and valid approaches to reality. When this mainstream of transcendentalism divides, as it does toward the end of the nineteenth century, it produces two rivers of thought. One, the approach to Spirit through intuition, nourishes idealism, progressivism, and social radicalism. The other, the approach to Nature through science, plunges into the dark canyon of mechanistic determinism. The one is rebellious, the other pessimistic; the one ardent, the other fatal; the one acknowledges will, the other denies it. Thus "naturalism," flowing in both streams, is partly defying Nature and partly submitting to it; and it is in this area of tension that my investigation lies, its immediate subject being the forms which the novel assumes as one stream or the other, and sometimes both, flow through it. The problem, as will appear, is an epitome of the central problem of twentieth-century thought. . . .

The works of Stephen Crane (1871–1900) are an early and unique flowering of pure naturalism. It is naturalism in a restricted and special sense, and it contains many non-naturalistic elements, but it is nevertheless entirely consistent and coherent. It marks the first entry, in America, of a deterministic philosophy not confused with ethical motivation into the structure of the novel. Ethical judgment there is, in plenty. To define Crane's naturalism is to understand one of the few perfect and successful embodiments of the theory in the American novel. It illustrates the old truth that literary trends often achieve their finest expressions very early in their histories. *Mutatis mutandis*, Crane is the Christopher Marlowe of American naturalism— and we have had no Shakespeare.

Crane's naturalism is to be found, first, in his attitude toward received values, which he continually assails through his naturalistic method of showing that the traditional concepts of our social morality are shams and the motivations presumably controlled by them are pretenses; second, in his impressionism, which fractures experiences into disordered sensation in a way that shatters the old moral "order" along with the old orderly processes of reward and punishment; third, in his obvious interest in a scientific or deterministic accounting for

* From *American Literary Naturalism, A Divided Stream* (Minneapolis: University of Minnesota Press, 1956), vii–viii, 66–67, 74–82. Reprinted by permission of the University of Minnesota Press.

events, although he does not pretend or attempt to be scientific in either the tone or the management of his fables. Crane's naturalism does not suffer from the problem of the divided stream because each of his works in so concretely developed that it does not have a meaning apart from what happens in it. The meaning is always the action; there is no wandering into theory that runs counter to what happens in the action; and nowhere does a character operate as a genuinely free ethical agent in defiance of the author's intentions. Crane's success is a triumph of style: manner and meaning are one. . . .

The Red Badge of Courage (1895), Crane's Civil War story, is the most controversial piece in his canon. It has been much discussed and most variously interpreted, and the interpretations range about as widely as they could. Is it a Christian story of redemption? Is it a demonstration that man is a beast with illusions? Or is it, between these extremes, the story of a man who goes through the fire, discovers himself, and with the self-knowledge that he is able to attain comes to terms with the problem of life insofar as an imperfect man can come to terms with an imperfect world? It is tempting to take the middle road between the intemperate extremes; but let us see what happens before we come to the paragraphs at the end that are invoked to prove each of the explanations:

> He felt a quiet manhood, non-assertive but of sturdy and strong blood. He knew that he would no more quail before his guides wherever they should point. He had been to touch the great death, and found that, after all, it was but the great death. He was a man.
>
> So it came to pass that as he trudged from the place of blood and wrath his soul changed. He came from hot plowshares to prospects of clover tranquilly, and it was as if hot plowshares were not. Scars faded as flowers.
>
> . . . He had rid himself of the red sickness of battle. The sultry nightmare was in the past. He had been an animal blistered and sweating in the heat and pain of war. He turned now with a lover's thirst to images of tranquil skies, fresh meadows, cool brooks.

It is not obvious whether the young man who thinks these thoughts is deluding himself or not. To judge the quality of his self-analysis we must look in some detail at what he has been through. The book opens with a scene at a Union encampment in which the uninformed arguments of the soldiers are described in a manner that recalls the mockery of "infantile orations" in *Maggie*. The phrase pictures a squalling child colorfully, while it conveys the author's private amusement at the image of a shouting politician. In *The Red Badge* there is continually a tone of mockery and sardonic imitation of men who are boisterous, crafty, arrogant, resentful, or suspicious always in an excess that makes them comical, and the author seems to delight in rendering the flavor of their extravagances. An element of the fantastic is always present, the quality apparently representing the author's feeling for the war, the situations in it, the continual and enormous incongruities between intention and execution, between a man's estimate of himself and the way he appears to others, between the motivations acknowledged to the world and those which prevail in the heart. It is with these last that the book is centrally concerned— with the problem of courage—and it is here that the meaning is most confusingly entangled with the tone.

In the opening scene the men are excited over a rumor that the troop is about to move, for the first time in months, and immediately the tone of mockery appears. A certain tall soldier "developed virtues and went resolutely to wash a shirt. He came flying back. . . . He was swelled with a tale he had heard from a reliable friend, who had heard it from a truthful cavalryman, who had heard it from his trustworthy brother. . . . He adopted the important air of a herald in red and gold." Another soldier takes the report "as an affront," and the tall soldier "felt called upon to defend the truth of a rumor he had himself introduced. He and the loud one came near to fighting over it." A corporal swears furiously because he has just put a floor under his tent; the men argue about strategies, clamoring at each other, "numbers making futile bids for the popular attention."

From this outer excitement we turn to the excitement in the heart of the youth who is to be the hero of the tale. He has crept off to his tent to commune with himself and particularly to wonder how he will act when he confronts the enemy. He has "dreamed of battles all his life—of vague and bloody conflicts that had thrilled him with their sweep and fire. . . . He had imagined peoples secure in the shadow of his eagle-eyed prowess." He had burned to enlist, but had been deterred by his mother's arguments that he was more important on the farm until—the point is sardonically emphasized— the newspapers carried accounts of great battles in which the North was victor. "Almost every day the newspapers printed accounts of a decisive victory." When he enlists, his mother makes a long speech to him—which is presented by Crane with no trace of mockery— but he is impatient and irritated. As he departs, there is a tableau described, for almost the only time in the book, with unqualified feeling:

> Still, when he had looked back from the gate, he had seen his
> mother kneeling among the potato parings. Her brown face, upraised,
> was stained with tears, and her spare form was quivering. He bowed
> his head and went on, feeling suddenly ashamed of his purposes.

Vanity amid dreams of Homeric glory occupy him thenceforth— until battle is imminent. Then he wonders whether he will run or stand; and he does not dare confide his fears to the other men because they all seem so sure of themselves and because both they and he are constantly diverted from the question by inferior concerns. When the first rumor proves false, its carrier, the tall soldier, in defense of his honor, "fought with a man from Chatfield Corners and beat him severely." (This tall soldier, whose name is Jim Conklin, has been identified symbolically with Jesus Christ by some critics.) In a similar instance, "A man fell down, and as he reached for his rifle a comrade, unseeing, trod upon his hand. He of the injured fingers swore bitterly and aloud. A low tittering laugh went among his fellows." This petty reaction alienates the boy. The tall soldier offers more theories, is challenged, and there are endless debates: "The blatant soldier often convulsed whole files by his biting sarcasms aimed at the tall one." Another soldier tries to steal a horse, is defied by the girl who owns it, and precipitates wild cheers from the men, who "entered whole-souled upon the side of the maiden. . . . They jeered the piratical private, and called attention to various defects in his personal appearance; and they were wildly enthusiastic in support of the young girl."

Approaching the first engagement, the youth perceives with terror that he is "in a moving box" of soldiers from which it would be impossible to escape, and "it occurred to him that he had never wished to come to the war . . . He had been dragged by the merciless government." He is further startled when the loud soldier, a braggart, announces with a sob that he is going to be killed, and gives the youth a packet of letters for his family. The engagement is described with terms of confusion: the youth feels "a red rage," and then "acute exasperation"; he "fought frantically" for air; the other men are cursing, babbling, and querulous; their equipment bobs "idiotically" on their backs, and they move like puppets. The assault is turned back, and the men leer at each other with dirty smiles; but just as the youth is responding in "an ecstasy of self-satisfaction" at having passed "the supreme trial," there comes a second charge from which he flees in blind panic: "He ran like a blind man. Two or three times he fell down. Once he knocked his shoulder so heavily against a tree that he went headlong." As he runs, his fear increases, and he rages at the suicidal folly of those who have stayed behind to be killed.

Just as he reaches the zone of safety, he learns that the line has held and the enemy's charge been repulsed. Instantly he "felt that he had been wronged," and begins to find reasons for the wisdom of his flight. "It was all plain that he had proceeded according to very correct and commendable rules. His actions had been sagacious things. They had been full of strategy. . . . He, the enlightened man who looks afar in the dark, had fled because of his superior perceptions and knowledge. He felt a great anger against his comrades. He knew it could be proved that they had been fools." He pities himself; he feels rebellious, agonized, and despairing. It is here that he sees a squirrel and throws a pine cone at it; when it runs he finds a triumphant exhibition in nature of the law of self-preservation. "Nature had given him a sign." The irony of this sequence is abundantly apparent. It increases when, a moment later, the youth enters a place where the "arching boughs made a chapel" and finds a horrible corpse, upright against a tree, crawling with ants and staring straight at him.

From this he flees in renewed panic, and then there is a strange turn. A din of battle breaks out, such a "tremendous clangor of sounds" as to make the engagement from which he ran seem trivial, and he runs back to watch because for such a spectacle curiosity becomes stronger than fear. He joins a ghastly procession of wounded from this battle, among whom he finds Jim Conklin, his friend, gray with the mark of death, and watches him die in throes that "caused him to dance a sort of hideous hornpipe." The guilt he feels among these frightfully wounded men, in this chapter which comes precisely in the middle of the book, should be enough to make him realize his brotherhood, his indebtedness, his duty; but his reaction as he watches the retreat swell is to justify his early flight—until a column of soldiers going *toward* the battle makes him almost weep with his longing to be one of their brave file. Increasingly, in short, Crane makes us see Henry Fleming as an emotional puppet controlled by whatever sight he sees at the moment. He becomes like Conrad's Lord Jim, romancing dreams of glory while he flinches at every danger. As his spirits flag under physical exhaustion, he hopes his army will be defeated so that his flight will be vindicated.

The climax of irony comes now, when, after a stasis of remorse in which he does indeed despise himself (albeit for the wrong reason of fearing the reproaches of those who did not flee), he sees the whole army come running past him in an utter panic of terror. He tries to stop one of them for information, and is bashed over the head by the frantic and bewildered man. And now, wounded thus, almost delirious with pain and exhaustion, he staggers back to his company—and is greeted as a hero! Henry is tended by the loud soldier, who has become stronger and steadier. Henry's reaction to his friend's care and solicitude is to feel superior because he still has the packet of letters the loud one gave him a day before, in his fear: "The friend had, in a weak hour, spoken with sobs of his own death. . . . But he had not died, and thus he had delivered himself into the hands of the youth." He condescends to his loud friend, and "His self-pride was now [so] entirely restored" that he began to see something fine in his conduct of the day before. He is now vainglorious; he thinks himself "a man of experience . . . chosen of the gods and doomed to greatness." Remembering the terror-stricken faces of the men he saw fleeing from the great battle, he now feels a scorn for them! He thinks of the tales of prowess he will tell back home to circles of adoring women.

The youth's reaction to his spurious "red badge of courage" is thus set down with close and ironical detail. Crane does not comment, but the picture of self-delusion and vainglory is meticulously drawn. In the following chapter Henry does fight furiously, but here he is in a blind rage that turns him into an animal, so that he goes on firing long after the enemy have retreated. The other soldiers regard his ferocity with wonder, and Henry has become a marvel, basking in the wondering stares of his comrades.

The order comes for a desperate charge, and the regiment responds magnificently, hurling itself into the enemy's fire regardless of the odds against it; and here Crane devotes a paragraph to a careful and specific analysis of their heroism:

> But there was a frenzy made from this furious rush. The men, pitching forward insanely, had burst into cheerings, moblike and barbaric, but tuned in strange keys that can arouse the dullard and the stoic. It made a mad enthusiasm that, it seemed, would be incapable of checking itself before granite and brass. There was the delirium that encounters despair and death, and is heedless and blind to the odds. It is a temporary but sublime absence of selfishness. And because it was of this order was the reason, perhaps, why the youth wondered, afterward, what reasons he could have had for being there.

Heroism is "temporary but sublime," succeeded by dejection, anger, panic, indignation, despair, and renewed rage. This can hardly be called, for Henry, gaining spiritual salvation by losing his soul in the flux of things, for he is acting in harried exasperation, exhaustion, and rage. What has seemed to him an incredible charge turns out, presently, to have been a very short one—in time and distance covered—for which the regiment is bitterly criticized by the General. The facts are supplemented by the tone, which conveys through its outrageous and whimsical language that the whole business is made of pretense and delusion: A "magnificent brigade" goes into a wood, causing there "a most awe-inspiring racket. . . . Having stirred this prodigious uproar, and, apparently, finding it too prodigious, the brigade, after a little time, came marching airily out again with its fine formation in nowise disturbed. . . . The brigade was jaunty and seemed to point a proud thumb at the yelling wood." In the midst of the next engagement, which is indeed a furious battle, the youth is sustained by a "strange and unspeakable hatred" of the officer who had dubbed his regiment "mud diggers." Carrying the colors, he leads a charge of men "in a state of frenzy, perhaps because of forgotten vanities, and it made an exhibition of sublime recklessness." In this hysterical battlefield the youth is indeed selfless and utterly fearless in "his wild battle madness," yet by reading closely we see that the opposing soldiers are a thin, feeble line who turn and run from the charge or are slaughtered.

What it all seems to come to is that the heroism is in action undeniable, but it is preceded and followed by the ignoble sentiments we have traced—and the constant tone of humor and hysteria seems to be Crane's comment on these juxtapositions of courage, ignorance, vainglory, pettiness, pompous triumph, and craven fear. The moment the men can stop and comment upon what they have been through they are presented as more or less absurd.

With all these facts in mind we can examine the Henry Fleming who emerges from the battle and sets about marshaling all his acts. He is gleeful over his courage. Remembering his desertion of the wounded Jim Conklin, he is ashamed because of the possible disgrace, but, as Crane tells with supreme irony, "gradually he mustered force to put the sin at a distance," and to dwell upon his "quiet manhood." Coming after all these events and rationalizations, the paragraphs quoted at the beginning of this discussion are a climax of self-delusion. If there is any one point that has been made it is that Henry has never been able to evaluate his conduct. He may have been fearless for moments, but his motives were vain, selfish, ignorant, and childish. Mercifully, Crane does not follow him down through the more despicable levels of self-delusion that are sure to follow as he rewrites (as we have seen him planning to do) the story of his conduct to fit his childish specifications. He has been through some moments of hell, during which he has for moments risen above his limitations, but Crane seems plainly to be showing that he has not achieved a lasting wisdom or self-knowledge.

If *The Red Badge of Courage* were only an exposure of an ignorant farm boy's delusions, it would be a contemptible book. Crane shows that Henry's delusions image only dimly the insanely grotesque and incongruous world of battle into which he is plunged. There the movement is blind or frantic, the leaders are selfish, the goals are inhuman. One farm boy is made into a mad animal to kill another farm boy, while the great guns carry on a "grim pow-wow" or a "stupendous wrangle" described in terms that suggest a solemn farce or a cosmic and irresponsible game.

If we were to seek a geometrical shape to picture the significant form of *The Red Badge*, it would not be the circle, the L, or the straight line of oscillation between selfishness and salvation, but the equilateral triangle. Its three points are instinct, ideals, and circumstance. Henry Fleming runs along the sides like a squirrel in a track.

Ideals take him along one side until circumstance confronts him with danger. Then instinct takes over and he dashes down the third side in a panic. The panic abates somewhat as he approaches the angle of ideals, and as he turns the corner (continuing his flight) he busily rationalizes to accommodate those ideals of duty and trust that recur, again and again, to harass him. Then he runs on to the line of circumstance, and he moves again toward instinct. He is always controlled on one line, along which he is both drawn and impelled by the other two forces. If this triangle is thought of as a piece of bright glass whirling in a cosmic kaleidoscope, we have an image of Crane's naturalistic and vividly impressioned Reality.

The Red Badge of Courage   Edwin H. Cady*

It has been variously asserted that Crane's way of imagining and constructing The Red Badge of Courage was realist, naturalist, impressionist, or symbolist. It would make a difference if it could be demonstrated that one of them, or any other, was the method. One would then expect to interpret particular parts, and the whole, in certain ways, and one's reading and response would be affected accordingly. But the conviction with which these various views have been urged by sensitive and intelligent critics might in itself warn the reader that no unitary view is exclusively right. The very secret of the novel's power inheres in the inviolably organic uniqueness with which Crane adapted all four methods to his need. The Red Badge's method is all and none. There is no previous fiction like it.

The narrative point of view, however, is nothing new. James and Howells had been developing the technique used in The Red Badge for years; they repeatedly displayed it with an easy virtuosity which Crane could hardly have missed in the big magazines. In the earliest pages of The Red Badge, the storyteller's point of view, the narrative line-of-sight along events which will afford the reader's perspective, is permanently established. The voice is that of a third-person, "objective" narrator—not a first-person, "subjective" teller who says "Call me Ishmael" or "You don't know me without you have read a book. . . ." But the point of view is located at almost the same place as if this were a first-person narrative: it is just behind the eyes of "the youthful private." The reader sees through Henry Fleming's eyes, and he is able to reflect backwards somewhat to record what goes on in Henry's mind (though never, of course, to overhear his

*From Stephen Crane, rev. ed. (Boston: Twayne, 1980 [1962]), 119–44. Reprinted by permission of Twayne Publishers, a division of G. K. Hall and Co., Boston.

"stream of consciousness"). But for the most part the reader is limited to seeing and hearing the life of the fiction as the narrator does; he can never "go behind" into the mind of another character.

These limitations make the experience afforded by the novel seem objective and thus credible, very intense, yet also somewhat detached and impersonal. The reader is not invited to "identify" wholly with young Fleming—a fact Joseph Hergesheimer recalled mourning over in his youth.[1] Fleming is part of a drama. He is to be subject to criticism, to judgment unintrusively unmoralized, established dramatically and ironically, but forcefully there. Essentially this is a perspective—but upon what? And to what end? What finally is the force of its proportion, its total form?

One way to begin to answer these questions is to notice some distinctions about the problem of point of view in this or any modern fiction which have not always been observed in discussing *The Red Badge*. At least four classes of "point of view" function in fiction. In simplest forms these are the author's, as he imagines and builds the work; the narrator's, which in any sophisticated fiction is not the author's way of looking at his work but an instrument of his technique in presenting it; the character's (or characters'), in the interplay of which—with one another and the narrator's viewpoints—lies a great deal of the craftsman's resource; and, finally, the reader's. Author's and reader's points of view are external to the novel. It may turn out that the reader's has been very skillfully played upon by the author who uses as instruments the internal points of view of narrator and characters.

The distinction in *The Red Badge of Courage* between the narrator's point of view and that of Henry Fleming, the sole character's view which the reader knows at all directly, is subtle for the reason already suggested. The narrator's point of view looks through Fleming's eyes. But though the reader sees what and as Fleming does, the reader is not he. Henry's point of view is that of his own experience; the reader knows it as, with the narrator, he goes reflexively "behind" for reports on that experience.

Material for observation of this experience is rich in the first four or five pages of the novel. It starts with a swiftly telescoped atmospheric registering of the context. Morning and early spring are telescoped in the first sentence:

> The cold passed reluctantly from the earth, and the retiring fogs
> revealed an army stretched out on the hills, resting. As the landscape
> changed from brown to green, the army awakened, and began to
> tremble with eagerness at the noise of rumors. It cast its eyes upon
> the roads, which were growing from the long troughs of liquid mud
> to proper thoroughfares. A river, amber-tinted in the shadow of its
> banks, purled at the army's feet; and at night, when the stream

had become of a sorrowful blackness, one could see across it the red, eye-like gleam of hostile camp-fires set in the low brows of distant hills.

It might, parenthetically, be possible to argue that the foregoing "one could see" establishes a narrative point of view distinct from Fleming's. But such an argument is unnecessarily messy and less than appreciative of Crane's artistic achievement. He handles point of view more like a movie camera than perhaps any predecessor had done. The reader stands to see somewhere back of Fleming's eyes. Sometimes the reader gets the long "panning" shot, sometimes the view only Henry could see, sometimes an interior view limited only by Crane's ignorance of methods Joyce would discover.

So the reader moves at once to a spirited, comic camp scene as tall Jim Conklin falsely reports imminent action. Then he retires with Fleming to ponder his emotions "in a little trance of astonishment" within the security of his hut. And suddenly his memory flashes back to the scenes and thoughts of his enlistment at home months before. The content of that flashback—seen by the reader through the narrator's double perception of what Fleming's point of view is now and what it was earlier—presents the basic problem of the novel.

The reader begins, then, with a perspective upon the perspectives of "the youth." They go back to dreams of battle and personal magnificence in war, dreams he has classed with "thought-images of heavy crowns and high castles"—the cloudy symbols of a high romance. Awake, this adolescent Minniver Cheevy "had long despaired of witnessing a Greek-like struggle. Such would be no more, he said. Men were better, or more timid. Secular and religious education had effaced the throat-grappling instinct, or else firm finance held in check the passions." On the farm, Fleming was a perfect neo-romantic.

Tales of "the war in his own country" inevitably began to move him, however. "They might not be distinctly Homeric, but there seemed to be much glory in them." In the face of his mother's Christian pacifism and her quietly effective ironic undercutting of his egotism, he eventually enlisted and left for camp with a soaring conviction "that he must be a hero." But the monotonous realities of camp life had taught him to concentrate on personal comfort and retreat "back to his old ideas. Greek-like struggles would be no more." Now, perhaps on the edge of the real thing, new possibilities of truth emerge. Maybe he will be a coward! "He felt that in this crisis his laws of life were useless. Whatever he had learned of himself was here of no avail. He was an unknown quantity. He saw that he would again be obliged to experiment as he had in early youth." When it turned out that the battle was not on the morrow, he had days to make "ceaseless calculations . . . all wondrously unsatisfactory." Examination of self and scrutiny of others were defeated. Only experience would help: "to go into the blaze, and then figuratively to watch his legs to discover their merits and faults . . . he must have blaze, blood, and danger, even as a chemist requires this, that and the other."

Except for the initial paragraph, the method and issues so far established are those of the realists. The emphasis on point of view, on vision, is theirs; and the establishment of a problem of knowledge, which will require an exercise in discovery and revelation, is theirs. So, too, is the pragmatic dependence on experience: answering the question by watching whether one's legs ran or stayed might have come straight from James's *Principles of Psychology*. And raising the issues of romanticism—the heroic, the glamorous, the egotistical, exalted and sentimental—was a confirmed habit of the realists. Anti-romanticism, the reduction by ridicule and irony of the romantic to the common, negative realism, was the first and always the easiest way for the realists to define themselves. Positive realism, finding the beauty, power, and meaning of life in the commonplace—a green farm boy among his peers in an unblooded regiment, for instance— was much more difficult. But the wrangling amateur military experts in the company street and the soldiers' hut are scenically presented— they talk and act—with a humorous precision dear to the heart of any lover of the common American man.

One does not read far into *The Red Badge of Courage*, however, without discovering that it is different from the traditional realistic novel. The extended and massive specification of detail with which the realist seems to impose upon one an illusion of the world of the common vision is wholly missing. Equally absent is the tremendous procession of natural and social "forces" characteristic of naturalism— of Frank Norris or Dreiser trying to be Zola. Detail is not absent, but it is comparatively sparingly deployed on a light, mobile structure; and it is used for intensive, not extensive effects. Reference to "forces" is there, but no effort at all to show them streaming in their mighty currents, floating the characters as tracers, as chips on the stream whose significance is to reveal the trending of the currents.

One of the more reliable ways, indeed, to distinguish romantic from realistic and both from naturalistic fiction is to examine the way each handles its characters. To the romancer the significance of his people is symbolic; they are representative men and women who reveal, by the doctrine of correspondence, spiritual truths (*viz.*, Chin-gachgook, Chillingworth, Goodman Brown, Captain Ahab and all his men). The reductive, agnostic realist, however, cannot believe in the spiritual sublimity, the ideality, of his characters. He levels his vision to the human, fascinated by the paradoxes of the common person:

his individuality, his commonplace mediocrity, the representative, perhaps universal, meaning of his "common" moral problems. To the naturalist, finally, humanity means only animality. This is the ultimate reduction. Where the romancer's concern was superhuman and the realist's humane, the naturalist's is infrahuman. And in a sense the naturalist joins hands with the romancer (no matter how the latter might cringe) again in looking not so much to what the man is as to what he can be made to reveal about realities far larger, stronger, more important and more abstract than man.

In this intent, too, Crane stands with the realists, but he stands historically in advance of them toward the coming future of the novel. The critics of his own day who wondered if Crane did not represent a "new realism" may have been more than a little right.[2] It was natural, if not inevitable, that the realism of the generation previous to Crane should develop to prepare the way for its own displacement. The shift was toward an increasingly psychological realism, and it was propelled by at least two major forces. One of these was the displacement of positivism from its dominance of late nineteenth-century thought. A decade like the 1890's, which began with William James's *Psychology* and ended with the unleashing of the new, electronic factors in physics which produced Henry Adams' image of "himself lying in the Gallery of Machines at the Great Exposition of 1900, his historical neck broken by the sudden irruption of forces totally new," was bound at the least to loosen the grip of positivism on the imagination. The second force, however, arose from the practice of realistic fiction itself. The more one confronted the mystery of men as persons living out their fates and struggling toward their deaths, the more one's scrutiny turned from the outward sign to the inward process itself. Howells noticed in 1903, when he was writing a novel Freudian in all but specifically Viennese terminology for the main concept, that all the realists had of late been turning to psychology. Indeed, many of them had been flirting with psychic phenomena as far-flung as the claims of spiritualism. What he did not seem to notice was that he himself had been working largely in psychological realism since *The Shadow of a Dream* in 1891.

For the better part of thirty-five years, Howells had fought at the foremost point in a great battle to capture American taste for realism. He had defined realism as the objective truth in art about the visible aspects of human life. But in 1903 he registered his realization that a change had occurred among the great realists of the world. God seems to love the game of the pendulum in man's affairs, he observed. And now "A whole order of literature has arisen, calling itself psychological, as realism called itself scientific . . . it is not less evident in Tolstoi, in Gorky, in Ibsen, in Björnsen, in Hauptmann, and in Mr. Henry James, than in Maeterlinck himself."[3]

It was like Howells to leave himself out of the account. The surprising thing is his so registering the change almost fifteen years after he had launched himself into it. What he apparently did not see was that what he called "the present psychologism" was not just a providential swing of the pendulum but a fairly predictable outcome of the earlier realism—and that it was already bridging the way for the interior, stream of consciousness, and therefore symbolic fiction which would succeed it. The realism of which Howells had been the chief American prophet had been, as he said, "scientific" in the mid-nineteenth-century sense of factualistic and "objective." It had also been intensely humanistic, fixing its focus on persons, on characters, in their human dimensions, qualities, conflicts, problems, and fates. The more it fastened on characters and the visible evidence of inner conditions, the more that realism would be tempted to "go behind" as James said. The further behind the veil of sense it went, the less normally and normatively visible its evidences would be. After a while it would no longer be the realist's appeal to the common vision which would win the reader's suspension of disbelief, but only a faith in the realist's honesty of covert vision secured, perhaps, by his faithfulness to that common vision in overt matters. The turn to psychology opened important and exciting vistas to the accomplished realist like Henry James. It also paved the way for the displacement of realism by such masters to come as Joyce, Anderson, Lawrence, and Faulkner.

The Red Badge of Courage was the first masterpiece of that transition, as Howells imperfectly saw while reviewing it. Most commendable, he said, was "the skill shown in evolving from the youth's crude expectations and ambitions a quiet honesty and self-possession manlier and nobler than any heroism had imagined . . . and decidedly on the psychological side the book is worth while as an earnest of the greater things that we may hope for from a new talent working upon a high level, not quite clearly as yet, but strenuously."[4] In a lifetime devoted to part-time criticism, Howells had a high batting average, but this time he hit only a part of the ball. He may have been told or have divined Crane's interest in the psychological. Crane was able to be overt about it from Greece, telling John Bass that "Between two great armies battling against each other the interesting thing is the mental attitude of the men." Or, as he explained himself to his English readers, people "think they ought to demand" of "descriptions of battle" that they be placed "to stand in front of the mercury of war and see it rise or fall . . . but it is an absurd thing for a writer to do if he wishes to reflect, in any way, the mental condition of the men in the ranks. . . ."[5]

"To reflect . . . the mental condition of the men in the ranks," representing them especially with one youth, is an exact definition of the achievement—and probably the intention—of *The Red Badge of Courage.* Its formal structure is rather simply Aristotelian. It has a beginning (Chapters I–IV), which gets the youth to real battle; a middle (Chapters V–XIII), which witnesses his runaway and return; and an end (Chapters XIV–XXIII), which displays his achievement of "heroism" at climax, followed by a certain understanding of it in a coda-like final chapter. The middle and end sections are replete with notations of Fleming's psychological responses to fear, stress, and courage. There are progressively at least ninety such notations of Fleming's state of nerves-mind-psyche (it is not at all clear that Crane had any coherent psychological theory to exploit). They occur in pairs or triads of alternating or developmental stages as well as singly and are sometimes recurrent. If only by mere weight, the ninety constitute a major part of the substance of a short novel.

Actually, of course, psychological notations count for far more than mere bulk in *The Red Badge.* They are fascinating in themselves. For instance, Crane recorded something he no doubt picked up from football (as psychologists are said to have done later, naming the phenomenon "scrimmage blackout"). In the depth of combat, Crane supposed, Fleming would pass into an absorptive trance in which he was conscious of little but performed with intense automatism in a "battle-sleep" during which he might occasionally "dream" impressions. Essential to the achievement of the novel are the psychological patterns Crane divined for Fleming's combat experience. One is the obverse of the other. In the one, fear leads to panic, panic to guilt, guilt to rationalization and eventually to frustration and acquiescence. In the other, resentment produces rage, and rage "battle sleep"; resolution, including willingness to die, follows and leads in turn to "heroism" and at last to adumbrations of emotional realism and modesty. Equally striking are Crane's observations of the complexities of individual-group relations.

If this psychologism carried Crane past realism, it also defined his sense of naturalism, at least for this novel. Philosophic naturalism in *The Red Badge of Courage* is not expounded. It is identified as a form of romanticism, a buttress to the ego, a means of escape from moral reality and responsibility. In the end it is rejected. It is referred to—in the final state of the novel more obliquely than directly—so often as to leave little doubt that Crane was quite aware of its patterns of explanation and their potential uses. But it is at last only a foil for the pragmatic, relativistic ideas toward which the novel finally points.

It may also indicate Crane's decision about naturalism at this point to note that he cut most of the explicit references to its ideas out of *The Red Badge* at various stages of revision. Before Crane's manuscript, in the Barrett Collection at Virginia, was laminated in a doubtless necessary effort to save its crumbling paper, it was possible to work out theoretically the existence of at least seven progressive states of *The Red Badge* text. Without being able to know what preceded the text which Crane's poverty preserved in canceled fragments on the versos of a later start, we have (on legal foolscap) the earliest draft. It existed in four states, having been revised in pen, in pencil, and at last in blue crayon. Unfortunately, I am informed, the essential color variations were lost in the lamination process: how very much too bad that no one thought to preserve the colors as they have been saved in the far more complex facsimile of *Walt Whitman's Blue Book!*[6]

Somewhere in the progression some leaves came out for the Bacheller syndicated text. And before the first edition there was a now lost typescript with nobody knows how much revision. At last, of course, Crane read and must in some degree have revised the galley proofs, which have also disappeared.

Rather boldly explicit in draft but variously suppressed and left implicit in the final text was Crane's association of philosophic naturalism with Henry Fleming's panic syndrome. One may guess that he thought to make the resultant theme central to the novel's development and then changed his mind.

Early in the morning of his first battle day, Fleming dashes, wild with curiosity, upon the scene of what he expects will be immediate combat. But it is bathos, nothing really is happening; and as the regiment presses on into a silently ominous landscape, his courage oozes away: "This advance upon Nature was too calm . . . absurd ideas took hold upon him. . . . It was all a trap." With this comes the idea associated throughout: he must become a prophet of the truth "Nature" reveals. "He thought that he must break from the ranks and harangue his comrades. . . . The generals were idiots. . . . There was but one pair of eyes in the corps." But fear of ridicule silences him as the tense ranks advance "to look at war, the red animal—war, the blood-swollen god." However, nature is no constant for Fleming; she varies with his psychic states. After his first and successful combat, he wakes from his battle-sleep with "a flash of astonishment at the blue pure sky and the sun gleaming on the trees and fields. It was surprising that Nature had gone tranquilly on with her golden process in the midst of so much devilment."

Fleming's later efforts to appeal to nature as a constant and as a source of comforting revelation (or rationalization) are therefore doomed. If one were to argue from *The Red Badge of Courage* about Crane's attitudes toward the naturalistic argument for man's animal irresponsibility toward duty and morality he would, in fact, have to conclude that Crane had considered but repudiated that argument.

Chapter VII is the first decisively interesting surviving example of Crane's revision of *The Red Badge*, and the revisions affect precisely this issue, shifting from explicit to implicit. This is the chapter in which Fleming is plunged from unworthy hope of personal justification into shame and self-pity by his deserted comrades' holding their line and repulsing the attack from which he had run. He seeks to "bury himself" in the thick woods, in nature. There he passes through swift changes of mood. "This landscape gave him assurance. A fair field holding life. It was the religion of peace. . . . He conceived Nature to be a woman with a deep aversion to tragedy." He shies a pine-cone at "a jovial squirrel" who dashes for safety: "The youth felt triumphant at this exhibition. There was the law, he said. Nature had given him a sign. . . . Nature was of his mind."

As he wanders on, however, other signs obtrude. In a swamp he sees "a small animal pounce in and emerge directly with a gleaming fish." And finally, in what at first seems "a chapel" in a pine grove, he finds the disintegrating corpse of a Federal soldier from a bygone battle, with "black ants swarming greedily upon the grey face." The present text ends abruptly with Fleming fleeing the horror and leaving "the chapel" to the "soft wind" and "sad silence" of nature—which ties in perfectly with an impressionistic bit of atmosphere about the onset of twilight which begins the next chapter.

Once, however, the text had been far more intellectually obvious, and Crane had kept it that way for quite a while. The manuscript, at least in its third state, was revised first in pen, then in pencil. In that minimally fifth revision Crane cancelled from the end of the chapter these words,

> Again the youth was in despair. Nature no longer condoled with him. There was nothing, then, after all, in that demonstration she gave—the frightened squirrel fleeting aloft from the missile. He thought . . . that there was given another law which far-overtopped it—all life existing upon death, eating ravenously, stuffing itself with the hopes of the dead. . . .[7]

That mood also passed. Shortly he is thinking as he heads back toward the battle that, because brambles restrain him, "Nature could not be quite ready to kill him." But, of course, that alternation was lost from the revised text.

Fleming's nightmare agony in the middle part of The Red Badge climaxes in Chapter IX with the macabre death of Conklin, "the tall soldier," and in Chapter X with Fleming's desertion of "the tattered man" on being asked where his own wound was. Crane tried hard to provide Fleming with reflections adequate to his shocked and shame-sodden state but he failed, cancelling, rewriting, and cancelling again. He had Henry reflect, in utter opposition to his old romantic ideas, that soldiers were really "Nature's dupes." Nature went seducing men with "dreams" of "glory," defeating their ingenuity of devices to stave off death by planting a treacherous sentiment in their hearts. "War, he said bitterly to the sky, was a makeshift created because ordinary processes could not furnish deaths enough." From earlier hints, Crane seems to have developed this and Fleming's derisive fury about it for five pages.[8] He cancelled the effort out only in the blue-crayon revision which appears to have gone to the typist.

That cancelled experience of Fleming's lay behind the returned motif of his exaltation of self-justification at seeing, at the beginning of Chapter XI, the routed troops on the road. That feeling is followed at once by his feeling like a sinner in Hell watching angels "with weapons of flame and banners of sunlight" when a disciplined column of infantry butts its glorious way through the chaos. Crane stops to put Fleming through nine progressive states of psychosomatic and imaginary response to his situation in the least dramatic (and so perhaps least satisfactory) chapter in the book. And it was clearly Crane's early intention to follow the "analytic" chapter with a twelfth which would bring to an ironic climax both the theme of natural irresponsibility and the several times repeated theme of Fleming's prophetic role toward his comrades and the world.

Since the relative slackness of the previous chapter makes it clear that discursive patches mar *The Red Badge*, it is not surprising that Crane suppressed his intended Chapter XII. He was right to do so, and the principal use of considering it is to see that in it he unmistakably derided the naturalistic diagnosis of Fleming's condition together with Henry's Dreiser-like urge to proclaim its gospel. And he left (now submerged) that rejection as the pivot upon which Fleming could turn again, now fit to be delivered by kindly (but by no means unique, as it turned out) fates to his outfit.

That aborted chapter begins, "It was always clear to Fleming that he was entirely different from other men," and now he consoles himself that his suffering has been "unprecedented" in the awful opposition of his tiny self to the universe. But then he sees that there is no malice really, "merely law," and that there were compensating principles—what might be called the squirrel's law recurred to him:

> Nature had provided her creations with various defenses and ways to escape . . . that the things might resist or hide with a security proportionate to their strength and wisdom. It was all the same old philosophy. He could not omit a small grunt of satisfaction as he saw with what brilliancy he had reasoned it all out.

Soon he is ready to avail himself of that brilliancy and apply his findings to the incident of his own flight from the battle: "It was not a fault; it was a law. It was—But he saw that when he had made a vindicating structure of great principles, it was the calm toes of tradition that kicked it all down about his ears." In bitter rebellion he then resolves to save mankind from the worship of "the gods of the ashes," and he begins to see himself "the growing prophet of a world-reconstruction. Far down in the pure depths of his being . . . he saw born a voice. He conceived a new world, modelled by the pain of his life, in which no old shadows fell darkening upon the temple of thought. And there were many personal advantages in it."

He thinks of "piercing orations" and "himself a sun-lit figure upon a peak." But gradually his enthusiasm burns out as he thinks of mankind's bovine habitude—"he would be beating his fists against the brass of accepted things." He rails abuse "in supreme disgust and rage. . . . To him there was something terrible and awesome in these words spoken from his heart to his heart. He was very tragic."[9]

Crane's irony is obvious from the bathetic anti-climaxes of this: "And there were many personal advantages . . . a sun-lit figure. . . . He was very tragic." But even though this has disappeared from the text, its irony remains operative in the pivotal next chapter. There Fleming suddenly sees that all-enviable, heroic-angelic column charging back from the fray "like terrified buffaloes." He feels "horror-stricken" and stares "in agony and amazement." Then, most significantly, "He forgot that he was engaged in combating the universe. He threw aside his mental pamphlets on the philosophy of the retreated and rules for the guidance of the damned." He loses himself in concern for the stricken angels, thinks absurdly of rallying them, tries to detain one to ask what happened, and gets his red badge of courage from the rifle-butt in the hands of a hysterical ex-hero. His knockout is virtually a death, and for a while after he goes "tall soldier fashion." His first day of combat draws on to sunset, and in the dark he is rescued by the selfless and faceless "cheery soldier" and delivered back to the 304th New York where he belongs.

There he is met with new cheer and sympathy. His lie about being shot readily believed, he is nursed and cared for by a suddenly mature, modest and no longer loud Wilson. In the morning he discovers that perhaps half the regiment had been missing after the action but turned up by morning with stories—" 'Jest like you done,' " Wilson tells Fleming. Then, in a very late, blue-crayon cancellation he thinks "with deep contempt of all his grapplings and tuggings with fate and the universe." He sees how ridiculous had been the cherished uniqueness and novelty of his thought. But he begins to feel self-respect returning, since he is safe and "unimpeached."[10]

It will take all the rest of the last part of the book to try that egotism in the fire of a real, if minor, heroism and reduce it to the human modesty achieved by Wilson on the first day. From this point forward, however, nature will be no more abstracted, personified, or capitalized in *The Red Badge,* and Fleming's recollections of his prophetic ideas and role will be merely embarrassed. He will be glad nobody else knows. Intellectually, that seems to be what there is to naturalism in the novel, and the symbolic or impressionistic uses of it are keyed to the intellectual.

It seems clear that *The Red Badge* is not a work of naturalism; and it is also certain that Fleming is *not* "guided by a naturalistic code of ethics." No more is a naturalistic "Henry's attitude . . . characteristic of Crane."[11] The true naturalist's truth must be that man is a part of nature and not other. Crane's sense of the indifference or hostility of nature to man was shared, for instance, by a Pilgrim Father (Brewster), a Massachusetts Bay Puritan (Winthrop), a rationalistic Calvinist (Edwards), a deist (Freneau, "The Hurricane"), by Melville (whatever he was), and by many varieties of non-naturalistic Darwinists. Like them, Crane did believe man was "other"—in Crane's case, man was human. That was a lesson Henry Fleming learned to see.

Then it becomes possible to say that *The Red Badge of Courage* is a unique work of psychological realism deeply affected in style by the fact that the author was an ironic, imagistic, metaphysical poet. And that brings one to the moot questions of Crane's impressionism and symbolism. If one could be sure of the qualities of these, it would be best to treat them apart. Since, in fact, their existence as well as their separability is obscure, it may be best to take them together. Actually, in Crane's case it might be impossible to define his impressionism and symbolism separately.

"Impressionism" was a potent and intensely controversial term in the 1890s. A war cry for those who sought escape from Victorianism, it stood for the liberation of the artist from the academy and tradition, from formalism and ideality, from narrative, and finally even from realism; for realism demanded responsibility to the common vision and impressionism responsibility only to what the unique eye of the painter saw. It was also a swearword for conservatives of every variety, of course. In painting there was a solid body of reference, forged in the heat of often vicious controversy, and a body of distinguished (no matter how controversial) examples to give substance to "impressionism."

But in literature the case was and is different. There was a rather vague breeze of the *avant garde* ghosting in the American literary atmosphere of the 1890s. In 1890 itself the Harpers published a volume of *Pastels in Prose from the French,* translated by Stuart Merrill with an introduction by Howells. It presented pieces by Baudelaire, Daudet, and Mallarmé, with a number of *chinoiseries* by Judith Gautier. The collection set Howells to musing about the Prose Poem, poetic prose, and poetry in prose and concluding that "the very life of the form is its aerial delicacy, its soul is that perfume of thought, of emotion, which these masters here have never suffered to become an argument."

Even if one assumed for the sake of the argument that Crane read the volume, what could it be said that he learned from it? The question resembles the unstudied one of whether, even as poet, Crane learned anything from the strikingly new poems Howells was publishing between 1891 and 1895 under such *avant-gardiste* rubrics as "Moods," "Monochromes," "Pebbles," and, in three cases, "Impression." On January 16, 1897, the *Chicago Record,* for example, damned *The Little Regiment* because it showed that "Mr. Crane is not a scientist. . . . He is above all an impressionist." But safely in England with Joseph Conrad and Edward Garnett, Crane could if he wished take pleasure in the fact that with them the epithet was a high compliment.[12]

Nevertheless, it was and is difficult to know just what Crane's "impressionism" means. In literature the term is so vague and so devoid of explicit example as not even to make an entry in Wellek and Warren, *Theory of Literature,* or in standard histories. Handbook definitions, when they occur, are not conspicuous for relevance to Crane. They seem roughly agreed that in literature "impressionism" means either absence of detail or else the effect of the author observing himself in the presence of life, not the life. Neither applies illuminatingly to the work of Stephen Crane. Yet it would be strange if there were nothing meant by all the often impressive critics who have applied the term to Crane; and of course that is not the case.

What they are talking about comes down, perhaps, to the vividness and intensity of Crane's notation of atmospheric textures and to the striking economy, *multum in parvo,* of his form. No doubt the effort to achieve psychological realism promoted what Willa Cather brilliantly defined as "The Novel Démeublé."[13] Howells's first attempts at it in *The Shadow of a Dream* (1890) and *An Imperative Duty* (1892) were strikingly "disfurnished" after *A Hazard of New Fortunes* (1890). Crane's own comment on literary aims is characteristically minimal and apparently innocent of the term "impressionism" until his significant work had been done—and Conrad, Garnett, Heuffer, and others had explained the situation to him. Even then he confined a striking use of it to painterly reference:

> The church had been turned into a hospital for Spanish wounded who had fallen into American hands. The interior of the church was too cavelike in its gloom for the eyes of the operating surgeons, so they had had the altar-table carried to the doorway, where there

was a bright light. Framed then in the black archway was the altar-table with the figure of a man upon it. He was naked save for a breech-clout, and so close, so clear was the ecclesiastic suggestion that one's mind leaped to a fantasy that this thin, pale figure had just been torn down from a cross. The flash of the impression was like light, and for this instant it illumined all the dark recesses of one's remotest idea of sacrilege, ghastly and wanton. I bring this to you merely as an effect, an effect of mental light and shade, if you like; something done in thought similar to that which the French impressionists do in color; something meaningless and at the same time overwhelming, crushing, monstrous.[14]

It has been persuasively argued that Crane must have learned much and adapted to his writing what he learned of French Impressionism.[15] Yet Linson, who should certainly have known, denies it flatly—and apparently by implication denies the name of "painter" to Vosburgh and the "Indians." Linson had been a fellow student of Gauguin but not wholly in sympathy with him. At least, however, Linson must be supposed to have known what Impressionism was about:

> To the oft repeated query as to Crane's use of color: "Did he get it from his studio associates?" My answer is "No." I was the only painter among his early intimates; one or two others he met casually with me. The rest were illustrators or journalists. . . . The Impressionism of that day was to him an affectation, and all affectation was dishonesty, uncreative, and thus dead from the start.[16]

That statement might, of course, be regarded at most as authoritative only through Crane's establishment of himself in England.

Taken at fullest value, however, Linson indicates the same things shown by Crane's remark about Oscar Wilde: Wilde was "a mildewed chump." Crane was having none of the official *fin de siècle*. But he might equally well have had nonetheless his own sort of impressionism; and one can catch him at it. In "War Memories," again, there is a peculiar little moment when one almost feels embarrassed for Crane:

> "But to get the real thing!" cried Vernall, the war correspond-ent. "It seems impossible! It is because war is neither magnificent nor squalid; it is simply life, and an expression of life can always evade us. We can never tell life, one to another, although sometimes we think we can."[17]

Those Shelleyan cries and the self-consciousness about expression and the real thing are out of character for Crane. And, as a matter of fact, they constitute a strategic insincerity. He is embarking on a long series of pictures which will not "tell life" but present it unmistakably to a reader.

Actually Crane had, quite consciously, mastered the solution to that (as presented) pseudoproblem long before. In the *New York World* for October 15, 1896, for instance, he had lightened a bit of journalism for himself with a touch of virtuosity:

> We, as a new people, are likely to conclude that our mechanical perfection, our structural precision, is certain to destroy all quality of sentiment in our devices, and so we prefer to grope in the past when people are not supposed to have had any structural precision. As the terrible, the beautiful, the ghastly, pass continually before our eyes we merely remark that they do not seem to be correct in romantic detail.
>
> But an odor of oiled woods, a keeper's tranquil, unemotional voice, a broom stood in the corner near the door, a blue sky and a bit of moving green tree at a window so small that it might have been made by a canister shot—all these ordinary things contribute with subtle meaning to the horror of this comfortable chair, this commonplace bit of furniture that . . . waits and waits.

The subject is the electric chair at Sing Sing, and the virtuosity is that he has solved the expressive problem in the act of describing it.

Not to choose any of the nature descriptions which set the atmospheric stage so perfectly over and again in *The Red Badge* or which tally Fleming's psychic gyrations, one bit of Crane's special impressionism, his way of conveying the real thing with extraordinary intensity, may stand for dozens. The 304th New York has not quite gone into action when nearby "Saunders" gets "crushed" by Confederates:

> The flag suddenly sank down as if dying. Its motion as it fell was a gesture of despair.
>
> Wild yells came from behind the walls of smoke. A sketch in gray and red dissolved into a mob-like body of men who galloped like wild horses.

With minimal but exact detail, in an aura of psychological, not objective, reality, the experience is precisely, forcefully communicated. The method is more poetic than traditionally novelistic, as has been variously observed. It is Crane's impressionism of texture. For the rest, the question has been most usefully approached through William M. Gibson's citation of the letter from Thomas Wolfe to Scott Fitzgerald dividing great writers into "putter-inners" and "taker-outers."[18] Crane belongs with Flaubert, Hemingway, and Willa Cather's ideal as a "taker-outer," and that trait perhaps is the other aspect of his impressionism.

Inescapably, when one considers Crane's abruptly vivid effects, the question arises whether they are just impressionistically textural or symbolic as well. In some senses, of course, they are immitigably symbolic, just as any word, any significant cluster of words, is symbolic in any literary context. But surely that is not what is meant when Crane is called a "symbolist," for it would distinguish him not at all from any other author. In fact, to make the point one last time, it is hard to say what species, if any, of "symbolist" Crane was. No systematic discussion of that subject appears to exist. Certainly, as visionist, he represented the opposite of Charles Feidelson's "symbolistic imagination" and so he represents the opposite of Mallarmé, Baudelaire, *et seq.*[19] Crane was, that is, intensely concerned with the vision of realities, objective and subjective, which he regarded as independent of language but ideally susceptible of "unmistakable" communication through words. The evidence seems clear that he had no notion of any linguistically self-contained and unique literary "reality" and that he would have found that notion laughably conceited. One might, of course, argue, as exponents of some antirational schools of criticism appear to do, that, regardless of what Crane thought he thought, he was a "symbolist" because all good literature is such and so successful authors are this (or that) because their literature is good. But arguments of that sort are not available to discussion.

Thoroughly discussable, however, is what has become virtually a school of Crane criticism which follows the original ideas of the single most energetic and embattled of Crane scholar-critics, Robert W. Stallman. One can scarcely avoid concentrating discussion of the master, his disciples, and their doctrine on the problem of the most famous image in *The Red Badge of Courage,* now almost the best known image in American literature: "The red sun was pasted in the sky like a wafer."

Stallman's intuition that this is the central characterizing symbol of the whole work, from which the nature and stature of its artistry and the substance of its meaning must be interpreted, was promulgated in a forty-nine page introduction in the *Omnibus* (175–224). For Stallman the key to it all is that the "wafer" means the form of bread, circular, crisp, almost parchmentlike, used in the celebration of the Eucharist in liturgical churches: "I do not think it can be doubted that Crane intended to suggest here the sacrificial death celebrated in communion." From this he argued back that Jim Conklin, the tall soldier who has died in the passages just preceding Crane's introduction of the image, is Christ, or a Christ-figure, and that the book then becomes, as Daniel Hoffman, accepting Stallman, said, "a chronicle of redemption." The contention is that, as in Christian doctrine, Fleming is somehow redeemed by the sacrificial death of Conklin in a symbolic or "apocalyptic" novel richly laden with Christian reference.

It should cause no wonder that such views have been not only doubted but challenged. A small critical war has been waged over them, with the balance appearing to turn firmly against them. The symbolist critics have obviously been useful in correcting overemphases on Crane's "naturalism," in stimulating study of his artistry, and in calling attention to achievements in that art which rise beyond what is usually subsumed under "impressionism." One thinks twice before rejecting the discoveries of well-informed, critically sensitive commentators. And it would be arrogant to deny that the childhood training and imaginative affinities of Stephen Crane should have led him to Christian imagery, or even perhaps to a pattern of Christian symbolism in *The Red Badge*. But, in all candor, many other critics simply cannot find such interpretations valid. The evidence adduced for the symbolic pattern breaks down at every point and at the first scrutiny. It is in fact not clear, first of all, that Crane as Crane is ever truly a symbolist: the test case may be "The Open Boat." Perhaps one needs to extend the sense of "impressionism" to take in what Crane does with images.

It would require a separate book to argue the problem out, but one can sketch the approaches to the problem by sticking to the wafer and Jim Conklin. To begin with, it was inherently improbable that Crane thought of a "wafer" as eucharistic. He had been reared in an antiliturgical, enthusiastically anti-Catholic church and had become hotly anticlerical. While one could not rule out his knowing of the wafer of the Mass, he was much more likely to have thought of the word as denoting a confection or, as various critics have pointed out, an item of stationery common to and typical of the nineteenth century. As messy, expensive sealing wax passed out of use, it was replaced by a useful imitation of paper or other substance. Round, with neatly serrated edges stylizing the irregularities of a wax seal, often a deep, solid red as wax had been, these often gummed "wafers" were used to seal letters, packages, documents, diplomas, etc. See definition 3 as opposed to definition 4 in the Merriam-Webster unabridged *Dictionary of the English Language*, Second Edition, for an unmistakable distinction between the stationer's (and Crane's) usage (no. 3) and the liturgical (and Stallman's) usage (no. 4). Joseph Hergesheimer, reading Crane, "thought of an actual red wafer, such as druggists fixed to their bottles; it had a definite, a limited size for me, an established, clear vermilion color."[20]

Visualizing *that* kind of "wafer" expunges religious significance from the image, and it removes certain embarrassments, too. If the image were to be taken as seriously sacramental, why was it red? And if one strained toward a metaphysical answer to that, why then, was it surrealistically "pasted"? Not to mention the most painful lapse in mere taste, there are embarrassments in the argument that the Lincolnesque Conklin is meant to represent Christ. As with the wafer, the connections seem hopelessly imprecise. Conklin does not bear the stigmata of Christ—even in his side. Christ's side was pierced after death by the spear of a professional soldier, iconography shows a neat, clean incision. Conklin's "side looked as if it had been chewed by wolves." Nor will it do to argue that the sign is Fleming's recognition scream, "Gawd! Jim Conklin!" Thirteen lines later, Conklin is saying, ". . . Lord, what a circus! An' b' jiminey, I got shot. . . ." Soldiers in *The Red Badge*, like real soldiers, frequently take the name of the Lord their God in vain—speaking not with symbolic portentousness any more than with blasphemous intent but simply as they speak (not in *The Red Badge*) obscenities for the registration of stereotyped and often comically inappropriate emotions.

The decisive difficulties with the Christian-symbolist reading of *The Red Badge*, it seems, are that there appears to be no way to make a coherent account of the symbols as referential to Christian doctrine and then to match that with what happens in the novel. The Christian doctrines of redemption and atonement, however central to orthodox faith, have ever been theologically obscure, intellectually mysterious. But they have always also been vital to Christian experience. And there just isn't any evidence of that, particularly as associated with the wafer and Conklin's death, in the after development of *The Red Badge*. There is textually no evidence that Fleming so much as perceives the "wafer." He mentions Conklin only once, informing Wilson of Jim's death, and they mourn briefly in the fashion of combat soldiers in the midst of death, ". . . poor cuss!" Restored to self-esteem on his safe return to the regiment, Fleming quickly soars into an arrogance unpleasantly contrasted with Wilson's quiet manliness. At the end he has self-admiration to place beside humiliation as objects of contemplation. But it is his desertion of the live but dying tattered man which stabs his conscience. Conklin's death is absent from his thoughts.

It may be, in short, that Crane had no notion conscious or unconscious of "redemption" for Fleming. That may not have been his point at all, and the fact that one can gather a great deal of religious reference—or any other sort of reference—from the text may imply no hidden cohesions of meaning. Or it may: perhaps it is more a matter of whether one cares for Miss Caroline Spurgeon's methods with Shakespeare or not.[21]

But in the end, the trouble with a "symbolic" reading of *The Red Badge* is that it assumes some sort of operative attitude toward a referential reality on the part of the artist. No matter how one qualifies it, a literary symbol must somehow be an image which points to something else, something usually conceptual. That "other" may be an established mythology accepted by artist and public; but nobody supposes that sort of integrative symbolism possible to Crane with

Christianity. Or the artist may be in revolt, and the symbols disintegrative of the mythology—as dominantly in Melville. Or the symbols may refer to an arcane, even unique, mythology of the artist—in which case the interpreter must either be blanked or find the key to the arcanum.

The arcane way of a Blake or Yeats seems foreign to the temperament and known ideals of Crane. But it may be that symbolistic investigation of that possibility and of the disintegrative functions of Crane's religious imagery might prove more fruitful than those which have hitherto apparently assumed integrative patterns. Howells may well have been deeply perceptive in remarking that Crane had not yet got into the secret of himself. It might be possible to divine part of that secret by guessing at where Crane's religious insights were, perhaps unconsciously, leading him. On the other hand, humanistic and naturalistic interpreters have no doubt been right in seeing how the vision of *The Red Badge* scouted and reduced traditional religious as well as romantic securities. Perhaps such should pay more attention to the imagery as symbol.

In any case, symbolic or not, Crane's imagery has obviously only begun to be comprehended. With a bewildering richness of reference (infraconceptual and so at first level imagistic and not symbolic), he wove a dense texture in *The Red Badge of Courage*. That, and not the often startling locutions, constitutes the triumph of its style. *The Red Badge* focuses only on three soldiers, Fleming and two who are obviously foils for him. One of them, Wilson, goes swiftly through the evolution from "loud soldier" to clear-sighted and therefore modest manhood which "The Veteran" testifies that Fleming also attained, perhaps by the end of the novel. But Wilson's transformation occurs while our eyes, which are with Fleming, are absent. Partly they are occupied with the death of "the spectral soldier," Jim Conklin.

If these common soldiers are representative as well as ordinary persons, Conklin is the representative sacrificed soldier, and he occupies in the novel a place equivalent to that of the Unknown Soldier in the national pantheon. His death deserves the emphasis its drama provides in *The Red Badge*. It is, as it must be, an occasion for shock and protest. Fleming incoherently registers it: "The youth turned, with sudden, livid rage, toward the battle field. He shook his fist. He seemed about to deliver a philippic. 'Hell—' " And nature, as it generally does in the novel, registers Fleming—the awful intensity but faceless frustration of the shock which cannot yet be grief: "The red sun was pasted in the sky like a wafer."

If style be taken as texture and form as structure, the question of the equal success of the novel's form depends on deciding the much-discussed problem of the ending. Does the novel end well? Does it end or just disappear? Is there a climax? Is the ending of the novel satisfactory, in short, in emphasis and substance?

Debate has raged since the early reviews, and much of it around the last chapter. Though many critics have not troubled to mention it, few would deny the real achievement of a climax in personal victory which comes at the end of the next to the last chapter. Jeered at by veterans, scorned by their general as "mud-diggers" and "mule drivers," barely surviving after a temporary desertion rate of nearly fifty percent on the first day, close to a "pretty success" which they had funked by a hundred feet a little earlier, the regiment had stood exasperatedly under a last pressure. Fleming, now a color-bearer, had resolved "that his final and absolute revenge was to be achieved by his dead body lying, torn and guttering, upon the field." His lieutenant had continued to curse, but it was now "with the air of a man who was using his last box of oaths."

Then the men are ordered to charge and at last, tough, determined, sacrificial, soldier-like, they really do. Fleming forces the way, banner in hand, and Wilson captures the colors of the enemy. There arose "wild clamorings of cheers. The men gesticulated and bellowed in ecstasy." They had even taken prisoners. Fleming and Wilson sat "side by side and congratulated each other." The narrative progression has been simple. Beginning in doubt about Fleming's—and the regiment's—courage, it had sunk to despair with his cowardice and Conklin's death. Now it rises to climax in their clear success, even, in a minimal sense, their heroism. The reversed curve is classic. And even more so is the reflective short downward curve of anticlimax at the end as the regiment is recalled and starts to wind its way back over the river and the men can suddenly realize that the battle is over.

As Fleming realizes this, his mind clears of "battle-sleep," and he is able to take stock. Crane trimmed quite a lot from the manuscript of the last chapter, much of it reflecting too exactly the naturalistic debates he also cut. But only one of the cuts was really important. What he was doing with Fleming, it seems clear, was not holding him up for judgment but rounding off the account of his experience. It was out of the question for Crane, insofar as he was a realist, to end a plot. It was neither with abstract structure nor with fable that he was concerned. The realists saw life as a continuum of the personal experiences of their characters. One broke in upon its flow at one significant point and left it at another. If in the course of this, one had any ulterior ideological motives, they should be planted out of sight and left for the reader to find.

As realist—psychological realist—as impressionist, perhaps even as metaphysician, Crane was, as we have seen, a visionist. The important thing was to see pellucidly and honestly. And what Crane is concerned with at the end of *The Red Badge* is what Fleming can see. By letting the readers see what Fleming sees, Crane will let them decide what to think of him. Henry struggles "to marshal all his acts. . . . From this present point of view he was enabled to look upon them with some correctness, for his new condition had already defeated certain sympathies."

Supposing that the defeated sympathies are the multitude of earlier romanticisms, what does Fleming's cleared sight now reveal in those three ultimate pages of the novel? That his "public deeds" were glorious and impart a "thrill of joy" to his ego. But that he has incurred real shame, however hidden, for "his flight" and real guilt for the tattered soldier, "he, who blind with weariness and pain, had been deserted in the field." This vision and the fear of some impossible detection balance his self-glorification with "a wretched chill of sweat" and "a cry of sharp irritation and agony."

In the end he sees that he is neither a hero nor a villain, that he must assume the burdens of a mixed, embattled, impermanent, modest, yet prevailing humanity. He has discovered courage:

> . . . gradually he mustered force to put the sin at a distance. And at last his eyes seemed to open to some new ways. He found that he could look back upon the brass and bombast of his earlier gospels and see them truly. He was gleeful when he discovered that he now despised them.
>
> With this conviction came a store of assurance. He felt a quiet manhood, non-assertive but of sturdy and strong blood. He knew that he would no more quail before his guides, wherever they should point. He had been to touch the great death, and found that, after all, it was but the great death. He was a man.

If capturing the enemy flag climaxes the action of *The Red Badge*, this discovery of manliness concludes its exploration of ideas. The third major theme could not be concluded, however, since Fleming was not dead. It was the continuing notation of Fleming's psychological states which could only be harmonized in a sort of fadeout chord as Milton had done with the last lines of "Lycidas." Trying to force more out of these last sentences than Crane put there has caused unnecessary trouble for critics.

As he trudged away from "blood and wrath" Fleming's "soul changed"—as it had changed sometimes three times in a page earlier in the novel, though with more prospect of duration (not permanence) this time. Crane tried to end this three times before he got it right. Finally he showed Fleming turning to a vision—"with a lover's thirst to images of tranquil skies, fresh meadows, cool brooks—an existence of soft and eternal peace." And a nature-image ends the book as one had begun it, the endlessly shifting nature registering the never settled psychological state in the last words. "Over the river a golden ray of sun came through the hosts of leaden rain clouds."

Was Henry Fleming then a hero? Well, yes—and no. It wasn't quite Crane's business to say so in *The Red Badge*, and he let it go to "The Veteran," which Eric Solomon very properly calls "A Gloss on *The Red Badge of Courage*."[22] There the reader sees that modesty, candor about his "flight," and a quiet courage to do what a man must do mark the veteran with the perspective of more battles and many years—as in two days they could never plausibly have marked "the youth." The ambiguities of Fleming's situation are natural. But Crane's irony bites only at his past delusions. He has become entitled to "images" of flowery peace.

The essence of that irony is that it would have been impossible for the early Fleming to judge whether the boy who had both "run" and borne the colors was hero or poltroon. He wouldn't, in fact, have known what he was talking about. He wouldn't have been able to see. From another point of view, Henry's heroism at its last is only common, the ordinary stock of courage among fighting men (or among truly living men and women), where what the visionless think "heroism" is as common as breathing. But from yet another point of view, the courage it takes to be human in the face of all the odds *is* magnificent, as only the extraordinarily sharp and realizing vision perceives. And it was Crane's sense of that in *The Red Badge*, as in much of the best of his work, which gives it an elevation and a pungency often tragic and always memorable. He talked about it overtly in "War Memories":

> On the morning of July 2, I sat on San Juan Hill and watched Laughton's division come up. . . . There wasn't a high heroic face among them. They were all men intent on business. That was all. It may seem to you that I am trying to make everything a squalor. That would be wrong. I feel that things were often sublime. But they were *differently* sublime. They were not of our shallow and preposterous fictions. They stood out in a simple, majestic commonplace. It was the behavior of men on the street. It was the behavior of men. In one way, each man was just pegging along at the heels of the man before him, who was pegging along at the heels of still another man, who was pegging along at the heels of still another man who—It was that in the flat and obvious way. In another way it was pageantry, the pageantry of the accomplishment of naked duty. One cannot speak of it—the spectacle of the common man serenely doing his work, his appointed work. It is the one thing in the universe which makes one fling expression to the winds and be satisfied to simply feel.

This passage was written at the end, when Crane was sick unto death and worn down to talking about it. In *The Red Badge of Courage* he was at a peak of his creative powers and could simply master the imaginations of readers with the power of an astonishing young genius presenting a masterpiece.

Notes

1. *The Work of Stephen Crane*, ed. Wilson Follett (New York, 1925–26), I, xi–xii.

2. See *New York Tribune*, January 20, 1987, and *Rochester Post Express*, February 22, 1897 (Stephen Crane Scrapbook, Clifton Waller Barrett Collection, University of Virginia Library) commenting on H. D. Traill, "The New Realism," *Fortnightly Review*, January 1, 1897.

3. "Editor's Easy Chair," *Harper's Monthly* CVII (June 1903): 146–50.

4. "Life and Letters," *Harper's Weekly* XXXIX (October 26, 1895): 1013.

5. John Bass, "How Novelist Crane Acts on the Battlefield," *New York Journal*, May 23, 1897; Crane, "With Greek and Turk, III," *Westminister Gazette*, June 4, 1897.

6. See Arthur Golden, ed. *Walt Whitman's Blue Book*, Vol. I. *Facsimile*. New York, 1968.

7. *The Red Badge of Courage* manuscript, Barrett Collection, p. 65; Cf. R. W. Stallman, *Stephen Crane: An Omnibus* (New York, 1952), p. 276.

8. Barrett manuscript, "SV" p. 75 on verso of "LV" p. 118; "SV" p. 76 on verso of "LV" p. 97; "LV" p. 85. (Cf. Stallman, *Omnibus*, pp. 291–92).

9. Barrett manuscript, "SV" p. 84 on verso of "LV" p. 113; p. 85 on p. 108; p. 86 on p. 112. (Cf. Stallman, *Omnibus*, pp. 298–300).

10. Barrett manuscript, p. 125. (Cf. Stallman, *Omnibus*, p. 317).

11. Winifred Lynskey, "Crane's *The Red Badge of Courage*," *Explicator* VIII (December 1949): 18.

12. See James Nagel, "Stephen Crane and the Narrative Methods of Impressionism," *Studies in the Novel* X (Spring 1978): 76–85. The essay may be supposed to abumbrate his forthcoming book on Crane and impressionism.

13. Willa Cather, *On Writing* (New York, 1949), pp. 35–43.

14. "War Memories," [December 1899] *Work*, IX, 245–46.

15. Joseph J. Kwiat, "Stephen Crane and Painting," *American Quarterly* IV (Winter 1952): 331–38.

16. Corwin K. Linson, *My Stephen Crane*, ed. E. H. Cady (Syracuse, 1958), pp. 46–47.

17. *Work*, IX, 201. *The University of Virginia Edition of the Works of Stephen Crane* (Charlottesville, 1970), VI, 222.

18. *Stephen Crane: Selected Prose and Poetry*, 1950; rev. ed., *Stephen Crane: "The Red Badge of Courage" and Selected Prose and Poetry* (New York, 1956; third edition, 1968), p. v.

19. Charles Feidelson, *Symbolism and American Literature* (Chicago, 1953), esp. pp. 44–76.

20. *Work*, I, x.

21. [Ed. Note: Caroline Spurgeon's *Shakespeare's Imagery, And What It Tells Us* (1935) is a notorious example of a critic forcing patterns of imagery into ingenious readings.]

22. *Modern Language Notes* LXXV (February 1960): 111–13.

Insensibility in
The Red Badge of Courage   William B. Dillingham°

When Henry Fleming, the youth of Stephen Crane's *The Red Badge of Courage*, charges ahead of his comrades and fearlessly carries his flag into the very jaws of death, he seems to be a romantic hero rather than the protagonist of a naturalistic novel. But for Crane appearance was seldom reality. Bearing the symbol of his country's cause, Henry is unquestionably courageous, but the underlying causes of his deeds are neither noble nor humane. Throughout his life Crane deeply respected heroic action. His attitude was, as Daniel G. Hoffman has said, that it was "among the very few means man has of achieving magnificence";[1] nevertheless, he considered courage the product of a complex of nonrational drives. The difference between the external act of courage and the internal process that leads up to that act created for Crane one of the supreme ironies of life.

The Red Badge has frequently been read as the story of how a young soldier achieves some sort of spiritual salvation. One critic sees Henry Fleming's "growth toward moral maturity";[2] another, his "redemption" through "humility and loving-kindness."[3] His initiation has been called the successful search for "spiritual and psychological order," the discovery of a "vision of pattern."[4] Some readings emphasize Henry's new sense of brotherhood and call the book the story of a young man's developing awareness of social responsibility.[5] Such views as these offer more insight than may be indicated by a brief quotation and comment, but they also tend to obscure the central irony of the novel, that of the nature of courage, by making Henry Fleming as distinctive and as individually interesting a character as, say, Raskolnikov, Huckleberry Finn, or Isabel Archer. The young soldier whom Crane seldom calls by name is, as Alfred Kazin has suggested, Everyman—or at least every man who has the potentiality for courage.[6] The chief purpose of the novel is to objectify the nature of heroism through Henry Fleming. Through witnessing his actions and changing sensations we discover the emerging paradox of courage:

° From *College English* 25 (December 1963): 194–98. Copyright © 1963 the National Council of Teachers of English. Reprinted with permission.

human courage is by its nature subhuman; in order to be courageous, a man in time of physical strife must abandon the highest of his human facilities, reason and imagination, and act instinctively, even animalistically.[7]

In developing and illustrating this paradoxical definition of courage, Crane used a simple structural arrangement. The novel is divided into two parts of twelve chapters each. The first twelve chapters tell of Henry Fleming's early insecurities about himself; his first battle, where he fights and then runs; his various adventures during his retreat; and finally his encounter with the fleeing soldier and then his wound. Chapter 13 begins with Henry's coming back to his own camp to begin anew, and the remainder of the book takes the reader through the battles of the next day, in which Henry fights with great courage.

The first part of the book deals with the anatomy of cowardice, which is in Henry the result of an active imagination and a disposition to think too much. Until he receives the head wound in Chapter 12, he is characterized by a romantic and thoughtful self-consciousness. In his anxiety about how he will conduct himself in combat, he speculates constantly about himself and the nature of battle: "He tried to mathematically prove to himself that he would not run from a battle" (p. 30).[8] Trying to comfort himself through reason, he makes "ceaseless calculations" for days. Finally he has to admit that "he could not sit still and with a mental slate and pencil derive an answer" (p. 35). Henry's "own eternal debate" is frequently interrupted by the terrifying images of his imagination. In the darkness he sees "visions of a thousand-tongued fear that would babble at his back and cause him to flee" (p. 44). This constant activity of Henry's reason and imagination compels him to feel isolated until he experiences a vague sense of unity with his fellows during the first battle. Here he becomes suddenly caught up in the fight almost by accident. In contrast to his insensibility in later battles, "he strenuously tried to think," but he is luckily carried along by the momentary excitement of his comrades. The first encounter with the enemy is very brief, and his courage is not seriously tested. In the second engagement, his imagination is rampant: "He began to exaggerate the endurance, the skill, and the valour of those who were coming" (p. 73). He imagines the enemy as dragons and sees himself as being "gobbled." No longer feeling enclosed in the "moving box" of his first encounter and now stimulated by wild imaginings, Henry runs in terror from the battle.

In "The Veteran," a short story written as a sequel to The Red Badge, Henry, now an old man, reminisces about his war experience and tells how his imagination and his reliance on reason compelled him to run: "The trouble was . . . . I thought they were all shooting at me. Yes, sir, I thought every man in the other army was aiming at me in particular, and only me. And it seemed so darned unreasonable, you know. I wanted to explain to 'em what an almighty good fellow I was, because I thought then they might quit all trying to hit me."[9]

After his retreat, he wanders behind the lines, still relying upon his reason and imagination, attempting to convince himself that he is the reasonable man, "the enlightened man," who "had fled because of his superior perceptions and knowledge" (p. 81). When he comes upon the group of wounded men, he is still debating his case. He then witnesses the death of his friend Jim Conklin. But even at this point he shows no significant change.[10] Shortly thereafter, his imagination still controls him as he magnifies "the dangers and horrors of the engagement" from which he fled (p. 104). Until he is wounded in Chapter 12, he is still rationalizing, still trying mathematically to prove to himself that his cowardice was "in truth a symmetrical act" (p. 104).

The episode in which Henry is struck by a retreating Union soldier occurs at the center of the novel both physically and thematically. The incident has frequently been called the ironic peak of the story. A Union soldier, not the enemy, gives Henry his wound, and unlike his comrades he is wounded with the butt of a gun, not with a bullet. Upon this highly ironic "red badge" Henry builds his courage. In addition to its function as irony, the wound serves as the chief symbol of the book. Significantly, the wound is inflicted on the *head.* Almost from the moment he is struck, Henry starts to set aside his fearful and potent imagination and his reason. Symbolically, the head wound is the damage the experience of war gives to these highest human faculties. The chaos of war teaches the necessity of insensibility. After the symbolic wound, Henry finds his way back to his regiment, and the last half of the book portrays a youth initiated into the ways of courage. From here on, Henry runs from himself; he escapes his essential humanity in order to avoid running in battle.

Henry's inner voices and visions, then, are obliterated by the head wound. Through one half of the story, his mind has been tried and found wanting. Henry's wound forces his attention to his physical being. The only voices now heard are those of the body. After he returns to camp, "he made vague plans to go off into the deeper darkness and hide, but they were all destroyed by the voices of exhaustion and pain from his body" (p. 120). When he awakes, "it seemed to him that he had been asleep for a thousand years, and he felt sure that he opened his eyes upon an unexpected world" (p. 127). The Henry Fleming who before looked into the future, saw imagined horrors, and speculated constantly about himself, now thinks little of the future: "He did not give a good deal of thought to these battles that lay directly before him. It was not essential that he should plan his ways in regard to them" (p. 136). He has become instinctively aware of a truth taught by intense experience, that man can and must cultivate a dullness which will serve as armor against the stings of fear and panic. The totality of Henry's war experience thus far has helped to show him that "retribution was a laggard and blind."

In contrast to the thoughtful and romantic boy of the first part of the book, the young warrior of the last twelve chapters is capable of unreason, even self-abandon. At the first sight of the enemy, he "forgot many personal matters and became greatly enraged" (p. 141). He becomes a prideful animal, seeking the throat of the enemy with self-forgetfulness. The feelings of the imaginative young soldier, who once thought of war as a glorious Greek-like struggle, now are constantly described in terms of bestiality, unreason, and even insanity. He "lost sense of everything but his hate" (p. 148). Suspending all thought, he fights as a "barbarian, a beast . . . a pagan" (p. 150). His actions are frequently described as "wild." He is "unconsciously" out in front of the other troops, looking "to be an insane soldier." "There was the delirium that encounters despair and death, and is heedless and blind to the odds. It is a temporary but sublime absence of selfishness" (p. 160). The selflessness implied here is not self-sacrifice but insensibility, which enables Henry to escape thoughts and suspend imagination, to get outside of himself while the emotions of rage and hatred control his actions. As he cultivates personal insensibility his mental position as an observer becomes more and more pronounced: "He was deeply absorbed as a spectator; . . . he did not know that he breathed" (pp. 184–5). Henry's self-abandon spreads to the others, who were "again grown suddenly wild with an enthusiasm of unselfishness" (p. 189). Henry is no longer aware of the personal element in the danger that he faces. Now he does not think of the enemy as attempting to kill him personally. He looks upon their bullets vaguely as "things that could prevent him from reaching the place of his endeavour" (p. 189). So separated from meditation and imagination is Henry that he finds it difficult after the battle to become himself again: "It took moments for it [his mind] to cast off its battleful ways and resume its accustomed course of thought. Gradually his brain emerged from the clogged clouds, and at last he was enabled to more closely comprehend himself and circumstances" (pp. 196–7).

Henry's change is thus the result of intensely dangerous experience which reveals to him intuitively the impersonal nature of the forces that defeat men. After glimpsing the powers of "strange, squalling upheavals" he is able to control his fear. This ability comes to men not through intellectual or spiritual processes but through habit in being exposed to violence. As Henry becomes more accustomed to battle and the sight of death, he no longer thinks about the implication of these overwhelming experiences. He sinks into a subhuman dullness and is thereby able to act courageously. He does not learn to know himself, as one critic asserts,[11] but to escape himself—to make his mind blank, to become a "spectator."

Otherwise, Henry remains essentially unchanged during the course of the novel. It is a mistake to think of him as having become rejuvenated through humility or in any way changed into a better person morally. He has simply adapted himself through experience to a new and dangerous environment.[12] When the last battle is over, he is the same prideful youth, bragging on himself as he reviews his deeds of valor. The Christian references, which have so frequently been a subject of controversy, do not point to "rebirth" or "salvation" for Henry. The pattern of religious imagery built up through the use of such words as "sacrifice," "hymn," and "cathedral" is part of the pervasive irony of the book.[13] Just as Henry is not "selfless" in the usual sense of the word, neither is he "saved" in the Christian sense. It is his body that is saved, not his soul. He is trained by war to realize, in contradiction of Christian ideals, that he must desert the mind and spirit and allow his physical being—even his animal self—to dominate. Through Henry, Crane is saying with St. Matthew that whosoever will lose his life will find it. But the Christian paradox is in direct opposition to Crane's. Henry finds and retains his physical life by losing that sensibility characteristic of the highest forms of life.

The evidence for a "naturalistic" interpretation of *The Red Badge* is overwhelming.[14] Creating, chiefly through irony, a considerable degree of aesthetic distance, Crane studies the change in the behavior of a soldier. Through half the book this character is a sensitive youth. But sensitivity is incompatible with physical courage and the ability to kill. In the center of the story occurs the symbolic head wound, which damages the youth's sensibility and causes him to rely more on the physical and instinctive, less on the mental. For the rest of the book, Henry is brave in battle, having arrived at that state of self-discipline which makes one in danger resemble more an animal than a man. An iconoclast, Crane enjoyed laughing as he destroyed the illusions of a former tradition. He does not rejoice that Henry has found courage; he does not change him into a better person. Nor does he mourn as did Wilfred Owen for the tenderness and the innocence that war destroys in those who must kill.[15] With a keen sense of the incongruity of things, he simply shows that courage has been misunderstood. In order to be a Greek (in a Greek-like struggle), one must be a barbarian.

Notes

1. Daniel G. Hoffman, *The Poetry of Stephen Crane* (New York, 1957), p. 150.

2. James B. Colvert, "Structure and Theme in Stephen Crane's Fiction," *Modern Fiction Studies*, 5 (Autumn 1959), 204.

3. Robert Wooster Stallman, introduction to *The Red Badge of Courage*, Modern Library (New York, 1951), p. xxxii.

4. Earle Labor, "Crane and Hemingway: Anatomy of Trauma," *Renascence*, 11 (Summer 1959), 195.

5. John E. Hart, "*The Red Badge of Courage* as Myth and Symbol," *University of Kansas City Review*, 19 (Summer 1953), 249–56. See also M. Solomon, "Stephen Crane: A Critical Study," *Mainstream*, 9 (January 1956), 25–42.

6. Alfred Kazin, *On Native Grounds* (New York, 1956), p. 50.

7. Although the focus of his article is somewhat different from the present discussion, James Trammel Cox also states this central paradox of *The Red Badge:* ". . . the selfless behavior of heroism paradoxically emerges only from the grossest, most infantile, animalistic, fiery hatred born of the vanity of egocentrism." "The Imagery of *The Red Badge of Courage*," *Modern Fiction Studies*, 5 (Autumn 1959), 219. Hoffman suggests the paradox in his treatment of Crane's indebtedness to Tolstoi: introduction to *The Red Badge of Courage and Other Stories* (New York, 1957), p. xii.

8. Page references are to *The Work of Stephen Crane*, ed. Wilson Follett (New York, 1925), I.

9. *Work*, I, 204.

10. For an opposite opinion, see Stallman, p. xxxiii.

11. Norman Friedman, "Criticism and the Novel," *Antioch Review*, 18 (Fall 1958), 356–61.

12. Crane never ceased to be interested in the molding influence of environment. His favorite situation shows man pitted against a new and quite different environment. In some cases, as in "The Blue Hotel" and "The Bride Comes to Yellow Sky," characters find it impossible to undergo the necessary change to survive and are either destroyed or disillusioned. In *The Red Badge* as in "The Open Boat," however, the chief characters manage to adapt to the dangerous new environment and thus to survive.

13. Two critics have made similar statements about the Christian imagery of the book: Bernard Weisberger, "*The Red Badge of Courage*," in *Twelve Original Essays on Great American Novels*, ed. Charles Shapiro (Detroit, 1958), pp. 104–105; and Cox, pp. 217–18.

14. Several naturalistic interpretations are available. See, for example, Winifred Lynskey, "Crane's *The Red Badge of Courage*," *Explicator*, 8 (Dec. 1949), 3; Richard Chase, introduction to Riverside Edition of *The Red Badge* (Boston, 1960); and Charles Child Walcutt, *American Literary Naturalism, A Divided Stream* (Minneapolis, 1956).

15. Owen's poem "Insensibility" is, however, a remarkably similar statement of the definition of courage:

> Dullness best solves
> The tease and doubt of shelling,
> And Chance's strange arithmetic
> Comes simpler than the reckoning of their shilling.
>
> Happy are these who lose imagination:
> They have enough to carry with ammunition.

Having seen all things red,
Their eyes are rid
Of the hurt of the colour of blood for ever.

"That Was at Chancellorsville": The Factual Framework of *The Red Badge of Courage*   Harold R. Hungerford*

The name of the battle in which Henry Fleming achieved his manhood is never given in *The Red Badge of Courage*. Scholars have not agreed that the battle even ought to have a name; some have implied that it is a potpourri of episodes from a number of battles.[1] Yet an examination of the evidence leads to the conclusion that the battle does have a name—Chancellorsville. Throughout the book, it can be demonstrated, Crane consistently used the time, the place, and the actions of Chancellorsville as a factual framework within which to represent the perplexities of his young hero.[2]

I

Evidence of two sorts makes the initial hypothesis that Crane used Chancellorsville probable. In the first place, Crane said so in his short story "The Veteran," which was published less than a year after *The Red Badge*. In this story he represented an elderly Henry Fleming as telling about his fear and flight in his first battle. "That was at Chancellorsville," Henry said. His brief account is consistent in every respect with the more extended account in *The Red Badge*; old Henry's motives for flight were those of the young Henry, and he referred to Jim Conklin in a way which made it clear that Jim was long since dead.

This brief reference in "The Veteran" is, so far as I know, the only direct indication Crane ever gave that the battle in *The Red Badge* was Chancellorsville. He appears never to have mentioned the matter in his letters, and his biographers recount no references to it. Such evidence as that cited above must be used with discretion; Crane might conceivably have changed his mind. But there is no good reason why he should have done so; and in any case, the clue given us by "The Veteran" can be thoroughly corroborated by a second kind of evidence, that of time and place.

No one questions that *The Red Badge* is about the Civil War;

* From *American Literature* 34 (January 1963): 520–31. Reprinted by permission of Duke University Press.

the references to Yanks and Johnnies, to blue uniforms on one side and to gray and butternut on the other clearly establish this fact. If we turn now to military history, we find that the evidence of place and time points directly to Chancellorsville.

Only three actual place-names are used in the book: Washington, Richmond, and the Rappahannock River.[3] Henry Fleming and his fellow-soldiers had come through Washington to their winter quarters near the Rappahannock River, and their army was close enough to Richmond that cavalry could move against that city. Such a combination points to northern Virginia, through which the Rappahannock flows, to which Union soldiers would come through Washington, and from which Richmond would be readily accessible. Chancellorsville was fought in northern Virginia.

Furthermore, the battle was the first major engagement of the year, occurring when the spring rains were nearly over. The year cannot be 1861; the war began in April, and soldiers would not have spent the winter in camp. Nor can it be 1862; the first eastern battle of 1862, part of McClellan's Peninsular Campaign, in no way resembled that in the book and was far removed from the Rappahannock. It cannot be 1864; the Battle of the Wilderness was fought near the Rappahannock but did not end in a Union defeat. Its strategy was in any case significantly different from that of the battle in *The Red Badge*. Finally, 1865 is ruled out; Lee had surrendered by the time the spring rains ended.

If we are to select any actual conflict at all, a *reductio ad absurdum* indicates the first eastern battle of 1863, and that battle was Chancellorsville. Moreover, 1863 marked the turning-point in the Union fortunes; before Gettysburg the South had, as Wilson remarked in *The Red Badge*, licked the North "about every clip" (p. 255). After Gettysburg no Union soldier would have been likely to make such a statement; and Gettysburg was the next major battle after Chancellorsville.

Like the evidence of "The Veteran," the evidence of time and place points to Chancellorsville, and it is therefore at least a tenable hypothesis that Chancellorsville and *The Red Badge* are closely connected. In the next three sections I shall present independent proof of that hypothesis by showing that the battle in Crane's novel is closely and continuously parallel to the historical Chancellorsville.[4]

II

The events preceding the battle occupy the first two chapters and part of the third (pp. 238–258). The opening chapter establishes the situation of the Union army. As winter passed into spring, that army was resting in winter camp across a river from a Confederate army. It had been there for some time—long enough for soldiers to build huts with chimneys, long enough for a new recruit to have been encamped for some months without seeing action. ". . . there had come months of monotonous life in a camp . . . since his regiment had come to the field the army had done little but sit still and try to keep warm" (p. 244). Such was the situation of the Army of the Potomac in April, 1863; it had spent a cold, wet winter encamped at Falmouth, Virginia, on the north bank of the Rappahannock River opposite the Confederate army. The army had been inactive since mid-December; its men had dug themselves into just such huts, covered with folded tents and furnished with clay chimneys, as Crane describes (p. 240). Furthermore, the arrival of a new Union commander, General Joseph Hooker, had meant hour after hour of drill and review for the soldiers; and Henry was "drilled and drilled and reviewed, and drilled and drilled and reviewed" (p. 245).

To this monotony the "tall soldier"—Jim Conklin—brought the news that "The cavalry started this morning. . . . They say there ain't hardly any cavalry left in camp. They're going to Richmond, or some place, while we fight all the Johnnies. It's some dodge like that" (p. 247). He had earlier announced, "We're goin' t' move t'-morrah—sure. . . . We're goin' 'way up th' river, cut across, an' come around in behint 'em" (p. 238). Of course Jim was "the fast-flying messenger of a mistake," but the mistake was solely one of dates; the infantry did not move at once. Many soldiers at Falmouth jumped to Jim's conclusion when eleven thousand cavalrymen left camp April 13 for a raid on the Confederate railroad lines near Richmond. No one in the book denied that the cavalry had left; and Jim's analysis of the flank movement was to be confirmed at the end of the book when another soldier said, "Didn't I tell yeh we'd come aroun' in behint 'em? Didn't I tell yeh so?" (p. 373). The strategy Jim had predicted was precisely that of Chancellorsville.

The Union army at Falmouth did not leave camp for two weeks after the departure of the cavalry, and such a period accords with the time represented in the book; "for days" after the cavalry left, Henry fretted about whether or not he would run (p. 249).

Finally Henry's regiment, the 304th New York, was assembled, and it began to march before dawn. When the sun rose, "the river was not in view" (p. 252). Since the rising sun was at the backs of the marching men, they were going west. The eager soldiers "expressed commiseration for that part of the army which had been left upon the river bank" (p. 253). That night the regiment encamped; tents were pitched and fires lighted. "When another night came" (p. 257), the men crossed a river on *two* pontoon bridges and continued unmolested to a camping place.

This description fits aptly the march of the Second Corps. Many of its regiments were mustered before dawn on April 28, and then marched west and away from the Rappahannock. The Second, unlike the other corps marching to Chancellorsville, was ordered not to make any special secret of its whereabouts and was allowed fires when it camped. The Second crossed the Rappahannock on *two* pontoon bridges the evening of April 30 and camped safely near Chancellorsville that night; all the other corps had to ford at least one river, without the convenience of bridges. Furthermore, by no means all of the army moved at once; two full corps and one division of the Second Corps were left behind at Falmouth to conduct a holding action against Lee.

It is clear from the text that at least one day intervened between the evening on which Henry's regiment crossed the bridges and the morning of its first day of fighting (pp. 257–258). If Crane was following the chronology of Chancellorsville, this intervening day of pensive rest was May 1, on which only the Fifth and Twelfth Corps saw fighting.

III

Action began early for Henry's regiment the next day, the events of which parallel those at Chancellorsville on May 2. The statements (pp. 258–279) about what Henry and his regiment did are clear enough. He was rudely awakened at dawn, ran down a wood road, and crossed a little stream. His regiment was moved three times before the noon meal, and then moved again; one of these movements took Henry and his companions back, for in the afternoon they proceeded over the same ground they had taken that morning and then into new territory. By early afternoon, then, Henry had seen no fighting. At last a brigade ahead of them went into action; it was routed and fled, leaving the reserves, of which Henry's regiment was a part, to withstand the enemy. The regiment successfully resisted the first charge, but when the enemy reattacked, Henry fled.

It might seem that tracing the path of Henry and his regiment before his flight would not be impossible, but it has proved to be so. The regimental movements which Crane describes loosely parallel the movements of many regiments at Chancellorsville; they directly parallel the movements of none.[5] Nevertheless, broad parallels do exist. Many regiments of the Second Corps moved southeast from Chancellorsville on May 2; many of them first encountered the enemy in midafternoon.

Furthermore, it can be demonstrated that the 304th, like the regiments of the Second Corps, was near the center of the Union line. In the first place, the "cheery man" tells Henry, and us, so (p. 312). His testimony deserves some credence; anyone who can so unerringly find a regiment in the dark should know what he is talking about. Moreover, the conversation of the soldiers before the assault (pp. 266–267) makes it clear that they were not facing the rebel right, which would have been opposite the Union left. Nor were they far to the Union right, as I shall show later.

The evidence given us by the terrain Henry crossed also points to a position at about the center of the Union line. During the morning and early afternoon he crossed several streams and passed into and out of cleared fields and dense woods. The land was gently rolling; there were occasional fences and now and then a house. Such topographical features, in 1863, characterized the area south and east of Chancellorsville itself. Further east, in the area held by the Union left, the terrain opened up and the dense second-growth forest thinned out; further west the forest was very thick indeed, with few fields or other open areas. But southeast of Chancellorsville, where the Union center was located, the land was cultivated to a degree; fields had been cleared and cut off from the forest by fences. Topography so conditioned action at Chancellorsville that every historian of the battle perforce described the terrain; if Crane knew the battle as well as I suggest he did, he must have known its topography.

Topography also gives us our only clue to the untraceable path of Henry's flight. At one point he "found himself almost into a swamp. He was obliged to walk upon bog tufts, and watch his feet to keep from the oily water" (p. 285). A man fleeing west from the center of the Union line would have encountered swamps after a few miles of flight. The detail is perhaps minor, but it corroborates the path Henry had to follow to reach the place where he received his "red badge of courage." He went west, toward the Union right held by the Eleventh Corps.

Henry's flight led him to the path of the retreating wounded soldiers, among them Jim Conklin. The scene of Jim's death (pp. 289–301) contains no localizing evidence, for Crane was concentrating upon the men, not their surroundings. Nevertheless, it is appropriate to Chancellorsville; the roads leading to the river were clogged with retreating Union wounded in the late afternoon of May 2. There were no ambulances near the battle lines, and many wounded men died as they walked.

By contrast, the scene of Henry's wound can be readily fixed. He received it in the middle of the most-discussed single action of the battle, an action which cost Stonewall Jackson his life and a major general his command,' almost surely won the battle for Lee, and generated thirty-five years of acrimonious debate. Even today, to mention Chancellorsville is inevitably to bring up the rout of the Eleventh Corps.

About sunset on May 2, 1863, Stonewall Jackson's crack troops attacked the predominantly German Eleventh Corps. The Eleventh, which was on the extreme right of the Union line and far from the fighting, was taken wholly by surprise, and many soldiers turned and ran in terrified disorder. The result was near-catastrophe for the Union; now that Jackson's men had turned the flank, the path lay open for an assault on the entire unprotected rear of the Union army.

Appropriately enough for such a battle, Jackson's men were halted by one of history's more extraordinary military maneuvers. For in a battle in which hardly any cavalry were used, a small detachment of cavalrymen held Jackson's corps off long enough to enable artillery to be dragged into place and charged with canister. The cavalrymen could do so because the dense woods confined Jackson's men to the road. The small detachment was the Eighth Pennsylvania Cavalry; the time was between 6:30 and 7 P.M. Theirs was the only cavalry charge at Chancellorsville, and it became famous not only because it had saved the Union army—perhaps even the Union—but also because no two observers could agree on its details; any historian is therefore obliged to give the charge considerable attention.

All these elements fit the time and place of Henry's wounding. Night was falling fast after his long afternoon of flight; "landmarks had vanished into the gathered gloom" (p. 308). All about Henry "very burly men" were fleeing from the enemy. "They sometimes gabbled insanely. One huge man was asking of the sky, 'Say, where de plank road? Where de plank road?' " A popular stereotype holds that all Germans are burly, and an unsympathetic listener could regard rapidly-spoken German as "gabbling." Certainly the replacement of *th* by *d* fits the pattern of Germans; Crane's Swede in "The Veteran" also lacks *th*. These might be vulgar errors, but they identified a German pretty readily in the heyday of dialect stories. Furthermore, plank roads were rare in northern Virginia; but a plank road ran through the Union lines toward the Rappahannock.

One of these fleeing Germans hit Henry on the head; and after he received his wound, while he was still dazed, Henry saw the arrival of the cavalry and of the artillery:

> Around him he could hear the grumble of jolted cannon as the scurrying horses were lashed toward the front. . . . He turned and watched the mass of guns, men, and horses sweeping in a wide curve toward a gap in a fence. . . . Into the unspeakable jumble in the roadway rode a squadron of cavalry. The faded yellow of their facings shone bravely. There was a mighty altercation. (pp. 309–310)

As Henry fled the scene, he could hear the guns fire and the opposing infantry fire back. "There seemed to be a great ruck of men and munitions spread about in the forest and in the fields" (p. 310).

Every element of the scene is consistent with contemporary descriptions of the rout of the Eleventh Corps. The time is appropriate; May 2 was the first real day of battle at Chancellorsville as it was the first day for Henry. The place is appropriate; if Henry had begun the day in the Union center and then had fled west through the swamps, he would have come toward the right of the Union line, where the men of the Eleventh Corps were fleeing in rout. The conclusion is unavoidable: Crane's use of the factual framework of Chancellorsville led him to place his hero in the middle of that battle's most important single action.

The first day of battle in *The Red Badge* ended at last when the cheery man found Henry, dazed and wandering, and led him back to his regiment by complicated and untraceable paths.

IV

The second day of battle, like the first, began early. Henry's regiment was sent out "to relieve a command that had lain long in some damp trenches" (p. 328). From these trenches could be heard the noise of skirmishers in the woods to the front and left, and the din of battle to the right was tremendous. Again, such a location fits well enough the notion of a center regiment; the din on the right, in the small hours of May 3, would have come from Jackson's men trying to re-establish their connection with the main body of Lee's army.

Soon, however, Henry's regiment was withdrawn and began to retreat from an exultant enemy; Hooker began such a withdrawal about 7:30 A.M. on May 3. Finally the retreat stopped and almost immediately thereafter Henry's regiment was sent on a suicidal charge designed to prevent the enemy from breaking the Union lines. This charge significantly resembles that of the 124th New York, a regiment raised principally in the county which contains Port Jervis, Crane's hometown; and the time of this charge of the 124th—about 8:30 A.M.—fits the time-scheme of *The Red Badge* perfectly.[6]

The next episode (pp. 360–362) can be very precisely located; Crane's description is almost photographically accurate. Henry was about a quarter of a mile south of Fairview, the "slope on the left" from which the "long row of guns, gruff and maddened, denounc[ed] the enemy" (p. 360). Moreover, "in the rear of this row of guns stood a house, calm and white, amid bursting shells. A congregation of horses, tied to a railing, were tugging frenziedly at their bridles. Men were running hither and thither" (p. 361). This is a good impression of the Chancellor House, which was used as the commanding general's headquarters and which alone, in a battle at which almost no cavalry were present, had many horses belonging to the officers and orderlies tied near it.

The second charge of the 304th, just before the general retreat was ordered, is as untraceable as the first. It has, however, its parallel at Chancellorsville: several regiments of the Second Corps were ordered to charge the enemy about 10 A.M. on May 3 to give the main body of the army time to withdraw the artillery and to begin its retreat.

The two days of battle came to an end for Henry Fleming when his regiment was ordered to "retrace its way" and rejoined first its brigade and then its division on the way back toward the river. Such a retreat, in good order and relatively free from harassment by an exhausted enemy, began at Chancellorsville about 10 A.M. on May 3. Heavy rains again were beginning to make the roads into bogs; these rains prevented the Union soldiers from actually recrossing the river for two days, for the water was up to the level of several of the bridges. "It rained" in the penultimate paragraph of *The Red Badge;* and the battle was over for Henry Fleming as for thousands of Union soldiers at Chancellorsville.

V

This long recitation of parallels, I believe, demonstrates that Crane used Chancellorsville as a factual framework for his novel. We have reliable external evidence that Crane studied *Battles and Leaders of the Civil War* in preparation for *The Red Badge* because he was concerned with the accuracy of his novel.[7] He could have found in the ninety pages *Battles and Leaders* devotes to Chancellorsville all the information he needed on strategy, tactics, and topography. A substantial part of these ninety pages is devoted to the rout of the Eleventh Corps and the charge of the Eighth Pennsylvania Cavalry. These pages also contain what someone so visually minded as Crane could hardly have overlooked: numerous illustrations, many from battlefield sketches. The illustrations depict, among other subjects, the huts at Falmouth; men marching in two parallel columns;[8] pontoon bridges; the Chancellor House during and after the battle; and the rout of the Eleventh. With these Crane could have buttressed the unemotional but authoritative reports of Union and Confederate officers which he found in *Battles and Leaders.*

If it is unfashionable to regard Crane as a man concerned with facts, we ought to remember that late in his life he wrote *Great Battles of the World*[9]—hack work, to be sure, but scrupulously accurate in its selection of incident and detail and in its analysis of strategy. One can do far worse than to learn about Bunker Hill from Crane.

VI

Two questions remain unanswered. First, why did Crane not identify the battle in *The Red Badge* as he did in "The Veteran"? One answer is fairly simple: no one called the battle Chancellorsville in the book because no one would have known it was Chancellorsville. No impression is more powerful to the reader of Civil War reports and memoirs than that officers and men seldom knew where they were. They did not know the names of hills, of streams, or even of villages. Probably not more than a few hundred of the 130,000 Union men at Chancellorsville knew until long afterwards the name of the four corners around which the battle raged. A private soldier knew his own experiences, but not names or strategy; we have been able to reconstruct the strategy and the name because Crane used a factual framework for his novel; and the anonymity of the battle is the result of that framework.

Of course the anonymity is part of Crane's artistic technique as well. We do not learn Henry Fleming's full name until Chapter 11; we never learn Wilson's first name. Crane sought to give only so much detail as was necessary to the integrity of the book. He was not, like Zola and Tolstoi, concerned with the panorama of history and the fate of nations, but with the mind and actions of a youth unaccustomed to war. For such purposes, the name of the battle, like the names of men, did not matter; in fact, if Crane had named the battle he might have evoked in the minds of his readers reactions irrelevant to his purpose, reactions which might have set the battle in its larger social and historical framework. It would have been a loss of control.

Why, with the whole Civil War available, should Crane have chosen Chancellorsville? Surely, in the first place, because he knew a good deal about it. Perhaps he had learned from his brother, "an expert in the strategy of Gettysburg and Chancellorsville" (Beer, p. 47). More probably he had heard old soldiers talk about their war experiences while he was growing up. Many middle-aged men in Port Jervis had served in the 124th New York; Chancellorsville had been their first battle, and first impressions are likely to be the most vivid. It is hard to believe that men in an isolated small town could have resisted telling a hero-worshiping small boy about a great adventure in their lives.

Moreover, Chancellorsville surely appealed to Crane's sense of the ironic and the colorful. The battle's great charges, its moments of heroism, went only to salvage a losing cause; the South lost the war and gained only time from Chancellorsville; the North, through an incredible series of blunders, lost a battle it had no business losing. The dead, as always, lost the most. And when the battle ended, North and South were just where they had been when it began. There is a tragic futility about Chancellorsville just as there is a tragic futility to *The Red Badge.*

Finally, Chancellorsville served Crane's artistic purposes. It was the first battle of the year and the first battle for many regiments. It was therefore an appropriate introduction to war for a green soldier in an untried regiment.

The evidence of this study surely indicates that Crane was not merely a dreamer spinning fantasies out of his imagination; on the contrary, he was capable of using real events for his own fictional purposes with controlled sureness. Knowledge of the ways in which he did so is, I should think, useful to criticism. For various cogent reasons, Crane chose Chancellorsville as a factual framework within which to represent the dilemma of young Henry Fleming. Many details of the novel are clearly drawn from that battle; none are inconsistent with it. Old Henry Fleming was a truthful man: "that was at Chancellorsville."

Notes

1. Lyndon Upson Pratt, in "A Possible Source for *The Red Badge of Courage,*" *American Literature*, XI, 1–10 (March, 1939), suggests that the battle is partially based upon Antietam. Lars Ahnebrink denies his arguments and favors elements from Tolstoi and Zola in *The Beginnings of Naturalism in American Fiction*, "Upsala Essays and Studies in American Language and Literature," IX (Upsala, 1950). Both argue from a handful of parallel incidents of the sort which seem to me the common property of any war; neither makes any pretense of accounting for all the realistic framework of the novel.

2. This study developed from a class project in English 208 at the University of California (Berkeley) in the spring of 1958 and 1959. I am grateful to those who worked with Crane in these courses; and I am particularly grateful to George R. Stewart, who was unfailingly helpful to me in many ways and to whose scholarly acumen and knowledge of the Civil War I am deeply indebted.

3. All references to the novel are to *The Red Badge of Courage and Selected Prose and Poetry*, ed. William M. Gibson, Rinehart Editions (New York, 1956); page references will be included in the text. Although this edition contains the manuscript passages excised from the first edition, I have based no conclusions upon them. For Washington, see p. 244; for Richmond, p. 247; for the Rappahannock, p. 329. Henry's reference to the Rappahannock may be an ironic twist on a journalist's cliché, but the twist itself—the original was Potomac—seems to me to be the result of conscious intent on Crane's part.

4. The literature on Chancellorsville is substantial. The most useful short study is Edward J. Stackpole, *Chancellorsville: Lee's Greatest Battle* (Harrisburg, Pa., 1958). The definitive analysis is John Bigelow, Jr., *The Campaign of Chancellorsville: A Strategic and Tactical Study* (New Haven, 1910). Orders, correspondence, and reports are available in *The War of the Rebellion: A Compilation of the Official Records of the Union and Confederate Armies*, ser. I, vol. XXV, parts 1 and 2 (Washington, D.C.,

1889). See also *Battles and Leaders of the Civil War* (New York, 1884), III, 152–243. The parallels presented below are drawn from these; all are in substantial agreement.

5. So flat a statement deserves explanation. I have read with great care all of the 307 reports of unit commanders in the *Official Records*. I have also studied more than a dozen histories of regiments which first saw action at Chancellorsville. Many show general parallels; none show parallels with the novel which I consider close enough to be satisfactory.

6. See Cornelius Weygandt, *History of the 124th New York* (Newburgh, N.Y., 1877).

7. Thomas Beer, *Stephen Crane* (New York, 1923), pp. 97–98. Corwin Knapp Linson, *My Stephen Crane*, ed. Edwin H. Cady (Syracuse, 1959), pp. 37–38, corroborates Beer's account.

8. Here the illustration seems to explain the otherwise inexplicable description in the novel (p. 252); Civil War soldiers rarely marched thus.

9. Philadelphia, 1901. *Great Battles* is not in the collected edition, *The Work of Stephen Crane*, 12 vols. (New York, 1925–1926), and apparently has never been discussed by scholars. It includes no Civil War battles, although Crane at one time considered an article on Fredericksburg, the battle immediately preceding Chancellorsville; see *Stephen Crane: Letters*, ed. R. W. Stallman and Lillian Gilkes (New York, 1960), p. 98.

Crime and Forgiveness:
The Red Badge in Time of War   John Fraser°

> War is waged by men; not by beasts, or by gods. It is a peculiarly human activity.[1]

In a period of such rampant formalism as our own it seems especially necessary to keep affirming, however unphilosophically, that literature is inseparable from life and that one can learn quite directly about the latter from it. The work that I am concerned with here seems particularly to invite such an affirmation, and it is largely that invitation that has prompted yet another article on so notoriously overanalyzed a novel, and so brief a novel at that.

If *The Red Badge of Courage* is brief, it also quivers with life in a way that partly accounts, no doubt, for the disproportionately large body of criticism that it has provoked. No other classic American novelist has so masterfully rendered the immediacy of consciousness, the impingement of data on the mind, the *creative* activity of the perceiving mind in respect to that data, the tricks and hiatuses and sudden shifts in direction that an ordinary mind is capable of. None, furthermore, has created an experiencing consciousness with so little

° From *Criticism* 9 (Summer 1967): 243–56. Reprinted by permission of John Fraser and the Wayne State University Press.

analytical guidance to the main changes of direction in it and yet with what feels like so high a degree of meaningful unconscious or semi-conscious logic informing those changes. And accordingly a very salutary tension can be set up for the reader between trying simultaneously to elucidate that logic and to preserve his own openness to the presented experiences. The novel is to a considerable extent, indeed, precisely "about" the dangers of mental rigidity and the disruption (sometimes for the worse, more often for the better) of premature orderings, so that it is especially ironical if in analyzing it one comes up with overly neat and academic formulations oneself. And the tension deserves to be especially acute at the present time.

To lecture to undergraduates on *The Red Badge* even three or four years ago was a somewhat disquieting experience. It felt strangely presumptuous, I mean, to be a well-fed academic ensconced behind a lectern and comfortably analyzing the intimate mental processes of a young man being shot at and breaking down under the strain of battle; and if one recoiled alike from the curiously pharisaical moralizings about them by a number of critics and from the sort of pattern-hunting and symbol-mongering by others that seemed to negate the intense reality of the rendered experience of battle, it was tempting to fall instead into a too easy neo-Nietzschean celebration of Man Fighting. Whatever one's approach may be, however, one's critical sincerity is surely being put to the test now that one is lecturing to young men who may themselves have to face death or mutilation in a war. And if studying literature is indeed directly relevant to living, here surely is a place where it should be demonstrable.

One major way in which the relationship obtains in fiction generally, I take it, is prognostically. That is to say, the sort of things that happen to this or that imagined character may sometime, in however subtilized a form, happen to *us*, and in works that matter we are presented either with workable modes of responding to them or with erroneous ones so explored as to enable us to formulate more workable ones for ourselves. Hence it is that any way of reading that draws us away from the vitality of the presented experiences is not simply a chance missed but an insidious psychological injury, in that because one has responded inappropriately to the imagined experience now, one will be the more likely to respond inappropriately to actual ones in the future. In the general spirit of these remarks I would like, then, to look once again at certain key aspects of Henry Fleming's experience of the complexities of battle and his coming to terms with them and with himself, since I judge the way in which he comes to terms to be a successful one with implications going considerably beyond the presented battlefield.

That Henry's accommodation to battle conditions is indeed es-

timable is still, it seems safe to say, by no means a truism. It would
be hard, for instance, to guess at the number of readers who have
learned from the introduction to the Riverside edition of the novel
that "Crane 'makes us see Henry Fleming as an emotional puppet
controlled by whatever sight he sees at the moment,' that when
Henry does return to the battle it is not as a valiant adult but 'in a
blind rage that turns him into an animal,' [and] that if there is 'any
one point in the book' it is that 'Henry has never been able to
evaluate his conduct'. . . ."[2] Faced with comments of that order,
moreover—faced, for instance, with such judgments elsewhere as
"Henry is unquestionably courageous, but the underlying causes of
his deeds are neither noble nor humane,"[3] and "Although Henry
does show courage there is decisive evidence that he is motivated
chiefly by animal fierceness and competitive pride"[4]—it is hard not
to feel that a certain naive liberalism is brought into play by the
novel for a good many readers. War is an abomination, Henry Fleming
adjusts himself wholeheartedly to war, therefore the mental processes
involved cannot be very creditable ones—thus, one suspects, the
unspoken argument runs, intensified perhaps by a feeling that improvement ought to involve introspection, increased self-understand-
ing (which is to say, in this case, understanding of one's errors), and
no doubt some kind of abnegation and general "withering into truth."
Viewed from such an angle, of course, Henry most decidedly doesn't
improve. Not only does he continue to delight throughout in the
thought of winning glory, he actually *does* win it, and does so when
by rights he should have been exposed in a very different sort of
light. After all, he has not only allowed his comrades after he rejoins
them to assume that he is respectably wounded, he has even had
the nerve to take advantage of his wounded-hero role to pick on the
chastened and now tenderly helpful Wilson. In fact he has become
positively *jaunty*. And yet—"who should 'scape whipping?" To speak
in the kinds of terms I have been employing is to feel the niggling
ungenerosity of the implied ethics when one stops and considers the
boy's age and inexperience, the shock of battle, the abrasive torments
of his wanderings behind the lines, and the fact that in its effects
the blow from the fleeing soldier's swung rifle butt is just as much
a wound as an actual graze from a bullet would have been. And a
good deal more is at issue than mere pharisaism.

To approach Henry in the kind of moral fashion I have sketched
in is especially ironical in that it is to approach him in very much
the terms in which he himself was operating up until the time when
he rejoined his regiment—and from which, I shall be arguing shortly,
he is thereafter very beneficially liberated. To complain as one critic
does apropos of Henry's encounter with the walking wounded that
"the guilt he feels among these frightfully wounded men . . . should

be enough to make him realize his brotherhood, his indebtedness, his duty; but his reaction as he watches the retreat swell is to justify his early flight,"[5] is in fact to miss the point by a very sizeable margin. The novel up to and including that episode has been a brilliant study of psychological disintegration as a direct result of certain ethical over-intensities, and Henry's abandonment of the tattered soldier in particular (quite properly it is the thought of *that* that returns momentarily to haunt him at the end of the novel) is produced directly by his crippling sense of guilt and dread of exposure. It is from those feelings too that he becomes liberated with what seem to me unquestionably beneficial consequences, and if one acknowledges those consequences one is in a position to move further into the moral significance of the novel.

That both George Wyndham and Joseph Conrad among the novel's admirers should have responded so sympathetically to the change in Henry bears witness to a good deal more, I take it, than the strength of certain *fin-de-siècle* preoccupations (I mean, the growing weariness with rationalistic and ego-denying democratic liberalism, and the reviving esteem for violent and physically dangerous action of one kind or another). Both men knew the stresses of violent action at first hand, and when Conrad reworked the basic situation of *The Red Badge* in *Lord Jim* he seems to me to have been testifying to a perception that Henry's restoration involves something considerably weightier than simply the attainment of military effectiveness. Henry *is* effective now, of course; he fights instead of running, he fights with great energy and success, and in the course of so doing he helps to rally his panicking comrades and save them from being overwhelmed. But "effectiveness" is too narrow a term, even though one may well feel that when fighting is called for the first necessity for a soldier is to fight as well as possible. Henry's change has also been unquestionably an improvement psychologically in a broader way, at least if one regards a unified state of consciousness as superior to a fragmented one. Henry back with his regiment is free of both the modes of estrangement displayed so brilliantly earlier—the emotional estrangement from his comrades and officers caused by his exacerbated broodings, and the stultifying self-estrangement, the inability to settle on any single reading of his circumstances and conduct and act accordingly, that had left him in a seemingly hopeless impasse just before he was engulfed by the fleeing soldiers and received his own "wound." And again, to speak in these terms is really to be speaking in moral ones too. "One can love and one can work" was one of Freud's definitions of health, I believe, and it is plain that the Henry who is back with his comrades—the Henry who can now take note of the change in Wilson, and can feel a healthy indignation on behalf of his unjustly abused regiment and "a love, a despairing fondness" for its flag—is far closer to other people and in a far better position to act in a conventional sense morally than the egotistically brooding youth of the earlier part. "He had been taught that a man became another thing in a battle. He saw his salvation in such a change." The change that in fact occurs can surely be summed up in a preliminary way by saying that a man—or at least much more of a whole one—is precisely what Henry has become; and when Crane writes of his comrades that "The impetus of enthusiasm was theirs again. They gazed about them with looks of uplifted pride, feeling new trust in the grim, always confident weapons in their hands. And they were men," there seems no reason to think that he is speaking ironically. True, Henry hasn't become impeccable—but then, why should he?

If, then, I am right about the improvements, we would seem to be invited to consider rather carefully the causes of Henry's breakdown in the first place, and the nature of the process by which he becomes liberated from them. This I now propose to do.

To say that in the first engagement Henry is basically in trouble because of the sort of Christian pacificism ingrained in him by his mother would be over-simple, of course; among other things it wouldn't allow for his disposition to preconceive situations overrigidly and then to be increasingly set off balance by the discrepancies between preconceptions and actualities. (E.g., "The youth stared. Surely, he thought, this impossible thing was not about to happen. He waited as if he expected the enemy to suddenly stop, apologize, and retire bowing. It was all a mistake.") But it wouldn't be a gross oversimplification, and I wish to try and refine upon it. More precisely—given Henry's romantic craving for distinction—the destructive tensions would seem to result from the clash in him between that Christian pacifistic ethic and the kind of neo-pagan ethic pointed to in the well-known and, in its essentials, twice-repeated assertion that "He had long despaired of witnessing a Greeklike struggle. Such would be no more, he had said. Men were better, or more timid. Secular and religious education had effaced the throat-grappling instinct, or else firm finance held in check the passions." And this is where the equally well-known supernatural imagery is invaluable as an index to the way in which the currents of Henry's feelings are flowing. That the forthcoming engagement presents itself to him almost exclusively in terms of an ultimate test of his moral worth is obvious enough; and that he has a sense of the test as taking place in some measure under the eyes of *someone* emerges in his lagging "with tragic glances at the sky" and reflecting that "he would die; he would go to some place where he would be understood." (See too his later reflection that the intelligently self-preserving squirrel at which he has thrown a pine-cone "did not stand stolidly baring his furry belly to the missile, and die with an upward glance at the sympathetic heavens.'') Yet the proliferation of the "infernal" imagery, and the impartial distribution with respect to the enemy and his own side of the comparisons to serpents, imps, monsters, dragons, and the like, surely indicates how much the reverse of innocent and "Greeklike" the military scene is appearing to the deeper reaches of his mind, and testifies to a growing unconscious anxiety as to the meritoriousness of the activities that he has commited himself to with such initial neo-pagan enthusiasm. He himself is entangled now with those balefully serpentine columns and those figures "dodging implike around the fires"; and when the fighting comes and he breaks, the fact that at that point the enemy onslaught figures to him in terms of ravening demonic monsters coming inexorably towards him bears witness, surely, to an overwhelming upsurge of guilt-feelings. The destructive power of the enemy's persistency is presumably heightened by his general feeling that if he himself is to be morally tested it must somehow be under "fair" conditions, and that conditions are proving increasingly very much the reverse of fair. That is to say, the failure of battle conditions to conform to his expectations functions as a further subliminal intimation that morally the battlefield is the wrong sort of place for him to be and that he was radically in error in his initial neo-pagan commitment to its values—though of course his conscious sense of the battle as a straightforward moral test isn't affected thereby.

Viewed in this general light, Henry's overwhelming perturbation and sense of guilt after he has broken don't call for much explication. It is significant in an obvious enough way when he conceives of his separation from the unbroken soldiers in such terms as, "He felt that he was regarding a procession of chosen beings. The separation was as great to him as if they had marched with weapons of flame and banners of sunlight." So it is too when we learn, apropos of the questioning of him by the tattered soldier, that "he was continually casting sidelong glances to see if the men were contemplating the letters of guilt he felt burned into his brow" and that "his . . . companion's chance persistency made him feel that he could not keep his crime concealed in his bosom. It was sure to be brought plain by one of those arrows which cloud the air and are constantly pricking, discovering, proclaiming those things which are willed to be forever hidden. He admitted that he could not defend himself against this agency." And when one puts these and all the other supernatural references together they point unmistakably (despite Crane's canny avoidance of any specific reference to the Christian deity[6]) to Henry's dominant sense of a supernaturally penetrated universe in which crimes are absolutely and inescapably crimes because known inescapably to *someone,* and so are almost certain to be visited by retribution.

What we see Henry getting liberated from, I suggest, is his whole disposition to view what he is up to in terms of such a universe and seek, unavailingly, to justify himself to it. The most revealing fact, it seems to me, is that after he has rejoined his regiment—and nothing, it should be recalled, has happened to validate his conduct in terms of his earlier set of rules—the supernatural imagery disappears virtually altogether, and with it his sense of his own worthlessness and the inevitability of his exposure. And the nature of the change in him gets spelled out in certain rightly much quoted passages that can be consolidated into a single one here:

> His self-pride was now entirely restored. In the shade of its flourishing growth he stood with braced and self-confident legs, and since nothing could now be discovered he did not shrink from an encounter with the eyes of judges, and allowed no thoughts of his own to keep him from an attitude of manfulness. He had performed his mistakes in the dark, so he was still a man. . . . He had been taught that many obligations of a life were easily avoided. The lessons of yesterday had been that retribution was a laggard and blind. . . . He had been out among the dragons, he said, and he assured himself that they were not so hideous as he had imagined them. Also they were inaccurate; they did not sting with precision. A stout heart often defied, and, defying, escaped. . . . Yesterday, when he had imagined the universe to be against him, he had hated it, little gods and big gods; today he hated the army of the foe with the same great hatred. He was not going to be badgered of his life, like a kitten chased by boys, he said. It was not well to drive men into final corners; at those moments they could all develop teeth and claws. . . . He had a gigantic hatred for those who made great difficulties and complications. . . . He had been to touch the great death, and found that, after all, it was but the great death. He was a man.

If my account thus far has been reasonably correct, Henry is no longer bothered by the presumed hostility of the "big gods and little gods" because he has ceased to bother about the "gods" in any Christian sense at all; and because he has ceased to bother about them he has ceased, too, to bother about retribution or to introduce supernatural values into the activities of battle. Hence the act of fighting is no longer some kind of ultimate moral testing of the self (is he in fact one of the "elect" or not?), and even death becomes simply death and not a stage en route to further judgment. We are not, it seems to me, being invited to react with patronizing irony when informed that "He saw that he was good. He recalled with a thrill of joy the respectful comments of his fellows upon his conduct."

And the fact that we can indeed refrain from so reacting testifies to a deeper moral validity in what has been going on, and brings me back to the question of the novel's "lessons."

I have not, of course, been arguing that *The Red Badge of Courage* is valuable because it demonstrates that to be a good soldier one should not be a good Christian. It demonstrates nothing of the sort, for Henry is not a *good* Christian at all. He is something more familiar to most of us, and perhaps more relevant, namely someone in whom certain religion-induced dispositions persist in a vulgarized form and without any strong accompanying affirmations and consolations, and who is in a state of muddle, perplexed by impulses towards a (seemingly) moral self-denial on the other, and by a conflict between a view of the world as rationally ordered and superintended and demanding reasonableness in return, and a view of it as not ordered at all. By putting an intellectual (albeit a very inept one) into the situation of battle where certain attitudes have much weightier direct consequences than they normally do, Crane has very usefully clarified the undesirability of that kind of muddle. He has also, it seems to me, effectively contributed to one's achieving an intelligent attitude towards war when one is in it, by treating it as a normal aspect of human existence. By "normal" I do not mean inevitable. Nor, of course, do I mean commonplace; part of the brilliance of the novel consists precisely in its continual demonstrations of the immense *strangeness* of battle. But war itself is treated by Crane, as it is by Tolstoy and Shakespeare and Homer, as a state in which so many of the deeper problems of existence are present that when one is in it it is no longer something to be set against "life," it *is* life; and he has brought out, I think, that if a value system is to be fully tenable it must somehow be adequate to both peace *and* war, not least because many of those problems are present in an intensified and paradigmatic form. The same kind of thing, as I have just indicated, can be said of other distinguished presentations of war.[7] But one of the temptations for the "enlightened" American consciousness is to pique itself on its moral superiority to foreign and less idealistic ones and hence quietly to slide non-protesting responses to war into the category of the morally underdeveloped. Crane, however, has dealt with war in terms that not only include that kind of consciousness but transcend it, and he seems to me to have effectively precluded the concession, "Well, perhaps as a matter of *expediency* a temporary transformation of the psyche may be necessary!"[8]—a concession which of course, with its moral reservations, thrusts one right back into the muddles of Henry's state before he breaks. In the terms of the novel there are not two moralities, a lower and a higher, but one, and it seems to me intellectually an eminently respectable one. I would like to develop that point.

That Henry has travelled from one intellectual position to another without passing through any kind of normal argumentation except of the most rudimentary kind[9] is essentially of no consequence if it can be granted that, contemplating the experiences presented in the novel, people with much better minds could arrive quite validly at the same position. It seems to me that they could, and that we are not in fact even compelled to choose in the novel between religion and mere naturalism. If we are indeed presented with a journey from a certain kind of Christianizing to a certain kind of naturalism, the naturalism is so rich that it is not only not "mere," it is in fact perfectly compatible with a superior—or at any rate an existentialist—way of being religious, even though the novel is manifestly written by someone who is in no sense a Christian himself. And this brings me to what is intellectually perhaps the most remarkable aspect of the whole remarkable book, namely that Crane, in a period in which absolutes were notoriously disintegrating, was able himself to assist in the process without in the least falling into the "amoral extremism or . . . sheer objectivism or romantic nihilism"[10] that have been imputed to him. In comparison to *The Red Badge*, *Lord Jim*, for example, seems philosophically crude, the product of someone who, driven out of the possibility of believing that there is some kind of supernatural sanction for values, can only fumble around with the notion that accordingly all values are simply the products of man-made systems and hence are all equally meaningless when one really reflects on them. Of course the events in *Lord Jim* to a considerable extent give the lie to the naive Marlovian pessimisms; in some sense it does indeed matter very much when a shipload of pilgrims are abandoned to a fiery or watery death, or when a native community is saved from predators. But in *The Red Badge* the language of events is a good deal clearer and more compelling, and I wish now to point out how in Henry's wanderings between his flight and his return to his regiment, events speak to him in such a way as to block his attempts to escape from ethical claims by invalid philosophical moves. It is to these moves that the term "naturalism" can properly be applied pejoratively.

What I have especially in mind are the "chapel" scene and the scene of the death of Jim Conklin. In the former, what is put a stop to is Henry's attempt to shut out the ethical exactions of the battle (and hence the torments of his own failure in terms of it) by reconceiving nature so that peacefulness and a quiet self-preservation become the "natural" order of things and the battle a mere remote aberration incapable of moral claims. The hideously solid corpse in the "chapel" serves as an irrefutable witness to the continuing reality of the battle, and the ants busily at work on its face furnish a reminder that predatoriness is as much a part of the natural as the reassuring self-preservation of the *sympathique* squirrel. Presumably they further serve as a subliminal reminder of the battle's scale, since what Henry then attempts is a conversion of it into something that is ethically harmless because vast and inhuman, a mere machine-like activity that one can remain emotionally detached from and in fact assert one's superiority to by contemplating it—by positively seeking it out, indeed—as an aesthetic spectacle. This second and very *fin-de-siècle* move, of course, is countered by the sudden confrontation not with ant-like distant figures but with the human warmth and decency and courage of the tattered soldier and the appalling fact of Jim Conklin. The comforting metaphor of the battle as an "immense and terrible machine" producing corpses vanishes when juxtaposed not with an anonymous corpse (however shocking and incongruously located) but with a man, and worse, a known man, going through the awesome and untranslatable act of dying.

It is in this latter scene, too, with its culmination in the wafer image, that Crane's dissolving of the conventional disjunction between "religion" and "naturalism" reaches its climax. There is, of course, an agreeable irony in the notorious attempt to appropriate the wafer image for conventional Christian purposes. Wafers are flat, and things to which they are pasted are also more or less flat, and what the image surely does is simultaneously destroy the numinousness of the sun as an external agent giving life to the earth and convert the bowl of the sky into an opaque surface holding the mind's eye back from penetrating into the space of the "heavens." In terms of the deeper currents of Henry's mind, in other words, we could hardly be further from that moment earlier when the quasi-patriarchical figure of the mounted general "beamed upon the earth like a sun" and three times in the space of some twelve lines exclaimed jubilantly "By heavens!"—and "the youth cringed as if discovered in a crime. By heavens, they had won after all!" Yet if Henry's fist-shaking protest now would seem to point to a rejection of the claims of the universe to being informed with a Presence whose severities must be respected because of its paternal benevolences,[11] it has just been unforgettably demonstrated that no diminishment of the mysteriousness and numinousness of life need be entailed therein. One of the most valid objections to certain ways of being religious is precisely that they *do* diminish those qualities. In *Paradise Lost,* for instance, it is especially noteworthy how unmysterious are the presented depths of the heavens and how commonplace their chief occupant, and how it is only in and through the consciousnesses of the two humans that one experiences any sense of genuine mysteries and profundities in existence. In *The Red Badge,* similarly, in contrast to the tritely physical supernaturalism of Henry's guilt-ridden imagery it is the truly marvellous, the sense of immense human loneliness and intensities in the face of existence, that gets reaffirmed in the account of the death of Jim Conklin.[12] In a very small compass one has been led from the ostensibly broad—and false—view of human activities, via the presences and pressures of men en masse and the greater intimacies of decent fraternal concern, to the impenetrable isolation of the individual confronting the unknown.

In the title of this paper I mentioned forgiveness, and it is concerning that that I wish to close. I have spoken already of the language of events and of how events in the novel speak to Henry, in a sense, humanly and judicially. What I wish to point out now is how they can comfort as well as lacerate, forgive as well as condemn. That Henry, apparently in a complete impasse after Jim Conklin's death, with every mental escape route blocked by his own arguings, is able to awake the following day a completely free man is certainly the strangest thing in the novel; and yet the mechanisms at work seem both entirely convincing and very heartening. Having witnessed the formidable ability of the mind to construct a reality in terms of which it appears hopelessly and permanently condemned, we now see the power of life to disown such a construction and relax abruptly the death-grip of the past. When Henry is overwhelmed by the fleeing men he is shocked out of his sense of the fixity of the battle lines and of his own uniqueness in running. With the blow from the rifle butt the seeming moral order of things is further loosened: in the place of Henry's doing unjust things to just people in an ostensibly just universe, someone else is now behaving unjustly to *him*—and doing so impersonally too, so that the blow seems to come simply from life itself like a random bullet, instead of like one of those carefully aimed retributive arrows he had been imagining earlier. And in his encounter with the cheerful soldier he is confronted with the demonstrated possibility of someone's having deserted like himself and yet being able to function with unabashed equanimity, good humor, and kindliness. It seems a profound gesture of benevolence from life, finally, that he should be guided so skillfully through the woods by his new companion in a manner that recalls, albeit in a wholly secular way, the loving figure of the Good Shepherd, and that on his arrival he should be welcomed with such tender consideration by his comrades, the latter changed both from what they had actually been earlier and from the implacable judges of his imaginings. Moreover, more than an illustration of Paul Tillich's formula about being accepted because unacceptable seems to be involved. In view of the fullness with which he has exposed himself to the tumults of existence, Henry in a sense has *earned* his acceptance and his subsequent wholeness and success. Especially significant in this connection, I think, is the episode at the end of the book in which the thought of his abandonment of the tattered soldier returns to haunt him and, after experiencing pain at it, he "gradually mustered force to put the sin at a distance. And at last his eyes seemed to open to some new ways." It is as if here were the final heartening affirmation of the change in him; quite rightly he is now able to reject the claims on him for a renewed sense of guilt that could be crippling in the same sort of way, though presumably not to the same extent, as the guilt he had felt after his first—and lesser—moral failure. The book, in sum, demonstrates that if one remains fully responsive to existence the possibility is always there of becoming to some extent "another thing,"[13] and not just in battle either.

The Red Badge of Courage, as I have indicated earlier, does not in the least mitigate the atrociousness of war. Indeed, to reread it is to be made more thankful than ever that one does not have to go into battle oneself, and more humblingly uncertain as to what one's own conduct would be under conditions like those faced by Henry Fleming. But to insist on the affirmative quality of Crane's treatment of war is not to diminish those facts. Crane has neither exploited war in the interests of nourishing a self-pitying fatalism about the inexorable destruction of the good and beautiful by life, nor indulged in a facile indignation about human brutishness and folly. Like B. Traven in The Death Ship—and like almost no other American novelist—he has succeeded in writing with unforgettable vividness about the atrocious in a way that yet makes it simply a part of life and not an indictment of it, or an indictment of "man," or any sort of indictment at all. In its psychological richness and its truly religious openness, The Red Badge is not only one of the most remarkable of American novels, it is one whose wisdoms seem especially valuable among the philosophical confusions of the present time. In exploring war as a closed situation in which an intellectual cannot escape from the moral claims of events merely by willing it—escape by focusing only on the kinds of events that feed his vanities—Crane has helped to show up the fashionable nihilisms of today as the effete and schizophrenic things that they are.

Notes

1. Frederic Manning, from prefatory note to The Middle Parts of Fortune: Somme & Ancre, 1916 (London, 1929).

2. Richard Chase, ed., quoting approvingly Charles Child Walcutt (Boston, 1960), p. xv. The passages from the novel quoted in this paper come from the Riverside edition.

3. William B. Dillingham, "Insensibility in The Red Badge of Courage," College English, XXV (December, 1963), 194.

4. Mordecai Marcus, "The Unity of The Red Badge of Courage," in Richard Lettis

et al., eds., *Stephen Crane's The Red Badge of Courage: Text and Criticism* (New York, 1960), p. 191.

5. Charles Child Walcutt, *American Literary Naturalism: A Divided Stream* (Minneapolis, 1956), p. 79.

6. Stanley Wertheim's "Stephen Crane and the Wrath of Jehova," *The Literary Review*, VII (Summer, 1964), 499–508, can help to bring home to one, if further evidence than that of the novel itself is needed, the kind of psychological mine field through which Crane was making his way.

7. See especially D. W. Harding's "The Poetry of Isaac Rosenberg," *Scrutiny*, III (March, 1935), 358–369, with its development of the thesis that "What most distinguishes . . . Rosenberg from other English poets who wrote of the [1914–18] war is the intense significance he saw in the kind of living effort that the war called out, and the way in which his technique enabled him to present both this and the suffering and the waste as inseparable aspects of life in war. Further, there is in his work, without the least touch of coldness, nevertheless a certain impersonality: he tried to feel in the war a significance for life as such, rather than seeing only its convulsion of the human life he knew." It seems significant that the best poetry to come out of that war was Rosenberg's and the best novel Frederic Manning's *The Middle Parts of Fortune*, and that the latter likewise was not a work of "protest." The nearest twentieth-century American equivalents are probably David Douglas Duncan's superb photographs from Korea assembled in *This is War* (New York, 1951).

8. Even Eric Solomon doesn't escape it in his sympathetic and perceptive "The Structure of 'The Red Badge of Courage'," *Modern Fiction Studies*, V (Autumn, 1959), 220–234.

9. E.g., "He searched about in his mind for an adequate malediction for the indefinite cause, the thing upon which men turn the words of final blame. It—whatever it was—was responsible for him, he said. There lay the fault."

10. Chase, p. xiv.

11. It is not, of course, a complete rejection at this point, as the continuance of the supernatural imagery testifies.

12. Concerning whom, it seems pertinent to add, one commentator has been able to assert bluntly, "His loyalty consists of braggadocio and clichés, and his death is without meaning." (Max Westbrook, "Stephen Crane and the Personal Universal," *Modern Fiction Studies*, VIII [Winter, 1962–1963], 351–360.) The remark testifies obliquely, I suspect, to the dehumanizations involved in the kind of symbol-hunting against which Westbrook is reacting.

13. That the change in Henry would be likely to be a lasting one seems suggested by the striking resemblances between it and what William James describes in *Varieties of Religious Experience* as "conversion."

Private Fleming:
His Various Battles   Marston LaFrance°

Crane's view of the human situation, set forth more clearly in *The Red Badge* than in his earlier work, is that man is born into an

° From *A Reading of Stephen Crane* (New York: Oxford University Press, 1971), 98–99, 104–24. © Oxford University Press, 1971. Reprinted by permission of Oxford University Press.

amoral universe which is merely the external setting in which human moral life is lived,[1] and that if moral values are to exist and man's life is to be meaningful, morality must be the creation of man's weak mental machinery alone; but even the best of men, the most personally honest, is prone to error and thus liable to bring misery upon himself and others because the mental machinery often distorts that reality which he must perceive correctly if his personal honesty is to result in morally significant commitment. Thus, Crane's essential subject, in *The Red Badge* as in the *Sullivan County Sketches, Maggie,* and the "Experiment in Misery," is man's weak mental machinery as it labours under the stress of some emotion, usually fear, to perceive correctly an area of reality which is not yet within the compass of the perceiver's experience. And if so, *The Red Badge* does have an obvious source which is available to anyone who wishes to investigate it; but the assumption of a naturalistic, a factually realistic, or a specifically literary context leads in the wrong direction. The real source of this novel and any other important Crane work seems to me simply the ironist's incredible awareness of human nature. Our amazement should not be directed at Crane's mastery of the techniques of naturalism, or knowledge of the Civil War, or Jamesian grasp of Western literature, but at so young a man's ability to create so superb a psychological portrayal as Henry Fleming.[2] . . . .

The novel opens with that sense of uncertainty which plagues Fleming until the last two or three pages. He hears Conklin's rumour that the regiment is about to engage in combat, and immediately withdraws to his hut to think about his own problems—and not at all about Conklin's rumour, by the way; he merely assumes the rumour will prove true (as it does not) and gives his whole attention to worrying about how he will act during his first battle. Thus, Fleming's intensely active imagination is presented at once: the really significant battles in this novel are already raging in full career within Henry's mind long before the first shot is fired in any external skirmish. He had dreamed of "bloody conflicts that had thrilled him with their sweep and fire"; and, like George Kelcey, his dreams feature great visions of personal glory in which he imagines "peoples secure in the shadow of his eagle-eyed prowess."[3] Henry had enlisted, had voluntarily fled his dull farm life, because of these vainglorious desires set in the impossibly romantic picture of war which his imagination has evoked from village gossip and luridly distorted news reports.

The flashback to the farewell scene can serve almost as a structural précis of the novel. Henry had "primed himself for a beautiful scene. He had prepared certain sentences which he thought could be used with touching effect" (p. 230). But his mother merely peels potatoes and talks tediously of shirts and socks. The result is Crane's usual deflation of vanity, comic here because of Henry's romantic and sentimental foolishness. Nevertheless, buried in his mother's prosaic commonplaces is precisely the view of himself and his duty to which Henry has to inch his way in painful experience throughout the remainder of the novel: "Yer jest one little feller amongst a hull lot of others, and yeh've got to keep quiet an' do what they tell yeh. . . . Never do no shirking, child, on my account. If so be a time comes when yeh have to be kilt or do a mean thing, why, Henry, don't think of anything 'cept what's right" (p. 231). Fleming is not the undiscovered Achilles of his grand illusions; he is just another lad who has to learn to be a man. And to be a man in Crane's world is to perceive the human situation as it is, accept it, and remain personally honest in fulfilling the commitments such a perception demands of the individual. The fact that Henry has to suffer the experiences of the whole novel even to approach this simple truth merely reveals, again, the most bitterly ironic aspect of Crane's psychological pattern: as in *Maggie* and the Sullivan County tales, the protagonist of *The Red Badge* also has to undergo all his suffering in order to perceive, to "see," a constant reality which is present and available to him before his progression through experience to the perception of it even begins.

Henry's weak mental machinery is at this point so busy with visions of glory and he is so impatient to leave that he hardly hears his mother's advice; but his shame, when he turns to see her praying and weeping among the potato parings, distinguishes him from Crane's earlier protagonists, and implies that eventually he will learn the truth of what he has just been told—that the real hero, in such a world as this, is the quiet, nameless man who can discern what is right and do it, simply because it is right and because he is a man.

Henry's education has already begun before the reader first encounters him. He has experienced the dreariness, boredom, filth, and part of the misery of a soldier's life. The prolonged inaction has left his imagination free to concentrate on that part of his problem which experience has not yet clarified for him, and thus he is first seen lying in his bunk trying "to mathematically prove to himself that he would not run from a battle" (p. 234). He contemplates the "lurking menaces of the future," in the only way he can, as these menaces exist within his own mind; and given Henry's imagination, it is no wonder that his thoughts scare him. When Conklin's rumour proves false and still more waiting has to be endured, Henry's tension becomes almost unbearable (p. 239); and his imagination evokes two illusions which Crane exploits throughout the novel: the notion that moral qualities exist in external nature—"The liquid stillness of the night enveloping him made him feel vast pity for himself. There was a caress in the soft winds; and the whole mood of the darkness, he

thought, was one of sympathy for himself in his distress" (p. 243)—
and the belief that he is unique, separated (at this point by fear)
from the other men in the regiment. After timidly broaching the hint
of fear to Wilson only to have the conversation end in an abrupt
quarrel, Henry "felt alone in space. . . . No one seemed to be
wrestling with such a terrific personal problem" (p. 245). Henry is
wrong, of course. The other men are also afraid; but without Henry's
imagination they fear only the *fact* of combat, and hence they can
play poker while he suffers. Henry no longer fears the actual fact:
"In the darkness he saw visions of a thousand-tongued fear that would
babble at his back and cause him to flee, while others were going
coolly about their country's business. He admitted that he would not
be able to cope with this monster" (p. 245). Such is Henry's state
of mind when he is suddenly awakened one morning and sent running
towards his first skirmish.

Crane introduces the "moving box" episode with the flat statement that Henry "was bewildered." Barely awake and intensely
excited, he has to use "all his faculties" to keep from falling and
being trampled by those running behind him. The passage in question
constitutes Henry's *first* reaction to this situation:

> he instantly saw that it would be impossible for him to escape from
> the regiment. It inclosed him. And there were iron laws of tradition
> and law on four sides. He was in a moving box.
>   As he perceived this fact it occurred to him that he had never
> wished to come to the war. He had not enlisted of his free will.
> He had been dragged by the merciless government. And now they
> were taking him out to be slaughtered. (p. 248)

This passage is pure rationalization without a hint of naturalism in
it. The "iron laws of tradition and law" are made by men and changed
by men. And Henry did enlist of his own free will; he was not dragged
to this commitment by any force except his own wish to go to war.
All that this passage really reveals is that Henry is so badly frightened
he is considering flight even before a shot is fired.

When Henry's curiosity leads him to charge over a rise only to
be confronted with still more inaction, Crane unambiguously presents
his basic trouble: "If an intense scene had caught him with its wild
swing as he came to the top of the bank, he might have gone roaring
on. This advance upon Nature was too calm. He had opportunity to
reflect. He had time in which to wonder about himself and to attempt
to probe his sensations" (pp. 249–50). Hence, a house acquires an
"ominous look," shadows in a wood are "formidable," and Henry
feels he should advise the generals because "there was but one pair
of eyes" in the regiment. In the afternoon he tells Conklin the truth
when he says, "I can't stand this much longer" (p. 252). Henry's

inner turmoil again obscures his perception: he no more grasps the significance of Wilson giving him the packet than he had heard his mother's advice. He soon witnesses the rout of some troops who run blindly back through his own regimental line, and he intends to wait only long enough to see the "composite monster" which has frightened these men. But when the charge finally comes, he does not run; he stays and fights.

This episode must have taken considerable thought, for Crane had to find a means of letting Henry engage in battle, an incident to which the four previous chapters have pointed, and still not undergo the unknown experience he fears. In other words, Crane's treatment at this point would commit him one way or the other: if Henry experienced the unknown here the result would be a short story; if this experience could be further delayed the result would be a novel. Crane solved his problem by having Henry fight this skirmish in a trance, a "battle sleep" induced by fatigue and rage; and because of this Henry later does not accept this combat as that attainment of the experience he has been anticipating.

Thus, Crane in this episode is able to repeat the irony of Henry's farewell scene. When the fight begins, Crane allows Henry to attain the real bearing of responsible manhood at war—for a few moments:

> He suddenly lost concern for himself, and forgot to look at a menacing fate. . . . He felt that something of which he was a part— a regiment, an army, or a country—was in a crisis. He was welded into a common personality which was dominated by a single desire. . . .
>
> There was a consciousness always of the presence of his comrades about him. He felt the subtle battle brotherhood more potent even than the cause for which they were fighting. It was a mysterious fraternity born of the smoke and danger of death.
>
> He was at a task. (p. 261)

This is a quiet statement, without any irony, of the ideal which Crane was to honour repeatedly in his writings about the Spanish-American War. But at this point Henry enters his battle sleep. Then, after the charge has been repulsed, and before Henry emerges from his trance, he feels "a flash of astonishment at the blue, pure sky and the sun gleamings on the trees and fields. It was surprising that Nature had gone tranquilly on with her golden process in the midst of so much devilment" (p. 265). And this statement implies the mature man's unsentimental view of nature as an amoral external mechanism. But then, when Henry emerges from his trance, his old weaknesses reassert themselves, and he is entirely unable to recall either the achievement or the perception which came to him at either edge of his battle sleep. Once again the reality he is seeking lies within his grasp; and once again his mental turmoil prevents his awareness of it.

This episode also contains some of Crane's famous animal imagery; and, provided it is read correctly, Crane's *use* of this very imagery argues against naturalism. Crane does not use animal images until Henry begins to slip into his battle sleep (p. 261); before this, there is only a single animal image in the three pages of this chapter: "the colonel . . . began to scold like a wet parrot" (p. 260). And, more important, there is no hint of such imagery in the above description of Henry's moment of manhood before his trance begins. But as Henry descends from full consciousness and becomes something less than a man he abruptly begins to perceive in terms of non-human images: he feels "the acute exasperation of a pestered animal, a well-meaning cow worried by dogs"; he rages like a "driven beast"; men "snarl" and "howl"; a coward's eyes are "sheeplike . . . animal-like" (pp. 261–2). And this sort of imagery ends when Henry regains full consciousness. This *use* of imagery is fairly consistent throughout the novel. Hence, the demands of dramatic propriety are as insistent here as they are in the flophouse scene in the "Experiment in Misery," and for the same reason: the primary function of the imagery in *The Red Badge* is, again, to represent the protagonist's agitated mind as it struggles from lurid distortions to an understanding that reality is, after all, but reality. The imagery in the novel always becomes most vivid when Henry's perception is most distorted, and such a state of mind is the extreme of the condition which Henry labours to transcend by applying his awareness, conscience, and force of will to his experience. Crane's use of such imagery in this novel, in short, strongly implies that he is a humanist, not a naturalist.[4]

When Henry awakens from his battle sleep to find that the charge has been withstood, he becomes vain in complacent admiration of his part in this success; and all his self-congratulation is illusory. Nothing is "over" for him; no trial has been passed. He uncritically admires actions which were done in a trance; and no Crane character ever feels such pompous self-satisfaction, even for real accomplishment, unless he is a vain fool. Complacency is a delusion in a world where nothing but death is final, where no ideal can ever be possessed because man has to reckon with externalities beyond his control, a stoic's world in which a continuous present poses a continuous demand upon man's moral and physical endurance. The attack is immediately renewed; and this time, after having seen so many others flee that he believes he will be left alone, Henry runs away. One must insist that he runs only nominally from the advancing enemy; what he really runs from is his own imagination. Crane's statement could hardly be more bluntly unambiguous: "On his face was all the horror of those things which he imagined" (p. 268).[5] Even as he flees, his busy mind rationalizes his flight in terms of his previous feeling of uniqueness (pp. 270–1), and thus he loiters in the rear long enough to learn that the line held and repulsed the charge a second time. Then, miserably ashamed, cringing "as if discovered in a crime," he moves into the forest.

Henry's journey through this forest, like Marlow's journey up the river into the heart of darkness, charts a pilgrimage within the mind. This moral forest clearly suggests the "direful thicket" through which the brave man of the poems has to plunge to find truth, and its "singular knives"—fear, guilt, shame, hatred of those who remained and fought, vanity, self-pity, rage, his suffering as he sympathetically experiences Conklin's death, the self-loathing evoked by the tattered man—slash at Henry's ego just as the brush and vines entangle his legs. This section of the novel probably required more virtuosity and sheer craftsmanship than any other because, in terms of Crane's structural pattern, no further progress can occur until Henry returns to face his commitment: the unknown experience is thus beautifully delayed while the protagonist undergoes an intense struggle within himself, the outcome of which merely returns him to the position from which he had fled when this section began.

Thus, Crane begins with considerable care. Henry's guilt first evokes rationalization of his cowardice as superior intelligence (p. 272), and from this premise his mind moves through anger at his "stupid" comrades who had "betrayed" him, to vanity, self-pity, and finally to a general "animal-like rebellion against his fellows, war in the abstract, and fate" (p. 273). The adjective is significant because with rationalization Henry has abandoned moral responsibility and again has become less than a man. Such is his state of mind as he enters the metaphorical forest of his inner self and the ensuing scenes portray his struggles to claw his way back up to the human condition again. His terrible journey through this forest can be divided into four parallel scenes or episodes—the craftsman's device of *Maggie* used here with much greater subtlety—which are easily identified: each begins with a specific illusion, a direction of Henry's thought which is followed until the pathway becomes blocked; when the illusion is destroyed, or when the barricade is encountered and Henry has to seek a new direction, the episode ends and the next one begins.

His first illusion arises directly from his attempts to rationalize his cowardice. It begins when he attempts to draw illusory justification from sentimentalized nature, and it expands to include an equally sentimental religious feeling. The "landscape gave him assurance. A fair field holding life. It was the religion of peace. It would die if its timid eyes were compelled to see blood. He conceived Nature to be a woman with a deep aversion to tragedy" (p. 274). He throws a pine-cone at a squirrel, and the squirrel, to Henry's immense satisfaction, runs away: "There was the law, he said [conveniently forgetting that a man is not a squirrel]. Nature had given him a sign" (p. 274). Although he then observes a "small animal" pounce into black water and "emerge directly with a gleaming fish," Henry needs stronger medicine and, moving "from obscurity into promises of a greater obscurity" (p. 275), he soon gets it. He blunders into the forest "chapel" with its "gentle brown carpet," its "religious half light"; and the way in which he perceives this mere hole in the woods should recall his earlier view of death as a means of getting "to some place where he would be understood" (p. 253). This sentimental religious feeling is thus equated with Henry's sentimental view of nature, and both illusions are brutally shattered when he finds a rotting corpse in the "chapel" where one would expect to find the altar. This putrid matter being eaten by ants does not suggest that death is any gateway to understanding, that nature has any aversion whatsoever to such tragedies, or that some sort of Christian doctrine is the theme of the novel.[6] Rationalization which overrides one's personal honesty can only lead to moral death (as George Kelcey also demonstrates); death literally blocks Henry's way at this point, and he has to find a new direction.

His new direction comes when out of curiosity he runs towards a great roar of battle. This first tentative step towards emerging from the forest is consciously determined, and Henry is aware that it is "an ironical thing for him to be running thus toward that which he had been at such pains to avoid"; but he now wants "to come to the edge of the forest that he might peer out" (p. 277). However, Henry then meets the tattered man—one of Crane's finest characters—whose question, "Where yeh hit, ol' boy?" causes him to panic; and his guilt and sense of isolation immediately lead him to another illusion: "he regarded the wounded soldiers in an envious way. He conceived persons with torn bodies to be peculiarly happy. He wished that he, too, had a wound" (p. 282). To reveal to Henry the real absurdity of such thoughts, to puncture this insane illusion, Crane lets him witness the appalling death of Jim Conklin. And if this seems too slight an accomplishment for so intensely written a scene, one should remember that this whole section of the novel is, after all, a virtuoso performance in prolonging the delay of Henry's actual experience of combat. Also, Conklin's death is as necessary to Henry's education as his parallel encounter with the corpse was. In its presentation of human suffering considered specifically against the infinite back-drop of the amoral universe this scene is a young author's first attempt at coping with a theme that immensely interested him; hence, as only one critic has noted, there is absolutely no irony in the portrayal of Henry in this passage. "Although Fleming cuts a rather pitiful figure under the towering sky, Crane's intention is not satirical. In fact this is one point in the book where the author seems to identify himself wholly with his character."[7] Henry rebels against the universe at this grotesque and meaningless death of a man he has known since boyhood, and his rebellion is simultaneously as futile, as absurd, and as understandable as the belief of the men in an open boat who think that fate will not drown them because they have worked so hard to get within sight of shore. The implicit truth behind the destruction of Henry's illusion is that man's position in this world is bleak enough as it is without wishing for any wounds to make it worse. Finally, it must be stated that the text offers no evidence of Conklin's death accomplishing anything else. Shortly thereafter, Henry commits his greatest sin: he deliberately deserts the tattered man who selflessly worries about others even when he is himself at the edge of the grave.

Because of the importance of the tattered man in Henry's journey to awareness, this episode can reasonably be considered a parallel scene comparable to the two just examined. That is, the desertion of this dying man is in itself Henry's illusion. His bitter and immediate self-loathing—"he now thought that he wished he was dead" (p. 290)—foreshadows what Crane makes explicit in the final chapter: the tattered man will always haunt Henry, not because of anything he does to Henry, but because of what Henry does to him. This desertion is the limit of Henry's penetration into the direful thicket of cowardice, selfishness, and immaturity; and as he can go no further, he must once more seek a new direction—metaphorically the only one left to him—a way out of the "forest" and back to his original commitment.

Henry's subconscious desire to find his way back is revealed by his envying the men of an advancing column so intensely that "he could have wept in his longings." He immediately pictures himself as "a blue desperate figure leading lurid charges with one knee forward and a broken blade high—a blue, determined figure standing before a crimson and steel assault, getting calmly killed" (p. 294). These asinine visions, in this context, are evoked by Henry's desire as a psychological thrust to counteract the opposing force of fear. Thus, Henry begins a debate with himself: he wants to go forward, his fear invents excuses, and his reason overcomes these excuses one by one as they are raised. This debate ends in defeat only because Henry believes there is absolutely no way in which he can return to his regiment with self-respect. And this belief, of course, turns out to be the illusion which forms the basis of his final episode in the forest.

However, Henry's mental debate itself accomplishes two important results: it enables Henry to transcend by an effort of will his

most absurd selfishness—his wish for the defeat of his own army—
and it sufficiently calms his mind for him to realize, for the first time
since his original flight, that his physical condition—hunger, thirst,
extreme fatigue—suggests he is actually "jest one little feller," ordinary, weak, fallible. His inner debate ends when he sees the very
men with whom he had lately identified himself flee back through
the woods in terror. He leaps into the midst of these panic-stricken
men *in an attempt to rally them,* and receives his red badge of courage
when one of them clubs him in the head with a rifle butt.

Crane probably seized upon this incident for his final title because
of the complex ironies woven into it, because of its centrality to a
story about courage and various sorts of wounds, and because Henry
has to win his way to manhood by struggle as one wins a badge:

> he does not receive his wound in flight, but in the performance of
> an act of courage! Henry is struck down (by a coward) while
> inarticulately striving "to make a rallying speech, to sing a battle
> hymn." He is in a position to suffer such a wound because he has
> originally fled from his regiment, but he is going against the current
> of retreating infantry, *towards* the battle, when he gains the red
> badge.[8]

He has already revealed his intent, his desire to return. The external
fact of the wound changes nothing whatsoever within Henry's mind.
Chance merely provides the means for which he has already been
searching, the means of returning to his regiment secure from outward
ridicule. He is guided back by the cheery-voiced soldier, a man who
helps others without vanity or even a wish for thanks, exactly as
Henry should have helped the tattered man. Henry tells his lie—
which ironically proves unnecessary—is nursed by Wilson and, being
both physically and emotionally exhausted, is put to bed in his friend's
blankets.

In terms of Crane's structural pattern, Henry is now back in his
original position and again about to confront the unknown, still untried
in battle—so he believes—still afraid. Nevertheless, the short story
has become a novel, and within Henry's mind a major battle has
been fought and won. Although he still does not know how he will
act when he confronts the unknown, the bitter experience of this
fantastic day's journey through the moral forest has brought Henry
to a secure knowledge of what he can *not* do when the time for this
confrontation comes, for him, on the morrow.

His actions the next morning, however, are not reassuring. His
vanity returns with his sense of security, he complains loudly, and
he treats Wilson quite shabbily. This reassertion of the old Henry is
demanded by dramatic necessity (if growth of character is contingent
upon awareness Crane cannot very well make much of a change in

Henry before he experiences actual combat), and Crane justifies it with great care by making it serve at least three functions. Henry's undesirable traits first provide a necessary contrast in order to emphasize the change which has occurred in Wilson, who has already had his baptism of fire:

> He seemed no more to be continually regarding the proportions of his personal prowess. . . . He was no more a loud young soldier. There was about him now a fine reliance. He showed a quiet belief in his purposes and his abilities. . . . And the youth saw that ever after it would be easier to live in his friend's neighborhood. (pp. 314–15)

Given Crane's technique of the parallel scene, this passage has to foreshadow the change which Henry will also undergo once he successfully faces up to his own commitment; it can have no other function.[9] Henry's vain foolishness at this point is also important as a contrast with his yesterday's view of himself—yesterday he had seen himself lower than all other men, and mocked by nature; today, like George Kelcey, he imagines himself "a fine creation . . . the chosen of some gods," and he considers nature "a fine thing moving with a magnificent justice" (pp. 319–20)—and because these absurdities allow Crane to show that Henry is now capable of perceiving the falseness of his position. His "pompous and veteranlike" thoughts are just as foolish, of course, as those he revealed during his flight; and neither passage presents Crane's own view of the universe and man's place in it.[10] But no one has noticed that these silly illusions form a carefully wrought sequence in themselves which begins with Henry's smug sense of power over Wilson because of the packet, rises to a climax of loud complaint, and ends suddenly when this swelling pomposity is "pierced" by a fellow soldier's lazy comment: "Mebbe yeh think yeh fit th' hull battle yestirday, Fleming." Henry is *inwardly* "reduced to an abject pulp by these chance words" (p. 325). Henry, in short, has assumed a vain pose and has been acting out his role as if the external view of himself were all that mattered; the laconic comment pierces this pose by abruptly awakening Henry's conscience, and the whole external pose collapses before this inner voice's inflexible command that Henry view himself as he really is. This whole sequence, finally, helps Henry prepare psychologically to face up to the coming fight.

When the battle comes, Henry turns his reawakened self-loathing and self-hatred upon the enemy, and he chooses to stay and fight rather than run again into that terrible forest: "He had taken up a first position behind the little tree, with a direct determination to hold it against the world" (p. 330). After making this willed commitment, Henry slips again into the trance of battle sleep, fights like a regular "war devil," and after the skirmish he emerges from his trance with the praise of his comrades ringing in his ears.

> He had fought like a pagan who defends his religion. Regarding it, he saw that it was fine, wild, and, in some ways, easy. He had been a tremendous figure, no doubt. By this struggle he had overcome obstacles which he had admitted to be mountains. They had fallen like paper peaks, and he was now what he called a hero. And he had not been aware of the process. He had slept and, awakening, found himself a knight. (p. 331)

Henry has thus successfully *passed through* the unknown, the feared experience, and *this* time because he has not run he accepts the fact, even though, again because of battle sleep, he has not actually *experienced* the unknown itself. Hence, he has a great deal to ponder about. The excellent irony of this crucial episode is *not* that Henry has become a hero in his battle sleep—Crane never offers the reader such an absurd definition of heroism—but that during this sleep Henry has successfully passed through the very experience upon which his imagination and fear have been intensely centered since the beginning of the novel; the monumental irony is that Henry has endured all his suffering, all the tortures of his imagination, over an action which is so easily done that one can do it superbly while in a trance. The implications which follow from this ironic deflation should be clear to the reader, even if Henry is not yet capable of sorting them out: if the feared unknown, the hideous dragon of war, can be successfully encountered while one is in a trance, then Henry's former imaginings, fears, concepts of knightly heroism, all such feverish activity of his weak mental machinery, stand revealed as absurd. Henry, in other words, for the first time since the novel began, is now in a position to learn authentic self-knowledge, to perceive the reality which is actually before his eyes to be seen, and to acquire the humility which Wilson has already attained.

Henry's subsequent actions immensely favour this conclusion. He accepts his own insignificance when he overhears his regiment of "mule drivers" ordered into an action from which few are expected to emerge alive. And, even though he knows the danger of the coming battle, there is no hesitation in Henry, no thought of flight. Hence, it follows reasonably from this deliberate courage that Henry should finally be able to experience actual combat in full possession of all his faculties. In fact, Crane insists upon Henry's awareness, both of the external and the inner reality, during this charge: "It seemed to the youth that he saw everything. Each blade of the green grass was bold and clear . . . all were comprehended. His mind took a mechanical but firm impression, so that afterward everything was pictured and explained to him, *save why he himself was there*" (pp.

338–9; my italics). The final phrase simply points to Henry's re-membrance of his past failures. The frenzy of this charge, not a blind rage of battle sleep, is described as a "temporary but sublime absence of selfishness. And because it was of this order was the reason, perhaps, why the youth wondered, afterward, what reasons he could have had for being there" (p. 339). Henry, like the other men, still shows anger, pride, wild excitement; but such qualities are good ones for a soldier to have because they help him stand and fight, they could hardly be omitted from any realistic presentation of men at war, they do not make these men less than human, and Henry never again loses his grip on his consciousness because of them. These men reveal anger and pride in this situation precisely because they are men who hold themselves responsible for their own actions and seek the good opinion of their fellow men. Henry has yet to learn that if a man satisfies his own sense of personal honesty, this is enough; the opinions of others, just one more externality, will vary with the several views which others take of one's actions. Chapter 21 prepares Henry for this stoic lesson.

The elated regiment returns from their charge, only to be taunted by veterans who observe how little ground was covered. Henry soon accepts the view that the extent of the charge was comparatively "trivial," even though he feels "a considerable joy in musing upon his performances during the charge" (a joy which is not unreasonable when we recall that only yesterday Henry had fled in panic from this same situation). When a general states yet another point of view—that the charge was a military failure, and the "mule drivers" now seem to him to be "mud diggers"—the lieutenant's defence of his own men implies that a military failure is in itself no criterion of the performance of the men doing the fighting. And the chapter ends with Wilson and Fleming being told of the praise they have received from the lieutenant and colonel of their own regiment. Wilson and Fleming have every right to feel pleased at this praise; and the fact that they "speedily forgot many things," that for them "the past held no pictures of error and disappointment," does not indicate that they are mere automatons at the mercy of external circumstance: it in-dicates that in their first flush of pleasure they have not yet assimilated and considered this praise in the total perspective which is specifically demanded by the several points of view presented in this very chapter. There is no time for assimilation of anything at this point because the novel immediately roars on into yet another battle, a final skirmish in which Henry's actions confirm the self-control he has recently acquired. During this fight all the men act like veterans by tending strictly to business and Wilson even captures an enemy flag; after the battle he holds this prize "with vanity" as he and Henry, both still caught up in the excitement of the moment, congratulate each other. The time for reflection and assimilation comes only with the final chapter when Henry walks away from the battle-field and is again free to probe into his own mind.

The endless critical squabbles which have arisen over this final chapter hinge upon a single question: does Fleming achieve any moral growth or development of character? Yet any Crane student should be able to answer this question almost without consulting this chapter at all—without reading Crane's description of Henry's change of soul which requires at least two pages in most editions. To claim that Fleming does *not* achieve any growth or development is to ignore many quite obvious statements of his gradual moral progress that are scattered throughout the novel, the entire function of Wilson's role, and the fact that Crane must have had some reason for endowing Henry—unlike the earlier protagonists—with awareness and a conscience. It is also well to remember that Crane is trying to be psychologically realistic: this is the *first* time Henry has full opportunity to reflect upon all the experiences which have crowded the past two days of his life, he is still a young lad not yet even twenty-four hours removed from the very nadir of self-abasement, and, like Wilson whose development preceded his own, Henry is still "capable of vanity. Even in the final chapter of the novel, Crane still writes as of a process that is going on. Fleming's mind, he says, 'was undergoing a subtle change'; nevertheless, the final paragraphs describe that change in detail, and the unmistakable traits of genuine maturity . . . are present."[11]

Crane devotes the first two pages, over a fourth of the chapter, to a careful preparation for the important matters which follow. The battle is over for the day, and, as the regiment ironically marches back over the same ground they had taken at great cost, the reader is taken directly into Henry's mind. He begins by rejoicing that he has come forth, escaped, from "a land of strange, squalling upheavals." The deliberately ambiguous language here should suggest *all* of Private Fleming's various battles, with the enemy, the "arrayed forces of the universe," and his own weaknesses. Then Henry attempts to consider all that has happened to him from the point of view of the new perspective he has attained by living through these past two days. And here Crane is again explicit, neither ironic nor ambiguous:

> he began to study his deeds, [both] his failures, and his achievements. Thus, fresh from scenes where many of his usual machines of reflection had been idle . . . he struggled to marshal all his acts.
>
> At last they marched before him clearly. From this present view point he was enabled to look at them in spectator fashion and to criticize them with some correctness, for his new condition had already defeated certain sympathies. (pp. 365–6)

Henry's "procession of memory" begins with the most recent events, his public deeds which are recalled with delight because they tell him "he was good." This recollection seems reasonable, so far as it goes; these public deeds, after all, have been good. But the next sentence reveals Henry's error a few moments before he himself corrects it: "He recalled with a thrill of joy the respectful comments of his fellows upon his conduct" (p. 366). Henry, in short, begins with his old error of judging himself by the opinion of others, by his external reputation. The entire remaining portion of his self-analysis consists of the assaults made upon this public image by the shameful recollections of his private deeds until, finally, an equilibrium is attained in which both public and private views of the self take permanent position in a realistic, balanced judgement. These emotionally powerful memories of his private misdeeds originally fell under three headings: his desertion from the regiment's first engagement, his "terrible combat with the arrayed forces of the universe," and his desertion of the tattered man. In the final version, the first act of desertion merged with the more vividly personal abandonment of the tattered man, and the resolution to the theme of Henry's battle with the universe was largely omitted.[12]

Thus, the great image which dominates these final pages as an inexorable "spectre of reproach" is the "dogging memory of the tattered soldier—he who, gored by bullets and faint for blood, had fretted concerning an imagined wound in another; he who had loaned his last of strength and intellect for the tall soldier; he who, blind with weariness and pain, had been deserted in the field" (p. 367). The great care with which Crane makes Henry recall all the ramifications of this incident implies the deep impression it has made upon the youth. He cringes when this spectre looms before him: "For an instant a wretched chill of sweat was upon him at the thought that he might be detected in the thing. As he stood persistently before his vision, he gave vent to a cry of sharp irritation and agony" (p. 367). If read correctly this passage does not reveal a selfish vanity; it reveals only the continuity of Henry's thought. He is still basking in the warmth of his public deeds when this private horror suddenly pierces and deflates, for him, his public image of himself. In order to live with this awful ghost Henry has to redress his own judgement of himself: he retains a concern for his external reputation—few men of any age desire to have their shameful deeds made public—but this vision finally forces him to accept the characteristic position of the mature man that his own inner view of himself is vastly more important than the external opinions of others.

Henry never entirely banishes this ghost—an attainment which would be as impossible in Crane's world as it would be in Hawthorne's—but he is able to place it in perspective, "to put the sin at a distance." An excised passage which follows reveals that Henry handles this sin as any intelligent man of conscience would handle it, as a means of trampling upon his own ego to prevent his committing such a sin again. "This plan for the utilization of a sin did not give him complete joy but it was the best sentiment he could formulate under the circumstances, and when it was combined with his success, or public deeds, he knew that he was quite contented" (p. 369). Henry is being neither vain nor callous in this decision; he is merely being practical and realistic. No better use of a past sin is possible in Crane's world. And if this sin is a real and permanent part of his past, so are his good actions during the day's fighting: if Henry is to see himself as he really is, he must consider both "his failures, and his achievements."

Once he attains this balanced view of himself, he is able to foresee "some new ways" of life for him in the future: "He found that he could look back upon the brass and bombast of his earlier gospels and see them truly. He was gleeful when he discovered that he now despised them" (p. 369). Henry's weak mental machinery, in short, has undergone considerable readjustment. His eyes have finally opened, and he is now able to begin perceiving correctly the reality which has been before him and largely unchanged since the novel began. Henry's personal honesty can now assert itself in morally significant action, and he is ready to begin the difficult practice of manhood in an amoral universe.

> *With this conviction* [my italics] came a store of assurance. He felt a quiet manhood, nonassertive but of sturdy and strong blood. He knew that he would no more quail before his guides wherever they should point. He had been to touch the great death, and found that, after all, it was but the great death. He was a man. (p. 369)

I am unable to find much irony in the closing paragraphs of the novel. Henry is exhausted from all his battles and gratefully marching to a rest. Only the most romantically obtuse reader at this point could believe in the actuality of "an existence of soft and eternal peace," but the image aptly describes how inviting the coming rest must seem to a weary young soldier. Certainly Henry is not fooling himself; his quiet confidence that he will "no more quail before his guides wherever they should point" would be meaningless if he really anticipated an existence of soft and eternal peace. And the final image seems to me merely an emblem of what has just happened to Henry. He has attained authentic self-knowledge and a sense of manhood after long and fierce battles with his own moral weaknesses; hence it seems entirely appropriate that Crane should end this tale with the image of a golden ray of sunlight appearing through hosts of leaden rain clouds. Irony has its function earlier in Crane's pattern, before the protagonist becomes aware of the reality he struggles to perceive correctly.

Notes

1. This view of the universe can reasonably be called naturalistic; but Crane's acceptance of it no more makes his work naturalistic than Matthew Arnold's acceptance of ultimately the same view makes his poetry naturalistic.

> If this seems a pessimistic view of nature, it is not only the logical end of Crane's concern with the subject, it is the logical end of America's concern. When Hawthorne and Melville questioned Emerson's view of nature as the benevolent image of the Over-Soul, they revealed an ambiguity in nature that begged closer inspection. Stephen Crane's examination showed nature to be as unmotivated as a machine with which man had come only accidentally in contact. (R. B. West, Jr., "Stephen Crane: Author in Transition," *American Literature*, XXXIV [May 1962], 227.)

2. James Colvert, "Stephen Crane: The Development of His Art," Ph.D. diss. (Louisiana State Univ., 1953), p. 145.

3. R. W. Stallman, *Stephen Crane: An Omnibus* (New York, 1952), p. 229. All further citations of *The Red Badge* in the text refer to this edition, which reprints Crane's deletions from earlier manuscript versions.

4. See Max R. Westbrook, "Stephen Crane and the Personal Universal," *Modern Fiction Studies*, VIII (Winter 1962–3), 353; "Stephen Crane and the Revolt-Search Motif," Ph.D. diss. (Univ. Texas, 1960), p. 183.

5. See Gordon O. Taylor, *The Passages of Thought: Psychological Representation in the American Novel 1870–1900* (New York, 1969), p. 126. There immediately follows a passage which should recall "The Black Dog" and "The Cry of a Huckleberry Pudding": "Since he had turned his back upon the fight his fears had been wondrously magnified. Death about to thrust him between the shoulder blades was far more dreadful than death about to smite him between the eyes . . . it is better to view the appalling than to be merely within hearing" (p. 269).

6. The symbolic function of this corpse is spelled out, unnecessarily, in a passage which Crane wisely cancelled (p. 276, n. 2).

7. Olov W. Fryckstedt, "Henry Fleming's Tupenny Fury: Cosmic Pessimism in Stephen Crane's *The Red Badge of Courage*," *Studia Neophilologica*, XXXIII (1961), 276.

8. Eric Solomon, "The Structure of 'The Red Badge of Courage,' " *Modern Fiction Studies*, V (Autumn 1959), 230–1. See also John J. McDermott, "Symbolism and Psychological Realism in *The Red Badge of Courage*," *Nineteenth-Century Fiction*, XXIII (Dec. 1968), 324–31.

9. The precise parallel between Wilson and Fleming is discussed by William P. Safranek, "Crane's *The Red Badge of Courage*," *Explicator*, XXVI (Nov. 1967), item 21.

10. Crane uses exactly the same device in a poem: two contrasting views of a morally neutral reality, the sea, are presented, and neither can legitimately be called Crane's own. See *The Poems of Stephen Crane*, ed. Joseph Katz (New York, 1966), p. 84.

11. Westbrook, "Revolt-Search," pp. 199–200.

12. Although the resolution of this excised theme (*Omnibus*, pp. 367, 369) is

presented ambiguously—Henry's "deity laying about him with the bludgeon of correction" for whom "no grain like him would be lost" can only be an illusion in Crane's amoral universe—Henry's conclusion resembles Crane's own view: "those tempestuous moments were of the wild mistakes and ravings of a novice who did not comprehend. He had been a mere man railing at a condition. . . . The imperturbable sun shines on insult and worship" (p. 367). See Fryckstedt, "Tupenny Fury."

The Red Badge of Courage: The "Religion of Peace" and the War Archetype

Jean Cazemajou[*]

> All Nature so calm in itself, the early summer grass so rich, and foliage of the trees . . . but fierce savage demons fighting there . . . rapid-filing phantoms through the woods.—Walt Whitman, "A Night Battle over a Week Since," notes dated 12 May 1863, in *Specimen Days* (1882).

Any examination of Stephen Crane's mental processes ought to begin by referring to his "irony of soul," a term he himself used in "This Majestic Lie," a story in *Wounds in the Rain.* He rejected one-sided views on human problems, for even if his dominant voice was one of dissent, he never fell into the trap of nihilistic iconoclasm. Irony often serves as a vehicle for a veiled but deeply-felt sense of justice; Crane's irony is of that kind.[1] What he seems to strive for in his work is the projection of a mental image to convey his personal conception of truth. Moving as he does in the sphere of abstractions and unresolved polarities, he often reduces his characters to a single feature in order to sketch their psychological progress along allegorical lines. This mythic approach to reality is a constant in his work: such primordial ideas as Mother, Child, Sin, Rebirth, War, and Peace operate in his writings as archetypal antagonists which evoke a dialectical tension. One consequence of this semantic structure is that in his writings no process of individualization is ever sufficiently complete to fill out the image of any character, even in Crane's most deeply wrought character studies. His artistic orientation precluded a sense of obligation to make his pictures picturesque or his characters thoroughly defined. That is one element of his comment on the genesis of *The Red Badge of Courage:* "It was essential that I should make my battle a type and name no names. . . ."[2]

Notions of war and peace in such a stylized and strangely con-

[*] From *Stephen Crane in Transition: Centenary Essays,* ed. Joseph Katz (DeKalb: Northern Illinois University Press, 1972), 54–65. © 1972 by Northern Illinois University Press. Reprinted by permission of Northern Illinois University Press.

stricted vision of the world—because of their recurring presence and their permanent influence on Crane's metaphoric fancy—provide the critic with two valuable tools for studying the writer's creative processes. Metaphoric war is notable in whatever topic Crane treated, whether it was urban life, adventure, or domestic relationships, because he always saw human existence in terms of conflict. In a coal mine near Scranton, Pennsylvania, miners at work are described as if they were waging some subterranean war:

> The place always resounds with the shouts of mule-boys, and there can always be heard the noise of approaching coal-cars, beginning in mild rumble and then swelling down upon one in a tempest of sound. . . . There is booming and banging and crashing, until one wonders why the tremendous walls are not wrenched by the force of this uproar. . . . It is war. It is the most savage part of all in the endless battle between man and nature.[3]

And the threat of death in "The Open Boat," hovering around the dinghy in the form of an omnipresent shark, is objectified as a bullet—"a gigantic and keen projectile." No matter where he may be, Crane is faithful to his idea that "the sense of a city is battle"—prefiguring in this central metaphor Edward Albee's vision of the city in *The Zoo Story*.[4] And domestic conflicts, especially those between mother and son, are projected as a version of war: in "An Experiment in Luxury" the mother is called "a spearswoman of the Philistines," and in *George's Mother* Mrs. Kelcey wields her broom like a lance when she cleans her apartment (p. 93).[5] Even the conduct of Whilomville's children, patterned on that of fictional heroes, is warlike in character. But in all these writings there always lurks a shadow of peace, dreamlike or nostalgic, in contrast to the figures of war. In most of Crane's works the two are linked together. In *The Red Badge of Courage* war and peace function simultaneously as factual realities and archetypal values.

The descriptive force of Crane's style may lead one to read that novel as if it were an introduction to the sound and fury of real combat. Specific details of camp life, preparations for attacks, charges and countercharges, captures of prisoners, and seizures of enemy flags serve to convey the illusion of verisimilitude. Indeed, these details sufficiently parallel reality to allow one scholar to argue convincingly that Crane had the Battle of Chancellorsville in mind when he wrote *The Red Badge of Courage*.[6] But the picture of battle given in the novel is blurred and limited in scope. It is not "war," but only war seen through the eyes of one raw recruit, a "youth." For him battle is chaos and confusion.

That is, however, only one possible view of war. The novel balances it with another, in which a world at peace continually intrudes on the smoke and destruction. Again, it is through the eyes of the youth that this antidote to war is visualized. He associates peace with images of rural harmony. Simultaneously frightened and fascinated by violence, Henry displays ambivalent tendencies. Tired of the routine of farm life, he is a dreamer soon carried away by the war hysteria that sweeps the land and reaches him first through the sound of a church bell ringing "the twisted news of a great battle" (p. 193). It makes him decide to escape from the monotony of chores by plunging into adventure. Soon after enlisting, however, he decides that endless drilling in camp is no better than "endless rounds from the house to the barn." And as the story unfolds a small number of flashbacks evoke the memory of peace, sharp and bright against the blurred image of battle: the warm farewell scenes of chapter 1, the crisp, gay circus parade of chapter 5, the cosy family meals and cool swimming parties of chapter 12—all introduce a universe in which everything is familiar and where a refreshing harmony of man with Nature prevails. These vignettes remind us of Whitman's glorification of life and the rebirth of Nature in his notes on the same battle.

Despite Crane's famous accuracy of detail, war and peace in *The Red Badge of Courage* function to a greater degree as archetypes than as realities. The novel invests both with the attributes of religious significance. For example, in a minute and highly evocative description of battle sounds, Crane introduces a reference to a war very different from the War between the States: "This uproar explained a celestial battle; it was tumbling hordes a-struggle in the air" (p. 237). Sketching the other side of the diptych: "This landscape gave him assurance. A fair field holding life. It was the religion of peace" (p. 234). In this way war and peace are cut off from ordinary experience and are raised to the level of primordial image.

This elevation is increased through the use of two emblematic figures borrowed from the farm: the cow and the horse. These two animals fulfill two opposing functions in Crane's symbology. The placid cow is associated with peace; the fierce horse is made representative of war. When in *The Red Badge of Courage* the peace archetype is centered around the image of "a fair field holding life," the gilded pageant of Henry's memory makes the cows on his farm appear with "a halo of happiness about each of their heads" (p. 206). Although this sanctification has its humorous connotations, it is not merely an occasional metaphor. In another passage, Crane identifies Henry with his quondam charges: "He developed the acute exasperation of a pestered animal, a well-meaning cow worried by dogs" (p. 223). This strange metaphor in fact becomes a structural device in the novel, serving both to represent peace and to group together pine forests, vast green fields, and cows as symbols of peace (p. 210).

Thus, one is tempted to say that Nature is simply a haven of peace in Crane's vision of the world, and many passages in *The Red Badge of Courage* seem to support this conclusion. Nature provides a wonderful backdrop for the hero's romantic regression into the bosom of the Mother of the Universe while he waits for his first battle to begin: "The moon had been lighted and was hung in a treetop. The liquid stillness of the night enveloping him made him feel vast pity for himself. There was a caress in the soft winds; and the whole mood of the darkness, he thought, was one of sympathy for himself in his distress" (p. 206). In the chapel-like forest, which welcomes Henry after he has made his "separate peace" in chapter 7, he projects "Nature to be a woman with a deep aversion to tragedy" (p. 234), and a religious serenity pervades this secluded place: "The trees began softly to sing a hymn of twilight. The sun sank until slanted bronze rays struck the forest. There was a lull in the noises of insects as if they had bowed their beaks and were making a devotional pause. There was silence save for the chanted chorus of the trees" (p. 236). But the forest is at best an ambiguous reality in this novel. Far from always being a haven of peace, it sometimes bristles with threatening fingers and vibrates with accusing voices: "He was obliged to force his way with much noise. The creepers, catching against his legs, cried out harshly as their sprays were torn from the barks of the trees. The swishing saplings tried to make known his presence to the world. He could not conciliate the forest" (p. 234).

Instead of being a specific setting, located precisely in space and time, this forest appears rather as a symbolic place reminiscent of the one in Genesis where Adam takes refuge after his fall and tries to hide behind trees in his flight from the face of God (Genesis, 3:8). Henry's Edenic vision which concludes the book is also fraught with Biblical overtones in which can be heard echoes of The Song of Songs: "He turned now with a lover's thirst to images of tranquil skies, fresh meadows, cool brooks—an existence of soft and eternal peace" (p. 318).

On the other hand, the horse remains central to Crane's concept of war: pilfering a horse (p. 205) is presented—ironically—as a typical act of war. The animal that one critic regards as the main symbol of aggressiveness in Crane's work appears invested with complex threats in *The Red Badge of Courage*.[7] At the beginning of the novel it appears in the centaurian image of "the gigantic figure of the colonel on a gigantic horse" (p. 203) as a means of announcing the impending holocaust. Epitomizing the potential danger of an annihilating onslaught, the simile of the "mad horse" conveys the fury of sudden attack (p. 312). Most of the time, the author refers to the eyes—or, rather, the "orbs"—of horses, or "dragons," advancing in battle formation (p. 203). But there is also elevation to abstract symbolism here, and war gradually becomes "the red animal . . . the blood-swollen god" (p. 213).

In this way the expressionistic quality of the novel brings into play an ancient world in which two abstract figures are opposed—the wargod, representing the animalism of bloody conflict, and the radiant goddess, the "anima" of Jung symbolized by the flag, which operates as a unifying and sheltering force in the chaos of battle. In chapter 19 the flag is endowed with feminine attributes, attracting as a maiden and protecting as a mother:

> It was a goddess, radiant, that bended its form with an imperious gesture to him. It was a woman, red and white, hating and loving that called to him with the voice of his hopes. Because no harm could come to it he endowed it with power. He kept near, as if it could be a saver of lives, and an imploring cry went from his mind. (p. 294.)

But whereas the flag never loses caste and always retains its godly virtues, even when reduced to shreds, the animalistic side of war occasionally loses all connection with a presumed deity. The "blood-swollen god" of war topples from his majestic throne into inferno where his very image is blurred by those of "savage demons" of the netherworld and "to the youth the fighters resemble[d] animals tossed for a death struggle into a dark pit" (p. 282). Seen through the eyes of a Methodist consciousness, this pit literally teems with reptilian menace. Crane once confessed that "priests who paint hell well, fill it with snakes instead of fire."[8] Only Melville's barren, solitary, withered wasteland in "The Encantadas"—also overrun with reptiles—surpasses The Red Badge of Courage in offering one of the most nightmarishly infernal pictures in American literature. Crane's war novel mentions serpents early, and they never really disappear from the scene. Thus on the morning of the first day of battle, the landscape appears to be soiled and violated by an ugly, ominous presence stretched across the belly of the earth: "When the sunrays at last struck full and mellowingly upon the earth, the youth saw that the landscape was streaked with two long, thin, black columns which disappeared on the brow of a hill in front and rearward vanished in a wood. They were like two serpents crawling from the cavern of the night" (p. 204).

That same simile reappears several times. It acquires its most fantastic significance when battle fury reaches a peak: "The blue smoke-swallowed line curled and writhed like a snake stepped upon. It swung its ends to and fro in an agony of fear and rage" (p. 282). But although snakes predominate, the teratology of The Red Badge of Courage includes monsters of divers kinds. Snakes easily turn into dragons, and Henry's adventure truly is a kind of dragon-hunt, a frenzied chase of "the beast that ascendeth out of the bottomless pit" in Revelation, (11:7). Shells are like "storm banshees" or seem to have "rows of cruel teeth" (pp. 218, 230). Still more frightening are the "smoke phantoms" that stifle the soldiers, restrict their vision, and bury them in a fuliginous world in which every object assumes grotesque shapes and where life itself becomes meaningless (pp. 216, 223). This chamber-of-horrors atmosphere is introduced even before the beginning of the battle, when the youth lies in his hut, torn by doubts and misgivings, tormented by the fear of a faceless monster: "In the darkness he saw visions of a thousand-tongued fear that would babble at his back and cause him to flee, while others were going coolly about their country's business. He admitted that he would not be able to cope with this monster" (p. 208).

But Crane's originality is not centered upon his handling of the horrible in war. That had been even more fully exploited by his contemporary, Ambrose Bierce, whose battle pictures are closer still to the Gothic tradition. Where *The Red Badge of Courage* goes the extra step is in pointing to the co-existence of the banal with the gruesome, not hesitating to undercut the significance of death on the battlefield with a simile such as "The men dropped here and there like bundles" (p. 224). While Crane tries his hand at a tale of initiation and demands that the hero defeat some fantastic monsters, he simultaneously applies the debunking lever of irony to challenge traditional concepts of heroism. Henry's qualifications for that kind of authentic bravery are indeed questionable. Appearing to his comrades as an admirable and almost inimitable "jimhickey" (p. 304), he has led the final charge, taken the bright colors to the front, and even participated in the conquest of the enemy flag. But deep down in the recesses of his soul he knows that he is closer to being an imposter than a jimhickey. At the very end of his ordeal the successive stages of his spiritual journey return to his mind, spelling shame more often than glory. The circular shape of this journey, which takes him back to the point at which he started, seems a parody of *The Pilgrim's Progress*, a series of trials in which the protagonist often makes wrong decisions.

At the beginning of his adventure, although he had plunged into the maelstrom of war on his own accord, Henry is deeply afraid of violence. This fear leads him to his panic and desertion in chapter 6. Then a series of encounters in no man's land serve to throw his instinctive flight into a moral perspective. Remorse sets in. Henry's meeting with mortally wounded Jim Conklin, who dies under his eyes, his rejection of the "tattered man," and his providential meeting with "the man of the cheerful voice" who takes him back to his regiment leave his conscience buffeted and sore. Then, a second time, the ambivalent force of violence plunges him into action. Swept by "the winds of battle," he is "not conscious that he [is] erect upon his feet"—and he fights like a "barbarian," a "beast" (pp. 282, 283, 284).

In *The Red Badge of Courage,* war is not the splendid and generous crusade that many Northern writers wanted their readers to see in the Civil War; nor is it the last stand for a lost cause that Southern writers glorified. Crane differs from most nineteenth-century authors of war stories in not offering Manichaean pictures of battlefields. In his book war is nothing but the outward manifestation of a dark force buried in the collective unconscious of man, "the throat-grappling instinct." That view of the Civil War as a catastrophe caused by a deep-lying flaw in human nature is very close to the one Melville offers in *Battle Pieces.* In this light the concluding episode of chapter 9 gives new significance to its final line, "The red sun was pasted in the sky like a wafer" (p. 246). The redness of the wafer is indeed a sign of sacrifice, but it does not point—as some critics believe— to the redemptive self-sacrifice of a Christ-figure.[9] It refers, intuitively rather than deductively, to the common archetypal image which is part and parcel of Aztec culture: the occasional need to sacrifice the life of a young man to the sun in order to preserve its life and brilliance.[10] This reference is reinforced by the ritual-like quality of many furious battle scenes in the novel, especially in such similes as "In front of the colors the three men began to bawl: 'Come on! come on!' They danced and gyrated like tortured savages" (p. 294).

Thus Crane, by depriving war of all of the conceptual adornments with which traditional religion and contemporary myth invest it, prepared the ground for a reassessment of its sociological significance. He did so, however, with no sense of carrying out a sociological inquiry. In the process of clarifying the personal drama of an isolated consciousness, he stumbled upon the dark impulses with which the collective unconscious had struggled for ages. It is in the constant swing from macabre war scenes to peaceful visions that *The Red Badge of Courage* develops its fundamental set of polarities; and they climax in the circus metaphor at the beginning of chapter 5, when the parade through the village street—a colorful vignette seen in retrospect—is followed by the infernal and spectacular fireworks of the circus of war:

> There were moments of waiting. The youth thought of the village street at home before the arrival of the circus parade on a day in the spring. He remembered how he had stood, a small, thrillful boy, prepared to follow the dingy lady upon the white horse, or the band in its faded chariot. He saw the yellow road, the lines of expectant people, and the sober houses. He particularly remembered an old fellow who used to sit upon a cracker box in front of the store and feign to despise such exhibitions. A thousand

details of color and form surged in his mind. The old fellow upon
the cracker box appeared in middle prominence.

Some one cried, "Here they come!"

There was a rustling and muttering among the men. . . .

Across the smoke-infested fields came a brown swarm of running
men who were giving shrill yells. They came on, stooping and
swinging their rifles at all angles. A flag, tilted forward, sped near
the front. (Pp. 220–221.)

The contrast between those two scenes is achieved mostly in terms
of painting, through a shift from a bright impressionistic tableau to
a blurred and confused panorama pierced by touches of expressionism.
A fundamental image takes shape here, the one that will transform
Henry into an invisible man: "In the battle blur his face would, in
a way be hidden, like the face of a cowled man" (p. 252). This
expressionistic distortion of appearance reaches its own climax as
Crane follows pictures of close combat with a bewitched world that
oscillates between the fantastic and the grotesque: "They in blue
showed their teeth; their eyes shone all white. They launched themselves at the throats of those who stood resisting" (p. 312).

The archetypal war described in *The Red Badge of Courage* was
fought against a "composite monster" (p. 220) that kept recurring
in his work afterwards—a fire-spitting, dragon-like monster containing
Biblical and primitive characteristics both, a Moloch that could not
be laid by the sheer force of arms. Thus, in war, true heroism is the
result of spiritual and not physical prowess and derives its might from
effacement rather than affirmation of self. So, although Henry failed
at Chancellorsville, as an old veteran in Whilomville he redeemed
himself by plunging into his burning barn to rescue his horses, dying
amidst the purifying flames.[11]

But *The Red Badge of Courage* is not Crane's definitive statement
on war. The way he realized his hypotheses was by going from dream
to experience, and until he had felt what war really was like he could
not be satisfied. Like one of the protagonists in his Spanish-American
War fiction, William B. Perkins—Ralph D. Paine in actual life—he
came out of his first battle giddy and bruised but "with his hat not
able to fit his head for the bumps of wisdom that were on it."[12]
From then on, the prosaic side of war introduced in *The Red Badge
of Courage* began to predominate in his work, replacing much of the
glamor in his own early imaginings. With a terseness that characterizes
his most famous poems, he eventually coined this aphorism: "War is
death, and a plague of the lack of small things, and toil."[13] Crane
never could attain the serenity and detachment needed to define
Peace. This concept he had to be content with relegating to the
remote and mysterious status of a fable—a "religion."

Notes

1. Vladimir Jankélévitch, *L'Ironie* (Paris: Flammarion, 1964), p. 39: "Ironiser c'est choisir la justice."

2. Crane to John S. Phillips, 30 December [1895], in R. W. Stallman and Lillian Gilkes, eds., *Stephen Crane: Letters* (New York: New York University Press, 1960), p. 84.

3. "In the Depths of a Coal-Mine," *McClure's Magazine* 2 (August 1894): 195–209.

4. "Mr. Binks' Day Off," *New York Press*, 8 July 1894.

5. References in parentheses are to Joseph Katz, *The Portable Stephen Crane* (New York: The Viking Press, 1969).

6. Harold A. Hungerford, " 'That Was at Chancellorsville': The Factual Framework of *The Red Badge of Courage*," *American Literature* 34 (January 1963): 520–31.

7. Daniel G. Hoffman, *The Poetry of Stephen Crane* (New York: Columbia University Press, 1957), p. 110.

8. "The Snake," *Pocket Magazine* 2 (August 1896): 125–32.

9. See, for example, various writings of R. W. Stallman beginning with his introduction to *The Red Badge of Courage* (New York: Modern Library, 1951); and Daniel Hoffman's introduction to the same novel (New York: Harper & Brothers, 1959).

10. This myth is particularly well analyzed in Georges Bataille, *La Part maudite* (Paris: Editions de Minuit, 1967), pp. 103–4.

11. "The Veteran," *McClure's Magazine* 7 (August 1896): 222–24.

12. "War Memories," *Anglo-Saxon Review* 3 (December 1899): 10–38.

13. "War Memories," p. 19.

Depersonalization and the Dream in *The Red Badge of Courage*

Robert M. Rechnitz*

Studies of *The Red Badge of Courage* continue to question whether the intention of the novel's final paragraphs is literal or ironic. Most of the recent critics lean toward a literal interpretation and assert that Henry Fleming gains a measured and realistic understanding of himself and his world.[1] James B. Colvert's conclusion is representative: ". . . .when he [Henry] sees them in spectator fashion . . . events in reality seem to fit into a comprehensible order."[2]

I believe that the possibility of Henry's gaining any such spectator-like objectivity is highly unlikely. In believing so, I am partially reverting to Charles C. Walcutt's judgment that the final four paragraphs of the novel

* From *Studies in the Novel* 6 (Spring 1974): 76–87. © 1974 by North Texas State University. Reprinted by permission of North Texas State University.

are a climax of self-delusion. If there is any one point that has been made it is that Henry has never been able to evaluate his conduct. He may have been fearless for moments, but his motives were vain, selfish, ignorant, and childish. . . .He has . . . for moments risen above his limitations, but Crane seems plainly to be showing that he has not achieved a lasting wisdom or self-knowledge.[3]

Walcutt suggests that Henry's ultimate understanding is clouded because it is distorted by the subjective delusions which have infused his perceptions throughout the novel. I depart from Walcutt, and take the position that Henry, in the course of his experience, exchanges his subjective delusions for a socially derived and sanctioned vision, an alleged objectivity, which is as far removed from reality as was his abandoned private vision. In exchanging private delusion for public, Henry finds a home in the army, just as Jim Conklin had before him, but the price is exorbitant. Becoming the good soldier, he becomes less the individual being; and he emerges in the concluding paragraphs in serene possession of an unauthentic soldier-self, ominously ready to follow his leader.

The little autonomy he possesses at the beginning is immediately threatened. He had entered the army intent upon realizing youthful dreams of glory. These private delusions are soon replaced by the incommunicable anguish and fears which are a natural part of the lull before the battle. Alone in the "light yellow shade" of his hut, he wonders whether he will have guts enough to stand and fight when his time comes.[4] His imagination, which is nourishing this private fear, gains its matter not from Henry's own limited experience but from that of his society. The veterans have told him of the enemy, "gray, bewhiskered hordes . . . tremendous bodies of fierce soldiery who were sweeping along like the Huns." Though Henry does not "put a whole faith in veterans' tales," he does tend to give greater credence to their reports than to the witness of his own senses. The tales of the veterans follow and displace his own observation of the rebel picket who had called him a " 'right dum good feller' " (p. 9).

This contest between individual and group perceptions, or, more precisely, between individual and social evaluation of personal perceptions continues throughout the novel. Much of the action depicts Henry's attempts to honor his personal interpretations, but the final outcome is foreshadowed in this present episode. The authority of personal interpretation crumbles under the massive testimony of the group. Eventually, Henry cannot believe his eyes.

He is by no means mere victim in this process. Henry is tempted to surrender his interpretive faculties to the group upon discovering that his fears are abated when leagued with those of his comrades. After hearing Jim Conklin say that he might run if the others did, Henry "felt gratitude for these words of his comrade. He had feared that all of the untried men possessed a great and correct confidence. He now was in a measure reassured" (p. 12). Henry can thus choose to sink his individuality in group anonymity and diminish his fear by partaking of the group's strength.

Since such a maneuver, demanding a surrender of autonomy, simultaneously appeals to and repels him, Henry compromises; he maintains an ambivalence toward his group allegiance, wryly dubbing his outfit "the blue demonstration" (p. 8). This ambivalence, this desire to assert his individuality and the equally pressing need to abandon it, runs through not merely the opening chapters but the entire book. Yet in the world of *Red Badge,* there can be no doubt whatsoever about the outcome. Henry must surrender his individuality for the sake of simple survival.

He does so, however, begrudgingly, his ambivalence always in evidence. For example, Henry relies upon and damns his officers with monotonous regularity. One morning, in the ranks of his regiment ready at last to march into the unknown under the red eyes of the enemy troops across the river, Henry gazes into the east, and in his need for leadership he sees against the sun "black and patternlike . . . the gigantic figure of the colonel on a gigantic horse" (p. 14). *Patternlike* is the key word here, the presence of the officer obliterating Henry's fear and confusion. But *black* is equally important, carrying as it does the threat of annihilation of self. This probability is forgotten though, as "the rolling crashes of an engagement come to his ears," and the officer, displaying beneficent self-control, "lift[s] his gigantic arm and calmly stroke[s] his mustache" (p. 14).

The threat of lost individuality is also forgotten when the men finally move into combat and Henry yields himself totally to the saving embrace of the group:

> He became not a man but a member. He felt that something of which he was a part . . . was in a crisis. He was welded into a common personality which was dominated by a single desire. . . . [The noise of the regiment] gave him assurance. . . . It wheezed and banged with a mighty power. . . . There was a consciousness always of the presence of his comrades about him. He felt the subtle battle brotherhood more potent even than the cause for which they were fighting. It was a mysterious fraternity born of the smoke and danger of death (p. 31).

Crane's description of the fearlessness his soldiers enjoy during this part of the battle is similar to an account of the loss of fear on the part of concentration-camp inmates given in Bruno Bettelheim's *Informed Heart.* Forced to stand in the cold without adequate clothing and any chance to help their dying friends, the prisoners confronted a "situation which obviously the prisoner as an individual could not meet successfully."

> Therefore, the individual as such had to disappear in the mass. Threats by the guards become ineffective because the mental attitude of most prisoners was now changed. Whereas before they had feared for themselves and tried to protect themselves as well as possible, they now became depersonalized. It was as if giving up individual existence and becoming part of a mass seemed in some way to offer better chances for survival, if not for the person, at least for the group.[5]

But just as the prisoners are unable to sustain their fearlessness and sense of power, so Henry soon feels his courage drain from him, and in the following exchange of fire he runs away. Henry's flight has been foreshadowed by more than his fearful anticipations before the battle. His perception of the officers as benign authorities who promise an end to chaos and the comfort he has derived from the ambience of the "blue demonstration" has been qualified by his growing suspicion that the officers are idiots who send the men "marching into a regular pen" (p. 23). The "blue demonstration" threatens to rob him of his will; marching into battle he sees "that it would be impossible for him to escape from the regiment. It inclosed him. And there were iron laws of tradition and law on four sides. He was in a moving box" (p. 21).

Consequently, though motivated by fear, Henry's flight has implications of which Henry remains unaware but which suggest themselves to the reader because of the traditional nature of the flight itself. Like a great number of American literary figures—Huck, Rip, Goodman Brown, the *persona* of "Song of Myself," an endless list of others—Henry abandons his society and lights out for the territories. One more romantic egoist, Henry resigns his membership in the society which would demand from him the relinquishment of his perfect freedom. Though he is most assuredly no student, he would seem to have imbibed his share of Transcendentalism from the very air of nineteenth-century America and would claim for himself Emerson's "infinitude of the private man."

But in the following moment, the reader is reminded that this is *Red Badge* and not Emerson's *Nature*. Henry enters the forest chapel and learns, most hideously, that the woods will no longer serve as nursery to the burgeoning soul:

> Near the threshold he stopped, horror-stricken at the sight of a thing.
> He was being looked at by a dead man who was seated with his back against a column-like tree. The corpse was dressed in a uniform that once had been blue, but was now faded into a mel-

ancholy shade of green. The eyes, staring at the youth, had changed to the dull hue to be seen on the side of a dead fish. The mouth was open. Its red had changed to an appalling yellow (pp. 43–44).

This scene marks the impasse at which, one after the other, the romantic heroes of the last half of the nineteenth century find themselves. Huck discovers that the Mississippi flows inexorably into the heartland of slavery, and James's Isabel Archer, to name only one other, discovers that the highroad of unlimited choice terminates within the walls of the Palazzo Roccanera. Henry Fleming learns to his horror that nature culminates in the forest chapel.

Nature and morality, once fused by the transcendentalists, are now divided, and the division has wide-ranging consequences. First, nature itself becomes foreign and treacherous. The branches in the forest chapel threaten to push Henry onto the corpse. Second, the individualism that Henry is capable of imagining as a substitute for his life in the army is no longer Emersonian, no longer expansive and life-enhancing, but isolating, atomistic. Self-reliance, drained of moral content by the time Crane is writing, has degenerated to mere selfishness. Whitman's "man in the open air" has become only a corpse propped against a tree. The third consequence is societal and needs a further paragraph of amplification.

Made aware of his experience with the corpse of the inadequacy of his individualism, Henry tries to rejoin the army. Marching up the road in a crowd of soldiers, Henry "regarded the wounded soldiers in an envious way. He conceived persons with torn bodies to be peculiarly happy. He wished that he, too, had a wound, a red badge of courage" (p. 49). This image appears in the first paragraph of chapter 9 and is paired at the end of the chapter with a highly similar image, the notorious: "The red sun was pasted in the sky like a wafer" (p. 53). The referent of "wafer" must remain a puzzle, but perhaps it is of little importance. The crucial fact about the sentence is its reductive effect. The setting sun is reduced to a trivial, two-dimensional dot merely pasted in the sky. This reduction may be considered as a further consequence of the lost transcendental fusion of nature and morality. Associating the paired images suggests, and added consideration confirms, that the image at the first part of the chapter is also perhaps reductive. To think of a wound as a badge is, indeed, to trivialize human suffering. Furthermore, we may say that if the nature-morality split diminishes nature, the same split brutalizes society. Henry knows that it is in society's eyes that a wound is a badge of courage. Society, stripped of morality, then, is not community, but is brutal collectivity. Consequently, Henry's hungering for a wound signifies a desire to surrender personal morality to the demands of collectivization, a sacrifice which perhaps Crane sensed might be increasingly demanded of men in the twentieth century.

Henry, on the other hand, has no comprehension of the moral implications of the wound, but he is a witness to its physical import when he sees Jim Conklin die. Conklin has served from the novel's opening as a warning, apparent only in retrospect, against whole-hearted identification with the group. Prior to their first battle, Conklin exhibits a blissful unconcern. This compliance with the dictates of the war machine marks him for destruction; and in the moments of his death, he remains in some hideous, indefinable way, a willing collaborator in the perverted mystic ceremony of war: "There was something ritelike in these movements of the doomed soldier. And there was a resemblance in him to a devotee of a mad religion, blood-sucking, muscle-wrenching, bone crushing" (p. 52). Like a "devotee of a mad religion," Conklin enacts the roles of both priest and sacrifice. The passive surrender of personal initiative in his early behavior culminates in a sort of self-destruction.

Having witnessed Conklin's death, Henry can no longer yearn for a red badge, that emblem of membership in the group, for he sees that the badge is deadly. He is forced in chapter 10 to take up the other alternative, which if not he then at least the reader already realizes is equally hopeless, his earlier atomistic individualism. In fact, so empty are the alternatives, that it is not until he is goaded into choosing by the mindless yammering of the zombie-like tattered soldier that Henry decides to run. But as the forest chapel scene demonstrated, individualism offers no adequate sanctuary, and in a short time Henry is led back to his regiment.

II

With Henry's return at the beginning of the second half of the novel, the dominant motif, that archetypal American movement of alternating escape and return, is several times repeated, even though there is no possibility of any genuine escape. The attempted escapes, however, are no longer physical; rather, they become a matter of allegiances and commitments. When Henry's individuality dominates, he curses the army. As the novel moves closer to its conclusion, he identifies increasingly with the army.

Quite understandably, Henry's initial loyalty upon returning is to the regiment. Wounded and exhausted, he sees in the figures of the sleeping men an image of content, and after having his wound dressed he sleeps among his comrades. But in chapter 14 he awakes: "He believed for an instant that he was in the house of the dead, and he did not dare to move lest these corpses start up, squalling and squawking" (p. 73). Only a moment passes before he realizes that "this somber picture was not a fact of the present, but a mere prophecy." The prophecy is accurate on two levels: first, of course, many of the men will be killed in the forthcoming skirmishes. But, second, the men are all doomed to die in a spiritual sense as they surrender themselves more and more to the demands of the army.

With some sort of recognition of this second meaning, Henry is unwilling to accept the officers' leadership. At the beginning of the new day's combat, furious at the evidence of the Union defeat, Henry cries out, " 'B'jiminey, we're generaled by a lot 'a lunkheads.' " Wilson, however in terms reminiscent of Jim Conklin's, defends the commanding general: " 'Mebbe, it wa'n't all his fault—not all to-gether. He did th' best he knowed. It's our luck t' git licked often,' said his friend in a weary tone. He was trudging along with stooped shoulders and shifting eyes like a man who has been caned and kicked" (p. 81). Wilson may have the better of the argument, but he is a beaten man. The great cost of what we may call his collective vision is but partially revealed in this passage.

It is more fully revealed as further instances of the collective vision are disclosed. In the following action, "deeply absorbed as a spectator" (p. 109), Henry observed the battle:

> The regiment bled extravagantly. Grunting bundles of blue began to drop. The orderly sergeant of the youth's company was shot through the cheeks. Its supports being injured, his jaw hung afar down, disclosing in the wide cavern of his mouth a pulsing mass of blood and teeth. And with it all he made attempts to cry out. In his endeavor there was a dreadful earnestness, as if he conceived that one great shriek would make him well (p. 110).

Though the events being described here are horrible, the style drains them of emotional content. This is precisely the cost of the collective vision—affectlessness. Throughout the novel, Crane's famous irony insists upon the unspeakable lesson: as he continues to surrender his autonomy to the overwhelming pressure of collectivization, modern man will most likely lose even the capacity to feel.

Another characteristic of the collective view might be noted here. Possibly, it is not so "enlarging and ruthlessly revealing" as critic James Colvert says.[6] On their way to fill the canteens, Henry and Wilson have a chance for a collective view of the battle:

> From their position . . . they could of course comprehend a greater amount of the battle than when their visions had been blurred by the hurling smoke of the line. They could see dark stretches winding along the land, and on one cleared space there was a row of guns making gray clouds, which were filled with large flashes of orange-colored flame. Over some foliage they could see the roof of a house. One window, glowing a deep murder red, shone squarely through

the leaves. From the edifice a tall leaning tower of smoke went far into the sky (p. 89).

It is true that this view is enlarging, but only in spatial terms, and with such a view one is bound to feel insignificant. But it should be noted that it is in such passages that Crane's style is at its most impressionistic. Though the view is broad, it consists of no more than a bundle of discrete images, for neither Henry nor the narrator supplies the conceptual strands which would weave the images into a fabric of meaning. The passage even suggests that meaning might be impossible to achieve on any plane more profound than the purely aesthetic one, impressionism having, as Richard Chase points out, "implications that are pessimistic, irrationalist, and amoral since its technique is to break down into a shimmering flow of experience the three dimensions that symbolized rationality and religious and social order in traditional art."[7]

Finally, on the psychological level, it must be noted that these paragraphs of the collective mass view follow immediately upon a passage that demands distancing and impressionism if one is to retain his sanity. Jimmie Rogers has been wounded: "He was thrashing about in the grass, twisting his shuddering body into many strange postures. He was screaming loudly. This instant's hesitation seemed to fill him with a tremendous, fantastic contempt, and he damned them in shrieked sentences" (p. 89). And off Henry and Wilson go with the canteens. The collective view here, then, seems motivated not by any desire to see reality, but rather to escape it. Motivation need not wholly determine perception, but it certainly qualifies it as we know. At any rate, all the considerations I am discussing here combine to suggest that the collective view may serve not only to humble a man but to delude and diminish him.

More references to man's diminished stature follow. The officers are referred to as "critical shepherds struggling with sheep." The regiment itself is lost in the noise of battle, the battle, in turn, lost in a world "fully interested in other matters" (p. 92). These images serve as background for Henry's and Wilson's crucial withholding from the men their knowledge of the great dangers involved in the impending charge. As a consequence, the virtues implicit in that decision are undermined. Without doubt, their choice to remain silent has elements of selflessness, loyalty, and certainly valor. But the context of the decision suggests that they remain mute also because they are feeling the pressures of the collective vision and its attendant, self-diminishing impressionism.

In the climactic battle of the book, Henry yields to those pressures. Charging across the field "like a madman," Henry undergoes the change he had yearned for before the battle. Unprotected and essentially alone, thirsting for help and protection, he finds it in the flag, "a creation of beauty and invulnerability . . . a goddess, radiant . . . that called him with the voice of his hopes. Because no harm could come to it he endowed it with power" (pp. 96–97). Unable to protect himself, Henry again chooses to submerge himself in the group; but this time he does so wholeheartedly, abandoning that remnant of individuality that had insisted earlier upon a wry aloofness from the group, derisively dubbing it the "blue demonstration." With the identification he makes now, Henry finds the strength to conduct himself nobly in battle, but there can be no mistake about the price he has unwittingly paid. The flag he carries, the emblem of group allegiance, does not belong to living men. The corpse from whom they wrest it tries to warn Henry and Wilson that to serve the flag is to die, but the warning is of no avail. "One arm [of the corpse] swung high, and the curved hand fell with heavy protest on the friend's unheeding shoulder" (p. 97).

In the final chapters, the ultimate consequences of Henry's un-qualified identification with the group unfold. This is accomplished primarily by a continued alternation of two points of view, the private and the collective, until Henry wholly surrenders his belief in the validity of his own perceptions and memories.

Having driven off the light contingent of rebels, the regiment, at the end of chapter 20, regains the "impetus of enthusiasm" (p. 102). But when they return to their line and the mockery of the veterans, they quickly lose it. Henry looks back at the ground they have just covered:

> He discovered that the distances, as compared with the brilliant measurings of his mind, were trivial and ridiculous. The stolid trees, where much had taken place, seemed incredibly near. The time, too, now that he reflected, he saw to have been short. . . .Elfin thoughts must have exaggerated and enlarged everything, he said.
>
> It seemed, then, that there was bitter justice in the speeches of the gaunt and bronzed veterans (p. 103).

Now the point is not that here, regarding his actions in spectator fashion, he is right and earlier wrong, for actually both impressions are correct. At the time of the battle, Henry's perception was accurate, the way was long and hard; in denying this, in accepting the point of view of the veterans, Henry betrays himself and his fellows. The glance of disdain he gives them is, however, not simply unjust. It is a tacit denial of the testimony of his own senses. Having made this, Henry is all the more vulnerable to the opinion of the general that the men are nothing but "a lot of mud diggers" (p. 104). Of course the men all rage at this unjust treatment. Their personal perceptions are still weighty enough to prevent their utter abasement by the opinion of the officer. But Crane is extremely shrewd at this point. If the men are able to maintain their personal points of view in the face of the officers' condemnations, they are not able to hold out against their praise. Told that the colonel said they deserve to be "major generals," Henry and Wilson are elated, "and their hearts swelled with grateful affection for the colonel and the youthful lieutenant" (p. 107). Given what Crane has told us about the psychology of the battlefield, we question whether the officers' praise has any meaning. But the real importance of the chapter lies in its revelation of the degree to which Henry's opinion of himself is becoming increasingly determined by the official version of his behavior.

Therefore, after the following victory and subsequent retreat (the logic of the battlefield remaining absurd to the end) when Henry remembers his behavior, his reflections are not easily acceptable as reliable judgment of his past:

> he began to study his deeds, his failures, and his achievements. Thus, fresh from scenes where many of his usual machines of reflection had been idle, from where he had proceeded sheeplike, he struggled to marshal all his acts.
>
> At last they marched before him clearly. From this present viewpoint he was enabled to look upon them in spectator fashion and to criticize them with some correctness, for his new condition had already defeated certain sympathies (p. 117).

By now there can be little doubt in our minds that viewing events in "spectator fashion" offers no assurance of discovering the truth. The spectator's way is the collective way, the way of the officers, remote, impressionistic, inhumanly dispassionate. Contrary to his opinion, Henry has not been "good," a moral term which has questionable validity as applied to men in the chaos of combat. And in a moment, his self-congratulations congeal as, in a "wretched chill of sweat," he recalls his desertion of the tattered soldier. "A specter of reproach came to him. There loomed the dogging memory of the tattered soldier—he who, gored by bullets and faint for blood, had fretted concerning an imagined wound in another; he who had loaned his last of strength and intellect for the tall soldier; he who, blind with weariness and pain, had been deserted in the field" (p. 117).

But this recollection, too, is inaccurate. It is true that Henry deserted him, and it is perhaps true that this was indeed profoundly criminal; but in being inaccurate, in constructing as he does here a sentimentalized version of the tattered soldier, a version replete with the sentimental cadences of the fundamentalist pulpit, he is being criminal again. He left the tattered soldier because of a complex of reasons and circumstances, which we can sum up by saying that he was being forced to take up the red badge of the mass man but chose at that desperate moment the alternative of atomistic individualism.

Perhaps the choice was wrong. It certainly served as no viable alternative. But in not adequately comprehending in this last chapter the stakes and circumstances that were then involved, and in "maturely" forgiving himself a little for that "sin"—without fully understanding its real nature—Henry runs a great risk of slipping ever more deeply into the role of mindless foot soldier. And we must consequently shudder when Henry, marching along with his fellows, knows "that he would no more quail before his guides wherever they should point" (p. 118). For we end almost where we began: to escape his fear of isolation. Henry will lose himself, not in the wryly dubbed "blue demonstration," but in something far more insidious, the "procession of weary soldiers" of the novel's final page.

III

Given the reading I have offered, it is impossible to take the final four paragraphs as either intentionally straightforward or ironic in tone. My insistence upon the wholly unambiguous implications of Henry's final commitment to his regiment nullifies the possibility of a straightforward reading and renders the irony so painfully obvious as to make of Crane a hopelessly inept artist. That being emphatically not the case, I conclude with Richard Chase that these paragraphs reflect Crane's embarrassment "about the necessity of pointing a moral."[8]

Yet, I would go further and suggest the possibility that Crane was a victim of more than just the demands of the reading public of his time. In including these final paragraphs, Crane is being strongly prompted to refuse to acknowledge the logic of his own art by a cultural force. In spite of the corpse in the forest chapel, the death of Emersonian self-reliance it symbolizes, Crane is compelled to insist upon his anti-institutional legacy, the anarchic dream of Emerson and Thoreau. Henry again escapes, if only in thought, to roam fields of clover and fresh meadows.

Crane insists in these last paragraphs upon Emersonian individualism, upon the impossible American dream of escape from history. Though it tear art works apart, as it does the last of this one, as it does the final fifth of *Huckleberry Finn*, and though it sink the nation, as it does the *Pequod*, the dream persists, measuring our institutions and, no less important, our lives. Having dramatized the forces in modern America which were increasingly demanding the subservience of human needs to those of the machine, Crane insists at the final moment—unconvincingly—that man might escape his self-imposed servitude. By doing so, Crane in effect redefines the dream, showing in the vastly limited possibility of its realization how precious is its vision of Emersonian individualism.

Red Badge, then, takes its place with those other works in our literature that constitute an evolving definition of that complex, protean American Dream of anarchic freedom. Wildly extravagant, certainly no proper goal if we are to survive as a free society, that dream must yet be cherished, indeed now more than in the past, as the profoundly valuable counterweight to the increasingly urgent search for community that is properly bound to occupy Americans in the decades to come.

Notes

1. See, for example, any of the following: Stanley B. Greenfield, "The Unmistakable Stephen Crane," *PMLA*, 73 (Dec. 1958), 562–72; John E. Hart, *"The Red Badge of Courage* as Myth and Symbol," *University of Kansas City Review*, 19 (Summer 1953), 249–56; Maynard Solomon, "Stephen Crane: A Critical Study," *Masses and Mainstream*, 9 (Jan. 1955), 32–41; and, of course, R. W. Stallman, Introduction to the Modern Library edition of *The Red Badge of Courage*. Other straightforward readings are to be found in the excellent Norton critical edition of *Red Badge*, eds., Sculley Bradley, R. C. Beatty, and E. H. Long, for example, the essays by Eric Solomon and Edward Stone. For two more recent straightforward readings see John Fraser, "Crime and Forgiveness: The Red Badge in Time of War," *Criticism*, 9 (Summer 1967), 243–56; and John J. McDermott, "Symbolism and Psychological Realism in *The Red Badge of Courage*," *Nineteenth-Century Fiction*, 23 (Dec. 1968), 324–31.

2. James B. Colvert, "Structure and Theme in Stephen Crane's Fiction," *Modern Fiction Studies*, 5 (Autumn 1959), 207.

3. Charles Child Walcutt, *American Literary Naturalism, A Divided Stream* (Minneapolis: Univ. of Minnesota Press, 1956), pp. 81–82.

4. Stephen Crane, *The Red Badge of Courage,* ed. Richard Chase (Boston: Houghton Mifflin, 1960, Riverside Editions), p. 4. Subsequent references to this edition will appear in my text.

5. Bruno Bettelheim, *The Informed Heart* (Glencoe: The Free Press, 1960), p. 137.

6. Colvert, p. 200.

7. Richard Chase, Introduction to *The Red Badge of Courage* (Boston: Houghton Mifflin, 1960), p. xii.

8. Ibid., p. xiii

Introduction:
The Red Badge of Courage   J. C. Levenson

The most important book that lies behind *The Red Badge* is Tolstoy's *Sebastopol*, which came into Crane's hands early and impressed him profoundly. It provided him a norm for realism in an account of war. Because it pointed the way in which he would go beyond the conventions of American realism, it reminds us that in the 1890s, as before and since, a fresh access to major European writing has helped young Americans to become strongly original. It even helped bring together the generations of American realists, for Howells, overwhelmed by his reading of Tolstoy in the mid-1880s, had become the first major critic in the English-speaking world to declare the Russian's central importance. Howells continued his ardent advocacy during the next decade and more as the reading public came to share his judgment. Nor did he conduct his advocacy in his critical writings only, as if it were only a matter of literary opinion. When young Theodore Dreiser met him, Howells urged the case so strongly that Dreiser, reporting the interview, concluded by quoting a Howells essay on Tolstoy: "I can never again see life in the way I saw it before I knew him. Tolstoy awakens in his reader the will to be a man; not effectively, not spectacularly, but simply, really. He leads you back to the only true ideal, away from the false standard of the gentleman, to the man who sought not to be distinguished from other men, but identified with them." Whether, five years earlier, Howells conveyed the same message to Crane in their first meeting, no one can know. There is a strong probability that he did so through the written word at least, and though the evidence is complex and takes the story back yet another five years, it gives an idea of Tolstoy's pervasive influence and his particular importance for Crane.[1]

Writing about the summer of 1888, when Crane was seventeen years old, Thomas Beer reported: "And a Canadian lady, nameless in the record, gave him a paper bound copy of Count Tolstoy's 'Sevastopol.' " In 1888, as the recognition of Tolstoy was quickening, three translations of *Sebastopol* had come out within two years. The paperback edition to which Beer refers, the translation of Laura E. Kendall, came out in the "Seaside Library" and was evidently intended for circulation in places like Asbury Park. Mrs. Kendall translated painstakingly from the Russian—her title-page refers to Count "Lyof"

° From *The Red Badge of Courage*, ed. Fredson Bowers, The University of Virginia Edition of *The Works of Stephen Crane*, vol. 2 (Charlottesville: University Press of Virginia, 1975), xl–xlvi, liv–lxix. Reprinted by permission of the University Press of Virginia.

Tolstoy—but she labored so hard at the task that she partly lost command of her native tongue. Her Russian-English dictionary style makes it difficult to get to Tolstoy, difficult enough so that quite possibly Crane would have tossed the book aside as he later did *La Débâcle.* He would not, however, have put down the fine translation from the French of Frank D. Millet, an American war correspondent whose clean idiomatic prose can hold the reader at every page. The Millet version, published in regular cloth binding by Harper's, lacks the supporting testimony of Beer that Crane had read it, but strong circumstantial evidence forces it into consideration. It had an introduction by Howells in which he praised Tolstoy for getting closer to human nature than any other writer. Howells praised the Russian's fidelity to "the life common to all men," and he singled out "Peace and War"—a locution also adopted by Crane for Tolstoy's novel—for its "great assertion of the sufficiency of common men in all crises, and the insufficiency of heroes." Howells' words seem to echo in the statement Crane later made when, speaking as the author of *The Red Badge,* he identified his own ideals with those of the Russian master: "I decided that the nearer a writer gets to life the greater he becomes as an artist, and most of my prose writings have been toward the goal partially described by that misunderstood and abused word, realism. Tolstoy is the writer I admire most of all." Even more they help explain Crane's words in the copy of *The Red Badge* which he gave to the older novelist: "To W. D. Howells this small and belated book as a token of the veneration and gratitude of Stephen Crane for many things he has learned of the common man and, above all, for a certain re-adjustment of his point of view victoriously concluded some time in 1892." At any rate the Tolstoy Crane admired was decidedly the author of *Sebastopol.* According to Beer, Crane as a nineteen-year-old college student was ready to declare Tolstoy the "world's foremost writer," and yet he apparently did not read *Kreutzer Sonata, War and Peace,* or *Anna Karenina* until well after finishing *The Red Badge,* and when he did read them, he expressed reservations about each of these works and tempered his enthusiasm accordingly. The judgment which he first made as a naïve boy, the mature writer confirmed with an assurance based on how the book stood up for him.[2]

What surely appealed to Crane was the way Tolstoy proved in his Crimean sketches how near a writer can get to life. Writing from the bastions of the besieged city, the young Russian officer, as he was then, proved sensitive to the whole multifarious world about him. In what he wrote, the action is at all points palpable; events register themselves on the senses without the mediation of received idea or hackneyed phrase. Some of the incidents, as Lars Ahnebrink first noted, may have been used by Crane: the overdramatic bestowal of letters to be sent home in case of death, the fraternizing of enemy troops during a lull, Vladimir Koseltzoff's inner struggle with cowardice. But incidents which have no parallel in *The Red Badge* seem equally close in feeling. The first of the book's three sketches, "Sebastopol in December, 1854," spans a fictive day from the first tinge of dawn till the dark of evening when, in the doomed city, "a regimental band is playing an old waltz, which sounds far over the water, and to which the cannonade of the bastions forms a strange and striking accompaniment." Everything is seen, heard, felt—the quietly courageous amputees and the newly wounded, screaming curses; the methodical surgeons at their work and the officer who calmly rolls a cigarette as shells go off around him; the archaic general who tells his troops, "Children, we will die, but we will not surrender Sebastopol," and the soldiers who reply, "We will die, hurrah!"[3]

Realism like this could be dangerous. Tolstoy, who began his book as a resolute patriot, ended with pictures of butchery and disarray that put him at odds with Tsarist censorship. But the danger did not lie merely with obvious content. The book was more powerful than censors could guess. Tolstoy himself believed so strongly in the importance of his convictions to his writing that he gave hardly more than a clue. But he lived up to the claim of having no hero but Truth, and in doing so he made a book which was unique in its being without a hero. Heroic acts were possible and men might sometimes be heroic, but the consistent pursuit of great purpose, such as traditionally defines heroism, is allowed to none of the characters. Nor is there, to put it somewhat differently, the consistent expression of great principles. The young Tolstoy had not yet framed the conception of history which in *War and Peace* delimits the powers of man or the vision of nature which transcends history. The world of *Sebastopol* far exceeds the comprehension of any character in the work, and the author gives no sign of knowing more than his characters. Committed to writing nothing but the truth, Tolstoy not only dissociated himself from the official point of view, but even took the youthful risk— *Sebastopol* is the early effort of a writer in his twenties—that he might subvert beliefs more fundamental than political allegiances. In fact, presenting the world as he did, he was undermining the rationalist assumption that man could in some degree understand and control his own destiny. Coherent meanings, in that world, seemed to occur only as parts happened momentarily to fit together. When Tolstoy juxtaposed waltzes and cannonades, oratory and anguish, the offense to ideologues and patriots should not conceal the greater threat to commonsense notions of how the world ought to work.

A brief digression may make it clearer how Tolstoy could help Crane move beyond the conventions of the older American realists. In contrast to *Sebastopol*, the *Personal Memoirs of U. S. Grant*, the finest realistic narrative to come directly from the Civil War experience, offered no offense to ideologues, patriots, or serious literary critics.[4] It was Howells' kind of book, as *The Red Badge* never was. For one thing, it began in history: Grant's clear, strong recognition of the political and social causes of the war makes it into a special phase of human history rather than a world that is simply given, behind which one can perceive no other way that things might be. Moreover, it had a clear, strong plot. From the moment of Grant's mustering volunteers at Galena, there is a consistent rising action. Grant grapples at first with bureaucratic tangles and undisciplined troops more than with the anarchic forces of actual conflict. But the scale of command gradually expands—from the Twenty-first Illinois Volunteers to the Department of the Tennessee to the armies of the West to the post of the general-in-chief of the Union armies. The military objectives become more difficult as well as more complex, yet Grant is able to impose his will and intelligence on events. The lucid imperturbable writing speaks for the same qualities in the man of action, and the book as a whole invites us to see the world as one in which heroic intelligence can master chaotic circumstance. There are no heroics, but Grant, for all his modesty, makes us see that a general can be a hero as judged not by archaic, but by widely held, current values. The book, which began in a couple of articles for the *Battles and Leaders* series, and which, heroically brought no completion by the dying Grant, became a best-seller, could not have escaped Crane's notice. No book should have appealed to him more, considering his pride in the military exploits of his Revolutionary ancestors, his having from early childhood played games of tactics and not just of fighting, his rise as a schoolboy cadet to the rank of captain, and his youthful hopes of going to West Point. But nothing in the record suggests that he responded in any way at all to a book which was everything that *The Red Badge* was not.

When commonly held values do not organize a literary work, other values come into play. In *Sebastopol* the controlling purposes of characters do not shape the action, but their collective authority as registers of experience brings out the objective ironies that are centers of meaning within the larger and seemingly incomprehensible world. As the fragmentary clarifications fall into a pattern, they suggest an implicit plot of discovery in which the young narrator arrives at his first decisive encounter with death. Tolstoy's last sketch ends with the deaths of two brothers. The older Koseltzoff thinks it is nonsense when he hears of the French assault, he feels pain for barely a moment when two bullets pierce his chest, and he reacts with little more than mechanical surprise when the doctor who examines him gives way to the priest. The priest offers comfort not so much by his prayer for the dying or his cross as by his falsehood to the effect that the Russian lines are holding. Mikhail Semenovitch, weeping with joy at the priest's lie, turns his last thought to his brother and wishes, "God grant him the same happiness!" Elsewhere in the battle the younger brother Vladimir (affectionately, Volodia) has had his taste of panic, but when he sees his orderly acting like a despicable coward, he feels his own courage flow back as if by a reflex. But it turns out that in the pinch the orderly fights and saves himself and, when he looks for his beloved lieutenant, sees no such man but only "a shapeless thing, clothed in a gray overcoat," lying "face to earth."[5] With these two episodes to which the whole narrative of *Sebastopol* has led, Tolstoy for all practical purposes defined the kinds of irony that were to be characteristic of Crane's writing about war: in the story of the older brother there is the ironic distance between delusion and fact, and in the story of the younger there is the ironic distance between character and event. Perhaps even more important than the lessons in irony is Tolstoy's ultimate nihilistic report on what war felt like. He let his narrative end in defeat, death, dispersal—the opposites of will, understanding, organized personal force such as might define not only heroism but life itself. For a realistic writer who wanted his reader to apprehend experience beyond the familiar, this was the last degree of otherness, beyond which there was nowhere to go. For Crane it was to be a theme to return to again and again throughout his career. . . .

In the last chapter of *The Red Badge* it turns out that his desertion of the tattered soldier is the "sin" which Henry Fleming must learn to live with and put at a distance, and the whole series of episodes leading up to the desertion allows him to say that he has "been to touch the great death and found that, after all, it was but the great death." These are the touchstones of his coming to manhood, and the narrative to this point warrants that they should be. In the second half of the novel, neatly complementary to the first, Fleming will go through a series of episodes in which he is the aggressor rather than the runaway, exploring rage rather than fear and learning in quite another sense how a man lives on close terms with death. In the second half, also, he attains a sense of comradeship based neither on the false fraternal sensations of mass behavior nor on terrible aware-ness of loss and betrayal: the friendship that develops between Flem-ing and Wilson is based on the shared experience of real events. The two halves hold together in that the test of maturity is for Fleming, having once run, to come back and fight another day. To get to his second half, however, Crane needed to invent a plausible and, if he could, a significant sequence of incidents that would bring the straggler back to his regiment. The success he eventually had in finishing the novel as he wanted conceals the difficulty he struggled with in the actual writing.

One reason for the difficulty, probably, was that he did not have his end precisely in view. He seems to have written with neither a detailed plan nor a scenario: no such working papers exist for *The Red Badge* or for any other of his novels except for the start of a plan and some deathbed notes for his unfinished novel, *The O'Ruddy*. With the *The Red Badge* he seems to have gone from draft to draft, writing ninety-some pages of a first draft before starting from the beginning on what became the final manuscript. He put plenty of effort into revision, but he did not plan. In his most circumstantial account of how he wrote his novels, he told a story which fits well with his discovery of how seriously challenging a subject he had taken up, his silent period of letting it germinate, and his testing the narrative among his studio friends as he went along. The interviewer for *The Illustrated American* reported:

> His method, he told me, is to get away by himself and think over things. "Then comes a longing for you don't know what; sorrow, too, and heart-hunger." He mixes it all up. Then he begins to write. The first chapter is immaterial; but, once written, it determines the rest of the book. He grinds it out, chapter by chapter, never knowing the end, but forcing himself to follow "that fearful logical conclusion;" writing what his knowledge of human nature tells him would be the inescapable outcome of those characters placed in those circumstances.[6]

Inescapable logic posed problems for Crane in two different ways. As for the narrative bridge he needed, he could at least be certain that there was a thematic coherence between the half of his novel that began in fear and ended with death, desertion, and despair, and the half that might begin in rage and end with Fleming's attaining a degree of control. He had a second plot, however, which seemed to get out of hand as he reached the climax of his novel. The plot was a plot of ideas, and it turned out that Crane, who could logically render the irrational surface of consciousness so well, had no such talent for dramatizing the intellectual progress of his central character. He got deeper into doing so than he intended. Eventually, in a victory of critical intelligence over instinct, he decided that his talent lay with understatement and he drastically cut and subordinated his second plot. But knowing that received ideas as well as unschooled emotions made the complications of Fleming's story, he did not present him as a creature of sensations only. Part of his aim was, to use once more the formulation of his final chapter, to tell how Fleming outgrew "the brass and bombast of his earlier gospels."

Brass and bombast meant in the first instance the dream of heroism that would account for so many excesses of emotion and behavior. In the opening chapter the words took on meaning in sensible terms: there was the frantic enthusiast who clanged the church bell "to tell the twisted news of a great battle," and then, when "the voice of the people" had done its work and Fleming enlisted, there was the "blue and brass" of his new appearance which he thought might flutter a schoolgirl's heart. The earlier gospels that he would have to relinquish would thus be the Homeric and chivalric tales from which he derived his grand illusions. Such definitions apply well enough to the whole novel to support the Q.E.D. of the ending. But in the course of the telling, Crane let the meanings shift and become more inclusive, as he fell into doing because he kept so close to the mind of his character. He let Fleming, despite the inadequacy of "mental slate and pencil," continually reflect on events, and before he was through, he had set up the stream of ideas as an expressive medium that vied with the stream of images. After his first skirmish, Fleming comments to himself: "It was surprising that nature had gone tranquilly on with her golden processes in the midst of so much devilment." The sentence cuts at once to the heart of Crane's metaphysics, which like his psychology depended on a simple, radical— and tenable—insight. Crane believed that, despite man's readiness to project ideas of order—and even attitudes toward himself—upon external nature, the universe is only a neutral backdrop to human activity. In asserting that nature could not provide sanctions for human value systems, he was in 1893 in an avant-garde of the tough-minded. William James's most eloquent statements of the argument were not yet set to paper, though others besides James could have cited the earlier American empiricist Chauncey Wright, who had long since described the natural universe as a background to human action that went on like the weather, doing and undoing.[7] Not that Crane knew the work of either philosopher; had he done so he might have handled his subject better. As matters stood, he was reduced to showing how, reacting to his own changeable situation, a man might regard nature in various ways. He showed how Fleming's ideas shifted with the *inner* weather, but he had no means, as he had with the irreducible finalities of the battle narrative, for conveying whether those ideas should be taken as valid. No doubt he would have liked to establish his irony on firmer ground and indicate subtly whether ideas were right or wrong, but he would not have denied that Fleming's philosophical divagations were, in the current jargon, ego trips. He would have liked the term, for he saw Fleming's adolescent reflections as consistently egotistical. The language in which Fleming frames his ideas expresses self-pity and self-congratulation in varying mixtures. It stands as the primary example of bombast in the novel as Crane was writing it.

Because Crane cut the key meditative passages out of the book, it is necessary to go to the surviving fragments of draft and manuscript, for only there can one see what the story was that forced itself into the narrative and eventually required of the novelist some of his hardest artistic decisions. First of all, they concern man and the universe rather than man and society. Fleming gives but one fleeting thought to the possibility that he was duped into his enlistment by a "merciless government." The book is as devoid of historical thought as it is of chronological or geographical location; though it flouts received ideas of patriotism or heroics, it does not call institutions into question. One reason lies in Fleming's (and Crane's) proclivity to jump at once to larger questions: "He rebelled against the source of things, according to his law that the most powerful should receive the most blame."[8] Secondly, the cut passages fill out the gamut of possible reactions which Fleming intellectualizes. In Chapter VII as it stands, the young man as he gets into the quiet of the woods personifies Nature as benign and maternal, "with a deep aversion to tragedy." When he casually tosses a pinecone at a squirrel and makes it run, he notes the squirrel's not "baring his furry belly to the missile" as earlier he might have noted that veterans do not expose themselves like duelists; seeing the squirrel's prudence in running away, he takes it as a sign that "nature was of his mind" and "reinforced his argument with proofs." After the encounter with the decaying corpse in the forest chapel, Crane did not originally leave the chapter with Fleming's illusions simply deflated. Instead of ending with the soft wind and sad silence that belonged to the landscape as well as the character, he went on:

> Again Fleming was in despair. Nature no longer condoled with him. There was nothing, then, after all, in that demonstration she gave—the frightened squirrel fleeing aloft from the missile.
> He thought as he remembered the small animal capturing the fish and the greedy ants feeding upon the flesh of the dead soldier, that there was given another law which far-over-topped it—all life existing upon death, eating ravenously, stuffing itself with the hopes of the dead.
> And nature's processes were obliged to hurry [MS 65.20–30]

Because we have the cancelled passage at the bottom of the manuscript page but not the discarded next page on which the chapter once continued, we see only the beginning of a meditation on death as the ultimate law. But Crane, having made his point with the chapel scene, was hardly strengthening his case. The problem seems to reverse itself when hindsight is available, and one asks not why he cut the passage but why he put it in.

The key word seems to be *despair*, especially since the next such deleted passage occurs in Chapter X, just after Fleming's betrayal of the tattered soldier and his momentary horrified wish that he were dead. There is one more turn to Fleming's immediate reaction to the event as he considers the tattered man's questions to be knife thrusts that foreshadow society's probing to come, from which he will not be able to escape. There the chapter now ends. But in Crane's original version, both draft and manuscript, Fleming's "old rebellious feelings" return and are directed "against the source of things"—"War, he said bitterly to the sky, was a make-shift created because ordinary processes could not furnish deaths enough." He goes on, we know from the draft, to accuse nature of inventing glory in order to seduce men to fight: "From his pinnacle of wisdom, he regarded the armies as large collection of dupes. Nature's dupes, who were killing each other to carry out some great scheme of life." He works himself into a rage, turning his "tupenny fury upon the high, tranquil sky," but the emotion is crossed with bitter self-congratulation that "among all men, he should be the only one sufficiently wise to understand these things." When purposeful action is balked, cosmic feelings come welling to the surface of consciousness, and from the depths of self-contempt, Fleming raises himself to a pinnacle of illusory wisdom.

When Fleming's consciousness is once again in touch with outward events, as it is immediately thereafter in Chapter XI, Crane had him repeat the same wild emotional swings. When he sees disorganized, fear-swept troops retreating, he takes comfort in supposing that their disorder vindicates his own flight. Yet when he sees an advancing column, he can so envy them as once more to wish himself a hero, even a dead hero. The surge of that old emotion lets him briefly feel "sublime," but as soon as he thinks of the difficulties of rejoining his unit, his "fire" begins to wane. Back then from heroic illusion through bafflement to self-hate. Because he can think of no answer to the questions which the world will surely ask, he is thrust back into confusion. The only salve for "the sore badge of his dishonor" would be a general defeat of the army, which would mean for him a vindication. But then he recognizes how murderous his wishes are and—"Again he thought that he wished he was dead." As a last hope it occurs to him that he might invent "a fine tale which he could take back to his regiment and with it turn the expected shafts of derision." But he cannot invent, he can only think of the barbs that will hit home. In whatever direction his mind casts, action is blocked.

At this point in the novel Crane brilliantly resolved the impasse in his plot, but in the writing he first took time—in his original Chapter XII—to let the impasse itself have ample expression. In a way the discarded chapter represented a false lead for him: instead of seeing the war from the inside, he was seeing his character from the inside. Feelings without an immediate context of fact raised the same doubts as facts without human response to them. But the chapter is nevertheless of great interest. If, as is probable, the impasse in Fleming's career was matched by an impasse Crane had reached in the composition of his novel, then the chapter is a unique document of the author's imaginative effort to find his way out. He groped his way through patterns of thematic development that in the following chapter he would handle as narrative incidents. At the very least the chapter stands as Crane's experiment with a kind of psychological system quite different from the others he suggested in the course of the novel, one for which he did not have a language, but which has to be taken seriously. The possibility is remote that he knew anything of Schopenhauer or of Nietzsche, but if he was inventing his own crude version of a birth of tragedy, he was also providing fresh evidence that the philosophers offer perfected models of the way others think. Crane depicted the illusion of the secure personality, clear-sighted, standing alone and able to hold out in its identity; in Schopenhauer's figure, it is like a small ship that successfully resists being engulfed by storm. In the midst of almost overwhelming turmoil, such a one sees underlying order and confidently maintains its own individuality. Counter to this is the psychology of the self which, thwarted in its worldly aims, sees the apparent order of things as false and, yearning for the collapse of formal limits and inauthentic order, wants to return to a primordial unity. In this scheme the personality lacks a sense of purposeful integration; feeling beset and pulled in all directions, it wants the relief of being restored to wholeness, absorbed into a totality that embraces all things. The two schemes underscore the connection of personality and culture, for whether they be called by Nietzsche's terms Apollonian and Dionysian or not, the psychological models correspond to basic cultural configurations.

Crane seems spontaneously to have developed this model in his draft. When the original Chapter XII picks up Fleming's stream of thought shortly after he has found himself totally blocked, he has made the jump to an illusory security:

> It was always clear to Fleming that he was entirely different from other men, that he had been cast in a unique mold. Also, he regarded his sufferings as peculiar and unprecedented. No man had ever achieved such misery. There was a melancholy grandeur in the isolation of his experiences. He saw that he was a speck raising his [tiny *deleted*] minute arms against all possible forces and fates which were swelling down upon him like storms. He could derive some consolation from viewing [his *deleted*] the sublimity of the odds.

> But, as he went on, he began to feel that, after all, [his rebellion, nature perhaps had not concentrated herself against him, or, at least, that *deleted*] nature would not blame him for his rebellion. He still distinctly felt that he was arrayed against the universe but he began to believe that there was no malice agitating [his *deleted*] the vast breasts of his space-filling foes. [He w *deleted*] It was merely law. [MS (d) 84.1–19; Va. 177.10–23]

Crane made it clear that the sense of uniqueness, by which Fleming asserted his individuality, was a matter of spiritual pride: "His egotism made him feel [safe *deleted*] secure for a time from the iron hands." The grand law which Fleming sees is that all things "fight or flee . . . resist or hide" according to how strong or wise they may be, and on this basis he feels justified in resisting the forces of exposure that pursue him. Presumably the irony is also intended whereby, following this higher law, Fleming hopes he may be saved from the iron hands of the merely "inevitable." One reason for thinking so is that in the paragraph before the inevitable seems to lose its inevitability, Fleming has allowed himself "a small grunt of satisfaction as he saw with what brilliancy he had reasoned it all out." Secure in such reasoning, he passes judgment on his own flight: "It was not a fault; it was a law." The whole meditative excursus which leads to this climax can be seen as a curious sublimation of the wish for general military defeat, which Fleming thought would be his moral vindication. Having ruled out that wish, he has built instead "a vindicating structure of great principles."

The second phase of this meditative chapter begins with the collapse of the vindicating structure. In Fleming's view "it was the calm toes of tradition that kicked it all down about his ears." Because men blindly stick to what the dead past has told them to believe, they will not accept his new wisdom. The enlightened calm of the reasoner gives way to vatic utterance as Fleming feels himself "the growing prophet of a world-reconstruction." Instead of explaining things as they are in the external world, he now speaks from "far down in the pure depths of his being," from "the gloom of his misery." With a quick swing from despair to self-intoxication, he is sure that all men will adhere to his new gospel. Instead of on a pinnacle of wisdom, he now sees himself "a sun-lit figure upon a peak" (at least he is gesturing, not preaching), and instead of his supposed wisdom being undercut by illogicality, his heart-wrung truth is undercut by bombast. But such bombast reaches its nadir only after he recognizes that his dream of freeing all men from false tradition, like his vindicating structure of reason, must collapse. When he recognizes that "he would be beating his fists against the brass of accepted things," he gives way to abuse and railing. When most carried away, however, he still remains egotistical: "To him there was something terrible and awesome in these words spoken from his heart to his heart. He was very tragic." Thus far the draft fragment, but of the surviving leaves from the discarded chapter in the later manuscript, a couple carry us further into Crane's original version—Fleming has reached a stage in which the suffering of the unheeded prophet passes beyond tragic bombast to pure incoherence. He possibly recalls that he was seeking a salve for "the sore badge of his dishonor," for he reuses the word and thus reminds readers of what has caused his perplexities: "For himself, however, he saw no salve, no reconciling opportunities. He was entangled in errors." He rages against "circumstances," bemoans his "martyrdom," fumbles in his "mangled intellect" (!) to find the ultimate cause, which is of course nature. In a perfect expression of disintegrated personality, he wishes his collapse upon the world: "He desired to revenge himself upon the universe. Feeling in his body all spears of pain, he would have capsized, if possible, the world and made chaos." But the trouble is that he has expressed suffering without in any way advancing the plot.

The treatment of tragic passion and moral confusion in this way was simply not Crane's style—quite literally not his style, as a couple of touches in the later manuscript suggest. Revising and embellishing as he rewrote, Crane began the chapter with the original opening sentence, but after stating Fleming's conviction that "his mind had been cast in a unique mold," he went on to elaborate not only the idea but also the image. The more he developed the image, the more he made the passage sound like authentic Crane: "Minds, he said, were not [all *deleted*] made all with one stamp and colored green. . . . The laws of the [wrong *deleted*] world were wrong because through the vain spectacles of their makers, he appeared, with all men, as of [the *deleted*] a common size and of a green color." This witty reference to dollar-bill conformity reminds us of the outside world and of the darts and barbs of public derision which had once been Henry Fleming's great fear, but such wit deflects attention from the boy's introverted thrashing around and from his inability to focus on anything outside himself. Similarly, intellectual agonies do not mix with humor, as another manuscript passage (for which we do not have the draft version) indicates. When the would-be prophet sees that he may not convert the human race, his mind, for a moment like the runaway soldier's, turns to other people: "He saw himself chasing a thought-phantom across the sky before the assembled eyes of mankind. He could say to them that it was an angel whose possession was existence perfected; they would declare it to be a greased pig." It is a literary if not a psychic impossibility that Henry Fleming, after chasing a greased pig on one page, should shake the foundations of the universe on the next.

Although it was not his style, the writing of this chapter gave a peculiarly direct expression of his method. The comment he made on his method of novel-writing suggests that the author represented his balked and floundering character with the help of firsthand knowledge: " 'Then comes a longing for you don't know what; sorrow, too, and heart-hunger.' He mixes it all up. Then he begins to write." The mixed-up quality of the original Chapter XII, which is to say the relative lack of conscious control, invites one to take with less qualification than otherwise Garland's remark that Crane's "mind was more largely subconscious in its workings than that of any man of my acquaintance."[9] But it was the craftsmanly and not the personal subconscious that he was talking about. No doubt there are personal disclosures here: where Fleming rails against the world, Crane can be said to hint a certain resentment of his own. The reference to minds stamped of a size and colored green suggests that money is not his measure, especially when put with Fleming's later comment on those who learned to reconcile themselves with the world and "accept the [cla *deleted*] stone idols and the greased pigs, when they contemplated the opportunities for plunder." Considering how poor Crane was while he worked on *The Red Badge*—poor enough to go without meals and once, at least, to have gone without shoes—the wonder is that the hints are so slight. More consciously but still not quite in control, he carried his analysis of youthful emotion back to childhood images. When Fleming decides that he will stand out against the "inevitable," he determines "to kick and scratch and bite like a child in the hands of a parent," and the Oedipal pattern of his revolt is emphasized by the superficially bowdlerized revision in the manuscript, "as a stripling in the hands of a murderer." In the manuscript there are more such primal images of the revolt against authority. When Fleming would, if possible, bring chaos back again, his next following thought is of impotence: "Much cruelty lay in the fact that he was [without power *deleted*] a babe." Since he cannot fight, he thinks of hiding:

> Admitting that he was powerless and at the will of law, he yet planned to escape; menaced by fatality he schemed to avoid it. He thought of various places in the world where he imagined that he would be safe. He remembered [once *deleted*] hiding once in an empty flour-barrel that [had *deleted*] sat in his mother's pantry. His playmates, hunting the [p *deleted*] bandit-chief, had thundered on the barrel with their fierce sticks but he had lain snug and undetected. They had searched the house. He now created in thought a secure spot where an all-powerful eye would fail to perceive him; where an all-powerful stick would fail to bruise his life. [MS 102.17–20; Va. 142.26–35]

This flight of imagination, despite its clinical refinement of detail, was wasted effort for Crane since he had already handled the theme of regression far more successfully in the episode of the forest chapel. But not all his efforts in this chapter repeated what had gone before. Of the trial imaginings that carried him forward to the turning point of his main plot, perhaps the most interesting occurred when Fleming concentrated "the hate of his despair" upon nature. For once the fear of shameful exposure, vague and confused, is transformed explicitly into the fear of death, comparatively a healthy emotion in itself and reasonably connected with his experience of nature: "He again saw [the grim *deleted*] her grim [He *deleted*] dogs upon his trail. They were unswerving, merciless and would overtake him at the appointed time. His mind pictured the death of Jim Conklin and in the scene he saw the shadows of his fate."[10] The clue to what he wanted next to do in his narrative was far more explicit than anything else which Crane's groping imagination had touched on. It pointed him away from inner drama and toward consciousness fastened to realities, and it may have suggested the incident by which he could pull together the most important motifs of this chapter and keep it from being simply a wasted experiment.

As Crane wrote the next chapter, all the pieces fell into place. The column whose advance Fleming had admired as heroic comes sweeping back in disarray. As in a fairy story, his wish for a general rout has come true even though he retracted it. Having struggled in his own mind against "forces and fates [th *deleted*] which were swelling down upon him like storms" and against other imaginary "space-filling foes," he now faces, in the words of the draft, an objective foe "coming storm-wise to flood the army." He is still the would-be hero, with an "impulse to make a rallying speech, to sing a battle-hymn," but in this situation his bombast fails him. Instead he inarticulately repeats the words "Why—why—," the same words that had been his inarticulate answer to the tattered man's sensitive probing. When no one will stop to answer him, he clutches the arm of a running soldier, and the frantic runaway, unable to break free, smashes him across the head with his rifle. The spurting blood gives Fleming his wished-for red badge, but it is not merely a badge. The heavy blow tests his will to live. His dreams are now acted out. Struggling with his pain, he is "like a man wrestling with a creature of the air"—only this is no phantom. Half unconscious, he has to try to raise himself from the ground in order not to be trampled. At last he succeeds, twisting himself to his hands and knees and then "like a babe trying to walk" to his feet. Lurching forward with head down and eyes on the ground, he "fought an intense fight with his body. His dulled senses wished him to swoon and he opposed them stubbornly, his mind picturing unknown dangers and mutilations if he fell upon the field. He went forward, Conklin-fashion. He thought of secluded spots where he could fall and be unmolested. To reach [them, *deleted*] one, he strove against the tide of his pain."

With Fleming's arrival at his Conklin-like struggle against death, the pattern is complete. The incident occurs on the last page of the surviving draft, though Crane probably wrote on to the end of the chapter. In rounding off the chapter, Crane had Fleming meet up with a cheerful soldier, talkative and friendly, whose questions help him to identify Fleming's regiment—no answers beyond the first inarticulate "Uh" are presented—and whose chatter supports the injured youth, that is, becomes the total content of his awareness, until he is in sight of his proper campfire. The cheerful soldier leaves without Fleming ever looking up and seeing his face. He appears mysteriously and goes mysteriously. There is a fairy-tale quality to his role, and indeed to Fleming he seemed "to possess a wand of a magic kind. He threaded the mazes of the tangled forest with a strange fortune." He is indeed a wish fulfillment, but the fulfillment is plausible, given the wish. Crane's great task in the narrative was to render events, internal as much as external, which could lead logically to the framing of the wish. Before Fleming could rejoin his unit, Crane had to find out, as it were, whether his character wanted to die more than he wanted to live, and once the image of Jim Conklin came to mind, the question could define itself.

From the groping of the original twelfth chapter, what remained in the eventual twelfth chapter (originally Chapter XIII), included two interesting vestiges. One was a reference back to discarded material. Caught in the swirl of the rout, Fleming "forgot he was engaged in combating the universe. He threw aside his mental pamphlets on the philosophy of the retreated and rules for the guidance of the damned." (In the manuscript Crane made the restoration to an objective world even clearer by adding: "He lost concern for himself.") Again, when Fleming is barely able to lurch and shuffle forward, he engages in interior argument once more, but this time it is specifically on the question of giving up or pressing on to safety: "He often tried to dismiss the question but his body persisted in rebellion and his senses nagged at him like pampered babies." The imagery of authority and rebellion, of adulthood and childishness, has been reversed. Instead of feeling inchoate rebelliousness and regressive longings, which could have made him want to yield to the physical blow and its effect, he fights to live. That means fighting against the forces of confusion, finding the irreducible purpose which, even in an imperfectly organized world, cannot be dispensed with.

In the original Chapter XIII Crane did much more than untangle the snarled materials of Chapter XII. Fleming had wished for a rout and the wish came true, he had wished for a wound and the wish came true, he had wished for a way to rejoin his unit and the wish came true. Events plausible in themselves connected with wishes plausible in themselves, and yet there is something fortuitous in the connection of wishes and fulfillments. Discrete incidents do not fall into a causal relation as that is traditionally conceived. So Fleming's wish to be a hero turns out in the event to be much different—and much less impressive—than anything he had dreamed. He consciously intends to stop the fleeing troops by his eloquence and he ends in fiasco. On the other hand, he does physically stop a soldier. By commonsense moral criteria he deserves no credit for willing what is evidently an accident: an impulse from the flux of inner impulses happens to connect by physiological reflex with a passerby who is part of the outward flux of events. Perhaps the impulse which causes the physical act is linked with the prior wish, but it cannot be demonstrated. When the discrete pieces are put together, they comprise a moral act which should not be undervalued. But should the actor feel anything but a distrust of his merits? The will is not enough to enact the event without the intervention of chance, a term which refers equally to Crane's dynamic psychology and his empiricist sense of the nature of things. In this respect the intervention of chance is comparable to the necessary intervention of grace in a theological view; in secular terms, it teaches the distrust of egotism. This scheme was Crane's great invention for putting together his psychological insights with his moral concerns. He would use it again to the same purpose in some of his best stories: "A Mystery of Heroism" and "Three White Mice" and "The Monster" recapitulate the situation in which an act can be measured only by figuratively watching the legs, not by examining the conscious will. The old-fashioned moral slate and pencil won't do. The experiment announced in the opening chapter of the novel came thus to its logical climax.

Crane had worked out a remarkably original narrative scheme for conveying his vision of the world and man, but he did not count on his readers to grasp his subtleties. "Trust their imaginations?" he was one day to be quoted; "Why, they haven't got any!"[11] No one can miss the fact that Fleming had one other wish fulfilled, the wish that he could invent a tale to take back such as would enable him to escape derision and public shame. The wound he sustained, whatever its possible moral or psychological significance, was not the badge of courage in any military sense. His making it so was a falsehood, and when he got back to his unit he would at the first opportunity turn it into a positive lie. Readers who want to discern in Fleming a moral redemption must settle for something considerably less. Psychological subtlety is not necessary to a recognition that his merits are less than saving. In Crane's novel the radical imperfection of man was as fundamental as the unpredictable disorder of the world which men experience.

Notes

1. Ellen Moers, *Two Dreisers* (New York: Viking, 1969), pp. 43–56, gives the most penetrating account of Tolstoy's impact on American culture in this period, citing Dreiser's interview with Howells and his use of the Howells passage in his subsequent article. She calls particular attention to the fact that the 1898 interview occurred as Dreiser was coming to his momentous decision to become a novelist.

2. Thomas Beer, *Stephen Crane* (New York: Knopf, 1923), p. 90. Of the translations available to Crane, that of Isabel F. Hapgood (New York: Crowell, 1888) does not seem to be in question. The Kendall translation (New York: George Munro, 1888) came out in a paperbound pocket edition, no. 1108 of the Seaside Library, and cost twenty cents. The Millet translation with Howells' introduction (New York: Harper and Brothers, 1887) would have cost Crane only seventy-five cents. It is also quite possible that when Howells met Crane in the spring of 1893, he might have given the young novelist a copy in reciprocation of Crane's earlier gift of *Maggie*. In any case Crane would have been interested in an edition introduced by the American novelist whom he most admired. Evidence for such hypotheses is worth seeking because of the intrinsic likelihood that the better written version would have influenced Crane. The Howells praise (*Sebastopol*, pp. 5–12) is echoed in Crane's letter to an editor of *Leslie's Weekly* (n.p., n.d.) about November, 1895 (*Stephen Crane: Letters*, ed. R. W. Stallman and Lillian Gilkes [New York: New York University Press, 1960,] p. 78). Crane's inscription in his gift copy for Howells of *The Red Badge* he backdated to August 17, 1895, more than a week before he received title-page proof, much less an advance copy (*Letters*, p. 62). The college boy's statement on Tolstoy, since Beer had little information on Crane's semester at Lafayette, may have come from one of his cronies at Syracuse and would in that case date from the spring of 1891. See Beer, *Crane*, p. 55.

3. *The Beginnings of Naturalism in American Fiction* (Uppsala and Cambridge: Lundequistska Bokhandeln and Harvard University Press, 1950), pp. 347–50; *Sebastopol*, Millet translation, pp. 43–44. The last paragraph of "December, 1854" in the Kendall and Millet versions is a fair sample of their difference:

Kendall:

The day is waning; the sun, which will soon disappear below the horizon, is shining through the grey clouds that surround it, and illumining with its crimson rays the ripples of the emerald sea, covered with boats and ships, and the white houses of the town. On the boulevard a band is playing a familiar waltz, to which the cannonade from the bastions forms a strange and weird accompaniment (p. 23).

Millet:

Day closes; the sun, disappearing at the horizon, shines through the gray clouds which surround it, and lights up with purple rays the rippling sea with its green reflections, covered with ships and boats, the white houses of the city, and the population stirring there. On the boulevard a regimental band is playing an old waltz, which sounds far over the water, and to which the cannonade of the bastions forms a strange and striking accompaniment (pp. 43–44).

4. 2 vols., New York: Charles L. Webster & Co., 1885.

5. *Sebastopol*, Millet translation, pp. 232, 235.

6. Herbert P. Williams, "Mr. Crane as a Literary Artist," *The Illustrated American*, xx (July 18, 1896), 126.

7. Cited in William James, *The Will to Believe* (New York and London: Longmans, Green & Co., 1897), p. 52.

8. Draft, p. 75.4–6. Crane scarcely changed the meaning when he made the sentence a little more stylish and the irony a little more subtle in his complete manuscript: "He rebelled against the source of things, according to a law, perchance, that the most powerful shall receive the most blame." Here, and throughout, my study depends on the research, analysis, exposition, and apparatus of Fredson Bowers' *The Red Badge of Courage: A Facsimile Edition of the Manuscript*, 2 vols. (Washington, D.C.: Bruccoli Clark Book, NCR/Microcard Editions, 1973). His definitive treatment of textual problems makes it possible to see in detail how the story grew under Crane's hand in the course of more than a year.

9. *Roadside Meetings* (New York: Macmillan, 1930), p. 206, quoting at length his own memorial article of 1900, "Stephen Crane: A Soldier of Fortune," *Saturday Evening Post*, CLXXIII (July 28, 1900), 16–17, reprinted in *The Book-Lover*, II (Autumn, 1900), 6–9.

10. Across that last sentence, just after the word "scene," Crane put a large question mark (Manuscript, p. 101.32).

11. Williams, "Mr. Crane as a Literary Artist," p. 126.

[Impressionism in *The Red Badge of Courage*]   James Nagel*

The point of view Crane employed in *The Red Badge* is basically that of a limited third-person narrator whose access to data is restricted to the mind of the protagonist, Henry Fleming, to his sensory apprehensions and associated thoughts and feelings. In typical Impressionistic manner, Henry's experiences are discontinuous and fragmented and result in a novel composed of brief units. These scenes do not always relate directly to juxtaposed episodes, nor do they always develop the same themes. Furthermore, Henry's view of the battle is severely limited. He knows nothing of the strategy of the battle; he frequently cannot interpret the events around him because his information is obscured by darkness, smoke, or the noise of cannons; rumors spread quickly throughout his regiment, heightening the fear and anxiety of the men. Often, preoccupied by introspection, Henry's mind distorts the data it receives, transforming men into monsters and artillery shells into shrieking demons that leer at him. In short, Henry's view of things is limited, unreliable, and distorted,

* From *Stephen Crane and Literary Impressionism* (University Park: Pennsylvania State University Press, 1980), 52–61, 87–92. Reprinted by permission of Pennsylvania State University Press.

and yet a projection of the working of his mind becomes a dramatically realistic depiction of how war might appear to an ordinary private engaged in a battle in the American Civil War.

In an important sense, narrative method is the genius of *The Red Badge*. Of their own, the central events of the novel are commonplace. What gives the novel its unique quality is the method of its telling, its restriction of information. As Orm Øverland has pointed out,

> throughout *The Red Badge* (except in the first paragraph where, as it were, the "camera eye" settles down on the camp and the youth, and the concluding one where it again recedes) we in our imagined roles as spectators never have a larger view of the field than has the main character.[1]

Many other Crane scholars have commented on this technique, and most of them invoke a visual metaphor, such as the "camera eye," to describe the method. Carl Van Doren, for example, wrote in the *American Mercury* in 1924 that Henry Fleming "is a lens through which a whole battle may be seen, a sensorium upon which all its details may be registered."[2] Although Van Doren is overgenerous in his analysis of how much of the battle Henry actually sees, he is essentially correct in classifying the methodology of its rendition. Indeed, even thirty years after its initial publication, *The Red Badge* must have seemed most remarkable, for no third-person novel in American literature previously published had so severely limited its point of view. That such restriction is Impressionistic has been well established by Sergio Perosa:

> *The Red Badge of Courage* is indeed a triumph of impressionistic vision and impressionistic technique. Only a few episodes are described from the outside; Fleming's mind is seldom analyzed in an objective, omniscient way; very few incidents are extensively *told*. Practically every scene is filtered through Fleming's point of view and seen through his eyes. Everything is related to his *vision*, to his *sense*-perception of incidents and details, to his *sense*-reactions rather than to his psychological impulses, to his confused sensations and individual impressions.[3]

There is somewhat more "telling" by the narrator than Perosa's comment suggests, and perhaps more interplay from Henry's "psychological impulses," but this formulation of the narrative method of the novel is essentially accurate. Although there are a few passages with an intrusive narrative presence, and a few other complicating devices involving temporal dislocations, the central device of the novel is the rendering of action and thought as they occur in Henry's mind, revealing not the whole of the battle, nor even the broad significance of it, but rather the meaning of this experience to him. The immediacy of the dramatic action is a product of the rendering of the sensory data of Henry's mind; the psychological penetration results from the mingling of experience with association, distortion, fantasy, and memory.[4] A further implication of this method, one that is unsettling but realistic, is that the world presented to Henry is beyond his control, beyond even his comprehension. His primary relation to it is not so much a matter of his deeds as of his organization of sensation into language and pattern.

No reading of *The Red Badge of Courage* can be complete, therefore, which does not deal with the significance of perception in the novel as both a methodological and thematic component. In this sense, the method of the novel is a rendering of Fleming's apprehension and his thoughts: its unifying and informing theme is the development of his capacity to *see* himself, in the context of war, more clearly. Henry's initiation into a nominal maturity becomes a function of his perception of life, death, and his own consuming, nearly incapacitating, fear.[5] After the opening of the novel, the concentration is on Henry's mind. In the first paragraph, however, before Henry has been introduced, an abstract, third-person narrator presents an establishing scene:

> The cold passed reluctantly from the earth and the retiring fogs revealed an army stretched out on the hills, resting. As the landscape changed from brown to green the army awakened and began to tremble with eagerness at the noise of rumors. It cast its eyes upon the roads which were growing from long troughs of liquid mud to proper thoroughfares. A river, amber-tinted in the shadow of its banks, purled at the army's feet and at night when the stream had become of a sorrowful blackness one could see, across, the red eye-like gleam of hostile camp-fires set in the low brows of distant hills (II, 3).

This paragraph contains not only objective descriptive details but a subjective and animating quality as well. The cold retreats "reluctantly," suggesting a desire to remain, to the discomfort of the soldiers; the fog, which has obscured the scene, now "reveals" the Union army in the hills; the army, personified into a composite and singular entity, "trembles" in response to rumors and casts its "eyes" across the scene. It is an opening filled with tension and ominous suggestion. As J. C. Levenson has pointed out, "the reader enters an animistic scene in which red eyes gleam beneath the low brows of hills and the whole world of consciousness is alive and active and menacing."[6] The characters, introduced in terms of their sensory indicators (the tall soldier, the loud soldier, the youth) to a narrative mind free of prior knowledge, behave nervously. Thus the opening ambience establishes the tone as well as the topography of the novel.

As soon as Henry Fleming is introduced, the center of intelligence becomes his: "There was a youthful private who listened with eager ears to the words of the tall soldier and to the varied comments of his comrades" (II, 4). From this point on, the central concern of the novel is the literal and figurative dimensions of his perception. The most obvious examples of this mode are narrative assertions about Henry's eyes and what he can see. The thrust of the novel is on Henry's mind rather than on the battle itself, and these comments are essentially revelations of character. For example, several passages reveal his egotistic conception of his superior vision, as when he concludes that "there was but one pair of eyes in the corps" (II, 25), or when, after his desertion, he feels that the limitations of his comrades "would not enable them to understand his sharper point of view" (II, 46). Of greater thematic significance are those passages which relate knowledge in terms of vision, as when Henry realizes that Wilson has changed from a "loud young soldier" to one of quiet confidence:

> The youth wondered where had been born these new eyes; when his comrade had made the great discovery that there were many men who would refuse to be subjected by him. Apparently, the other had now climbed a peak of wisdom from which he could perceive himself as a very wee thing (II, 82).

Significantly, Wilson's development of insight, of true self-knowledge, precedes Henry's. Wilson, who functions in some ways as Henry's alter-ego in the second half of the novel, has experienced his perceptual initiation by Chapter 14; Henry's does not come until Chapter 18, at which point it is formulated in terms of a similar visual metaphor:

> These happenings had occupied an incredibly short time yet the youth felt that in them he had been made aged. New eyes were given to him. And the most startling thing was to learn suddenly that he was very insignificant (II, 101).

For Henry, this passage has a function beyond its metaphoric value. For the first time he is able to see clearly:

> It seemed to the youth that he saw everything. Each blade of the green grass was bold and clear. He thought that he was aware of every change in the thin, transparent vapor that floated idly in sheets (II, 105).

The psychological implication of Henry's transformation is that his preoccupation with fear, and his projection of heroic stature for his brave deeds, had obscured reality and prevented him from seeing himself in context. Now that he sees himself as one with his fellows, as an individual no more significant than any other, within the impersonal machinations of war, he develops the capacity to comprehend his environment: "His mind took mechanical but firm impressions, so that, afterward, everything was pictured and explained to him, save why he himself was there" (II, 105). The conclusion of the novel, which marks a juncture not in the battle but in Henry's development, continues the concentration on vision. In the final scene, Henry's "eyes seemed to open to some new ways. He found that he could look back upon the brass and bombast of his earlier gospels and see them truly" (II, 135). In visual terms, there is no doubt that Henry has undergone significant development: he has relinquished his dreams of "Greek-like struggles" as well as his fear, which had become "the red sickness of battle," in favor of a more mature and balanced picture of himself as part of humanity.

As might be expected from the narrative stance of the novel, there is a stress on sensory faculties. The reader, like the viewer of an Impressionistic painting, is presented with an array of sensational details from a scene: the colors, sounds, feelings of a given experience.[7] In Chapter 3, for example, after a visual passage in which Henry keeps "his eyes watchfully upon the darkness" (II, 21), other senses come into play: the smell of the pines is pervasive; the sounds of insects and axes echo through the forest; and Henry's sensations of touch become acute:

> His canteen banged rhythmically upon his thigh and his haversack bobbed softly. His musket bounced a trifle from his shoulder at each stride and made his cap feel uncertain upon his head (II, 22).

But the predominant sensory emphasis is on vision, so much so that Harold Frederic, himself a skilled novelist, called *The Red Badge* a "battle painting" in his review in the New York *Times* in 1896.[8] Sensitive to Crane's narrative method, Frederic remarked that as readers "we see with his [Henry's] eyes, think with his mind, quail or thrill with his nerves." Frederic concluded that this method of "photographic revelation" accounts for the fascination of the novel. Frederic's comments have more than figurative significance, for there is a good deal of narrative "picturing." One expression of this device is subjective, generated within Henry's mind, as in the opening chapter: "His busy mind had drawn for him large pictures, extravagant in color, lurid with breathless deeds" (II, 5). The method is essentially expository, evoking no coordinate image but rather a generic sense of the workings of Henry's mind.[9] Paradoxically, most of the passages labeled pictures by the narrator constitute internal rather than external renderings. In general, when Henry is confused and under stress, his mind seeks resolution through imaginative portraits. One such instance occurs in Chapter 11, in which Henry, filled with guilt for his desertion and remorse for the death of Jim Conklin, sees "swift pictures of himself, apart, yet in himself . . ." (II, 64). The first image he conjures is of himself in a heroic moment of death, standing bravely, "getting calmly killed on a high place before the eyes of all." He imagines as well the "magnificent pathos of his dead body." This image temporarily expiates his sense of shame and for a few moments "he was sublime." He constructs a more sustaining image of himself at the front of battle, then loses confidence in his capacity for heroic action (II, 65). Thus one function of narrative picturing is the projection of Henry's internal fantasy, creating visual correlatives for his heroic striving and compensatory fears of cowardice and death. So it is with Henry's "visions" and "pictures" in the opening chapter and his "dreams" throughout the novel.

To some extent, Henry is forced to imaginative picturing to find coherence and unity in his experience, for his sensory data is confused and incomplete. During the battle in which he deserts, smoke blankets the battlefield, as it does often, and allows him only "changing views" of the action (II, 41). One of his central problems throughout the novel is that he cannot perceive enough to construct a reliable interpretation of his situation: his comrades appear to him as "dark waves" and the enemy as "grey shadows" in the woods (II, 69). A "clouded haze" obscures almost every important scene. In the absence of congruent information about the events, Henry's mind interprets the limited data in terms of his fear. He never has access to all he would like to see:

> The youth leaned his breast against the brown dirt and peered over at the woods and up and down the line. Curtains of trees interfered with his ways of vision. He could see the low line of trenches but for a short distance (II, 89).

In another scene, in which Henry is so close to the rebel troops that he can momentarily distinguish the features of individual men, his view is changed before he can act:

> Almost instantly, they [the Southern troops] were shut utterly from the youth's sight by the smoke from the energetic rifles of his companions. He strained his vision to learn the accomplishment of the volley but the smoke hung before him (II, 114).

It is clear throughout the novel that given limited information, Henry must struggle to understand his circumstances. After one battle, in which it seemed to him that he had covered a great deal of ground, he has an opportunity to survey what has actually happened: "He discovered that the distances, as compared with the brilliant measurings of his mind, were trivial and ridiculous" (II, 117).

In most cases, however, Henry is not allowed to reflect upon the accuracy of his interpretations, and his fears and visions distort the data he receives. The most dramatic of these instances come during battle, and most of them involve Henry's perception of battle objects as dragons and monsters of various kinds. The first such image exemplifies his distortions: "From off in the darkness, came the trampling of feet. The youth could occasionally see dark shadows that moved like monsters" (II, 15). When he next peers across the river at the enemy camp fires, he sees them as "growing larger, as the orbs of a row of dragons, advancing." Even when his own regiment moves through the darkness the men appear to be "monsters" which strike Henry as "huge crawling reptiles." As a result, the early part of the novel is filled with "serpents," "monsters," "battle-phantoms," "dragons," and other fantastic manifestations of "war, the red animal, war, the blood-swollen god."[10] Significantly, Henry's distortions are consistent until Chapter 18, when he experiences a dramatic epiphany and "new eyes were given to him." Previously he had been capable of almost surrealistic projections, as when he imagines that the artillery shells arching over him have "rows of cruel teeth that grinned at him" (II, 42), or later, when coming upon some of his comrades in the forest,

> his disordered mind interpreted the hall of the forest as a charnel place. He believed for an instant that he was in the house of the dead and he did not dare to move lest these corpses start up, squalling and squawking (II, 80).

After his moment of recognition, in which he perceives his insignificance and loses much of his fear, there are no such distortions. It is then that he can see his earlier errors of interpretation: "Elfin thoughts must have exaggerated and enlarged everything, he said" (II, 117). He is still subject to sensory restriction and obscuring, as when a scene becomes a "wild blur" as he dashes across a field (II, 108), but he no longer creates monsters out of shadows.

Indeed much of the narrative emphasis is on his improved capacity to perceive:

> His vision being unmolested by smoke from the rifles of his companions, he had opportunities to see parts of the hard fight. It was a relief to perceive at last from whence came some of these noises which had been roared into his ears (II, 122).

As the narrator makes explicit, Henry's new sight is more than a literal clarity of apprehension; it involves cognitive factors as well. In the final chapter,

> gradually his brain emerged from the clogged clouds and at last he was enabled to more closely comprehend himself and circumstance. . . . He understood then that the existence of shot and counter-shot was in the past. . . . Later, he began to study his deeds—his failures and his achievements. . . . At last, they marched

> before him clearly. From this present view-point, he was enabled
> to look upon them in spectator fashion and to criticise them with
> some correctness. . . . (II, 133).

The novel concludes with a visual emphasis. As Henry's "eyes seemed
to open to some new ways," he is able to reflect on his earlier ideas
and "see them truly" (II, 135).

In an important sense, *The Red Badge* is a novel of the growth
of Henry's visual capacities. The narrative method, alternating from
objective apprehensions presented in the manner of a motion picture
camera[11] to the subjective rendering of his distortions, emotions,
fantasies, and memories, is the single most innovative device in the
novel. As J. C. Levenson has commented, Crane's

> radical breakthrough came from his premise that mental life pri-
> marily consists in witnessing the vivid immediate presences within
> one's own mind, that is, in the flux of consciousness. So far as
> consciousness is concerned, self-projected images have equal status
> with sense data.[12]

For Henry Fleming these "self-projected images" consist of both
evocations generated out of internal need and interpretative distortions of genuine sensory data, and he is largely unable to distinguish
between them.

Beyond these narrative methodologies, which dominate the novel,
there are several other strategies that play a role in individual scenes.
If the flashback technique can be theoretically reconciled with Impressionism in fiction as a narrative projection of thought, it is more
difficult to establish congruence with Impressionism of moments that
jump forward, even if they present a future, retrospective time:
"When he thought of it later, he conceived the impression that it is
better to view the appalling than to be merely within hearing" (II,
42). It is even more difficult to understand intrusive passages as part
of an Impressionistic novel, and there are a few of them in *The Red
Badge*. One such passage occurs in Chapter 3: "But the regiment
was not yet veteran-like in appearance. Veteran regiments in this
army were likely to be very small aggregations of men" (II, 22). It
seems unlikely that this comment can be read as the narrator's
statement of Henry's thoughts since he is a raw recruit who has yet
to see his first battle and knows little of the size of battle-torn
regiments. The later image of "guns squatted in a row like savage
chiefs" (II, 38) again seems to derive from beyond Henry's frame of
reference. But such passages are rare and do not substantially qualify
the Impressionistic method that dominates the novel. It should be
noted, however, that there is more variation of narrative logic than
has generally been acknowledged. There is even one passage of direct
thought as in stream of consciousness: "The youth pitied them [a

group of artillery gunners] as he ran. Methodical idiots! Machine-like fools!" (II, 43). Here, in an intensely emotional moment, the intervening narrative consciousness disappears to render Henry's thoughts precisely as they occur.

Despite these variations, the basic method of the "showing" of *The Red Badge of Courage* is Impressionistic and consists of the sensations and thoughts of a private engaged in a battle he does not comprehend and cannot even clearly see. The drama of the novel is epistemological, a matter of perception, distortion, and realization which finally culminates in Chapter 18 with Henry's epiphany. The genius of the novel is its use of a narrative method that underscores the perceptual themes, that forces the reader to participate in the empirical limitations of the central character, and that creates a psychological reality on a level never before achieved in the American novel.

In general, there is a good deal of subtlety in Crane's handling of the narrator as an intermediary consciousness between character and reader. The obvious function of the narrator is to describe the scene; another more intricate role is to formulate and present the mental activity of the protagonist. The narrator presents thought without alteration, without comment, without verification that the thought has external validity; the presumption is that narrative assertions articulate the thoughts of the character. This methodology stresses the limitation of sensory perceptions and the reduced reliability of interpretations of experience. The meaning of data is often as much a product of interpretation as it is of physical reality. As Peter Sloat Hoff described Impressionistic narration,

> the reader is placed at the same epistemological level as the confused characters who serve as centers of consciousness. The reader becomes to some degree a receiver of temporally fragmented sense impressions rather than organized narration. The information which reaches the reader of an Impressionistic novel is potentially incorrect, for it often comes through an observer who may be mistaken, and it is information often broken and distorted.[13]

The mode of unreliable narration describes almost exactly Crane's means of presenting Henry Fleming's heroic view of himself, the plains rushing eastward in "The Bride Comes to Yellow Sky," and Maggie's view of Pete as a knight.

The close identification of the narrator's mind with a character has many unreliable manifestations in *The Red Badge*. One of those already noted is the narrator's insistence in rendering sensory impressions without correction, even in the case of distance, hence the formulation that "once he [Henry] saw a tiny battery go dashing along the line of the horizon. The tiny riders were beating the tiny horses" (II, 38). This scene represents the simplest form of unreliability in Impressionism in that it is the projection of raw, apprehensive data from the mind of a character. But it is also possible for the narrator to render subjective, judgmental thought as well, as is the case in *The Red Badge* when the lieutenant urges Henry to keep up with the ranks: "He [Henry] mended his pace with suitable haste. And he hated the lieutenant, who had no appreciation of fine minds. He was a mere brute" (II, 25). The irony of this passage results from the reader's sense of Henry's self-revelation, that the human weakness is not so much the lieutenant's brutishness as Henry's grandiose view of his own "fine mind."

The result of this mode in *The Red Badge* is a continuous pattern of distorted judgments by Henry projected faithfully by the narrator. In general, these statements reveal the extent to which Henry's mind, driven by doubt and shame, reconstructs the data of reality to create a context in which his actions can be seen in their most positive light. After Henry deserts, he begins to reflect that "his actions had been sagacious things. They had been full of strategy. They were the work of a master's legs" (II, 45). The narrator does not suggest the bias of Henry's view; the reader, seeing Henry's interpretation in context, must supply the countering qualification of Henry's delusions. The novel is replete with ironic assertions that point to Henry's immaturity, innocence, and distorted self-view.[14] Indeed, they build throughout the novel to a moment just before Henry's epiphany in Chapter 18, at which point they reach their most profound delusion: "He had been a tremendous figure, no doubt. . . . He had slept and, awakening, found himself a knight" (II, 97). After his epiphany, the narrative irony ceases. What the handling of this device suggests for Impressionism is that irony is a function of distance, of knowledge, of point of view; given the same data that Henry himself receives, the reader's interpretation is impossible to reconcile with Henry's. The resulting tension, born of interpretive distance, becomes one of the dominating factors in the novel. . . .

Metaphors of perception generate the fundamental theme of *The Red Badge* in terms that explicitly link the novel to the development of Literary Impressionism in America. From the beginning of the novel Henry's most significant problem is his inability to formulate and sustain a realistic conception of himself and the conditions of war. Severely limited in experience, his mind resorts to fantasies of glory based on his reading about classical battles, and these conceptions compete for dominance with his fears of cowardice and death, his uncertainties about himself, his dread of the unknown. This mental conflict finds appropriate expression in his illusions of himself, restricted vision, and eventual perceptual growth.

Henry's underlying problem in the novel is not simply his effort to control his fear, as some critics have argued,[15] but rather to perceive and interpret himself and his situation with some degree of assurance. His insecurities are born of a need to understand himself. Since his father is dead, he has no role model to emulate; since war is unknown to him, he can only fantasize about it. Even Henry's fantasies and visions are essentially deductive, deriving from a heroic portrait of war. However, his attempts to understand himself and the specific circumstances of "his" war are basically empirical and inductive: "He saw that he would again be obliged to experiment as he had in early youth. He must accumulate information of himself . . ." (II, 10). His understanding must commence in total ignorance; early in the novel he is forced to the realization that "as far as war was concerned he knew nothing of himself" (II, 10).

Attempting to learn, Henry "tried to observe everything" (II, 23). When his regiment moved in the night, "he kept his eyes watchfully upon the darkness" (II, 21). When a skirmish began, "his eyes grew wide and busy with the action of the scene" (II, 28). His view is less than complete, however, presenting him with confused and incomplete data and inspiring in him a sense of isolation. This feeling, when mingled with his earlier heroic conceptions, casts him as a singular viewer of reality: "There was but one pair of eyes in the corps. He would step forth and make a speech. Shrill and passionate words came to his lips" (II, 25). As this passage suggests, Henry's attempts to see more clearly are compromised by his self-congratulatory illusions. Before he had left home, in thinking about the war "he had seen himself in many struggles. He had imagined peoples secure in the shadow of his eagle-eyed prowess" (II, 5), a fantasy that presents heroism in terms of vision. Now, actually confronting battle, he must also deal with an antithetical vision "of a thousand-tongued fear that would babble at his back and cause him to flee while others were going coolly about their country's business" (II, 20).

This conflict has its first manifestation in Henry's desertion. As the images of monsters and savage gods suggest, Henry's mind, driven by fear, has metamorphosed the enemy into "redoubtable dragons" and "red and green monster[s]"; his compatriots who stand their ground are certain to be "initial morsels for the dragons"; his brigade will be "gulped into the infernal mouth of the war-god" (II, 41–43). These visions so dominate his mind that it is impregnable, and he is cognitively "blind" when he runs. Later, the danger passed, he attempts to assess what has happened, and the pride of his earlier heroic notions replaces his fear. His blindness continues, but the obscuring thoughts are now complex rationalizations contending that he had acted more wisely than his comrades: "He, the enlightened man who looks afar in the dark, had fled because of his superior perceptions and knowledge" (II, 45). Pride, as well as delusion, is expressed in terms of vision, and his superiority over his fellows seems to him to indicate that they will not be able to comprehend his enlightened perspective: "Their density would not enable them to understand his sharper point of view" (II, 46).

If Henry's fear, which prompts him to perceive enemy forces as monsters and dragons, generates his impulse to flee, his continuing inability to see himself and battle clearly dominates the center of the novel. Henry is not alone in his problems: Jim Conklin had earlier rejoiced in a similar pride in his superior "prowess of perception" (II, 16) and now he was dead; Wilson, brash with confidence, had also believed in his own supreme perception: "He was sprightly, vigorous, fiery in his belief in success. He looked into the future with clear, proud eye" [sic] (II, 19). But Wilson had quavered in his resolve and, anticipating death, had given Henry an envelope to be returned to his parents.

Henry's experience with Wilson in the second half of the novel, beginning with Chapter 12, reveals that during Henry's absence from the regiment his "loud" comrade has undergone substantial growth. Wilson ministers to Henry's wounds with sensitivity and compassion, sacrificing his blanket at night, cooking for him in the morning. Henry is aware of Wilson's development:

> He was, no more, a loud young soldier. There was about him now a fine reliance. He showed a quiet belief in his purposes and his abilities. And this inward confidence evidently enabled him to be indifferent to little words of other men aimed at him (II, 82).

But the vehicle by which Wilson has achieved his sudden maturity is expressed in a metaphor of vision that expresses the theme of epiphany: Henry

> wondered where had been born these new eyes; when his comrade [Wilson] had made the great discovery that there were many men who would refuse to be subjected by him. Apparently, the other had now climbed a peak of wisdom from which he could perceive himself as a very wee thing (II, 82).

Wilson's "new eyes," which inspire humility and confidence and yet reveal to him his insignificance, are apparently the result of an epiphany born of the frantic activity of war which accelerates growth and allows significant character alterations within a short time. Henry's reflections indicate that the key to Wilson's transformation was the perspective from a "peak of wisdom" which revealed that he was one with his fellows.[16] It is significant that although he observes

Wilson's development, this awareness does not, for some time at least, inspire a corresponding change in Henry himself.

In fact, although he rejoins his regiment after his desertion and walk with the wounded men, and after the death of Conklin and his own blow to the head, Henry persists in a self-serving rationale. He contemplates using the envelope to embarrass Wilson, despite his sense of Wilson's new humility (II, 85). He rejoices that "he had performed his mistakes in the dark" (II, 86) and never, until his subsequent appearance in "The Veteran," reveals the truth about what he did. As a new battle begins, his view again constricts: "Curtains of trees interfered with his ways of vision. He could see the low line of trenches but for a short distance" (II, 89). As he hears praise for his supposed bravery in the previous battle, however, he begins to change: "He became suddenly a modest person" (II, 91). This state of mind is temporary, for soon after, in the "chaos" of his mind, he begins to feel that "he had been a tremendous figure, no doubt" (II, 97).

As he moves into the key epiphanic episode, Chapter 18, his perceptual difficulties at first continue, his view "blurred by the hurlying smoke of the line" (II, 100). But in the rush of activity, Henry's perspective is suddenly transformed and he undergoes a maturing of self-awareness: Henry feels that "he had been made aged. New eyes were given to him. And the most startling thing was to learn suddenly that he was very insignificant" (II, 101). Henry's "recognition" improves his perception literally and figuratively. As the battle begins anew, his ability to perceive his environment is markedly improved:

> It seemed to the youth that he saw everything. Each blade of the green grass was bold and clear. He thought that he was aware of every change in the thin, transparent vapor that floated idly in sheets. The brown or grey trunks of the trees showed each roughness of their surfaces. And the men of the regiment . . . all were comprehended. His mind took mechanical but firm impressions, so that, afterward, everything was pictured and explained to him, save why he himself was there (II, 105).

Although it is significant that Henry has achieved a new level of insight, in accord with the psychological reality of the novel, perceptual growth is neither total nor invariable. Henry has seen, for the first time, the limitations of his importance, and he has begun to see his environment more clearly, yet the flux of life brings new circumstances. In a mad rush at the enemy, Henry charges with his eyes nearly closed and the scene becomes a "wild blur" to him (II, 108). Looking across a "clouded haze" to the battlefield, he must depend on his "misused ears" for information (II, 112). Later, in the heat of battle, smoke obscures the field and Henry "strained his vision to learn the accomplishment of the volley but the smoke hung before him" (II, 114).

For all of these difficulties, Henry's epiphany has brought a new awareness. As he surveys the battlefield after the conflict, he realizes that his emotional pitch during the action distorted his view: "Elfin thoughts must have exaggerated and enlarged everything, he said" (II, 117). His new confidence also allows moments of unimpaired vision, and he sees clearly the number and alignment of the troops (II, 122). In the final chapter, looking back upon his actions, Henry is capable of a more mature and balanced evaluation:

> His mind was under-going a subtle change. . . . Gradually his brain emerged from the clogged clouds and at last he was enabled to more closely comprehend himself and circumstance. . . . Later, he began to study his deeds—his failures and his achievements. . . . At last, they marched before him clearly (II, 133).

This new visual capacity informs and qualifies the conclusion of the novel and gives meaning to its final image. Henry's eyes "open to some new ways," and in viewing his previous indiscretions he can "see them truly" and "despise" them. He has gained control of his fear; he has come to know and accept death: "He was a man." In the most telling comment in the novel, "it came to pass that as he trudged from the place of blood and wrath, his soul changed." Henry's epiphany has not been simply a matter of understanding battle: it has fundamentally altered him as a human being. As a result, the concluding image creates optimism: "Over the river a golden ray of sun came through the hosts of leaden rain clouds" (II, 135).

The story of Henry Fleming's growth in The Red Badge of Courage is no chronicle of confrontations with Deterministic forces, as a Naturalistic reading would require, nor even a Realistic account of combat. Rather, it is a record of Henry's progressive intensification of vision to a moment of epiphany in which he sees his world and himself in a larger perspective. The novel is basically a story of psychological adjustment to reality in which Henry achieves a reconciliation of his romantic visions with his new awareness. He does not suddenly perceive all truth for all time, for such a conception, as Donald Pizer suggests, would be reductive: "The Red Badge presents a vision of man as a creature capable of advancing in some areas of knowledge and power but forever imprisoned within the walls of certain inescapable human and social limitations."[17] But the novel does document an epistemological process in which a young boy makes gains in self-knowledge, in his ability to perceive his environment, and in his attempts to achieve a balance that keeps thought and emotion in constructive proportion. Even so, for Henry the "truth" is ultimately tentative, relativistic, solipsistic, but as close to reality as a single human being, insignificant yet egoistic, can ever come in an Impressionistic novel.

Notes

1. Orm Øverland, "The Impressionism of Stephen Crane: A Study in Style and Technique," *Americana Norvegica, I*, ed. Sigmund Skard and Henry R. Wasser (Philadelphia, 1966), p. 256.

2. *Stephen Crane: The Cultural Heritage*, ed. Richard W. Weatherford (Boston, 1973), p. 329. Originally published in *American Mercury*, 1 (Jan., 1924), 11–14.

3. Sergio Perosa, "Naturalism and Impressionism in Stephen Crane's Fiction," in *Stephen Crane: A Collection of Critical Essays*, ed. Maurice Bassan (Englewood Cliffs, N.J., 1967), p. 88.

4. For further comments on this point, see Frank Bergon, *Stephen Crane's Artistry* (New York, 1975), pp. 2, 5, and Milne Holton, *Cylinder of Vision: The Fiction and Journalistic Writing of Stephen Crane* (Baton Rouge, 1972), p. 8.

5. See Perosa, p. 93.

6. J. C. Levenson gives a detailed and perceptive reading of this paragraph in his introduction to *The Red Badge, The Works of Stephen Crane* (Charlottesville, 1970), II, xiv.

7. See, for example, *Works*, II, 15.

8. See *Heritage*, p. 116. Originally published in the *New York Times* (Jan. 26, 1896), p. 22.

9. For further examples, see *Works*, II, 6, 10, 31, 50, 66, 67, 88, 129.

10. See *Works*, II, 15, 16, 20, 32, 35, 41, 42, 69.

11. See E. H. Cady, *Stephen Crane* (New York, 1962), p. 120.

12. Levenson, p. xlvi.

13. Peter Sloat Hoff, an unpublished paper delivered at the Literary Impressionism session of the 1975 Modern Language Association convention.

14. See *Works*, II, 46, 47, 49, 67, 75, 87, for further examples.

15. See Stallman's comments in *Stephen Crane: An Omnibus* (New York, 1952), p. 288.

16. See John W. Rathbun, "Structure and Meaning in *The Red Badge of Courage*," *Ball State University Forum*, 10, No. 1 (1969), 12–13, for a similar observation.

17. Donald Pizer, "Nineteenth-Century American Naturalism: An Essay in Definition," *Bucknell Review*, 13 (1965), 14.

Violence as Ritual and Apocalypse
Harold Kaplan*

The naturalist obsession with violence can, when conditioned by an imaginative sensibility and raised to the level of revelation—

* From *Power and Order: Henry Adams and the Naturalist Tradition in American Fiction* (Chicago: University of Chicago Press, 1981), 121–27. Reprinted by permission of the University of Chicago Press.

emerge in the form of ritual observations and ceremonial drama. Stephen Crane had that kind of sensibility, tightening what is loose allegory in Norris, and in *The Red Badge of Courage* he developed a poetry of violence that singles that book out in the mainstream of naturalist fiction.

Crane did not need to know the Civil War personally because he knew it so well imaginatively; all that he needed were the naturalist myths that fed his imagination. His book is powerful, standing out above the works of Norris, London, and even Dreiser, not because it documents the life of camp and battle but because it is highly focused on primitive mysteries in battle and death.

Crane is clearly attempting to give a religious coloring to these revelations. Nature contains a god, and his service is sacrifice and death. War is nature's stormy Mount Sinai, "war, the red animal— war, the blood-swollen god" (RB 23).[1] All that nature contains of great force, pain, death, extreme physical effort, and ultimate physical collapse are given their high ground of revelation in war. It is there that these naturalist truths meet and converge on a metaphysical level. And when Henry Fleming is most absorbed by the battle, he knows war in this way: "He himself felt the daring spirit of a savage, religion—mad. He was capable of profound sacrifices, a tremendous death" (RB 103).

But since Henry is entirely oblivious of the political or moral justifications of this war, his battle crisis reveals only the cosmic processes of survival and death. Here can be found naturalism's nearest approach to religious transcendence, and it occurs at the boundaries of biological fate. And this is the essence of naturalist heroism: to approach the mystery of nature depends on the will to confront its most savage truth, sacrificing a mundane safety. Crane mentions "profound sacrifices," but it is clear that these sacrifices have no specific moral purpose. The value is metaphysical and personal, and the antagonist is not a human being but natural violence and death.

Violence possesses awesome meaning here because it opens toward death. The major confrontation with naturalist mystery is not in battle itself, for it comes to Henry Fleming when he is running away from battle. The scene is described in explicitly religious terms:

> he reached a place where the high, arching boughs made a chapel. He softly pushed the green doors aside and entered. Pine needles were a gentle brown carpet. There was a religious half light.
>
> Near the threshold he stopped, horror-stricken at the sight of a thing. [RB 41]

The "thing" is a dead man, seated with his back against a tree, and the chapel containing that thing expresses the lucid power of Crane's imagination. Crane of course complicates the religious references with the irony that is characteristic of all his writing, but here the irony is complex, not obviously reductive. Nothing of the shock of physical death is withheld; the eyes of the dead man have "the dull hue to be seen on the side of a dead fish," and

> Over the gray skin of the face ran little ants. One was trundling some sort of bundle along the upper lip. [RB 41]

In the midst of all this horror, "The dead man and the living man exchanged a long look." Then the scene draws softly to a close, as if it had brought spiritual comfort:

> The trees about the portals of the chapel moved soughingly in a soft wind. A sad silence was upon the little guarding edifice. [RB 42]

A fuller initiation into the mystery of death takes place later, in the prolonged agony of Henry's friend, Jim Conklin. As he walks beside Henry in the parade of the wounded, Jim is dying on his feet, staring into the unknown: "he seemed always looking for a place, like one who goes to choose a grave" (RB 47), and, already spectral in his look, he says, "don't tech me—leave me be" (RB 49). The dying man is preparing himself: "there was something ritelike in these movements of the doomed soldier" (RB 49). When the place and the moment are finally reached, there is an effect of ennoblement and transfiguration: "He was at the rendezvous . . . there was a curious and profound dignity in the firm lines of his awful face" (RB 49, 50).

The dignity might reflect natural process: Conklin's last moment is like the falling of a tree, "a slight rending sound." But, with his mouth open, "the teeth showed in a laugh" (RB 50). The laugh dismisses a sentimental primitivism, and Conklin, when he falls, reveals the side of his body, which looks "as if it had been chewed by wolves." Fleming at this moment shakes his fist at the battlefield, getting out only one word, "Hell——." Following this is a line that has stirred debate among various critics as to its serious or ironic implication: "The red sun was pasted in the sky like a wafer."[2] Given the context, it would seem absurd to miss the irony of this reference to Christlike dying and to the Communion. Still, if Crane is here employing his characteristic irony, he is at the same time confirming the universal ritual modes for confronting the experience of death.

The allusion to Christ emphasizes the vulnerability of the religious imagination, a pathos that is frequent in naturalist writing. Here irony and pathos come together in the seeming laugh of the dying man, enforcing his stoic dignity. He dies as a tree falls, and he has chosen his place to die after walking for a long time with a horrible wound in his side. There is not only a natural mystery here but a moral lesson. Conklin himself has no doubt transcended the motivation of pride in his personal bearing, but Fleming seems to have learned something from it, and this is related to the ostensible theme of Crane's book, the "red badge" of an initiation into courage. Just as the mystery religions of nature reached their deepest revelations in death, so here a specifically naturalist ethic is death-oriented. Almost immediately after Conklin's death, which might have confirmed him more than ever in his desire to run away, Henry begins to envision, instead, a return to his comrades, among whom, restored to self-respect by leading a charge in battle, he sees himself "getting calmly killed before the eyes of all. . . . He thought of the magnificent pathos of his dead body" (RB 55).

The awe and fierce dignity of Conklin's death confirmed that "magnificent pathos." It is a death-pathos now linked to the spirit of "a savage religion" requiring "profound sacrifices." The forest chapel of death, where ants trailed over the dead soldier's lips, affirmed the harsh terms of a soldier's religion, and further, and conclusive, emphasis is placed on Henry's redemptive initiation in battle: "He had been to touch the great death, and found that, after all, it was but the great death. He was a man" (RB 109). The values of this manhood are vitalist, and Crane views their implications with detachment: "He had been where there was red of blood and black of passion, and he was escaped. . . . He saw that he was good" (RB 107). Did the "good" reside in Henry's escape or in his authentication by blood and passion? At that margin of experience it is not possible to distinguish between survival and authenticity, or self-realization.

Critics have argued about this conclusion of Crane's story. Some have accepted Fleming's apotheosis in courage, while others continue to challenge the notion that Crane was seriously attempting to define a code of virile honor. I doubt, myself, that Crane was capable of writing a line describing subjective human commitments without leaving the door open for implicit irony. He was that kind of naturalist—indeed, in his uncorrupted detachment he resembles Flaubert or Joyce—and it is from that perspective, with a lucidity that is almost inevitably ironic, that he viewed the male-oriented vitalism of hunting, fighting, and survival. In this he presents a precise contrast with Adams's cult of the Virgin. Yet it might seem that, moved by the same intellectual needs as Adams, Crane was led to a parallel sexual vitalism but one almost inevitably "machoist" in tendency (later to be elaborated in the works of Hemingway and Norman Mailer).

The naturalist ethic in which the red of blood and the black of passion are the banner of manhood and lead the way to the "good" finds easy reinforcement in the group. The battle ordeal and the natural laws of pain and death set the conditions for the "subtle battle brotherhood" of the men who fight together. In the end, after

both loss and victory, the regiment has become "a mysterious fraternity born of the smoke and danger of death" (RB 31). The brotherhood
of soldiers expresses the force of the vitalist cult as it might be applied
to nations, races, and classes. These are collectivities committed to
historic conflict and survival. Promoting the ethic of conflict, they
learn to translate danger into fraternity; perhaps they even invite
violence in order to learn fraternity.[3]

In Crane's completely clear view of this theme, the only suffering
that exceeds physical suffering, and could make the latter welcome,
is that of the moral outcast. Similarly, the only emotion that can
compete with fear is shame. After Henry Fleming has run from battle,
his fear lessens and he is gradually possessed by the self-ostracism
of the moral refugee. As he walks among the wounded, he encounters
the "tattered man," and the latter's desire to compare wounds probes
into his cowardice. "The simple questions of the tattered man had
been knife thrusts to him. They asserted a society" (RB 53). What
Henry needs now is a wound of his own, and he longs for it, his
"red badge of courage." The blow he receives from another fleeing
soldier gives him what he wants, and he is able to return to his
regiment. The wound is unworthy, but the link between its sign and
his self-respect has been emphasized. Now he has the chance to
redeem himself in another battle, and he does.

The power of emulation thus matches the power of pain and
death. It is perhaps this equation in naturalist thought that is the key
to some of its deepest political implications. Nature's force and process
are absorbed and dominated by the social process, but this in turn
is ruled by natural law. In an army the reasons for valuing courage
and the ability to endure pain and face death are obvious. Nevertheless, Crane's descriptions of the army as a social unit and a moral
force establish it as something much greater than an instrument for
winning wars. His imagery is, as usual, concise and telling: "It [the
regiment] inclosed him. And there were iron laws of tradition and
law on four sides. He was in a moving box" (RB 21). The army as a
thing, a box, alternates with images of the army as a serpent, a dragon,
a monster. The interesting question is how this imagery supports
rather than undercuts the army's function as a disciplined moral
instrument, capable of collective judgment: "The regiment was like
a firework" (RB 31), Crane writes, a thing ready to explode with its
force. The point is actually to eliminate a traditional concept of
judgment. This collectivity, enforcing behavior, is viewed as power
in itself in its ability to evoke emulation, fear, shame, and pride.

The "naturalness" of this power is emphasized by the clarity
with which Crane saw that to bring up the cause for fighting would
have no relevance. There is no war here in the ordinary political
and geographic sense. There are two armies, but they are distinguished

only by the color of their uniforms. And the generals, who think they have control over the battle, actually do not. They send only inconsistent and incomprehensible orders, and they preside over actual confusion; for, whether running away or running forward, "the running men . . . were all deaf and blind" (RB 28).

Accordingly, when the group power of the army is not a prisonlike enclosure of tradition and law, it becomes simply a "floodlike force." Either way, the species dominates, absorbs, and transcends individual instincts and all personal interests, including survival itself. The group is not led but driven, both from within and from without; it either compulsively obeys tradition or anarchically surrenders to chaos. The army as a mob is as definite a force as the army under discipline. Nothing really distinguishes this society from simple organic or mechanical force except the spirit of emulation. If the approach of battle reveals to Henry that "he knew nothing of himself" and that "he was an unknown quantity" (RB 11), it also reveals that there is not much to know beyond the realities of fear and courage, strength and weakness. For the rest, "he continually tried to measure himself by his comrades" (RB 14); it was their good opinion he wanted. Henry's mind is at times filled with conventional battle romanticism, with notions of breathless deeds observed by "heavy crowns and high castles," but this traditional idealization of war is treated as a thin layer of childlike fantasy superimposed on more basic forces: the "moving box" of the army and the "throat-grappling" instinct for battle.

Still, as I have noted, these more basic forces are themselves the source of idealizations, of purely naturalist values. One is the vitalist virtue of proven manhood, of macho courage. Another is Henry's feeling of sublimity in the presence of "tremendous death" or in "the magnificent pathos of his [own] dead body" (RB 55). This might be called the moral code of Thanatos, calling for "an enthusiasm of unselfishness," "a sublime recklessness . . . shattered against the iron gates of the impossible" (RB 103). The highest virtue learned in naturalist conflict thus seems to be self-immolation. Behind war, "the blood-swollen god," stands death, a greater god, and the question that needs review is the extent to which the naturalist myth finds itself in service to the gods of *greatest* strength. The death pathos has no rival in its power to stir human emotions; recognizing this, Crane went further than most naturalist writers in appreciating the primitive compulsions of attraction and dread that death exerts.

Let us then trace the clear outline of Crane's naturalist values. Primordial violence, "the red animal," releases the most elemental and unsocialized passions and instincts. But since in Crane's work this occurs in the context of opposed armies, it results in elemental socialization. Henry Fleming's only defense against the fear of death, and perhaps against the attractions of death, is the approval of his comrades. He knew his greatest despair when he was alone, isolated from the rest of the army. Confronting death, he comes back to the army and experiences great relief, as if here was the only alternative to metaphysical panic. Social membership is almost as absolute as death, and it receives from death a kind of existential sanction, giving to Henry all the confidence of being that he can have. In all of this the crisis of violence is indispensable, for it proves the need for high group discipline and, in a naturalist paradox, juxtaposes primitive savagery with highly organized behavior. The battle scene brings together the reality of power and conflict and a primitive social ethic at its point of inception. In fact, if one wonders why the ethos of naturalist political movements, whether fascist or communist, is imbued with authoritarian discipline, the most direct answer would be that, in assuming the universality of group conflict as the premise for their existence, they needed to organize and motivate themselves like armies.

Redemptive Violence

In *The Red Badge of Courage*, a novel of war, where the opportunity to expose social illusions and oppressions was most available, Crane chose to concentrate on primitive collective psychology and instinctual experience. He pointedly avoids the social and historical issues of the Civil War. The deepest reading of Crane, I myself believe, emphasizes a tragic naturalism or a pessimism directed at both natural violence and social rule. But it is arguable, to a degree limited somewhat by his ironic sensibility, that Crane, in both *Maggie* and *The Red Badge of Courage*, is a vitalist in whom high respect for truth fuses with stoic faith in nature. Certainly he traces the growth of a neoprimitive, stoic religion of nature in his characters, as in Henry Fleming's inchoate respect for the gods of death and war. Essential to it is the ordeal, the arena in which the hero finds value in pain, violence, and even death—accepts them as productive of good. The ethos that naturalism develops is thus based on the struggle for survival, and it features that combination of sacrificial and stoic virtues described by Lovejoy as "hard primitivism."[4] Nietzsche was the modern teacher of these stoic values when he said, in making his own great claim to naturalist revelations, that he would rather perish than renounce the truth that "life sacrifices itself—for the sake of power!"[5] The various forms of redemptive or cathartic violence expressed in the works of Crane and Hemingway and by many later disciples, in both fiction and film, are specifically Nietzschean motifs in the modern myth of power.[6]

Notes

1. Quotations from *The Red Badge of Courage* are from *The Red Badge of Courage*, ed. Sculley Bradley et al., rev. ed. (New York: Norton, 1976).

2. For this debate, see R. W. Stallman, ed., *Stephen Crane: An Omnibus* (New York: Knopf, 1952), pp. 223–24.

3. Authority for this statement can be found in the works of one of the best students of modern responses to violence. Hannah Arendt writes as follows:

> As far as human experience is concerned, death indicates an extreme of loneliness and impotence. But faced collectively and in action, death changes its countenance; now nothing seems more likely to intensify our vitality than its proximity. Something we are usually hardly aware of, namely, that our own death is accompanied by the potential immortality of the group we belong to and, in the final analysis, of the species, moves into the center of our experience. It is as though life itself, the immortal life of the species, nourished, as it were, by the sempiternal dying of its individual members, is "surging upward," is actualized in the practice of violence. [*On Violence* (New York: Harcourt, Brace & World, 1970), p. 68]

4. Arthur O. Lovejoy, in Arthur O. Lovejoy and George Boas, eds., *A Documentary History of Primitivism and Related Ideas* (Baltimore, 1935), pp. 9–11.

5. *Thus Spake Zarathustra*, trans. R. S. Hollingdale (Baltimore: Penguin Books, 1962), p. 136.

6. There are strong political analogies here; the therapeutic justifications of political terrorism in the writings of Frantz Fanon come first to mind. The fact that during the civil rights movement his ideas were frequently echoed in statements of the blacks' need to assert self-respecting manhood is general testimony to the popular influence of his thinking. A more complex implication is found in the mood and actions of Israelis since the Holocaust and in the very bitter criticism often directed at the passivity of the Jews before the Nazis, suggesting that there were more virile and noble ways to be slaughtered.

The Red Badge of Courage and Social Violence: Crane's Myth of His America
Robert Shulman[*]

The Red Badge of Courage is Crane's response to the underlying violence, turmoil and savagery of post-Civil War America. Crane, however, has still not received enough credit for conveying through the war world of his novel the inner meaning of the social, political, racial and economic realities he transformed into the myth of war in *The Red Badge*. By "the myth of war" I mean the timeless, larger-than-life, suggestive quality that emerges from Crane's dominant

[*] From *Canadian Review of American Studies* 12 (Spring 1981): 1–19. Reprinted by permission of the *Canadian Review of American Studies*.

imagery of war and fog, from his disorienting irony and failure to provide clear connectives, from his sense of anarchic breakdown and uncertainty, and from the savage violence, shifting shapes, and diminished, groping protagonist that together give *The Red Badge* its distinguishing energy. This configuration constitutes a "myth" in the sense that it embodies a dominant imagery and set of emotionally charged attitudes that express the meaning of life not only for the author but also for a significant number of others in his culture.[1]

Whereas Henry Adams and W. E. B. Dubois wrote directly about chaos, brute power and the political, racial, economic and technological forces that were violently transforming post-Civil War America, Crane deals with these tendencies indirectly, by implication, in the language not of social and political analysis but of poetic metaphor or myth. At first Crane's novel seems an unlikely candidate for the approach I am suggesting.[2] The Civil War setting, for example, is an embarrassment. But unlike Tolstoy in *War and Peace*, Zola in *The Debacle*, or Stendhal in the battle scenes of *The Charterhouse of Parma*, Crane is not primarily interested in rendering with circumstantial realism a period thirty years in the past. His primary commitment is to render the psychology of battle, especially the inner rhythms of perception, fear and fantasy; to test inadequate views of heroism, identity and human nature; to probe the modern epistemological situation; and to establish for himself what will suffice. Although he researched Chancellorsville, *The Battles and Leaders of the Civil War*, and looked at Brady's photographs, instead of a complex rendering of the Civil War in particular, Crane is mainly interested in the testing of a young American Everyman—in the timeless, universal drama of a young man confronting the existential facts of death and fear, and the perhaps more time-bound drama of perceptions often beautifully warped by emotion and self-interest in a fog-shrouded inner and outer world where knowledge is shifting and uncertain. One result of this emphasis on the inner drama, on the flow of perceptions and feelings, and the relative neglect of sustained, external social specification is a novel that moves through metaphors toward universals. We recall the boy, the battle, the forest, the fog, the fear, the attack and retreat, the waiting, the flag, the sun. They are all sufficiently particularized to be compelling but they nonetheless have much of the generalized quality of Bunyan or a Methodist tract, much more internal probing than in Bunyan or a Methodist tract to be sure, but nonetheless generalized and universal, not particularly America in 1863. Crane's book, then, is indebted to fictional conventions rooted in Pilgrim's journey through a troubled world and in the transformed imagery and techniques of his own Methodist tradition.[3]

As a novel "about" the Civil War, *The Red Badge* thus leaves something to be desired, because Crane's main interests are elsewhere.[4] The general, universal, timeless quality he achieves and his moving psychological and epistemological drama nonetheless emerge from his imaginative transformation of the world he knew, not only the inner world of the self but also in part the conflict-ridden America of his own lifetime, the world which strongly conditioned his view of the self and existence. The significant events of Crane's personal life—his father's death, for example, or his own complex reaction to and against his family's Methodism—took place in the larger context of post-Civil War America. Crane's response to his religious upbring-ing made him especially sensitive to violent tendencies in the Amer-ican society of his lifetime, just as some of the deepest impulses of the larger society affected his identity and outlook and thus his creation of *The Red Badge*. One mark of a great writer is his ability to sense the undercurrents of his culture and to create imaginative forms to give them meaning. Part of Crane's achievement is that in the war world of *The Red Badge* he did exactly that.

Since *The Red Badge of Courage* is Crane's major creation and since of all his important works it has seemed the most remote from the America of his lifetime, however, I need to provide enough historical analysis to make Crane's novel at least partially available for a culturally oriented criticism. Because I think it is important to place this novel back into a history many people still want to see as prettier than it was, I call attention to the social, political and historical implications of Crane's basic image of war, his unsettling irony, and his sense of the chaos and violence of existence.

In America the sense of violent conflict and anarchic breakdown that animates *The Red Badge* reached a climax during the strike-ridden, depression years 1892–94 when Crane was conceiving and writing his novel. But these were not the first war-like years of Crane's lifetime. He was at a crucially impressionable age during 1877, a "year of violence" as Robert V. Bruce characterizes it.[5] Severe public dislocations, cataclysmic events that disturb parents, can deeply affect their children. For Kenneth Keniston's young anti-war activists of the 1960s, it was the Bomb and their parents' response to it that dominated their earliest memories.[6] For American children during the 1960s, the series of political assassinations, ghetto uprisings and the war in Vietnam, all with their immediate and cumulative impact, will probably function in the same way. For Stephen Crane, the violent events of 1877 are prime candidates. Crane was six, and in a minister's family in New Jersey the talk could not have avoided the burning and killing from Pittsburgh to San Francisco, the battles between Federal troops and urban crowds as close by as Maryland and Pennsylvania, the railroads shut down across the country and a spontaneous general strike broken with troops and bloodshed; in the nearby coal mining country, more strikes, the devastation of poverty, and the recent violence of the Molly Maguires (Crane's uncle lived in Molly Maguire country)—all this the culmination of four years of economic depression, wage cutbacks, and watered stock, with the specter of anarchism or communism seriously invoked, along with the troops, who had to be recalled from their assaults on the Sioux to take care of uprisings closer to home.[7]

During the next ten years as the corporations began to consolidate, economic warfare was not confined to rebates, stock manipulation and ruthless competition, but, as in the formation of Standard Oil, often involved direct physical violence. As the corporations fought among themselves, during the 1880s labor struck repeatedly against the prevailing twelve hour day, low wages and company domination.[8] In the background was anxiety about class war, a concern Bellamy drained of its threat in his concept of society peacefully organized as an industrial army. In the violent years immediately preceding *The Red Badge of Courage* (1895), however, the unions talked of organizing an army to fight against Pinkerton strikebreakers, the Populist platform invoked the specter of class war and "terrible social convulsions," and the conservative Supreme Court agreed—it saw in the income tax "an assault upon capital," a forecast of "a war of the poor against the rich."[9]

In particular, the violence of American life, often explicitly the violence of industrial war, dominated public consciousness at precisely the time Crane was publishing his *Sullivan County Sketches* in the *New York Tribune* the year before he began writing *The Red Badge of Courage*. "A Day of Rioting. Bloody Work at Homestead. Twenty Killed in a Battle Between Strikers and Pinkerton Men," the *Tribune* headline read on July 7, 1892. Three days later, in an issue that contained one of Crane's stories, the front page was still dominated by Homestead ("Denial by the Leaders of Locked-Out Men at Homestead of a Report Cannon Are Being Shipped to Them"), and when news from Homestead slackened, it was immediately replaced by banner headlines reporting "A Battle Between Miners. Men Shot and a Mill Blown Up in the Coeur D'Alene Region" (July 12, 1892), a story that continued in mid-July and was itself replaced by news of the assassination attempt on Frick and the "riots," burning, killing and pitched battles between miners and troops in Tennessee, as the miners, repeating what they had done a year earlier, attacked the prison stockades housing convict labor the owners used to keep wages down (see, for example, the front page articles on August 14, 16 and 19, 1892). Interspersed among these stories were front page headlines: "The Troops Ordered Out. Civil Authorities Powerless in Erie Country. Loaded Freight Cars Worth $100,000 Burned in the Railroad Yards Near Buffalo. The Switchman's Strike Threatens to Spread to

Several Great Systems. Freight Traffic Blocked" (August 16, 1892; see also August 19, 1892).

In the midst of these events the threat of race war was also presented in front page headlines. Our knowledge of these armed black uprisings has been almost totally suppressed, but "Negroes Rise in Arms," the *Tribune* wrote on July 13, 1892. "A Mob Attacks the Jail in Paducah, Ky. They Open Fire on the Sheriff's Posse and Kill One Man. Expectation of a Lynching the Cause of the Attack" (p. 7). To prevent the lynching, from two to three hundred Negroes armed with Winchesters attacked the jail, were repulsed, and attacked again a few hours later. The National Guard was called out, a posse of seventy-five whites armed themselves with shotguns and revolvers from the local hardware stores, and at least fifty Negroes were arrested for carrying arms.

The protection of alleged rapists was not the only motive for armed black resistance. The threat of lynching against a black who had killed a white man, apparently in self-defense, brought an armed crowd of blacks to the jail in Jacksonville, Florida (July 8, p. 1). And a few weeks later, a front page story from New Orleans confirmed "that there is truth in the sensational reports that the negroes at Kenner (La.) have banded together for mutual protection and an aggressive movement against the white population there" (August 8). The whites had successfully kept the blacks from voting for Governor in the April elections, and black leaders had organized an armed counterattack, including the alleged shooting of a judge. A few months later, another front page headline read, "Negro Rising in Texas. Stafford's Point Said to Be in the Hands of an Armed Mob" (February 16, 1893).

Armed blacks across the country were fighting back and were giving substance to Frederick Douglass' warning the month before Jacksonville, Paducah and Kenner. "Negroes May Make Bombs Too," the front page headline had read, and the story went on, " 'If the Southern outrages on the colored race continue, the negro will become a chemist. Other men besides Anarchists can be goaded into making and throwing bombs.' So said Frederick Douglass, the colored ex-minister to Hayti, at the Palmer House this morning. 'This terrible thirst for the blood of men must cease in the South,' he went on, 'or as sure as night follows day there will be an insurrection. Anarchists have not a monopoly on bombmaking and the negro will learn to handle the terrible instrument of destruction unless the wrongs committed against him cease' " (May 8, 1892).

"The wrongs"—the lynchings, beatings, degrading stereotypes and psychological devastation; the Jim Crow laws, loss of civil rights and economic serfdom—all have been well publicized, with the more obvious examples reported throughout Crane's lifetime, and Crane himself having firsthand knowledge through his unsuccessful attempt to save a black man from a lynch mob in June 1892.[10] White attacks on blacks contributed significantly to the climate of violence of Crane's period, but it is the armed black counterattacks that need to be emphasized to correct the impression that blacks passively accepted injustice and to suggest that race war as well as industrial or class war were active possibilities in the public's consciousness during Crane's lifetime.

The violence of industrial war, and the battles, burning, lynching and killing of often overt race war against blacks and Indians were intensified during 1893–94 by what contemporaries felt was the worst depression in the country's history, at precisely the time Crane was writing and rewriting *The Red Badge of Courage*.[11] As a context for the anarchic violence in *The Red Badge*, we should recall that during the depression of 1893–94 the public image of war was fused with a widespread sense of social breakdown and anarchy. The entire railroad strike supporting the Pullman workers, for example, was unequivocally reported under such massive front page headlines as "Coming Near to Anarchy. Mobs Rampant in Chicago" (July 7, 1894). And a month earlier the bloody, nationwide miner's strike was as a matter of course presented as a military operation: "A Vast Army Stops Work. The Miners' Strike Begins" (April 22, 1894). That strike of 130,000 men continued to involve the sort of "anarchic" violence that had been building up for months. "A Mob Applies the Torch. Terror and Ruin in the Wake of 600 Striking Miners Looting Stores, Destroying Corporation Property and Burning Coal Tipples. A Battle in Which the Mob is Worsted and One Probably Killed," this from Bridgeport, Connecticut, on January 28, 1894. Headlines about "riots," dynamiting, burning bridges and battles with the militia filled the papers almost daily.

"Strikers Become Demons," the *Tribune* reported in an especially revealing story, "An Official of the Frick Co. Stoned to Death. His Body Thrown Into a Furnace. A Day of Riot, Destruction and Bloodshed in the Coke Regions. A Report that 10 Hungarians Have Been Killed or Fatally Injured" (April 5, 1894, p. 1). The Frick official, the story went on to say, "was brutally murdered by 200 riotous Hungarians. . . . The murderers were pursued. . . . One of the fleeing Huns was shot and instantly killed." Through a web of associations with the immigrant Anarchists of the Haymarket, the foreign bomb-throwers of Paris and the striking Huns of Pennsylvania and Chicago, nativist sentiment became increasingly overt in reports of the industrial wars and "anarchic" violence of 1892–94.[12]

Anarchy had come home to roost, and Americans were not allowed to forget its horrors. Since Anarchism has always been an insignificant political force in America, it is important to stress that during Crane's lifetime the fear of anarchy was intense, widespread and rooted in the material interests of corporate owners, in the built-in frustrations of middle-class citizens uneasily involved in a rapidly expanding urban, industrial world, and in the long-term tensions resulting from the conflict between systematic, repeated depressions, with their attendant failures and unemployment, and the prevailing belief in individual responsibility for success and failure.[13] During this depression itself, moreover, the strikes, "riots," burning, business failures, mass unemployment and arbitrary use of Federal troops did signify genuine, large-scale breakdown or, more precisely, an intensification of the often violent conflict integral to the ordinary workings of the American economic and industrial process.

From the major battles of 1877 and the corporation wars and labor strikes of the 1880s to the depression and acute industrial and racial warfare of 1892–94, whatever its other qualities, the America of Crane's lifetime was marked by fighting, battles, armies, irrational prejudice and a deepening sense of anarchy and dislocation. Because of his reaction to his religious upbringing, Crane was well-situated to respond to and transmute the reality and imagery of war from his society into the war world of his novel. His father was a respected Methodist minister, his mother was a leader in the WCTU, and his maternal uncles, great uncles and grandfather were influential Methodist clergymen. Their theology, however, was significantly more severe than Crane's father's. In *The Feminization of American Culture* Ann Douglas demonstrates that during the nineteenth century women and ministers lost their earlier positions of influence and created a counter ideology of domesticity.[14] As in Crane's immediate family, the ministry and religion became increasingly feminized. In moderating the intensities of his wife's family's frontier, fire-and-brimstone Methodism, Crane's father was thus part of a larger movement.[15] Crane saw his father as a man "so simple and good that I often think he didn't know much of anything about humanity."[16] Crane nonetheless drew strength from his father even as he rejected Jonathan Crane's feelings about human innocence and the need to abstain from smoking, drinking, gambling and the other *Popular Amusements* the Reverend Crane opposed in his books and sermons. Although Jonathan Crane preached "about the fiery pit," in the view of Daniel Hoffman the central opposition in Crane's thought is between his father's God of love and his mother's family's God of wrath and damnation.[17]

After his moderate father died when he was eight, Crane was raised by a devout mother whom he loved and whose views he saw as narrow but not "as narrow as most of her friends or her family" (*Letters*, p. 241). He spent a lifetime rebelling against her opinions. What is important for our purposes is that as part of his rebellion against his family's religious milieu, Crane seems to have been unusually sensitive to the violence around and within him, a violence both sides of his upbringing deplored and thus made attractive. In both the moderate and evangelical traditions Crane emerged from, disorder, anger and the forceful expression of passion were perceived as deeply threatening both to the balanced and the subordinated self.[18] The threat of uncontrolled instincts and the need for order and restraint were basic to his parents' campaigns against the temptations of dancing, intoxication, smoking and the other instinctual pleasures they opposed. But just as Crane was drawn to the popular amusements his parents campaigned against, in forming his own identity he was also imaginatively compelled by the emotional unrestraint and violence of the underside of city life; he was especially fascinated by the immoderate violence of war and the disorder of strikes and the violent upheavals of American social and economic life.[19]

It was not, however, a simple process of rejection. In his mother's family's tradition the injunctions about discipline, restraint and the need for a loving redeemer appealed strongly to fears of death and damnation and were couched in an imagery and with a ferocity Crane both reacted against and embodied in a secular way in the demonic imagery and violence of *The Red Badge*. Alive in his tradition, that is, was a violent preaching of the need for gentleness, submission and salvation, a preaching whose intensity and imagery undercut its own imperatives about restraint, to say nothing of the conflicts with the moderate Protestantism Crane associated with his father. In Crane's view, "upon my mother's side, everybody as soon as he could walk, became a Methodist clergyman—of the old ambling-nag, saddle-bag, exhorting kind" (*Letters*, p. 94). As his poetry and fiction show, however, Crane was attracted as well as repelled by their sense of existence. Crane's sensitivity to American violence is thus rooted both in the imagery, attitudes and intensities of his forebears as well as in his reaction against them.

Crane, moreover, was raised in a tradition that generated unacknowledged violence by bending the will of children and training them to deny their passions and hostilities and to love and fear their parents and later God. Crane, however, never succeeded in finding a God to love or to whom to subordinate himself.[20] In the moderate Protestant tradition in which he was raised, moreover, children were taught selflessness and love—an emphasis that conflicted with adult demands for masculine aggressiveness. The ideal of selfless love was thus both compelling and a source of conflict and guilt because of the contradictory imperatives of adult male identity. Raised as a "feminized" minister's son by an older sister and a devout mother, no wonder Crane was alert to the violence within him and his society. By the time of *The Red Badge* the conflicts between what he had been taught and what he had experienced also powerfully motivated him to test the received values of heroism, patriotism and the image of man as formed in the loving image of God. Crane needed to get beneath the received verities to show life as he felt it really was.

Crane was also prepared to respond to the war-like realities of his period in part by the Methodist sense of Christian warfare. In his immediate family tradition Christian soldiers marched onward in battle against the demons of rum, tobacco and gambling. Crane himself went beneath such genteel surfaces to the demonic energy that drove Protestant Americans in their warfare on the battlefields of everyday life. In the process, Crane recaptured his forebears' sense of man's demonic nature and of the earth as a wayfaring and warfaring for Christian soldiers.[21] But he did not recapture the animating faith of his parents and relatives. True, in *The Red Badge* characters sometimes do selflessly care for others, usually to point up Henry Fleming's shortcomings, and at the end, having touched the bottom of his own mindless savagery, Henry may be in a position to move forward with a measure of confidence. But this secular affirmation may also be ironic and we may be intended to see it as another of the repeated instances of Henry's self-congratulation and self-delusion.

For Crane himself, the guilt inseparable from his rebellion also contributed to his secular reanimating of the demonology of his tradition. Much more pervasive than the possible but in any case muted affirmations is Crane's version of the fiends and the smoke-filled, hell-like possibilities of unredeemed human existence.[22] In *The Red Badge* Crane faces up to the reality of this sense of life without recourse to the affirmative beliefs of his tradition. Because for him the old religious certainties no longer exist, he gives us a world in which the sky is blue but empty and in which in a "religious halflight" the chapel of the woods is filled with rotting corpses.[23]

His sensitivities made acute by his response to his religious upbringing, Crane created an imagined world that also draws on and gives meaning to dominant impulses in the larger American society in which he lived. The connection between novel and society is not a direct, one-to-one, allegorical relation but is indirect, deep and pervasive. Crane, that is, has created a metaphor or myth for the fear and sense of breakdown, the preoccupation with anarchy and the very real violence of his society. Metaphor brings together unlikely or widely separated areas of experience and through imaginatively charged language makes us see an underlying connection. Myth is similar to metaphor but is more fully developed and complex. Myth, moreover, touches the values and basic preoccupations of large numbers of people in a culture and through a shared imagery and set of attitudes puts into perspective the deepest concerns of the culture.[24] It is in this sense that Crane's image of war and sense of anarchy and breakdown function as a metaphor or myth for significant currents and undercurrents of his society. Although we can discount any one of the memorable features of *The Red Badge* as accidental or insignificant, cumulatively they establish a meaningful, clarifying and imaginatively intensifying relation with Crane's contemporary society.

The image of war is at the heart of Crane's myth of his America, as it was at the center of the public reality of his society. In *The Red Badge*, Crane thus gives us a compelling war world characterized by battles, smoke, chaos and demons. Begrimed figures typically grope through the fog, fiend-like shapes emerge and disappear, and no one has a sense of pattern or meaning. Fear is the dominant emotion, and at his moment of heroism Henry Fleming behaves with the instinctual savagery of a gored beast. The pervasive smoke, chaos, killing, irrationality and fear are appropriate metaphors for the violence, disorder and passions of Crane's period, with its headlines of burning, terror and killing, its undercurrents of anxiety and deep-rooted animosities, its widespread image of war and battle, and its intensifying sense of anarchy and breakdown. For some, like Crane himself, moreover, this configuration speaks to the continuities and transformations of a Protestant faith that has lost its assurances but not its hold on the dark side of the self.

The imagery of war in *The Red Badge* emerges from the society upon which it reflects. Society at large informs Crane's recurring image of "riotous surges" as the men "pitched upon each other madly" (p. 123) or his sense that "wild yells came from behind the walls of smoke. A sketch in grey and red dissolved into a mob-like body of men" (pp. 30–31). The sense of "strange and ugly fiends jigging heavily in the smoke" (p. 124) also answers both to the transformed imagery of Crane's religious heritage and to the sense of demonic upheaval as fiendish strikers kill and burn. At key moments as well "the regiment was a machine rundown" (p. 112) or "it was the whirring and thumping of gigantic machinery" (p. 123) or "the battle was like the grinding of an immense and terrible machine to him. . . . The torn bodies expressed the awful machinery in which the men had been entangled" (pp. 50, 52), an imagery rooted in the gigantic chaos of a machine world breaking down. Crane's war world is animated from subterranean sources but they are in part shaped and given urgency by the larger American world Crane is also responding to and illuminating.

To shift from content and the imagery of war, one of Crane's basic techniques is to blur fixed outlines. From the snake-like image of the army and the mysterious "red, eyelike gleam" of the enemy camp fires in the opening paragraph to the blurred shapes moving in and out of the fog during the battles, almost nothing in *The Red Badge* is hard-edged, stable or easy to grasp physically, intellectually or emotionally. Reinforcing this technique are the dislocating irony and absence of explicit evaluations and connectives. Crane deliberately withholds direct, authorial commentary, so that we are never fully certain of his attitude toward any one of Henry's reactions. He also systematically refuses to supply logical and evaluating transitions. We look in vain for words like "because," "then," "less important," "but"—the entire vocabulary of reasoned discourse which implicitly assures us that things make sense. Throughout the novel, finally, Crane may intend any one statement to undercut itself ironically. For all of these reasons characters and readers are unsettled, they can take almost nothing for granted or at face value, and the uncertainty generates a very real strain. In his ironic outlook and his technique of blurring fixed outlines, Crane is both responding to and reflecting on the uncertainty, instability and anxieties of the culture at large, not in a direct but in a deep and subtle way.

Crane's myth of his America comes to a focus in the person of Henry Fleming, an almost nameless character, cut off from others and from his own "higher" mental powers. This little man, variously unsettled, pretentious, anxious, groping and savage, is a fitting protagonist for Crane's myth of American disorder and violence, of America's pervasive warfare and the lack of certainty his troubled times communicated. Henry Fleming is "an infernal fool" (p. 96) in the full sense of each of these charged words. He gropes through a smoke-filled hell-on-earth. He is "a war-devil" who "fights like th' devil" and "looks like th' devil" (pp. 97, 91, 79). As opposed to the ideal of selflessness, when Henry momentarily does forget himself, he becomes "a barbarian, a beast" (p. 97), an animal or devil. During the dominant part of his journey his vision is limited and his instincts are savage, "like a dog" with "his teeth set in a cur-like snarl" (pp. 96, 94).

Compounding the limits of the suspect human mind at the mercy of distorting personal needs is the nature of the outside world itself. The external human world is defined by the pervasive smoke, violence and instability. The external natural world is serenely indifferent to this spectacle: "It was surprising" to Henry but not Crane "that nature had gone tranquilly on with her golden processes in the midst of so much devilment" (p. 38). The divine world either does not exist or is so remote, empty and indifferent as to be nonexistent. Supremely empty and remote, "the blue, enamelled sky" looks down on the "dark smoke as from smoldering ruins" (p. 98).

The outer smoke and fog Henry gropes through also image his inner confusion. Henry's emotional turmoil, his fear, insecurity and need to think well of himself, affect the workings of his mind. This modern American Everyman lacks the emotional and intellectual capacity to make sense of his shifting, violent world. Henry nonetheless has intellectual pretentions. He has a number of theories, including "his theory of a blue demonstration" (p. 22), his image of "the red animal, war, the blood-swollen god" (p. 25), and "his mental pamphlets on the philosophy of the retreated and rules for the guidance of the damned" (p. 69). But none of his theories or philosophies explains what he needs to know. They only highlight his intellectual pretentions and the unreliability of a mind moved by inner and outer forces it does not and perhaps cannot understand. Through most of the novel Henry Fleming, the "infernal fool," is "bewildered" (p. 22) or self-important or self-deceiving. The only coherence in his world, moreover, is ironic, as when he sees "a coherent trail of bodies" (p. 105). He receives his red badge of courage when he vainly asks, "why—why" and receives in answer a blow on the head from one of his own comrades (p. 70). He may or may not have grown as a result of his immersion in battle—the over-all rhythm of the novel is open to contradictory interpretations. But at best Henry Fleming represents an image of man diminished from that in "Song of Myself" or "Self-Reliance."

The deemphasis on rationality and spirituality, the stress on savagery and deviltry, and the entire reduced status of Crane's protagonist derive from and reflect on American society as well as the diminished state of Crane's religious faith. Crane's great-uncle, the Bishop Jesse T. Peck, would recognize in Henry Fleming and his world an image of unregenerate man but he would have trouble finding the redemptive affirmations that complement his views of hell fire and human depravity expressed in his "rules for the guidance of the damned," *What Must I Do to Be Saved?* In a more secular vein, the earlier confidence and celebration of human and divine power were rooted in a basic confidence in America, an assurance that was not basically shaken even as writers like Emerson and Whitman tempered their views as they grew older. But Henry Fleming's groping, uncertainty, fear and mindlessness image an America quite different from Emerson's Concord or the New York of "Crossing Brooklyn Ferry."

In a general way, Crane's sense of America is thus closer to Melville's than to either a contemporary's like Howells or to that of predecessors like Emerson and Whitman. But when we look at the particulars of Crane's configuration, we realize that for all his general affinities with Melville, Crane is responding imaginatively to the surfaces and undercurrents of his own period. In his confused, fear-stricken protagonist; in his imagery of war, fog, chaos and demons; and in his unsettling irony, his technique of blurring clear edges, and his systematic undercutting of certainty, Crane has transmuted the prevailing image of war from his society and his religious tradition into his novel. He has simultaneously rendered his society's widespread sense of fear, breakdown and uncertainty.

In the violent war world of *The Red Badge* Crane, that is, has created an enduring myth that draws on, universalizes and puts in perspective the immediate violence of militia and Federal troops, of Pinkerton strike breakers and corporate warfare, of lynchings and the armed counter-attacks of black men, of the subjugation of the Indians, entire industries shut down, cities under martial law, workers and police killed, dynamite exploding, and men either baffled and unemployed or deeply uncertain about their position in a rapidly changing urban, industrial world. The pervasive image of war—the violence, anxiety, economic dislocation, and racial and ethnic hatred—were not peripheral or sporadic but were at the center of men's consciousness and dominated public life repeatedly during Crane's formative years and during the time immediately preceding his creation of *The Red Badge of Courage.* His response to his religious upbringing disposed Crane to respond powerfully to the imagery and reality of violent war and anarchic breakdown in the society at large. *The Red Badge of Courage* is not "about" these central tendencies and events, but in the novel Crane does successfully transform into the universality of art the dominant imagery and much of the inner meaning of an exceptionally troubled era in American life.

Notes

1. In preparing this article, I wish to acknowledge aid from the American Philosophical Society and the National Endowment for the Humanities.

2. See, however, Jay Martin, who argues that "it was what Crane learned from American society . . . rather than what he learned from Zola, Tolstoy, and others, that was the essential source of his ability to evoke war and the bewildered and pretentious reaction to war in *The Red Badge." Harvests of Change: American Literature 1865–1914* (Englewood Cliffs, N.J., 1967), p. 62.

3. For the relation between Crane's Methodist tradition and his use of generalized figures in his poetry, see Daniel G. Hoffman, *The Poetry of Stephen Crane* (New York, 1957), p. 65.

4. Daniel Aaron, for example, recognizes that *The Red Badge* is a novel opposed to war, not particularly *the* War, but since Aaron is mainly concerned with *the* War, he cannot fully value *The Red Badge. The Unwritten War: American Writers and the Civil War* (New York, 1973), pp. 211–18.

5. *1877: Year of Violence* (Indianapolis, 1959).

6. *Young Radicals* (New York, 1968).

7. In addition to Bruce, see Samuel Yellen, *American Labor Struggles* (New York, 1936), pp. 3–38, and John R. Commons, et. al., *History of Labor in the United States* (New York, 1918), II, 181–91.

8. See Samuel Eliot Morison, *The Oxford History of the American People* (New York, 1965), pp. 762–63; William Miller, *A New History of the United States* (New York, 1968), pp. 257–81; and Philip Taft and Philip Ross, "American Labor Violence," in *Violence in America,* ed. Hugh Graham and Ted Robert Gurr (New York, 1969), pp. 287–94.

9. The *New York Tribune*, July 10, 1892, p. 2; "The Omaha Platform, July 1892," in *A Populist Reader*, ed. George Brown Tindall (New York, 1966), p. 91; and the Supreme Court quoted in Harold U. Faulkner, *Politics, Reform and Expansion 1890–1900* (New York, 1959), p. 185.

10. See C. Vann Woodward, *The Strange Career of Jim Crow* (1955; New York, 1966); W. E. B. Dubois, *The Souls of Black Folk* (1902) in *Three Negro Classics*, ed. John Hope Franklin (New York, 1970), and *Black Reconstruction* (New York, 1935); Mark Twain, "The United States of Lyncherdom" (1901) in *Mark Twain on the Damned Human Race*, ed. Janet Smith (New York, 1962), pp. 96–104; Richard Wright, *Black Boy* (New York, 1945); NAACP, *Thirty Years of Lynching in the United States, 1889–1918* (1919; New York, 1969). For Crane's encounter with the lynch mob, see R. W. Stallman, *Stephen Crane: A Biography* (New York, 1968), pp. 10–11.

11. On the Depression of the 1890s, see Samuel Resnick, "Unemployment, Unrest, and Relief in the U.S. During the Depression of 1893–1897," *Journal of Political Economy*, LXI (Aug. 1953), 324–45, and Charles Hoffman, "The Depression of the Nineties," *Journal of Economic History*, XVI (June 1956), 137–52. On the war against the Indians, see Richard Hofstadter and Michael Wallace, eds., *American Violence: A Documentary History* (New York, 1969), p. 279, and the *New York Tribune*, April 5, 1894, p. 1; March 31, 1893, p. 1; and July 16, 1892, p. 5.

12. For this web of association with the Paris and Haymarket anarchists, see the *Tribune* for the early months of 1894, when the front pages were dominated by stories of anarchist murders and bombings in France, the massive police hunt for the anarchists, and the sensational trials of the bomb-throwers. The stories established a powerful connection with the Haymarket, since Pentecost, the lawyer of the Haymarket anarchists, had his appointment as a New York City assistant district attorney revoked, and through early January 1894, front page stories about him were juxtaposed with accounts of the murders perpetrated by the French anarchists. Later, the same juxtapositions connected anarchist murderers, striking miners and Coxey's army (see, for example, April 28, 1894, p. 1). And just as the Pullman boycott was beginning, massive front page headlines told of the anarchist slaying of President Carnot of France (June 25, 1894), so that the "anarchy and violence" of the strike had a clear connection with foreign murderers and the destruction of the state.

13. On the material interests of corporate owners, see, for example, United States Strike Commission, *Report on the Chicago Strike of June–July, 1894* (Washington, D.C., 1895), pp. xliii–xliv, pp. 145, 152, 159; Yellen, pp. 123–24; Hofstadter and Wallace, p. 152; and William Miller, p. 277. For an analysis of the middle-class response, see John Higham, *Strangers in the Land: Patterns of American Nativism 1860–1925* (New York, 1969), pp. 53–55, and Richard Sennett, "Middle-Class Families and Urban Violence: The Experience of a Chicago Community in the Nineteenth Century," in *Nineteenth Century Cities*, ed. Stephen Thernstrom and Richard Sennett (New Haven, 1969), pp. 386–420. For an analysis of the intellectual consequences of this situation, see David W. Noble, *The Progressive Mind, 1890–1917* (Chicago, 1970). Noble argues that "The intellectual history of the United States between 1890 and 1917 is best understood as the expression of a profound cultural crisis caused by the rapid urbanization and industrialization of the nation during the nineteenth century" (p. 1). See also Robert H. Wiebe, *The Search for Order 1877–1920* (New York, 1967), a perceptive study of 'the underlying dislocations, tensions and groping toward order in post-Reconstruction America, "a society without a core' . . . afflicted by 'a general splintering process' . . . incapable of facing the challenge of urbanization, industrialization, and immigration," a society that experienced "a fundamental shift in . . . values, from those of the small town in the 1880s to those of a new, bureaucratic-minded middle class by 1920." The quotations are from Donald Davies' summarizing "Foreword," pp. vii, viii.

14. Ann Douglas, *The Feminization of American Culture* (New York, 1977).

15. On the Reverend Jonathan Crane, see R. W. Stallman, pp. 3–5, and Hoffman, pp. 48–51.

16. *Stephen Crane: Letters,* ed. R. W. Stallman and Lillian Gilkes (New York, 1960), p. 243.

17. The quotation is from Stallman, p. 5. See Hoffman, particularly Chapters III and IV.

18. See Philip Greven, *The Protestant Temperament: Patterns of Child-Rearing, Religious Experience, and the Self in Early America* (New York, 1977), especially "The Evangelicals: The Self Suppressed" and "The Moderates: The Self Controlled," pp. 21–261. See also Jonathan Crane's representative statement of the moderate view quoted in my note 20.

19. See, for example, such stories as "Maggie," "An Experiment in Misery," "Men in the Storm," "An Eloquence of Grief," and the other *New York City Sketches of Stephen Crane,* ed. R. W. Stallman and E. R. Hagemann (New York, 1966) as well as such works as "In the Depths of a Coal Mine" and "Nebraskans' Bitter Fight for Life," in *Stephen Crane: Uncollected Writings,* ed. Olov W. Fryckstedt (Uppsala, 1963), pp. 121–31. Fryckstedt's introduction and notes fully document Crane's involvement in the political, social and economic life of his times. See also Crane's 1894–95 letters to Willis Brooks Hawkins—Nos. 90 and 98, p. 65 and pp. 69–70, give the tone—as well as No. 13, "To the Manager of the American Press Association," p. 11; No. 135, "To S. S. McClure," pp. 107–08; No. 88, "To Wickham W. Young," p. 64; and the letters cited under index entry "opinions on . . . politics, poverty . . . wealth," in *Stephen Crane: Letters,* p. 358.

20. I have been outlining the moderate style of Protestant child-rearing described by Greven, pp. 151–261. Crane's father belongs in this moderate tradition. Jonathan Crane, "gentlemanly in controversy and charitable in judgments" (Stallman, p. 5), nonetheless believed that "appetites and passions may ally themselves to thought, but in themselves are void of thought, and know only to press onward. Man's duty and safety demand that they be subjugated, taught to obey" (quoted in Hoffman, p. 50). Although Crane's mother was raised in the strict evangelical tradition, Crane was spared the full force of this style of child-rearing. In his early years in the busy Crane household his sister Agnes, fifteen years his senior, had much of the responsibility for raising him (Stallman, p. 3). Crane, however, was intimately familiar with the evangelical outlook of his mother and her family, as Daniel Hoffman shows in convincing detail.

21. For the relation between Crane and his maternal relatives, particularly his great-uncle, Bishop Jesse T. Peck, see Hoffman, pp. 52–92, especially pp. 62–64.

22. See, for example, Jesse T. Peck's *What Must I Do to Be Saved?* quoted in Hoffman, pp. 62–63.

23. Stephen Crane, *The Red Badge of Courage: An Episode of the American Civil War* ed. Fredson Bowers (Charlottesville, Va., 1975), p. 47.

24. For this view of myth, see Henry Nash Smith, *Virgin Land: The American West as Symbol and Myth* (New York, 1957), p. v.

The Red Badge of Courage:
Text, Theme, and Form
Donald Pizer[*]

During the last several years, Hershel Parker and his former student Henry Binder have argued vigorously that The Red Badge of Courage which we have been reading since 1895 is a defective text.[1] Crane, they believe, was forced by his editor Ripley Hitchcock to eliminate from the version accepted by D. Appleton & Co. an entire chapter as well as a number of important passages—particularly from the close of the novel—in which he underlined with biting irony the fatuousness and wrong-headedness of Henry Fleming. It is therefore the original and uncut version rather than the censored version of The Red Badge, Parker and Binder maintain, which we should be reading. In response to this contention Parker arranged for the uncut version of The Red Badge to be included in the prestigious, widely used, and in general textually responsible Norton Anthology of American Literature and Binder has published the version in a separate volume.[2]

This effort to rescue Crane's uncut draft of The Red Badge from exclusively scholarly use (the omitted portions of the novel have been known and available since the early 1950s) would have little significance except for the coincidence of Parker's editorial involvement in the Norton anthology and thus its presence in that widely circulated form. For there is no direct external evidence that Crane cut The Red Badge under pressure from Hitchcock. There are only inferences and assumptions derived from long-known collateral external evidence and from the critical belief that the uncut novel is the superior work of art—the novel which presents Crane in the form of his initially more honest and powerful intentions rather than in the emasculated and muddled form of these intentions in the first edition. The Appleton text, Parker, Binder, and yet another Parker student Steven Mailloux argue, is hopelessly flawed because of the unintentional ambivalences created in its themes and form by Crane's destruction, through his omissions, of his previously consistent and clearly evident contemptuous attitude toward Henry.[3] Thus, if we wish to read "the Red Badge that Crane wrote"[4] rather than the one forced upon him by Hitchcock's desire for a less negative portrait of a Civil War recruit, we must read it in the form available to us in the Norton Anthology and Binder's edition.

I have already discussed elsewhere the weaknesses in the argument from external evidence that Crane was forced by Hitchcock

[*] From South Atlantic Quarterly 84 (Summer 1985): 302–13. Reprinted by permission of Duke University Press.

to cut *The Red Badge*.[5] I would now like to tackle the more prob-lematical but equally vital issue of the argument from internal evidence that the ambivalences and ambiguities in the 1895 Appleton text constitute proof that Crane was forced to warp the themes of the novel through his revision and that the more immediately clear and consistent uncut draft is thereby the superior text. I have found it best in undertaking this task to concentrate initially and for a good deal of my paper on a portion of the novel which Crane wrote early in his composition of the work and which he left uncut and unrevised in its printed version—the first two paragraphs of *The Red Badge*. By demonstrating the purposeful and thematically functional ambiv-alences in this passage and then in the revised novel as a whole I wish of course to demonstrate that Crane's intent from the first was toward the expression of the ambivalent nature of Henry's maturation under fire and that his revision and cutting were toward the refinement of this intent. And I would also like to push on to a demonstration of the thesis that the presence of major thematic ambivalences in *The Red Badge* can be explained to a large degree by their apt relationship to major changes occurring at that time both in Crane's ideas and in the history of American thought.

Here are the first two paragraphs of *The Red Badge of Courage*:

> The cold passed reluctantly from the earth, and the retiring fogs revealed an army stretched out on the hills, resting. As the landscape changed from brown to green, the army awakened, and began to tremble with eagerness at the noise of rumors. It cast its eyes upon the roads, which were growing from long troughs of liquid mud to proper thoroughfares. A river, amber-tinted in the shadow of its banks, purled at the army's feet; and at night, when the stream had become of a sorrowful blackness, one could see across it the red, eyelike gleam of hostile camp-fires set in the low brows of distant hills.
>
> Once a certain tall soldier developed virtues and went resolutely to wash a shirt. He came flying back from a brook waving his garment bannerlike. He was swelled with a tale he had heard from a reliable friend, who had heard it from a truthful cavalryman, who had heard it from his trustworthy brother, one of the orderlies at division headquarters. He adopted the important air of a herald in red and gold.[6]

The opening paragraph of the novel describes the coming of spring to an army which has been in camp for the winter.[7] One major stream of imagery in the paragraph is that of awakening—awakening both after the cold of night and the fogs of dawn and after the brown of winter. The army awakens eagerly and expectantly—life is more than the cold and darkness of sleep, and in daylight and warmth passage can be made (the roads now "proper" rather than liquid mud) in the direction of one's destiny. The setting and its images are those of the beginning of a journey in which the emotional cast or coloration of the moment is largely positive; something is going to happen, and this something is better than the death in life of coldness, darkness, and immobility. The opening of the novel thus suggests that we are to be engaged by an initiation story, since both the initial situation and its images are in the archetypal form of an awakening to experience. Out of the blankness and emptiness of innocence, youth advances through experience to maturity and manhood.

Of course, the journey will have its difficulties. Indeed, without these it would not be an initiation journey. One is of those others in life who have aims different from ours and who therefore appear before us as the contradictory, belligerent principle in experience. So there is in the first paragraph the image of a mysterious and potentially dangerous enemy whom one sees in the night. But perhaps the greater difficulty will be in knowing in truth both the nature of the journey as it occurs and its full meaning at its conclusion. This difficulty is anticipated in the first paragraph by three references to the difficulty of knowing which are expressed through images of seeing and hearing. Fogs often obscure the landscape, the army hears only rumors, and the river is in shadow. The only unequivocally clear image of knowing is that the immediate avenue of movement—the roads—are now passable. Moreover, both the awakening and opposing forces are given an animal cast (the army "stretched out on the hills"; the "low brows" of the distant hills where lies the enemy), which suggests the limited rational equipment of those seeking to know.

The first paragraph of *The Red Badge of Courage* reveals Crane in a typically complex interweaving of images. Although the images in the paragraph imply that Henry's adventures may shape themselves into an initiation story, they also suggest that Henry himself will be an inept and inadequate interpreter of what has happened to him, that he will be unable to see and know with clarity and insight. And since the narrator will choose to tell the story through Henry's sense of its nature and importance rather than with a clear authorial underlining of meaning, we as readers will be left in a permanent state of ambivalence or ambiguity. Are we to respond to Henry's experiences principally in their symbolic character as milestones in the archetype of initiation, or are we to respond to them, because of Henry's limited understanding, as fog-ridden, shadowy, and misunderstood markers on a dimly perceived road?

The second paragraph reinforces and extends the notion that we are to have difficulty fully comprehending Henry's experiences. The first paragraph rendered the distinction between a possible progressive movement through time and the difficulty of knowing what occurs in time by means of symbolic and potentially allegorical images. The second paragraph increases our sense that the conventional means of evaluating experience are not to be trusted but does so now by means of the narrator's ironic voice in his reporting of such efforts. A tall soldier goes to wash a shirt with a belief that this enterprise requires virtue and courage. (As always in Crane's narrative style, the terms describing an action—here "developed virtues" and "went resolutely"—though superficially authorial in origin are in fact projections into the third person narrative voice of the doer's own estimation of his action. It is the soldier who believes he is behaving virtuously and resolutely, not Crane.) The statement, beginning as it does with major values and ending with the minor task to which these have been applied, is couched in the classic form of ironic anticlimax. One may think that it takes virtue and courage to wash a shirt, but there is a sharp and large distinction to be made between the actual character of the act and one's estimation of it. The implication which this distinction has for the general nature of self-knowledge, for the estimation of the worth of our acts, is that we will generally both aggrandize the significance of the event and overvalue our own attributes in relation to it.

The remainder of the paragraph contains two further implications for the problem of knowledge, both of which are also expressed in habitual forms of Crane's irony. The "tale" which the tall soldier has heard is rendered suspect despite the soldier's belief in its truth by Crane's account of its distant source and by his ironic repetition of the reliability, truthfulness, and trustworthiness of each of the tellers in the tangled history of its transmission. Much of what we learn about experience from our fellows is tainted by the difficulty of communicating accurately both what has occurred and what lies in store for us. Group knowledge, in short, is as suspect as personal self-evaluation.

As a further indication of the complications inherent in the acquisition and transmission of knowledge, the tall soldier—in his belief that he has something important to tell—begins to play a traditional role. He carries a banner and adopts the air of a herald. Man, when he has something to communicate, will adopt various roles to dramatize the worth both of his information and of himself. But the role will often obscure the emptiness and valuelessness of that which is being communicated. In short, Crane appears to be saying in this paragraph, the process of gaining and transmitting knowledge is warped by powerful weaknesses within both human nature and social intercourse. And the knowledge communicated by this process—that which we believe is true about ourselves and our fellows—is thus suspect.

The two opening paragraphs of *The Red Badge of Courage* constitute a paradigm for the themes and techniques of the novel as a whole. In its events and in much of its symbolism, the novel is a story of the coming of age of a young man through the initiatory experience of battle. But our principal confirmation of Henry's experiences as initiation myth is Henry himself, and Crane casts doubt—through his ironic narrative voice—on the truth and value of Henry's estimation of his adventures and himself. And so a vital ambiguity ensues.

The initiation structure of *The Red Badge* is evident both in the external action of the novel and in a good deal of the symbolism arising from event. A young untried soldier, wracked by doubts about his ability to perform well under fire, in fact does flee ignominiously during his first engagement. After a series of misadventures behind his own lines, including receiving a head wound accidentally from one of his own fellows, he returns to his unit, behaves estimably in combat, and receives the plaudits of his comrades and officers. On the level of external action, *The Red Badge* is thus a nineteenth-century development novel in compressed form. In such works, a young man (or woman) tries his mettle in a difficult world, at first believes himself weak and unworthy in the face of the enormous obstacles he encounters, but finally gains the experience necessary to cope with life and thus achieves as well a store of inner strength and conviction. Much of the symbolism in *The Red Badge* supports a reading of the work as developmental fiction, for one major pattern of symbolism in the novel rehearses the structure of the initiation myth. Henry is at first isolated by his childlike innocence. But after acquiring a symbol of group experience and acceptance (the red badge), he is guided by a supernatural mentor (the cheery soldier) through a night journey to reunion with his fellows; and in the next day's engagement he helps gain a symbolic token of passage into manhood (the enemy's flag).

But much in the novel also casts doubt on the validity of reading the work as an initiation allegory. Chief among these sources of doubt is Crane's ironic undermining at every turn of the quality of Henry's mental equipment and therefore of the possibility that he can indeed mature. Whenever Henry believes he has gained a significant height in his accomplishments and understanding, Crane reveals—by situational and verbal irony—how shallow a momentary resting place he has indeed reached. A typical example occurs after the enemy's first charge during the initial day of battle, when Henry grandiosely overestimates the character of a minor skirmish. ("So it was over at last! The supreme trial had been passed. The red, formidable difficulties of war had been vanquished" [p. 34].) This ironic deflation of Henry's self-evaluation continues unrelieved throughout the novel and includes as well Henry's final summing up, when, after in effect merely having survived the opening battle in the spring of a long campaign (with Gettysburg to follow!), he concludes that "the world was a world for him, though many discovered it to be made of oaths and walking sticks" (p. 109).

In addition, Crane casts doubt on the depth of Henry's maturity at the close of the novel by revealing Henry's exercise in sliding-door conscience. Henry, at the end of the second day's fighting, is still troubled by two of his less estimable acts—his desertion first of his unit and later of the tattered soldier. But what troubles him most is less the intrinsic nature of these acts than that they might be discovered, and when he realizes that this is not likely, he "mustered force to put the sin[s] at a distance" (p. 109) and revels instead in his public accomplishments. It was this aspect of Henry's intellect—his conscience-troubled rationalizations of his behavior and his closely related fury at fate for having placed him in conscience-troubling situations—which Crane, after concluding the first draft of the novel, realized he had overdone and thus cut heavily in the interval between the draft and publication.

Crane also undermines the initiation structure of *The Red Badge* by including in the novel two major counterstructures. Initiation is essentially a mythic statement of a faith in the potential for individual growth—that the forward movement of time is meaningful and productive because through experience we acquire both the capacity to cope with experience and a useful knowledge of ourselves and the world. But *The Red Badge* also contains two major structures which imply that time is essentially meaningless, that all in life is circular repetition, that only the superficial forms of the repetition vary and thus are capable of being misunderstood as significant change and progress. One such symbolic structure is that of the rhythmic movement of troops. The novel begins with the advance to battle by Henry and his regiment, it ends with their departure from battle, and the body of the work contains a series of charges and countercharges, advances and retreats. Since these movements occur in an obscure landscape in connection with an unnamed battle, and since little meaning attends the various movements aside from their impact on Henry and his regiment, significance is attached to the fact of movement itself rather than to movement in relation to a goal or direction. One of the symbolic structures of *The Red Badge* is therefore of a flow and counterflow of men, a largely meaningless and directionless repetition despite Henry's attribution of deep personal meaning to one of its minor phases, a moment of flow which he mistakes for a moment of significant climax.

Another such circular symbolic structure is even more consciously ironic in character. Henry runs on the first day of battle because of

two psychic compulsions—an animal instinct of self-preservation and
a social instinct to act as he believes his comrades are acting. On
the next day—in a far more fully described series of combat experiences—Henry responds to battle precisely as he had on the first
day, except that he now behaves "heroically" rather than "cowardly."
Again an animal compulsion (that of the cornered animal made vicious
and powerful by anger and fear at being trapped) is joined with a
social one (irritation at unjust blame attached to the regiment) to
produce a similar "battle sleep" of unconsciousness in action. These
underlying similarities in Henry's battle performances reveal not only
Crane's attack on the conventional notions of courage and cowardice
but—in their role as "equal" halves in a balanced symbolic structure—his belief that life is essentially a series of similar responses
to similar conditions in which only the unobservant mistake the
superficially different in these conditions and responses for a forward
movement through time.

These two powerful drives in *The Red Badge*—the initiation plot,
structure, and symbolic imagery, and the undercutting of a development myth by a variety of ironic devices which imply that the belief
that man can adequately interpret the degree of his maturity is a
delusion—these two drives come to a head in the final chapter of
the novel. The second day's battle is over, and Henry has behaved
well in his own eyes and in those of his fellows. Yet he continues
as well to overvalue his accomplishments and deny his failings. The
imagery of the conclusion reflects this ambivalence. Henry, now that
the battle is over, thinks of "prospects of clover tranquility" (p. 109).
But in fact it is raining, and "the procession of weary soldiers became
a bedraggled train, despondent and muttering, marching with churning
effort in a trough of liquid mud under a low, wretched sky. Yet the
youth smiled, for he saw that the world was a world for him . . ."
(p. 109). In this passage, the fatuousness of Henry's conception of
what awaits him and therefore of what he has achieved is inherent
in the sharp distinction between Henry's belief and the permanent
condition of the group to which he belongs, of all mankind, in effect,
despite his conviction that he lies outside this condition.

It might thus be argued that Crane wishes us, at this final moment,
to reject completely the validity of an initiation experience for Henry.
Yet, in the final sentence of the novel, added after the completion
of the full first draft, Crane wrote: "Over the river a golden ray of
sun came through the hosts of leaden rain clouds" (p. 109). This
flat, bald imagistic statement reaffirms the essential ambiguity of the
work as a whole, despite the possibility of reading the final chapter
as a confirmation of one position or the other. For the image is not
attributed to Henry; it occupies a paragraph of its own, and is the
narrative voice's authoritative description of a pictorial moment rather

than of Henry's suspect response to the moment. And the narrative voice wishes us to be left, as a final word, with the sense that life is truly ambivalent—that there are rain clouds and that there is the sun. The darkness and cold (and lack of vision) of the opening images of the novel are part of the human condition, but the promise of daylight and spring warmth and of vision which are also present in the opening images have in part been fulfilled by the ray of sunlight.

I would now like to explore the implications of Crane's ambiguity in *The Red Badge of Courage* for his career and for his place in American literary and intellectual history. Crane's career can be divided into the usual three major phases, of which *Maggie* (1893) is the principal work in the first phase, *The Red Badge* in the middle period, and the novellas of 1897 and 1898 (of which I shall discuss "The Open Boat") the most important work of the last phase.

Maggie has always been rightfully considered the most naturalistic of Crane's works. Each of its characters is locked in a prison of self-delusion from which he never escapes. Maggie believes that Pete is a chivalrous knight who will rescue her from poverty and the oppression of her home; Pete believes that he is a formidable lover and that he has behaved well toward Maggie; Jimmie believes that his family honor requires defense; and Mary Johnson believes that she has been a Christian parent to Maggie. These delusions are made so grossly evident by the distinction between a character's self-conception and the circumstances of his life—between Mrs. Johnson's notion of the home she has created and the actual nature of that home— that we are left with little doubt that one of Crane's principal intents in the novel is to depict the overpowering role of emotional self-interest in the handicapping of the capacity to see life and oneself fully and clearly. No one knows anything of truth in *Maggie*—neither what they are nor what he or she wants to believe about himself and the world at large. Some are destroyed by this limitation (Maggie goes to her death); some are in decline (Pete and Mrs. Johnson); and some continue on their way (Jimmie). But all are locked into a world of blindness which effectively thwarts any possibility of growth based on understanding. Although the physical setting of *Maggie* is a slum, its symbolic setting is a surrealistic hall of mirrors, where the characters see only grotesque versions of themselves, versions, however, which they accept as real. And since there are no exceptions to this principle in *Maggie*, it must be assumed that Crane, at this stage of his career, believed self-delusion to be the universal human condition, with only its degree and level of sophistication a matter of variation.

"The Open Boat," written some five years later, is at the other end of Crane's depiction of the human condition. The allegorical context of the story, however, does not differ radically from the slum of *Maggie;* here, too, life is principally a matter of coping with the destructiveness present in all existence. The four men in the open boat find the sea (the immediate setting of their lives) dangerous; the sky (God) empty; and the shore (society) unknowing. But unlike the characters of *Maggie* in their absolute social and emotional isolation, the four men in "The Open Boat" come to rely on each other—to lean heavily on each other in order both to bear their condition and to survive it. Much in the story details a growth in their mutual interdependence, from a sharing of duties in the boat to a sense of comradeship which all feel. In the end, after the adventure is over, Crane tells us that the men, hearing the sound of the sea at night, "felt that they could then be interpreters."

Few readers have viewed this closing line as ironic. Our sense of a successful resolution of the adventure for its survivors, of something gained through the experience, is too great to cast doubt on the "reliability" of this final statement. Thus, the principal question to be asked of the statement is what indeed can the men now properly interpret? Crane replies to this question within the story as a whole, and his answer also replies, in a sense, to the issues raised by *Maggie.* There is no God, he appears to be saying, and isolation is therefore the quintessential human condition. But within this unchanging situation men can both establish temporary communities based on mutual need and entertain compassion for those ranges of human experience which also reveal man's essential loneliness. To be more precise, the correspondent learns, within the story, that there are no temples to cast stones at in blame for their fate, but that the men can establish a "subtle brotherhood" in their mutual understanding and aid on the boat, and that his realization of these truths of experience can at last bring him to a recognition of the universal pathos surrounding the soldier of the legion, alone and dying far from home.

"The Open Boat" thus suggests that Crane has come some distance from *Maggie.* We are still battered by life, and some, like the oiler, are mercilessly destroyed. But we can now understand this condition and, to some extent, through our understanding, lessen its effect on us, both physically and emotionally. We need not all be victimized by the human capacity for self-delusion; some of us have the capacity to mature, under pressure, to understanding. Which returns us to *The Red Badge of Courage.* In relation to Crane's career, the novel, in an image appropriate to its setting, is a kind of battleground in which the two views of human nature and experience which I have identified as flourishing in *Maggie* and "The Open Boat" struggle for dominance, without either succeeding in gaining the day. The plot and a good deal of the symbolic structure of the novel imply growth on Henry's part in coping with the eternal "war" which is human experience. But Crane's ironic voice and other symbolic structures imply that Henry is as self-deluded at the close of the novel as he is uncertain about himself at the opening. The theme of the value of social union in *The Red Badge* has something of the same ambivalence. Henry does gain a sense of a "subtle battle brotherhood" (p. 31) at various times during combat, and his return to his regiment is depicted as a productive reunion. But at other times, when he opposes the blind obedience which "union" requires of him, he is described as locked into a "moving box" (p. 21) of social and psychic compulsion as viciously destructive as is the Johnson household in imposing its values and demands on its weakest members.

The Red Badge of Courage is thus a work whose ambivalences and ambiguities are an appropriate and probably inevitable reflection of those of its author at that particular moment in his career. Crane in the novel was "working out" his then divided and uncertain notion of the balance of emphasis to give to the human capacities both for self-delusion and for insight and understanding.

The Red Badge of Courage also reflects in its ambivalences a major moment of transition in the history of American belief—that of a period in American thought when, broadly speaking, there was a movement from nineteenth-century certainties to modern doubts, from a willingness to affirm large-scale notions about the human enterprise to an unwillingness to do more than represent the immediacies of experience itself.

The origins of this state of mind in the 1890s lie less in the events of the decade itself than in the realization by a generation coming of age during the decade of changes which had been occurring in the American scene and American belief since the Civil War. In brief, and with some of the melodramatic overemphasis and overgeneralization inherent in the art of intellectual history, young writers of the 1890s were now no longer sure of two transcendent faiths which had buttressed American belief for over a hundred years. The first was a faith in human nature in general—or more specifically in the Christian notion of man as God's special creature as that notion was refined and extended by late eighteenth-century Enlightenment idealism and early nineteenth-century romantic transcendentalism. The second was a more specialized faith in America as a world in which the Edenic possibilities of man could indeed flourish—that in this new-found-land man's capacity for productive self- and national development could best be realized.

Challenging these two faiths in the 1890s were the growing awareness of the impact of a Darwinian explanation of man's origin on the belief that man was principally a reflection of God's own capacity for wisdom and goodness, and the growing awareness that American society in its present state of development was indeed an apt symbolic reflection of man as a jungle, rather than an Edenic, creature. The animal degradation of life in the slums and factories and the cut-throat character of economic life everywhere made such an endorsement of the metaphor of America as jungle so obvious than even the popular mind could grasp the analogy.

Yet always—along with these realizations—there remained a powerful vestige of a continuing faith, one that took many forms but which had in all its shapes an emotional center of belief that America was indeed a new birth for the best that was in man—that the experiment could yet succeed. It is out of this tension between old belief and new doubts that a work such as *The Red Badge of Courage* emerges in the mid-1890s. And as so often occurred in the Americanization of the nineteenth-century great debate between faith and doubt, the specific poles of tension among writers of the 1890s were less within religious or even social categories of belief than within epistemological ones: can man know and translate into experience the great transcendent truths of life? If one can posit the two extremes in the American version of the debate, they might thus be Emerson's celebration of man's capacity to grasp intuitively the large truths analogically present in experience (that is, in nature) and the early Hemingway's lack of confidence in all but the concrete immediacies of experience itself, of his immense distrust of all large abstractions which men seek to impose on life.

Henry's experiences in *The Red Badge of Courage* appear to confirm, in their symbolic analogue to an awakening at dawn and a concluding ray of sunshine after battle, the great nineteenth-century faith in the human capacity for growth and development through a self-absorbed projection into life. But the novel also contains an equally powerful edge of "modern" doubts about the capacity of man to achieve wisdom, doubts expressed in the "modern" form of an ironic undercutting through voice and structure of the protagonist's belief that the traditional abstraction of courage is real and can be gained. It is thus an irony of a different kind that in seeking to universalize his story, to have it be not a depiction of a specific battle but an expression of a permanent human condition, Crane in fact also brought his account of Henry Fleming closer to the specific state of mind of his own historical moment—to the uncertainties about the possibility for growth and self-knowledge which had begun to gnaw at the American consciousness in his own time.

The Red Badge of Courage therefore plays seemingly contradictory roles in relation to the career of its author on the one hand and its historical moment on the other. In relation to Crane's career, the novel lies between Crane's deeply pessimistic view of man's blindness in *Maggie* and his far more affirmative sense in his later novellas of man's capacity to grow in insight and moral courage through experience. In relation to American thought, however, the novel affirms an earlier nineteenth-century faith in man's ability to mature while offering as well a modernistic critique of man's fatuous belief in his own ability to evaluate correctly both himself and experience. But this paradox, this cross-stitching, so to speak, of past and present in the work, in which it looks both backwards and forwards depending on whether one adopts a biographical or historical perspective, is one of the major sources of the novel's richness and permanence. *The Red Badge of Courage* is not a work flawed in its ambivalences. Rather, as its first two paragraphs suggest, it holds them in meaningful suspension to reflect what in the end is perhaps the modern temper in its essence—not so much a reaffirmation of faith or an announcement of the triumph of doubt as a desire to explore the interaction between these two permanent conditions of man.

Notes

1. See Binder's "The *Red Badge of Courage* Nobody Knows," *Studies in the Novel* 10 (Spring, 1978): 9–47 and Parker's comments on *The Red Badge* in his "Aesthetic Implications of Authorial Excisions," in *Editing Nineteenth-Century Fiction*, ed. Jane Millgate (New York, 1978), pp. 99–119 and "The New Scholarship," *Studies in American Fiction* 9 (Autumn, 1981): 181–97.

2. Ronald Gottesman et al., ed., *The Norton Anthology of American Literature*, vol. 2 (New York, 1979) and Henry Binder, ed., *The Red Badge of Courage* (New York, 1982). Parker is one of the editors of the *Norton Anthology*.

3. See Mailloux's *Interpretive Conventions: The Reader in the Study of American Fiction* (Ithaca, N.Y.: Cornell University Press, 1982), pp. 160–65, 178–91.

4. Binder, "The *Red Badge of Courage* Nobody Knows," p. 10.

5. " 'The *Red Badge of Courage* Nobody Knows': A Brief Rejoinder," *Studies in the Novel* 11 (Spring 1979): 77–81.

6. *The Red Badge of Courage*, A Norton Critical Edition, ed. Donald Pizer (New York, 1976), p. 5. Citations from this edition will hereafter appear in the text. The text of *The Red Badge* in the Norton Critical Edition is that of the 1895 Appleton edition conservatively emended, principally to correct typographical errors.

7. The reading of *The Red Badge of Courage* which follows has been evolving in my own thinking about the novel and about Crane's career and his times for some years. See, for example, my "Stephen Crane's *Maggie* and American Naturalism" and "Late Nineteenth-Century American Naturalism" in my *Realism and Naturalism in Nineteenth-Century American Literature* (Carbondale, Ill., 1966); "A Primer of Fictional Aesthetics," *College English* 30 (April 1969): 572–80; "Nineteenth-Century American Naturalism: An Approach Through Form," *Forum* (Houston) 13 (Winter, 1976): 43–46; and my edition of *American Thought and Writing: The 1890s* (Boston, 1972). I have also drawn upon my awareness of the vigorous debate in Crane studies on the nature, role, and worth of the ambiguities in *The Red Badge*. For a survey of the debate, see my "Stephen Crane," in *15 American Authors Before 1900: Bibliographical Essays on Research and Criticism*, ed. Earl N. Harbert and Robert A. Rees (Madison, Wisc., 1984), pp. 128–84.

Fighting Words: The Talk of
Men at War in *The Red Badge*   Alfred Habegger[*]

The chapter in "The Open Boat" where the shipwrecked men study and comment on the tantalizing movements of a group on the beach exhibits an interesting variety of direct discourse. The speakers are not identified; their speeches seem less inhibited than the rest of what gets spoken on the tiny dinghy; and the "conversation" suggests a group thinking out loud rather than four speakers voicing their individual thoughts. Although each line of "dialogue" responds to the preceding lines, the attention of all four men is focused exclusively on people who are out of earshot. The prevailing decorum that rules self-expression on the boat having been set aside, the passage as a whole turns into a cascade of eager collective commentary, a genuine prose choral ode that shifts in tone from excited hope to angry resentment. The latter feeling is directed at the man on shore whose attention-getting signal, the whirled garment, remains maddeningly indecipherable and ineffective. Eventually, one of the men declares, "No! He thinks we're fishing. Just giving us a merry hand. See? Ah, there, Willie."[1]

As far as I know, those three concluding words have not drawn comment, even though their meaning seems no clearer than that of the rotated jacket. Nearly everyone I have asked to explain the words has replied that the speaker is making his point to Billie the oiler. When I proposed a query about this passage to the editor of a journal devoted to the elucidation of American speech, I received the same clarification:

> Since *Willie* is an alternative diminutive for *William*, isn't it most reasonable to assume that "Willie" is a vocative address to Billie the oiler? Also, my memory is that Crane was pretty sloppy about details; even if he wasn't thinking of the "Willie" as a variant of "Billie," he may well have been thinking of the same character. In any case, for one of the men to call Billie "Willie" would be a perfectly natural thing, it seems to me.

This is evidently the obvious explanation, and yet it is far from satisfactory. In my own experience of American speech, "Billie" and "Willie" are definitely not interchangeable. Within the passage, I can think of no reason why any of the men should abruptly address himself to one particular person rather than the group. Why would Crane have the speaker single out another by name when there is no need to establish the names or identities of the speakers them-

[*] This essay was written specifically for this volume and is published here for the first time by permission of the author.

selves? And why would the speaker of the three mysterious words suddenly abandon ordinary functional speech, especially in addressing a working man? To do so would be to commit a pointless faux pas, like saying "Behold!" Anyway, the oiler surely has his mind on the shore scene already.

The moment we reflect on the mysterious exclamation it becomes clear that it must mean something well beyond the signification of the individual words. To solve this puzzle we need to bear in mind Crane's skill in representing hoots, jeers, catcalls, threats, surly challenges, and similar utterances. "Ah, there, Willie" was at one time an immediately recognizable formula expressing derision and defiance. I am not certain whether "Willie," by itself an insulting term for a homosexual man, a "Willie-boy," was a necessary part of the phrase. Neither do I know just when the phrase was in vogue, how it got started, how it was uttered, or even what it precisely meant—whether it served as a challenge to combat, a taunt directed at a person seen as a sissy, a victorious crowing, or something else. But it was definitely a rude expression of personal defiance. We know this to be the case because of the variation James Thurber rang on the phrase in his fine 1943 put-down of Salvador Dali, "The Secret Life of James Thurber." This sketch exposed the vanity and pretensions of Dali's memoirs of childhood by contrasting them with the homeliness of Thurber's own early recollections. Dali had known girls named Galuchka and Dullita and remembered the comforts of the womb; Thurber's first memory was of accompanying his "father to a polling booth in Columbus, Ohio, where he voted for William McKinley." The only romance in Thurber's childhood came from his fascination with idioms not meant to be taken literally—skeleton key, leaving town under a cloud, crying one's heart out, all ears. In his conclusion, after having vindicated his "secret world of idiom" in the face of Dali's phony glamor, Thurber taunted his rival with the idiom that had become as antiquated and homely as Thurber's boyhood in Columbus—"Ah there, Salvador!"[2]

What we have in Crane's "Ah, there, Willie" is an example of local speech, speech so genuinely historicized that it remains misunderstood, or even unnoticed, by later readers. One of the chief points to be made about the soldiers' talk in The Red Badge of Courage is that this "historical" novel does not contain one single instance of speech that is as local, as historical, as the locution I have considered in "The Open Boat." Historicized talk is always hard for later generations to follow, but all the talk in Crane's Civil War novel is easily comprehended. Anyone who immerses himself or herself in letters or journals from the early 1860s will at once realize (though the point is evident anyway) that Crane was no more concerned to reproduce the exact talk of Civil War combatants than he was to establish battle coordinates. Yet the reviews of the novel tell us that its first readers regarded it as fascinatingly historical. The narrative took them back to the Civil War in a way no other account had succeeded in doing. Paradoxically, Crane achieved this illusion of verisimilitude partly by means of his soldiers' talk, which was manufactured with more skill than the author has been given credit for. This talk contributed to the novel's air of historicity, and it contributes even more to the question the novel investigates: How do fighting men express their thoughts?

In discussing Crane's representation of speech, I will not be concerned with talk that is metaphorical rather than literal—"the courageous words of the artillery and the spiteful sentences of the musketry."[3] Neither will I have much to say about the many passages in which Henry Fleming's unarticulated thoughts are rendered in language and imagery he himself would not have used. "Minds, he said, were not made all with one stamp and colored green" (54). "He had been out among the dragons, he said" (72). The diction, the absence of quotation marks, and the familiarity of the narrative convention these sentences follow all announce that "said" is not to be taken literally. (Obvious as the convention may be, Crane himself called attention to it in one sentence: "But [Henry] said, *in substance*, to himself that if the earth and the moon were about to clash, many persons would doubtless plan to get upon roofs to witness the collision" [38; italics mine]). I am confining my attention here only to those passages that represent *spoken* language, whether that language is recorded in direct discourse or summarized by Crane in what is traditionally called indirect discourse.

Although I will also ignore the much-discussed problem of "dialect," taking this term to refer to the presentation of regional or uncultivated speech through nonstandard orthography, it will be necessary to comment briefly on the generalized countrified traditionalism of the soldiers' talk. Some of their statements—"Well, I swan" (104), "I'm a gone coon" (21), "Be keerful, honey, you'll be a-ketchin' flies" (41)—surely had an old-timey feel for Crane's first readers. Perhaps the same was true for "kit-an'-boodle" (8, 68), "jim-hickey" (96), "chin-music" (77), "skedaddle" (14, 16), "fresh fish" (7), "fight like hell-roosters" (75), "smart as a steel trap" (47). Most of the mild oaths and curses probably had an old-fashioned flavor by 1895— "make way, dickens [i.e., devil] take it all" (40), "by ginger" [i.e., Jesus] (62), "Great Jerusalem" (63). The fact that Crane was able to introduce undisguised profanity into the next-to-last charge—"Where in hell yeh goin'?" and "Gawd damn their souls" (89)—tell us that the various euphemistic oaths were not simply an evasive concession to public taste. They also contributed to the picture of life in the 1860s as seen from the 1890s.

The character with the strongest rural twang is the tattered man, whose speech—"a reg'lar jim-dandy" (46), "there's a bat'try comin' helitywhoop" (44), "first thing that feller knowed he was dead" (47)—shows none of Henry's anxiety at being taken for a greenhorn. Even so, humor and irony are well within the tattered man's range:

> "Oh, I'm not goin' t' die yit. There too much dependin' on me fer me t' die yit. No, sir! Nary die! I *can't!* Ye'd oughta see th' swad a' chil'ren I've got, an' all like that."
> The youth glancing at his companion could see by the shadow of a smile that he was making some kind of fun. (47)

Here the bitter countrified drollery with which Crane's yokel speaks is beyond Henry's appreciation.

One could cite a few other instances of expressions that probably struck readers in 1895 as colorful and old-fashioned—"a hull string of rifle-pits" (22), "sore feet an' damn' short rations" (14, 15), "back in winter quarters by a short cut t'-morrah" (23), "could tear th' stomach outa this war" (80, 106), "sech stomachs aint a-lastin' long" (7), "Gee-rod [Jesus God], how we will thump 'em" (14). Framed by Crane's terse, up-to-date, and highly individualized prose, these and other locutions and speeches helped give the soldiers' talk a slightly quaint, historical feel. The novel had an overwhelming impact not because it revived the history of battles and leaders and official political rhetoric, but because it achieved an effect analogous to that of the new social history of our own time, which tries to revive the unofficial voices, the unexpressed experiences. Of course, Crane was chiefly interested (in this respect also, perhaps, resembling some of our own historians) in generating an *illusion* of factual excavation and reconstitution. It was the glaring disparities between his language as narrator and that of his characters that helped turn his trick.

To single out the more colorful speeches for attention, however, is to convey a very misleading impression of Crane's soldiers' talk, which is for the most part flat and inexpressive, even a little dull. "Billie—keep off m' feet. Yeh run—like a cow" (16). "We're allus bein' chased around like rats. It makes me sick" (77). Mebbe yeh think yeh fit th' hull battle yestirday, Flemin'." "Why, no, . . . I don't think I fit th' hull battle yestirday" (76). A general, elated that the center of his line has held, says, "Yes—by Heavens—they have! . . . . Yes, by Heavens, they've held 'im! They've held 'im" (34). Most of the men's speeches have the same flagrant shapelessness and ordinariness. This is as true for the garrulous cheery-voiced man who guides Henry to his regiment as for tongue-tied Henry himself.

In fact, rather than trying to make his characters sound interesting,

Crane deliberately spotlights their inexpressiveness by showing again and again how poorly their words match their thoughts and feelings. After Henry's regiment has repulsed the first charge, he preens himself on having lived up to his ideals; all he says, however, is "Gee, aint it hot, hay?" (30). When he seems "about to deliver a philippic," he can only say, "Hell—" (45–46). His intense effort to deliver a "rallying speech" only produces "Why—why—what—what's th' matter?" (57).[4]

Since it is only in rare instances that Crane reveals the thoughts of other characters, he is debarred from making a similar demonstration of their failure of expression. Hence he uses a much riskier technique to call attention to the soldiers' inarticulateness: He contrasts their flat speech with his own remarkable language. Thus when the regiment breaks out in "crows and cat-calls" at the fat soldier who attempts to "pilfer" a horse, all we hear the men saying is "Gin' him thunder" and "Hit him with a stick" (12–13). When "a black procession of curious oaths" comes from Jim Conklin's lips, we hear nothing but another man's questions: "Well, why don't they support us? Why don't they send supports? Do they think—" (27). The same thing happens in Chapter 1, where, after being told that Jim Conklin and Wilson "had a rapid altercation, in which they fastened upon each other various strange epithets," we hear speeches on the order of "Oh, you think you know—" and "Huh" (9). Similarly, there is often a striking disparity between the claimed and the exhibited tone. Henry yells "in a savage voice," but the words he utters are merely "Well, yeh needn't git mad about it" (15). Crane went to remarkable lengths to make his characters sound dull.

This inarticulateness, so pervasive and obvious in Crane's narrative, has to do with much more than an illusory realism of speech. Crane is also saying something about the social and moral constraints on expression. From the second paragraph on, he shows that unrestrained speech brings a risk of combat and inadvertent self-ostracism. That is why the action begins with overly free speech, Conklin returning to camp "swelled with a tale" and Wilson responding with rage at his "words" (1, 9). The resulting bickering between two soldiers identified at this point as the tall one and the loud one is in part a conflict between two exemplars of unconstrained speech— an expansive tall-talker and a hectoring loudmouth. Thus Jim speaks "pompously," with "the important air of a herald," "with a mighty emphasis," and the "garment" he waves "banner-like" (1, 9) resembles the meaningless signal of the man on shore in "The Open Boat." Jim has an answer for everything, as when he later produces "a heavy explanation" (19) of the troop movements: "I s'pose we must go reconnoiterin' 'round th' kentry jest t' keep 'em from gittin' too clost, or t'develope'm, or something" (20). It is clear this bluffing windbag doesn't know the meaning of *reconnoiter* and doubtful whether he grasps the technical military sense of *develop*.

Only after Conklin has sustained his mortal wound does his speech ring true: "I thought mebbe yeh got keeled over. There's been thunder t' pay t'day. I was worryin' about it a good deal" (42–43). There is a grim humor in the fact that his effort to conceal a wound that has the appearance of being "chewed by wolves" (45) confers on him a newfound gift for restrained and dignified speech. Crane's allusion to the Spartan boy who was chewed to death by a fox hidden under his cloak shows that Conklin has acquired laconic speech the hard way.

Although Wilson begins by ordering Conklin to shut up, he too learns to express himself in a fashion contrary to his original way of talking—and contrary to that of all the other men as well. Once Wilson has been compelled to acknowledge before Fleming his own fear and cowardice, he is no longer "pricked" by the "little words" that "other men aimed at him" like bullets (68). He speaks with relative candor and even becomes a peacemaker, calming a quarrel between men "stung" by one another's "language" (69). Although he is the target of several gibes, he does not seem to be particularly injured by them. In this, Wilson is contrasted with Henry, who remains fearful that others might somehow discover his shameful acts. Henry's "tender flesh" is repeatedly "stung" (93) by taunts, and when he and Wilson hear themselves dismissed as "mule-driver" and "mud-digger," it is Henry who sustains a wound: "arrows of scorn . . . had buried themselves in his heart" (100). Wilson acquires his relative invulnerability from his imprudence in disclosing his fear to Henry before the first action; he now has nothing more to hide. Henry, meanwhile, is compelled by a combination of moral weakness and the accidents of war to conceal his desertion of both the regiment and the tattered soldier. One man turns into a kind and candid speaker and another into a lying braggart.

Thus, unlike Conklin and Wilson, Henry must continue to talk in a tongue-tied and dishonest manner, using speech to deceive others as well as himself. At the beginning he did not dare express his "outcry" (19) that the stupid generals were marching the men into ambush. Near the end, recalling his shameful treatment of the tattered man, he can only utter "a cry of sharp irritation and agony" followed by a covering "outburst of crimson oaths" (107). He has not changed for the better, and in the few instances when his tongue seems unloosed his speech is notably hollow, as when he finally expresses the thoughts that have been on his mind from the beginning and delivers "a long and intricate denunciation of the commander" (75). Such talk is foolish and dangerous, and he lapses back into his uneasy state of silence after being "pierced" by the "words" of a "sarcastic" voice (76). What we see in *The Red Badge* is an account of arrested development, an explanation, partly moral and partly circumstantial, of inexpressiveness in speech. We follow the process by which an untried youth turns into the kind of man who will never be able to speak his mind truthfully.

The fact that Henry and Wilson develop in opposite ways shows that, contrary to what some critics have argued, Crane's novel offers more than a systemic account of war or language.[5] Crane is telling a partly traditional story of an individual's moral and social *Bildung*, highlighting his development through scenes that contrast him with others following different moral pathways. The chapter in which Henry hands back Wilson's packet of letters makes the key differences clear. This packet, like Wilson's original "melancholy oration" revealing his terror, places "a small weapon" in Henry's hands. To use this weapon would be "to knock his friend on the head" (70–71). Although Henry thinks he is acting with magnanimous forbearance, he is obviously deceiving himself, since, as Crane's language makes apparent, Henry does in fact wound Wilson on the head, an injury he renders by withholding speech:

> "Wilson!"
> "What?". . . .
> "Oh, nothin'," he said.
> His friend turned his head in some surprise. "Why, what was yeh goin' t' say."
> "Oh, nothin'," repeated the youth. (70)

In this way, Henry requires Wilson to articulate his own former cowardice by asking for the letters. In the act of speaking out, he incurs a head wound resembling the one that Henry has received: "Dark, prickling blood had flushed into his cheeks and brow" (73). Fittingly, the end of this episode consists of Henry's complacent daydreaming about the "stories of war" (73) with which he will entertain his mother and the schoolgirl back home. One man learns how to speak painful truths; the other remains silent while daydreaming about the self-flattering stories he will tell elsewhere.

It is surprising how many soldiers are wounded in the head in Crane's novel, and how often their head injuries are linked to the capacity to speak. When the babbling man is grazed on the head by a bullet, he responds by saying, "Oh" (28). Another man has his jaw supports shot away, "disclosing in the wide cavern of his mouth, a pulsing mass of blood and teeth. And, with it all, he made attempts to cry out. In his endeavor there was a dreadful earnestness as if he conceived that one great shriek would make him well" (100). The tattered man apparently gets his mortal wound after a friend, Tom

Jamison, blurts out that his head is bleeding. Another man in the tattered man's regiment dies after being shot "plum in th' head":

> Everybody yelled out t' 'im: 'Hurt, John? Are yeh hurt much?' 'No,' ses he. He looked kinder surprised an' he went on tellin' 'em how he felt. He sed he didn't feel nothin'. But, by dad, th' first thing that feller knowed he was dead. . . . So, yeh wanta watch out. Yeh might have *some queer kind 'a hurt yerself.* (47; italics mine).

Finally there is the cheery-voiced man's comrade, Jack, who answers a stranger's question at the wrong time:

> "Say, where's th' road t' th' river?" An' Jack, he never paid no attention an' th' feller kept on a-peckin' at his elbow an' sayin': "Say, where's th' road t' th' river?" Jack was a-lookin' ahead all th' time tryin' t' see th' Johnnies comin' through th' woods an' he never paid no attention t' this big fat feller fer a long time but at last he turned 'round an' he ses: "Ah, go t' hell an' find th' road t' th' river." An' jest then a shot slapped him bang on th' side th' head. (61).

In all these accounts there is an association between a terrible head wound and the articulation of thought through speech.

Hence Henry himself is struck and injured on the crown of his head while attempting to deliver a rallying speech or ask a question. This red badge of courage marks his inability thenceforward to speak the truth about himself and the war. The tattered man has it right: Henry has sustained "some queer kind 'a hurt" in his capacity to communicate through speech. *The Red Badge* tells the story of an irreparable moral injury.

Because we cannot know exactly what goes on in the minds of the other characters, it is difficult to answer with perfect certitude a question similar to the one that agitates Henry in Chapter 1—does he resemble the other soldiers in his systematic untruth? Certain features of the narrative, however, invite us to regard Henry as representative or typical. He is identified chiefly as "the youth," and the deceptive silence that characterizes him even more strongly at the end than at the beginning seems to be the new order of the day. It is significant that the final instances of direct discourse in the novel are all rude put-downs designed to end acts of communication.

> "Oh, shet yer mouth."
> "You make me sick."
> "G'home, yeh fool." (107–8)

These statements, the last that anyone makes in the novel, tell us exactly what Henry's inability to talk about his experience leads us to suspect about the place of language in the society of soldiers: The use of language has sustained a mortal injury. Henry has become a man among men by learning how important it is never to tell the truth about himself.

Does Wilson also become a member of this society? The concluding exchanges between him and Henry suggest that Wilson has become an outsider by virtue of developing the ability to talk. Like Crane's own father, Wilson is now "a dog-hanged parson" (77). One particular exchange sums up the final positions of the two young men relative to speech. "Well, Henry, I guess this is good-bye-John," says Wilson, and Henry answers, "Oh, shet up, yeh damn' fool" (91). There seems to be nothing mawkish or embarrassing about Wilson's speech; in fact, his slightly humorous invocation of the colloquial phrase, "good-bye-John," keeps sentiment at a safe enough distance. Even so, Henry orders him to cease speaking, in this way expressing his solidarity with the final sentiment of the other men: Whatever it is you have to say, keep it to yourself.

In Henry's eyes, the worst social injury that can happen to a man is to be turned into a "slang-phrase" by another man uttering "a humorous remark in a low tone" (54) to a group of men. Now, alternating between complacency at his public image and an incommunicable anxiety about his proven treachery, Henry has joined the group whose identifying speech act is the silencing jeer directed at outsiders. Wilson, however, is well on his way (as his name tells us) to being the butt of someone's "Ah, there, Willie."

Notes

1. Stephen Crane, *Prose and Poetry* (New York: Library of America, 1984), 897.

2. James Thurber, "The Secret Life of James Thurber," *New Yorker* 19 (February 27, 1943): 15–17.

3. *The Red Badge of Courage: An Episode of the American Civil War*, ed. Henry Binder (New York: Norton, 1982), 39. Subsequent citations are to this edition. Of those who have considered the representation of speech in the novel, W. M. Frohock, "*The Red Badge* and the Limits of Parody," *Southern Review* 6 (1970): 137–48, comments on Crane's use of free indirect discourse and Fleming's "bucolic" speech. Robert L. Hough, "Crane's Henry Fleming: Speech and Vision," *Forum* (Houston) 3 (1962): 41–42, shows that the inconsistencies in Crane's reproduction of Fleming's colloquial speech testify to Crane's lack of interest in the accurate recording of actual talk.

4. See Amy Kaplan's treatment of the inadequacy of storytelling in "The Spectacle of War in Crane's Revision of History," *New Essays on The Red Badge of Courage*, ed. Lee Clark Mitchell (Cambridge: Cambridge University Press, 1986), 91–94.

5. Hence the inadequacy of Christine Brooke-Rose's deconstructive reading: "*The hero/the monster, running to/running from, separation/membership,* and *spectator/spectacle* . . .* are intertwined with each other and caught up in the opposition that subsumes them—that of *courage/cowardice*" ("Ill Logics of Irony," in *New Essays on the Red Badge of Courage*, ed. Lee Clark Mitchell (Cambridge: Cambridge University

Press, 1986), 129. One is appalled and fascinated by this essay's reliance on Paul de
Man's statement that "a narrative endlessly tells the story of its own denominational
aberration" (p. 141). Without being aware of the irony, Brooke-Rose relied on a man
now known to have concealed his Nazi collaborationism in order to construct her
argument that Fleming's cowardice and savagery are exemplary for all men. It seems
wiser, as well as more faithful to the text (Binder's), to recognize an "essentialist"
moral demarcation between Wilson and Fleming.

Crane, Hitchcock, and the Binder Edition of *The Red Badge of Courage*

James Colvert*

Henry Binder's edition of *The Red Badge of Courage* is now a
decade old, and though only a few scholars have accepted it as
authoritative, even fewer have raised arguments against the theory
that brought it into existence. By a kind of default, then, it is still a
contender, though not as strong as it once seemed to be when it
occupied a prestigious place in the *Norton Anthology of American
Literature*, was reviewed in *American Literary Scholarship* as a major
breakthrough in Crane scholarship, was reported in a front-page story
in the *New York Times*, was offered as an Alternate Selection by
Book-of-the-Month Club, and was placed by *Choice* on its 1983 list
of *Outstanding Academic Books*.[1] But if it has slipped from these
heights in the estimation of most readers, it is nevertheless still on
bookstore shelves in the recent (1987) Avon Books mass market
paperback issue, recommended by prominent cover captions as "The
Only Complete Edition from the Original Manuscript" and the "*Red
Badge* as Crane Actually Wrote It!"

The manuscript version is indeed *one* version of the *Red Badge*
as Crane "actually wrote it," but the question, of course, is whether
it is the *Red Badge* he wanted Appleton and Company to publish—
the novel as it stood before he struck out the endings of three
chapters, removed one entirely, and deleted passages from two others,
including the final chapter. Binder thinks it is. He argues in "*The
Red Badge of Courage* Nobody Knows" that scholars, who have studied
the manuscript since it was added to the Barrett Collection at the
University of Virginia in the early fifties, have been wrong in thinking,
as most do, that Crane marked out these endings and removed whole
pages from his book to improve the narrative pace and eliminate
tedious redundancies.[2] Crane was in effect "forced" to cut these

* This essay was written specifically for this volume and is published here for the first
time by permission of the author.

crucial passages, he writes, and far from improving the book, severely damaged it. What happened, he says, is that Ripley Hitchcock, Appleton's enterprising editor, sensing a strong commercial potential in the war story but realizing that the hero's bitter, "near-blasphemous" reflections on fate, nature, and cosmic law would offend readers, ordered Crane to cut these crucial passages as a condition of publication. Crane, obscure and penniless, with no other prospects of publication in sight, consented, perhaps without realizing how much damage Hitchcock's ordered expurgations would do to the novel. The true, authoritative text, then, is that of the manuscript as it existed in the spring of 1894, which represents Crane's fullest and best conception of the novel, before he cut Henry Fleming's "blasphemous" tirades against nature and the cosmos and before he half-heartedly attempted to soften the dialect speech of his characters on the advice of his friend and mentor, Hamlin Garland. The proper task of the textual editor, as Binder saw it, was to return the novel to this pristine form. Restoring to the Barrett manuscript material recovered from a few pages scattered among several different libraries, filling in lost passages whenever possible from fragments of an earlier draft, reconstituting the deleted chapter, and rescuing a considerable number of details Hitchcock allegedly ordered out as objectionably realistic or vulgar, Binder reconstituted the text almost as it existed (a few pages are unrecoverable) in April 1894. His edition—essentially the novel as it stood before Crane showed it to any editor or publisher—includes all of the material from the reassembled manuscript that does not appear in the 1895 book form.

It is impossible to discuss the Binder edition without taking into account Hershel Parker's contribution to the enterprise. Parker, Binder's former teacher, first conceived the plan for the edition, which he outlined briefly in his 1976 review of Fredson Bowers's Center for Editions of American Authors (CEAA)-approved text of the *Red Badge* and his facsimile edition of the Barrett manuscript. The arguments he sketched out in a paragraph in this article became the basic premises of the theory Binder sets out in his rationale. Parker was a member of the editorial board of the *Norton Anthology* when it selected the Binder text for its second edition (1979); he organized, as guest editor of *Studies in the Novel*, a special Crane issue that appeared as a kind of combined announcement and celebration of the new text; and he has for a decade conducted a vigorous "campaign" for its scholarly recognition.[3] His several lively, boldly speculative (and sometimes caustic) essays, along with Binder's comprehensive history and analysis, have undoubtedly influenced the thinking of a good many scholars, for example the contributors (Parker among them) to an excellent recent (1986) collection of new essays on the novel, all of which cite the Binder edition as authoritative.[4] The most recent evidence of Parker-Binder influence is a note in the splendid new two-volume edition of *The Correspondence of Stephen Crane* (1988) that states that Hitchcock "forced" Crane to "excise key passages" that "slowed the pace of the action but contributed to the structural and thematic unity of the novel."[5]

Several critics have commented skeptically on these arguments. Edwin Cady noted early the extreme conservatism of a textual theory that "would allow Crane little ground for legitimate rewriting and arrives at a very chthonic *Red Badge* indeed."[6] Regina Domeraski, referring to the excisions in the manuscript, suggests that at the time of the revision Henry's philosophical ruminations "may have sounded a false note for Crane because they are often uncharacteristically verbose and rambling and spell out feelings and ideas that he suggests far more skillfully in a few words or with a telling image elsewhere in the book."[7] But by far the most formidable critic of the Binder edition—in fact, the only critic who has laid out a fully developed argument against it—is Donald Pizer. In a brief but cogent article published the same year the edition first appeared in the *Norton Anthology,* Pizer challenged the theory on the grounds of its almost exclusive reliance on conjecture, surmise, and unwarranted hypothesis. As he notes, there is nothing in the correspondence between Crane and Hitchcock to suggest that the editor ever demanded excisions in the novel, nothing to suggest this in Crane's letters to anyone else or in the memoirs of the people who knew him, nothing in the record that states or implies that the author ever wanted the book republished in its 1984 form, and no evidence that Hitchcock ever made similar demands on any other authors whose books he edited.[8] In a later essay examining the effects of the excisions on the novel itself, Pizer questioned the Parker-Binder contention that the cuts undermined its structure and coherence. In revising the final chapter, he argues, Crane's intention was to change the character of the hero, who in the 1894 version learns nothing from his experiences on the battlefield and at the end is still as self-deluded and morally perverse as ever. In the Appleton version, Henry's moral perversity is significantly qualified by glimmerings of a developing moral consciousness, and in this double-mindedness is more complex psychologically than the Henry of the early version, not less, as Parker and Binder argue. In Pizer's view, the intentional ambiguity of its ending aptly expresses changes occurring in the mid-nineties "both in Crane's ideas and in the history of American thought"; it reflects the author's own conflicting and divided idea "of the balance of emphasis to give to the human capacities both for self-delusion and for insight and understanding."

The cogency of Pizer's criticism of the major premises of the Parker-Binder theory—its unwarranted conjectures about Hitchcock's

motives and actions as Crane's editor and its argument that the
Appleton text is incomplete and incoherent—calls the authority of
the Binder edition into grave question. Pizer charges that the Parker-
Binder preference for the simpler, more certain concept of Henry's
character in the manuscript version ignores certain biographical and
historical realities that help to explain Crane's alterations in the last
chapter. The revised *Red Badge* "reflects in its ambivalences," Pizer
writes, "a major moment of transition in the history of American
belief—that of a period in American thought when, broadly speaking,
there was a movement from nineteenth-century certainties to modern
doubts, from a willingness to affirm large-scale notions about the
human enterprise to an unwillingness to do more than represent the
immediacies of experience itself."[9] One of the main problems with
the Parker-Binder theory, in short, is that it is unhistorical.

Pizer addresses the question broadly, in terms of the changing
dynamics of late nineteenth-century thought and feeling. I would like
to address it more narrowly by considering how fatally dependent
their theory is on distortions of more particular biographical and
historical circumstances and events as well as on certain unwarranted
assumptions about Crane's aesthetics.

II

The notion that Hitchcock or Appleton (or both) would have
found the manuscript version blasphemous is crucial to the Parker-
Binder theory. Parker's statement of this key premise shows how in
his view it relates to other arguments in the theory:

> Appleton's probably leaned hard on Crane to make him take out
> the blasphemy. Blasphemy it was, though it seems tame to us:
> making fun of the notion that not a sparrow falls, etc., having a
> character defy the Universe—why, in *Maggie* they even removed
> a line saying "as God says" when it meant "as it says in the Bible."
> I think it is a pretty good bet that Hitchcock said the ironic ending
> had to go, that there had to be an inspiring ending. So Crane took
> out philosophical sections where Henry had alternately praised and
> condemned the Universe and put in a sentence of specious upbeat
> religiosity which was obviously at war with the meaning of the
> manuscript. ("Over the river a golden ray of sun came through the
> hosts of leaden rain clouds.")[10]

Binder is more circumspect; Parker's vehement "blasphemy"
becomes Binder's cautious "near-blasphemy," and his mild "may
have" substitutes for Parker's certain "But blasphemy it was." But
their point, the point without which their whole theory tumbles to
the ground, is the same: that Hitchcock saw offense to good religion
in the excised interior monologues and ordered their expurgation as

a condition of publication. These "near-blasphemous tergiversations concerning cosmic determinism," Binder says, "may have struck the Appleton editor . . . as the most patently questionable material in the original story." In these passages, "Henry rebels against or bitterly accepts a variously named cosmic agency—'nature,' 'the powers of fate,' 'the source of things,' 'a God,' 'the Great Responsibility'—as the ultimate cause of his own actions." The sacrilege is compounded, Binder argues, by Henry's assumption of a special, personal relation to these powers, which he perceives in his delusion as sometimes malevolent and brutally hostile, sometimes kind and tenderly solicitous. The cumulative effect of these cuts, Binder believes, is to prepare for a new ending to the novel, "to change Henry Fleming from a youth who rebels against the 'powers of fate' . . . to a youth who undergoes a change of character in battle."[11]

A brief account of some of these excised passages might help bring the issue into focus. The first is the 160 or so words ending Chapter seven, of which Binder was able to restore about half. It follows immediately on the famous scene in which Henry discovers the rotting corpse in the peaceful little chapel-like bower, which he enters in a serene, complacent mood to commune with a kindly mother nature who has just assured him by the example of the flight of the frightened squirrel from his casually tossed pinecone that his panicky desertion of the battlefield was in accordance with her immutable law. But when he encounters in horror a rotting corpse in this little bower of peace and kindness, this comforting illusion is rudely dispelled. The Appleton chapter ends with Henry stopping at the end of his panicky flight to gaze back at the seemingly peaceful little bower in awe and confusion. In the manuscript, the chapter continues with a return to Henry's philosophical ruminations. Nature, he now thinks, "no longer condoled with him"; the sign of the squirrel had been false; there was another law "that far-over-topped it," signified by the greedy ants feeding on the flesh of the dead soldier, "all life existing upon death, eating ravenously, stuffing itself with the hopes of the dead." The excised ending of Chapter ten, which follows immediately upon the scene in which he deserts the suffering tattered man, elaborates on his bitter conviction that nature is a deadly deceiver, creating the illusion of glory to entice men to their deaths. In his feeling of helplessness before its power, he turns "in tupenny fury upon the high, tranquil sky," and thinks he "would have like to have splashed it with a derisive paint." Chapter twelve, which Crane removed in its entirety, is a rambling six-page philosophical fantasy in which Henry, reviewing again his thoughts about the irresistibility of nature's law and reflecting on the irrelevancy of man-made law in a world governed by the indifferent law of nature, imagines himself as "the growing prophet of a world-reconstruction," the creator of "a new world modelled by the pain of his life."

There are so many objections to the argument that Appleton would have felt compelled to censor all this that it is hard to know where to begin. In the context of Crane's irony, in the context of literary and intellectual history, and in the context of the narrative from which they were plucked, these themes and attitudes, even as they touch on the "new thought" unfolding from Darwin, Spencer, Draper, and other advanced thinkers of the latter part of the nineteenth century, were commonplace by the mid-nineties. It is extremely doubtful that Hitchcock would have supposed that Appleton's readers, even their "sometimes finicky" readers, as Binder describes them, could have found these ideas offensive. (Parker's word for them is "dangerous.")[12] Fleming's rebellious thoughts against "God, country, and all humanity" and his "questioning of cosmic justice" are of course familiar themes in Judeo-Christian story and myth, freely dramatized in classic American literature since the time of the earliest puritans. If Hitchcock and Appleton found Henry's jejune vision of himself as a rebel against cosmic law objectionable, what can we suppose they thought of Ahab's vow of vengeance on nature, of his conviction that he is God's equal, or of his overweening assertion that he would "strike the sun if it insulted" him? Or, again, of Hester Prynne's belief that her adultery was divinely sanctioned, or of Chillingworth's stated opinion that free moral choice is illusion, that men are driven not by will but by "dark necessity"? By Crane's time the tragic fate of the young scientist Aylmer in Hawthorne's "The Birthmark," whose ambition is to "lay his hand on the secret of creative force, and perhaps make new worlds for himself," had long been a familiar parable of the dire consequence of man's rebellion against nature. Hitchcock would have no reason to suppose that the orthodox-minded readers would not have understood Henry's similar presumption, that he is "a growing prophet of world-reconstruction," in the same way. By comparison with the blasphemous contentions of Ahab, Aylmer, Hester, and others in classic American literature, Henry's railings against nature—preposterous railings, as Crane's blatant and scoffing irony would have signalled to the most "finicky" of Appleton's readers—are merely the petulant outbursts of a presumptuous youth, as indeed Crane intended them to be.

Parker and Binder must characterize Crane's editor and publisher as rather exceptionally censorious to make credible the alleged objections of the latter to Henry's philosophical posturing in the original form of the *Red Badge*. As a consequence their account of the literary climate in which Hitchcock operated is clearly unbalanced, though oddly sketchy, considering how crucial it is to their argument. Their theory simply assumes (as it must, indeed) that the nineties were unequivocally and unrelievably repressive, as Parker's brief characterization reveals:

> The members of the American literary establishment were a remarkably homogeneous set of males of British ancestry and conventional upper-middle-class education, and for all the nominal allegiance they paid to literary realism, they were aesthetically timid to the point of prizing tameness over originality, and morally timid to the point of routinely censoring themselves in advance of publication. So eminent a novelist and theorist of realism as William Dean Howells valued the decorum of American letters, and the majority of the reading public depended upon the editors to keep unnecessary unpleasantness out of their homes.[13]

The "morally timid" Hitchcock suppressed references to "the powers of fate" and the treachery of nature, and the decorum-minded Hitchcock slashed out "vulgar" or excessively "realistic" matter. Thus Binder conjectures, the editor excised as suggestive of swearing the expression "rooty-tooty-tooty-too" from the tattered soldier's report that someone said to him during the battle, "Yer shot, yeh blamed, infernal, tooty-tooty-tooty-too." Likewise the deletion of the word "bath" in the sentence "It was the soldier's bath" describing awakening troops rubbing their sleepy eyes. "We can guess," Binder observes, explaining this, "that to any responsible editor of the time, baths, even for soldiers in battle, were an issue not to be dealt with irreverently."[14]

It is true, of course, that literary men like Hitchcock and Howells and publishers like Appleton worked under certain constraints. Profanity in fiction was of course tabooed in the mid-nineties, and the restriction was generally accepted by writers and publishers as a reality of the literary profession. Richard Watson Gilder, the editor of the staid *Century Magazine*, achieved a permanent place in the mythology of repressive editors when he rejected Crane's *Maggie* as profane and "too honest," and even the dean of American realists, William Dean Howells, expressed regrets in print that Crane used profane language in his 1893 *Maggie*. Appleton was clearly committed to the prevailing sense of publishing propriety and decorum, as this statement of its standards confirms: "The duty of a publisher involves reasonable watchfulness that nothing immoral, indecent or sacrilegious should be printed, and there the responsibility ends."

But what neither Parker nor Binder acknowledges is that these conservative and repressive forces had long been challenged by new ideas, new forms of expression, and new subject matter, and that Appleton and Company, which Parker thinks "leaned hard on Crane" for his radical ideas, had been in the vanguard of the challengers for more than thirty years before the *Red Badge* came across Hitchcock's desk. It was Appleton, in fact, that introduced Darwin's *On the Origin of Species* to American readers in 1859 and reprinted the book thirty-eight times during the last half of the century, despite violent and continuing attacks from scholars and religious leaders. "In enjoying the distinction of being the first to introduce Darwin's theories to American readers," the historian Gerard Wolfe writes, "Appleton also had to face the consequences of a storm of disapproval from fundamentalist religious leaders and conventional scholars. The publisher was deluged with hundreds of threatening letters" and "suffered for years from the stigma cast upon them for having published" Darwin's works. Appleton also published in the last quarter of the nineteenth-century the works of Thomas Henry Huxley, beginning with *Man's Place in Nature* in 1863, and issued his nine-volume *Collected Essays* in 1893, about the same time Crane began writing the *Red Badge.* In their lists were books by such advanced thinkers as John Tyndall, Sir Charles Lyell, and Herbert Spencer. The company published its first book by Spencer in 1860 and released in 1864 his *First Principles,* the first in the ten-volume series *Synthetic Philosophy* issued by the firm.[15]

Appleton also published and kept in print all through the last quarter of the century John William Draper's influential and controversial *The History of the Conflict between Religion and Science,* which, like the Darwin books, were anathema to orthodox religionists, including the Pope, who publicly condemned it. "Characteristic of the advanced thought of the time," Wolfe writes, "is Draper's strict determinism: 'Men do not control events. . . . Events control men.' "[16] It seems hardly credible in view of this that Appleton would force Crane, as Binder claims, to delete the word "fierce" in the sentence "The red sun was pasted in the sky like a fierce wafer" because it "intended to characterize the powers of fate at one of the most extreme moments of Henry's rebellious anger."[17]

Convention-bound though Appleton was in some respects, the publisher was hardly as narrow and intolerant in the matter of ideas as the Parker-Binder theory assumes. Hitchcock was undoubtedly following policy when he asked Crane to remove the profanity in *Maggie* in preparation for Appleton publication in 1896. But it doesn't seem likely that he would have felt obliged to expurgate references in Crane's novel to the "powers of fate" on behalf of a publisher who had been disseminating radical thought in America for thirty years and who had defended Darwin, Spencer, Huxley, and others against hundreds of would-be censors, including a bishop and a pope. Parker's incidental comment on Howells's regard for literary decorum is indicative of his general tendency to simplify history for the benefit of his theory. We get a better sense of the complex dynamics of this decade of transition from nineteenth- to twentieth-century thought and feeling when we observe that Howells was also surprisingly responsive to the new sense of things powerfully represented in Crane's work. Howells's introduction to Tolstoy's *Sebastopol*, recognized as an important model for the *Red Badge*, shows that despite his reservations about Crane's novel (he thought it weak because it was not authenticated by real-life experience of war), he was in accord with the critical spirit of its vision. "We are all so besotted with dreams and vanities that we have come to think that the right will accomplish itself spectacularly, splendidly; but Tolstoi makes us know that it never can do so. . . ." Howells describes Tolstoy's "The Cossack" in terms almost exactly applicable to the *Red Badge*—as "that epic of nature, and of a young man's sorrowful, wandering desire to get into harmony with the divine scheme of beneficence."[18] Howells understood, as Hitchcock and Appleton understood, and as their common readers undoubtedly would have sensed (excepting a few like General McClurg, who took the novel as an insult to heroic soldiering) that Henry's anguished and helpless introspection is a version of the old puritan's anxious pondering over the meanings of nature's ambiguous signs, blended with a more recent awareness of the irresistible laws of nature and of the uncertain power of human perception to account for the reality they bind.

III

Ripley Hitchcock, Appleton's cultivated and liberal-minded literary advisor and editor, author of several books on American art and on the history of the early American West as well as a scholarly study of De Quincey, figures crucially in the Parker-Binder theory. It was he, presumably, who engineered the "maiming" of Crane's masterpiece, a skillful entrepreneur, in Binder's portrait, who specialized in the profitable business of simplifying and sanitizing books other publishers found unsuitable for a popular audience. In Parker's somewhat darker view he was calculating and devious, an "exemplary diplomat who routinely took extreme liberties as editor," who "had a habit of getting his way when he wanted changes made, but getting his way in his own good time." In any case, he tampered ruthlessly with texts. He cut and rearranged Edward Noyes Westcott's *David Harum*, severely condensed Theodore Dreiser's *Jennie Gerhardt*, and slashed, with ruinous effect, Crane's *Red Badge* and *Maggie*.[19]

Unfortunately almost no documentary information about the Crane-Hitchcock relationship has survived. For the first five months of the period in which the *Red Badge* was being prepared for publication, Crane was on a journey through the West and Mexico as a roving correspondent for the Bacheller Syndicate, but only a few brief, cryptic notes have survived from this time, all of them from Crane to Hitchcock. We know nothing for a fact about what Hitchcock said or didn't say about the novel. All is inference, surmise, hypothesis, and simple guesswork, as Binder acknowledges in his response to Pizer's criticism on this point: "the most important evidence and documents relating to the actual process of the cuts in *Red Badge* do not exist." The reason, he says, is that Hitchcock made his demands in his New York office in person in the summer of 1895, after Crane returned from his Western trip. Lacking these documents, Binder notes, touching crucially on the method underlying his theory, our knowledge of "the working relationship between Crane and Hitchcock in the final stages of preparing *Red Badge* for publication must be inferred from other related circumstances."[20]

What Parker infers about Hitchcock is that he operated according to a secret agenda designed to handle his youthful author as a potentially troublesome adversary. "One of the oddities of Crane scholarship," he writes, "is that the relationship between Crane and Hitchcock has proved so elusive. For what it's worth, I felt I understood their encounters better when I began envisioning them in an edgy dance in which, by the rules, each partner had, now and then, to approach the other closer than he wanted to."[21] According to Parker, the "edgy" game began in January 1895, when Crane submitted the manuscript of his novel (the manuscript now in the Barrett Collection, he contends) to Hitchcock, shortly before the correspondent departed on his Western journey for Bacheller. Hitchcock was already familiar with the story in its severely shortened newspaper form as published by the Bacheller Syndicate a few weeks before, but none of the objectionable philosophical passages appeared in this version, which had been cut to about one-third of its full length, and the unheroic ending of the original had been lopped off to give the story a reassuring ending, the scene in which Henry and his friend Wilson celebrate their heroic charge against the enemy. Parker imagines how sharply Hitchcock was "taken aback" when he read the "threatening" long version of the story:

> Hitchcock, reading the full manuscript, could not have escaped learning that it was ironic—not after he encountered on page 74, all blatantly, Fleming's wistful, envious yearning for a wound just big and bloody enough to impress his fellows (and not, any reader would understand, big enough to hurt much: "He wished that he, too, had a wound, a little warm red badge of courage." (Crane may already have lined out "warm.") Two or three years before [when he submitted his manuscript of his slum novel to the editor], Hitchcock had found *Maggie* too threatening to publish, and now he was finding problems with the war story that he could not have anticipated from reading the newspaper clippings. The problems could be dealt with, he plainly decided, but they would have to involve

some negotiations with the volatile author—negotiations best delayed until the author was in Hitchcock's office.[22]

Hitchcock's first step in the "edgy dance" was to accept the novel
for publication in a letter that reached Crane in Lincoln, Nebraska,
in early February. "What suggestion Hitchcock made is uncertain,"
Parker conjectures (the letter has been lost), "but one can make a
fairly safe guess": he asked Crane to find another title, as Parker
infers from a cryptic sentence in Crane's answering letter: "I shall
have to reflect upon the title."[23] Hitchcock said nothing in this letter
about the massive cuts he already knew he would demand when the
author could be confronted in his office, nor did he mention them
when he sent the manuscript to Crane in New Orleans, ostensibly
for final revision. When Crane returned to New York in May, Hitchcock went over the manuscript with him, citing at last the blasphemous
philosophical tirades he wanted cut, presumably before he presented
a contract for Crane's signature on June 17. When the offending
Chapter twelve and chapter endings had been duly removed, the
editor then ordered a typescript made. When it was ready, the editor
went over the text with Crane again, ordering out several other
impious passages in Chapters sixteen and twenty-five, intent now on
reversing the plot to show Henry in a favorable light in the last scene
of the book. The conjecture that the cuts in Chapters sixteen and
twenty-five were made in the typescript explains, of course, why they
are not crossed out in the Barrett manuscript.

To credit all this, we must make three unlikely assumptions: first,
that Hitchcock would have considered Henry's rebellious thoughts
against nature unpublishable in the literary climate of the nineties,
which, as I have already said, is improbable; second, that the version
of the novel Crane submitted to the editor was the manuscript version,
with Chapter twelve and the chapter endings still in place; third,
that Hitchcock in these circumstances would have gone to such
devious lengths to conceal his determination to force the expurgations.
The assumption that the author submitted his original manuscript to
Hitchcock rather than, as Fredson Bowers argues, a typescript is
crucial to the theory of the Binder edition, since it must assume that
Crane expurgated the Barrett manuscript *after* Hitchcock read it in
its uncut state. Otherwise, of course, Hitchcock would never have
seen the expurgated passages he supposedly ordered out. Binder and
Bowers's arguments on this point from their comparisons of the variant
texts of the manuscript, the newspaper version, and the Appleton
book version are technical and inconclusive: It is granted on both
sides (though tacitly on Binder's) that the shortened Bacheller newspaper version was set from a typescript, not from the original manuscript; but Bowers concludes from his analysis of the variants that

Crane submitted the carbon copy of the Bacheller typescript to Hitchcock, while Binder concludes from his that Crane submitted the uncut manuscript. The evidence for these intricate textual analyses is somewhat conflicting, and the argument finally comes to rest on statistical interpretation, that is, on the number of variants that argue for or against manuscript or typescript.[24] But Binder's argument seems to leave more unanswered questions. Why would Crane have given Hitchcock the much marked up and dog-eared manuscript if a typed copy had already been made for the Bacheller printers (he would have presumably ordered a carbon, knowing that he would need it for submission to some house for regular publication)? How could Hitchcock, thoroughly alert supposedly to all the "objectionable" implications of Henry's rebellious thoughts against nature and the cosmos, have overlooked the most crucial of these passages (in Chapters sixteen and twenty-five) during the first cutting session? If this most critical action in the "maiming" of the text was merely an afterthought, would there have been any necessity for such devious maneuvering as Parker envisions?

A clear example of Parker's straining to picture Hitchcock as an inveterate censor is his conjecture that the editor was so "taken aback" by his discovery of the ironic import of the title that he jumped ahead of his waiting game and requested (or demanded) a change in the title of the novel in his acceptance letter. If it is true, as Parker says, that what "bothered Hitchcock about the title . . . was probably its blatant irony in the context of the entire manuscript,"[25] why would he suppose that merely changing the title would make it any less ironic? In arguing his point, Parker curiously twists one of the few documentable facts in the scant record of the transaction. It is indisputable that the editor mentioned the title in his letter of acceptance. But as Crane's note about the New Orleans revision clearly shows, the issue was not the irony at all, but the length; Hitchcock simply thought it was too long. "As to the name," Crane wrote, responding at last to Hitchcock's request for a shorter title, "I am unable to see what to do with it unless the word 'Red' is cut out perhaps. That would shorten it."[26] Parker's odd comment is that "Crane's laconic offer to shorten it by a three-letter word was disingenuous," meaning, I suppose, that it was a calculated gesture in the ongoing "edgy dance."[27]

The attitudes and strategies Parker envisions in his account of Hitchcock strike other false notes. There is no reason to suppose that the editor should have thought Crane's characterization of Henry Fleming "threatening" or "dangerous," no reason to think that he would feel compelled by Crane's supposed "volatility" to devise such devious, unnecessary, and uneconomical strategies for mangling his novel. Hitchcock almost certainly talked it over with him when Crane returned to New York from Mexico in the late spring of 1895, and he almost certainly suggested improvements of various kinds in the normal course of his editorial duties. He could have advised Crane, for example, to strike the egregious sentence "It was the soldier's bath," or to suggest that the dull and repetitious cogitations about nature at the end of Chapter seven ruined the effect of the last sentence of the Appleton version of the chapter: "A sad silence was upon the little guarding edifice," a poetic evocation of the ambivalence of nature, which Henry at that crucial instant senses in the immediacy of sight and sound. Yet, as it must be acknowledged, he could have been responsible as well, for distant and unrecoverable reasons, for the regrettable loss of some effective touches in the excised material, the loss, say, of the fine sentences on pastoral vistas and corpses at the beginning of the last chapter, one of which presents this striking image: "The fence, deserted, resumed with it careening posts and disjointed bars, an air of quiet rural depravity"—vintage Crane, as the late R. W. Stallman would have called it. It is odd and regrettable that it was struck out, and not even the Parker-Binder theory can account for it, unless of course "depravity" could be supposed to be one of the finicky Hitchcock's taboo words.

What seems more probable than these envisionings is that Crane struck out the tediously abstract and repetitive philosophical passages in the manuscript when he reviewed it prior to ordering the Bacheller typescript, that he submitted the carbon of this to Hitchcock (as Bowers argues), and that he marked out 1,250 or so words in Chapters sixteen and twenty-five of this typescript copy in New Orleans ("the great number of small corrections" he mentioned in his letter to Hitchcock.)[28] If this is close to what actually happened, it must be that he realized when he re-read his novel in New Orleans in late February or early March (he probably had not read it since he cut the chapter endings and removed Chapter twelve sometime in 1894) that the simple pessimistic certainty of man's diminishment implied in the original ending was no longer in accord with his growing sense, as Pizer expresses it, "of man's capacity to grow in insight and moral courage through experience."[29] He then took out the remaining youthful rantings in Chapter sixteen and altered the final chapter to reflect this growing new conviction.

IV

As I have already noted, Parker and Binder, in conceding the absence of direct, concrete evidence that Hitchcock tampered with the text of The Red Badge of Courage, necessarily rest their case on the cogency of the inferences they draw from "other related circumstances."[30] Thus the alterations Hitchcock ordered in Crane's Maggie:

A Girl of the Streets and Dreiser's *Jennie Gerhardt,* those he proposed
for Crane's *The Third Violet,* and those he actually made himself in
Westcott's *David Harum* suggest almost certainly, they think, that he
"routinely took extreme liberties" with literary texts and "had a habit
of getting his way" with Appleton authors.[31] As Binder puts it, "If
these related consistencies regarding . . . Hitchcock's known editorial
practices with other authors, and his specific dealing with Crane [over
Maggie and *The Third Violet*] did not exist, the cuts in *Red Badge*
would be mysterious indeed."[32]

But there are two serious problems with their arguments from
these parallels. First, they violate the very "related circumstances"
test Binder himself invokes. Second, they overlook or distort historical
and biographical facts and evidence. What Hitchcock did in editing
Maggie, as Pizer argues in addressing the "related circumstances"
test (he does not use the phrase), was quite different from what
Parker and Binder claim he did in editing the war novel. In the case
of *Maggie,* Hitchcock asked the author to remove oaths and profanity—"words that hurt," as Crane referred to them; as Pizer puts
the matter, the editor "was not interested in altering basic contents
or themes of *Maggie;* he was interested rather in achieving a superficial
verbal decorum."[33] But according to the Parker-Binder theory, his
intent in editing the *Red Badge* was to change the meaning of the
book by censoring its presumably offensive philosophical and religious
ideas. It is hard to know what to make of Parker's claim that he first
became aware of Hitchcock's nefarious role in mutilating the war
novel when he "at last realized that the same familiar pattern of
expurgation was working in *Red Badge* that worked a few months
later in *Maggie.*"[34] The patterns are not the same.

Similar objections can be raised against the Parker-Binder charge
that the editor took "extreme liberties" when "he cut, rearranged,
and rewrote the late Edward Noyes Westcott's *David Harum* and
condensed Theodore Dreiser's *Jennie Gerhardt.*" The facts in the
matter of the revision of *David Harum* confirm the literal accuracy
of Binder's statement. Hitchcock did cut out many redundant episodes,
he did shuffle chapters, and he did add transitions to fill gaps left by
these operations; but the circumstances, once again, are remote from
those surrounding his editing of the *Red Badge. David Harum,* the
first and only novel of a Syracuse, New York, banker and businessman,
had been rejected by six publishers before it came to Hitchcock; one
declared it "vulgar," another commented on the hero's "bad English,"
and still another (Walter Hines Page) judged that its extraordinary
length (the submitted manuscript was almost a foot high) made it
unmarketable. In his letter of acceptance Hitchcock advised Westcott
to shift the order of several chapters and to eliminate several more—
about thirty thousand words all told—and the author readily con-

sented.[35] Westcott died six months before the book was published, and Hitchcock finished the pruning task the author had begun.

Binder includes most of these facts in his account, but his language and emphasis hint strongly of certain editorial improprieties; the changes Hitchcock made in the manuscript, mostly after Westcott's death shortly after the book was accepted, Binder writes, "could not have been authorial, but they were extensive, and it is certain that Hitchcock engineered them."[36] Not "authorial"; "extensive" cuts; "engineered"—such are the terms of suggestion. But as the facts show, nothing about the alleged censoring of the "blasphemous" *Red Badge* can be convincingly inferred from the editing of this otherwise unpublishable amateur novel. Again the rule of reasonable inference drawn from "other related circumstances" seems to have been suspended for the convenience of argument.

The issue with Dreiser's diffuse and sprawling *Jennie Gerhardt*, which Hitchcock edited for Harper's in 1911, was also its length, and it is true that Hitchcock insisted, despite Dreiser's protest, on cuts. But many of the dozen or so people who read it in script complained about its length and repetitiveness, including Dreiser's wife, who helped him cut one longer version to a bulky 723 pages. When it was published, it had been cut to 425 pages. Neither theorist offers evidence or even claims that the editor's aim was to suppress offensive ideas, vulgarity, or unseemly realism, as it allegedly was in the editing of the *Red Badge*. Nevertheless, Binder can declare "that there is consistency in Hitchcock's calling for cuts . . . in *Jennie Gerhardt*," and Parker can write that, referring to the drastic pruning, "Comparatively speaking [Hitchcock] was taking few liberties with *The Red Badge of Courage* and, later, with *Maggie*," as though something significant is to be inferred from a "related circumstance."[37]

Quite as irrelevant are their interesting conjectures about concealed significances in Hitchcock's 1896 letter accepting Crane's *The Third Violet* for Appleton publication. Binder, who discovered this important letter, cites it in his essay as further confirmation of Hitchcock's inclinations to alter the texts he edited, as well as, for Parker at least, his characteristic deviousness. Crane wrote this perky little summer resort romance in the fall and winter of 1896 when he was living in rural Hartwood, New York, with his brother Ed and rapidly becoming famous as the author of the *Red Badge*. It is not a strong book, as almost everyone has acknowledged, including Crane himself. "I have finished my new novel—'The Third Violet'—and sent it to Appleton and Co., as per request," he wrote a friend on the same day he mailed the manuscript to Hitchcock, "but I've an idea it won't be accepted. It's pretty rotten work. I used myself up in the accursed 'Red Badge.' "[38] Nevertheless, Hitchcock took it immediately, though he expressed certain doubts:

I wish you were here in the city for I should like to talk over the story with you. I should make any suggestions with the greatest diffidence, for your picture of summer life and contrasting types and your glimpses of studio life are so singularly vivid and clear. I have found myself wishing that Hawker and Hollended [Hollanden] were a trifle less slangy in their conversation, and that the young lady who plays the part of the heroine was a little more distinct. You will pardon these comments I am sure, for I think you know my appreciation of your work and the value I set upon the original flavor of your writing. Sometime, perhaps, we can talk the matter over. It will probably not be desirable to publish before March or April so that there will be plenty of time for the proof reading.[39]

As Pizer notes, it is hard to find editorial impropriety in this, and impossible to see in it a desire "to change the substance and direction of a novel."[40] Binder curiously relegates the letter to a footnote and in his analysis ignores Hitchcock's significant expression of appreciation for the uniqueness of Crane's work and his acknowledgment of proper constraints on his role as an editor ("I should make any suggestions with the greatest diffidence"). Parker, ever suspicious of Hitchcock's suave courtesy, seems certain that this is simply a cover for his characteristic deviousness. The important thing, as Parker sees it, is that "Hitchcock made it clear that he was going to require revisions in *The Third Violet* even though he couched the delay as a desire to allow 'plenty of time for the proof reading.' "[41] Binder sees it as a peremptory summons: "His tone was deferential, but Crane knew the meeting was not to be denied," as Binder thinks Crane acknowledged when a few days later he wrote Nellie Crouse (a young woman with whom he was carrying on a flirtation through the mails): "I have a new novel coming out in the spring and I am . . . obliged to confer with the Appleton's about that."[42]

But there is more to the story than Parker and Binder tell. In context, Crane's complaint to Miss Crouse about being "obliged" to confer with Appleton's reveals more about his relationship (or hoped-for relationship) with Miss Crouse than with his Appleton editor. For he also noted in the same passage that he was "obliged" to confer with the publisher S. S. McClure, who was "having one of his fits of desire to have me write for him," and confessed that he was "dejected" over the impending inconvenience of a trip to the city.[43] But these are concealed boasts that seem to have little to do with either Hitchcock or McClure; they are more like courtship maneuvers, tactics of a clever young writer trying to impress an intrigued young woman with weary allusions to his growing literary fame and the consequent tedium of having to confer with eager editors and anxious publishers.

The rest of the story also suggests that Crane was far more

independent in his dealings with Hitchcock than Parker and Binder acknowledge. If the editor intended his letter as a polite notice to report for instructions for revising *The Third Violet*, "a meeting which could not be denied," as Binder says, then the author's response must have disappointed him. For Crane did indeed deny it. He was in New York the day after he wrote Miss Crouse and was there for two weeks. He consulted with McClure about writing war stories for *The Little Regiment* and made a trip to Virginia to inspect the battlefield at Fredericksburg. But he did not call on Hitchcock. As he explained in a letter of oblique apology two days after he returned to Hartwood, he had discovered in New York that his burgeoning celebrity made certain unpleasant demands on his privacy, and he had fled the city in confusion:

> I fear that when I meet you again I shall feel abashed. As a matter of truth, New York has so completely muddled me on this last visit that I shant venture again very soon. I had grown used to being called a damned ass but this sudden new admiration of my friends has made a gibbering idiot of me. I shall stick to my hills.

So much for "a meeting which could not be denied." Actually it was Crane, not Hitchcock, who made the rules for handling his new novel, as the next paragraph of his letter shows:

> I think it is as well to go ahead with The Third Violet. People may just as well discover now that the high dramatic key of The Red Badge cannot be sustained. . . . The Third Violet is a quiet little story but then it is serious work and I should say let it go.[44]

This does not sound much like an humble, powerless author trying to conciliate an overbearing and intrusive editor. It is possible, as Fredson Bowers has suggested, that Hitchcock did hope to get Crane to do "a structural and narrative reworking, and perhaps one of tone," but differences between the McClure Syndicate text of the novel, which ran as a serial in several newspapers in late 1896, and the Appleton text show that he "did nothing about the novel [for book publication] except to prune and vary its style."[45] It seems almost certain that Parker and Binder are mistaken in their reading of Hitchcock's letter as an attempt to require revision in *The Third Violet*, but even if they are right, his attempt obviously failed.

V

The argument that Crane surrendered to demands for an expurgated *Red Badge* involves as a matter of course an interpretation of Crane's character and motives. If Hitchcock was the savvy, entrepreneurial editor bent on wringing maximum profits out of the *Red*

Badge, then Crane was the ambitious, gifted but inexperienced young artist willing to sacrifice the integrity of his work to the demands of the marketplace in order to get it before the public. The argument is that in 1895, when Hitchcock came into his life, he was too desperate—financially, emotionally, and creatively—to refuse his editorial intrusions. Having "no celebrity and no power," as Binder writes, "he was apparently willing to abide by extensive suggestions for revision. . . Editorial requests, with Crane taking only a limited interest in carrying them out, are the only explanation for the kinds of cuts that were made in the story."[46] Parker writes: "Crane was a kid and he wanted the book published. He really messed it up. . . My feeling is pretty strong . . . that after Garland criticized the MS [of the *Red Badge*] Crane probably yielded halfheartedly to one or another advisor, gradually losing his sense of the work as an aesthetic unity and relinquishing his practical control of it in order to get it into print, however maimed."[47]

Once again the argument invokes the principle of inference from a "related circumstance," Crane's alleged expurgation of his book of poems, the 1895 *Black Riders,* on orders of his publishers, Copeland and Day. In this case, however, unlike the cases of *David Harum, Jennie Gerhardt,* and *The Third Violet,* there is indeed a "related circumstance." Crane's surrender to Hitchcock in the matter of the *Red Badge* is anticipated and made plausible, Parker and Binder argue, by the fact that he gave in to Copeland and Day's demand that he cancel a number of poems about God, nature, and "the powers of fate," presumably for the same reasons the Appleton editor demanded expurgations of similar materials in the war novel.

Crane, or one of his friends, submitted the poems in the spring of 1894, and Copeland and Day held them for several months, apparently uneasy about a considerable number of unorthodox religious and philosophical themes, including several on the idea that nature is inherently malevolent and God is unjust or malicious or cruelly indifferent. In response to Crane's prodding, they finally offered to publish the poems, but only if the poet would agree to omitting a number of the most objectionable of the verses, which they apparently specified in a long list (the letter and list are lost). Crane objected vigorously:

> We disagree on a multitude of points. In the first place I should absolutely refuse to have my poems printed without many of those which you just as absolutely mark "No." It seems to me that you cut all the ethical sense out of the book. All the anarchy, perhaps. It is the anarchy which I particularly insist upon. From the poems which you keep you could produce what might be termed "a nice little volume of verse by Stephen Crane," but for me there would be no satisfaction. The ones which refer to God, I believe you

condemn altogether. I am obliged to have them in when my book is printed. There are some which I believe unworthy of print. These I here with enclose. As for the others, I cannot give them up—in the book.

In the second matter, you wish I would write a few score more. It is utterly impossible to me. We would be obliged to come to an agreement upon those that are written.

If my position is impossible to you, I would not be offended at the sending of all the retained lines to the enclosed address.[48]

The publisher's response to this is also lost (another of a myriad of examples of how the absence of documents in Crane's history opens wide spaces for conjecture and hypothesis), but we know from Crane's reply that they agreed to publication—apparently on Crane's terms. He accepted their offer of ten percent of the sales, gave them a title, "The Black Riders and other lines," and closed with an intriguing sentence: "I am indebted to you for your tolerance of my literary prejudices."[49] But Copeland and Day balked again. Three weeks later they sent him a list of seven poems that they strongly advised omitting from the volume and cited three of the seven that they would refuse to publish under any circumstances. If Crane responded to these new demands, no letter exists to prove it, but several days later he sent the publishers a one-sentence note: "Dear sirs: I enclose copy of title poem," referring to a revision of the version the publishers already had in hand, "Black riders rode forth."[50] Curiously, none of the seven poems listed as objectionable appeared in the book, though Crane could have assured their inclusion by simply requesting it.

Parker and Binder take this sequence of events to mean that Crane simply surrendered. Despite "the staunchness of his protest," Binder writes, "he must have found that the publisher could be equally firm, for he compromised concerning the selection for *Black Riders,* apparently conceding the final say to the editors."[51] "Crane capitulated," Parker writes. "He did not even negotiate for the inclusion of the four poems that Copeland and Day had not absolutely refused to publish. He wanted to keep the ethical sense and the anarchy, but he wanted, all forgivably, to be in print."[52]

But did he surrender? Did he sacrifice "ethical sense and anarchy"? What seems more plausible is that he won. Crane's tough reply to Copeland and Day's first letter seems to suggest that the list of poems they found objectionable was long, almost certainly longer than the seven named in their second list (Crane refers to "many of those which you just as absolutely mark 'No.' "). What seems to confirm this is the fact that a great many of the kind of poems Crane insisted on—poems about God, poems celebrating "anarchy" and "ethical sense," appear in *The Black Riders.* The publishers, I suggest, yielded to Crane's demands, as evidenced by his

expression of appreciation for their "tolerance" of his "literary prejudices." At least a dozen of these rescued poems are explicitly about
God, and several others refer to Him indirectly. In a few He appears
as the benign and loving God of the hymn book, but in poem after
poem He appears as vicious, traitorous, unjust, a raging bully; or,
alternately, indifferent and careless; or, in one poem, dead. Several
turn on the idea that His existence or nonexistence is unknowable.
Some express the speaker's rebellion and rejection, even hatred of
Him. Nature appears in some as universally malevolent, as in the
title poem itself, "Black riders came from the sea." There are a
number implying "ethical anarchy," if Crane meant by this phrase
scornful, ironic rejection of conventional notions of piety and virtue.

Joseph Katz, who edited the poems, believes like Parker and
Binder that the publishers wanted to "cut all the ethical sense out
of the book," and again like Parker and Binder sees the one-sentence
response to the publishers' second list "as evidently a curt note of
capitulation."[53] But, as he observes correctly, at least two of the four
poems in the final list the publishers offered to print (which Crane
did not bother to rescue) "would have taken on connotations of
blasphemy" in the overall context of the book, which suggests that
Crane's earlier protest was almost totally effective. In the end, the
publisher lifted its interdiction on all but three of the poems originally
listed for expurgation. We will probably never know why Crane didn't
bother to ask for the inclusion of the four the publisher reluctantly
agreed to include. But it is clear, as Katz says, that "their omission
did not change the character of the book. Undoubtedly, Crane's hasty
addition of 'Black riders came from the sea,' submitted after his
capitulation, assured that."[54]

In view of all this, it is impossible to make sense of Parker's
claim that The Black Riders was "shamefully expurgated," that Crane
"abjectly" capitulated to censorship, that "all the 'ethical sense' and
'anarchy' had been purged from the book." And his claim that Crane
pretended to be "ecstatic" about it after it was published in an
unconscious attempt to avoid compounding the "shame" and "dishonor" of his surrender seems to be mere fantasy.[55]

VI

In arguing their theory of the reconstituted text of the Red Badge,
Parker and Binder have made a valuable contribution to Crane studies
by calling attention to questions in the history of the novel's composition, revision, and publication that have been hanging unanswered
for decades. The manuscript versions—the fragmentary preliminary
draft and the trimmed-down final draft—have been casually cited,
commented on, and speculated about since the early fifties, when

John T. Winterich and R. W. Stallman issued editions of the novel with selected passages from them bracketed in the text or cited in footnotes. But not until Binder published his careful reconstruction of the manuscripts in 1979 were scholars actually able to see it in its original form, essentially the form Crane gave it in his first round of revisions in the spring of 1894. It is a fascinating book in this early form, invaluable for what it shows about the development of Crane's mind and art as he refined the theme and ruthlessly excised the windy and repetitive "adolescent ontological heroics," as Parker aptly describes them. Readers of the *Red Badge*, even those "reluctant, skeptical souls" Parker chides for refusing to acknowledge the manuscript version as representative of Crane's final intention—or, rather, what the theorists think should have been his final intention—are indebted to them for making it available.

But it is not likely that its authority will ever be generally accepted. Binder's claim that unwarranted editorial intrusiveness is the only way the massive deletions can be accounted for is of course highly partisan. Pizer's explanation for the cutting of the interior monologues as a sharpening of the ambivalence of Henry's moral development, an ambivalence implicit in the fundamental structure of the novel, is far more plausible than the Parker-Binder "blasphemy" theory. Domeraski speaks for many critics when she explains that Crane removed the interior monologues because he found them too abstract, verbose, and repetitious. Even those writers who nominally declare allegiance to the Binder text often advance critical ideas that the narrowing and unhistorical theory cannot accommodate. The "maimed" text theory assumes, for example, that the superior power of the early version owes much to the clarity of Henry's characterization, where he appears finally as indisputably unredeemed. Howard C. Horsford, who identifies with the Parker-Binder school of thought, notes nevertheless that in "Crane's representation Fleming is not so much a conventionally developed character, with a stable and distinct central being, as a welter of conflicting subjective sensations," a view of Crane's art closer to Pizer than to Parker or Binder. Horsford, unlike the theorists who argue that the "incoherent" Appleton text, closely considered, is essentially uninterpretable, thinks that Crane's ironic vision is clear enough, "whether one accepts the originally published version or the manuscript as the more nearly authoritative," and agrees with Domeraski (and others) that "turgid writing suggests reasons why he may have excised the [abstract philosophical] passages."[56]

It may be that the inadequacy we feel in the Parker-Binder rationale is its bedrock assumption that the ultimate value of the novel is its supposedly radical moral vision. It insists that the ethical implications of the state of Henry's mind at the end of the book is what matters most of all for Crane's art. It matters, of course, but not so much perhaps as academic criticism (including my own) has often supposed. Crane's earliest critics, men like Conrad, H. G. Wells, Harold Frederic, Edward Garnett, and Ford Madox Ford, who read the novel within weeks of its English publication in 1896 and recognized it at once as a pivotal book in the history of modern literature, hardly mention plot or characterization or ethical themes. Conrad and Garnett, much as they admired Crane's radical new method, nevertheless felt its "natural limitation," as Garnett wrote—its inability to probe as deeply as some into "rich depths of consciousness that cannot be more than hinted at by the surface." Crane's genius was for capturing the poignant feeling of the instability and uncertainty of things as suggested ambivalently in the fleeting apprehension of surfaces. Garnett continues: "in a few swift strokes he gives us an amazing insight . . . and he does it all straight from the surface; a few oaths, a genius for slang, an exquisite and unique faculty of exposing an individual scene by an odd simile, a power of interpreting a face or an action, a keen realizing of the primitive emotions—that is Mr. Crane's talent."[57] This is essentially the point Andrew Delbanco (another critic who acknowledges the authority of the Binder edition) makes when he observes that what is truly radical in Crane is his power to replicate "the pure experience of the eye" without recourse to the traditional seeing, and his consistent refusal "to provide a conceptual context for purely sensory experience. . . . In Crane's fictive world, the senses admit smell and color and shape—fractional impressions from which one can only guess at the meaning of the whole—or indeed, whether there is any meaning to the whole at all."[58]

The Parker-Binder theory cannot accommodate such ideas; it insists on the primary importance of "conceptual contexts," on ethical and psychological coherency, a sense of rounded-out completion— Henry is either reformed or he is not. The theory, which focuses largely on forces in the contemporary environment—various Victorian literary inhibitions—cannot account for Crane's 1895 expurgations as signs of his burgeoning distrust of simplistic assumptions about human character and of his rapidly growing awareness of the enormous expressive power of "fractional impressions." Its focus misses entirely those qualities in his writing that most interest us, and obscures, in its insistence that Crane's art reached its maturity in the 1894 manuscript version of his novel, a crucial moment in the history of his discovery of his unique powers. The value of the Binder edition as evidence for this moment is incalculable—however doubtful the theory that brought it into existence.

Notes

1. Hershel Parker reviews the history of the edition in his "Aesthetic Implications of Authorial Excisions: Examples from Nathaniel Hawthorne, Mark Twain, and Stephen Crane," *Editing Nineteenth Century Fiction*, ed. Jane Millgate (Boston: Garland, 1978), 99–119.

2. *"The Red Badge of Courage* Nobody Knows," *Studies in the Novel*, 10 (1978): 9–47.

3. The special Crane issue of *Studies in the Novel* (see note 2 above) includes in addition to Binder's essay several others on Crane's texts and related topics: Steven Mailloux, *"The Red Badge of Courage* and Interpretative Conventions: Critical Response to a Maimed Text," 48–63; Parker (with Brian Higgins), "Maggie's 'Last Night': Authorial Design and Editorial Patching," 64–75; David J. Nordloh, "On Crane Now Edited: The University of Virginia Edition of *The Works of Stephen Crane*," 103–19.

4. Lee Clark Mitchell, "Introduction," *New Essays on The Red Badge of Courage*, ed. Lee Clark Mitchell (New York: Cambridge University Press, 1986), 16.

5. Stanley Wertheim and Paul Sorrentino, *The Correspondence of Stephen Crane*, 2 Vols. (New York: Columbia University Press, 1988), I, 173.

6. Edwin H. Cady, *Stephen Crane*, rev. ed. (Boston: Twayne Publishers, 1980), 25.

7. "A Note on the Text," *The Red Badge of Courage* (New York: Bantam Books, 1983), 133–34.

8. " '*The Red Badge of Courage* Nobody Knows': A Brief Rejoinder," *Studies in the Novel*, 11 (1979): 77–81.

9. *"The Red Badge of Courage:* Text, Theme, and Form," *South Atlantic Quarterly*, 84 (1985): 311.

10. *Flawed Texts and Verbal Icons: Literary Authority in American Fiction* (Evanston, Ill.: Northwestern University Press, 1984), 158.

11. *"The Red Badge of Courage* Nobody Knows," in *The Red Badge of Courage*, by Stephen Crane, ed. Binder (New York: Avon Books, 1982), 126, 129.

12. "Getting Used to the 'Original Form' of *The Red of Courage*," in *New Essays*, 35.

13. "Getting Used to the 'Original Form,' " 26.

14. *"The Red Badge of Courage* Nobody Knows," 130–31.

15. The historical information about Appleton and Company is from Gerard R. Wolfe, *The House of Appleton* (Metuchen, N.J.: Scarecrow Press, 1981), 42–49.

16. Wolfe, 192.

17. *"The Red of Courage* Nobody Knows," 130.

18. Leo Tolstoi, *Sebastopol.* Introduction by W. D. Howells (New York: Harper & Brothers, 1887), 10. In an article in the special Crane issue of *Studies in the Novel*, which preceded the publication of Binder's text (see note 3 above), Steven Mailloux, also Parker's former student, undertakes to explain how the "maimed" *Red Badge* could achieve the status of a classic. This happened, according to Mailloux, because readers, conditioned by the conventional nineteenth-century realistic war novel to expect a reassuring moral growth in the hero, naturally gave this interpretation to the ambiguous Appleton ending. The actual incoherence caused by the "maiming" was not discovered until close-reading New Critics discovered it in the mid-forties. Mailloux cites Tolstoy's *Sebastopol* as one of the classic realistic war novels that helped establish the conventional idea that war is morally educative (others are the war novels of Zola, Stendhal, and De Vigny). But *Sebastopol*, which Crane drew on heavily for style and

ideas, clearly does not show anyone achieving moral maturity. As J. C. Levenson notes, it is "a book which was unique in its being without a hero. Heroic acts were possible and men might sometime be heroic, but the consistent pursuit of great purpose, such as traditionally defines heroism, is allowed to none of the characters." (*The Red Badge of Courage: An Episode of the American Civil War*, ed. Fredson Bowers, Volume II of The University of Virginia Edition of *The Works of Stephen Crane* (Charlottesville: University Press of Virginia, 1975), lxiv.) Like Henry, the soldiers Mikhaloff, Kalouguine, and Volodnia are driven in war by fear, vanity, and delusions of heroic grandeur, and all move through the world of death and destruction of Sebastopol in the critical light of Tolstoy's irony. Their brooding fears, daydreams of military greatness, and cruel selfishness, we can hardly doubt, are the chief sources of the psychology of Henry Fleming. Like Crane's hero in the Appleton version, Tolstoy's characters are in the end morally ambivalent:

> Where is the traitor? Where is the hero? All are good and all are bad. It is not Kalouguine with his brilliant courage, his gentlemanly bravado, and his vanity—the chief motive power of all his actions; it is not Praskoukine, an inoffensive cipher, although he fell on the battlefield for his faith, his ruler, and his country; nor timid Mikhaloff; nor Presth, that child with no conviction and no moral sense, who can pass for traitors or for heroes. (121–22)

This is the complex psychology, as Pizer argues, that Crane was aiming for in his revision. The manuscript version presents a simpler Henry—still all bad in the end, or even worse, as Parker and Binder suggest; but in the Appleton he is more like a Tolstoy character, both good and bad.

19. "Getting Used to the 'Original Form,' " 38, 39.

20. "Donald Pizer, Ripley Hitchcock, and *The Red Badge of Courage*," *Studies in the Novel*, 11 (1979): 218.

21. "Getting Used to the 'Original Form,' " 35.

22. "Getting Used to the 'Original Form,' " 36–37.

23. Crane to Hitchcock, [early February 1895], *Correspondence*, 97.

24. Although Bowers suggests that Crane had the Bacheller typescript made in the fall of 1895, shortly before the novel appeared in the cut newspaper form, no one actually knows for certain when he made these key alterations. Crane revised the book after Garland read it in early April, and it may have been then, as Pizer thinks likely, that he cut the chapter endings and removed Chapter twelve. Unless more evidence turns up, we will never know exactly when he made these cuts, but the important point for the present argument is that he almost certainly made them before Hitchcock ever saw the novel.

25. "Getting Used to the 'Original Form,' " 37.

26. Crane to Hitchcock, March 8, 1895, *Correspondence*, 100.

27. "Getting Used to the 'Original Form,' " 37.

28. In his essay, pp. 168–69, Binder specifically challenges this point, which he finds strongly implied in Bowers's statement that in New Orleans Crane cut passages containing "the introspective examination of the youth's states of mind," and that the deletion of these 1,250 or so words "had an important effect on the shape of the latter part of the book." But Binder says it is "impossible to think that Crane drastically and illogically changed a novel that had just been accepted and then referred to the changes as "small corrections." The key terms in Binder's response are obviously interpretive. What Crane might have meant by "small" we can only guess, but they were small in comparison with the much larger excisions of this kind he made earlier.

Nor is it beyond belief that Crane could have thought of these abstract and inert representations of Henry's thought—already brilliantly evoked, as Domeraski says, "in telling images elsewhere"—as "small corrections."

29. "Text, Theme, Form," 313.

30. Henry Binder, "Donald Pizer, Ripley Hitchcock, and *The Red Badge of Courage*," 216–23.

31. "Getting Used to the 'Original Form,' " 38.

32. "Donald Pizer, Ripley Hitchcock, and *The Red Badge of Courage*, 219.

33. " '*The Red Badge of Courage* Nobody Knows': A Brief Rejoinder," 78.

34. "Aesthetic Implications of Authorial Excisions," in *Editing Nineteenth Century Fiction*, 112.

35. Gerard R. Wolfe, *The House of Appleton*, 281.

36. "*The Red Badge of Courage* Nobody Knows," 126.

37. "Getting Used to the 'Original Form,' " 39.

38. Crane to Curtis Brown, December 31, 1896 [for 1895], *Correspondence*, 161.

39. Hitchcock to Crane, January 6, 1896, *Correspondence*, 174.

40. "A Brief Rejoinder," 79.

41. "Getting Used to the 'Original Form,' " 38–39. Parker consistently attributes devious motives for delays in publication.

42. "*The Red Badge of Courage* Nobody Knows," 138.

43. Crane to Nellie Crouse, January 12, 1896, *Correspondence*, 181. A passage in a similar vein in another letter to Crouse is taken as evidence that Crane disliked Hitchcock, a notion that underlies Parker's theory that their relationship was marked by suspicion and hostility. This idea originated with R. W. Stallman. Referring to a passing remark in another letter to Nellie Crouse in which Crane humorously characterizes Hitchcock as somewhat stuffy in comparison with a good fellow from Buffalo also named Hitchcock (Crane to Crouse, January 6 [1896], *Correspondence*, 171), Stallman comments, "Though Ripley Hitchcock may not have known it, Crane disliked him." (R. W. Stallman, "Stephen Crane's Letters to Ripley Hitchcock," *Bulletin of The New York Public Library*, 60 (1956): 320.) Stallman does not say, however, that Crane resented him for expurgating the *Red Badge*, as Parker and Binder argue. The notion, incidentally, is accepted by the editors of the *Correspondence*, who also take Crane's remark as evidence of his "resentment" of the editor for his alleged editorial interference (173). But all this is extremely doubtful. Crane apparently trusted and admired Hitchcock, as attested by the fact that later that year he named him, along with his "literary fathers" Howells and Garland, as one of his literary executors (see Crane to William Howe Crane, November 29, 1896, *Correspondence*, 265).

44. Crane to Hitchcock, January 27, [1896], *Correspondence*, 191.

45. Stephen Crane, *The Third Violet*, ed. Fredson Bowers, Vol. III of the University of Virginia Edition of *The Works of Stephen Crane* (Charlottesville: The University Press of Virginia, 1975), 333.

46. "*The Red Badge of Courage* Nobody Knows," 124.

47. *Flawed Texts*, 158.

48. Crane to Copeland and Day, September 9 [1894], *Correspondence*, 73–74.

49. Crane to Copeland and Day, September 27, 1894, *Correspondence*, 74–75.

50. Crane to Copeland and Day, October 30, 1894, *Correspondence*, 77.

51. "*The Red Badge of Courage* Nobody Knows," 136.

52. "Getting Used to the 'Original Form,' " 34.

53. *The Poems of Stephen Crane,* ed. Joseph Katz (New York: Cooper Square Publishers, 1971), xxviii.

54. Katz, xxxi. Katz apparently thinks the omission of the two poems, which would have "taken on connotations of blasphemy" in context, is evidence of "capitulation" and that the "hasty addition" of the title poem was all-important in preserving the character of the book. But there are many other such poems in the published volume. Crane's six-word note accompanying this last-minute submission ("Dear sirs: I enclose copy of title poem") probably appears to be a "curt note of capitulation" only because his reply to the publisher's letter listing the seven poems is missing. In his December 15 letter to Copeland and Day Crane stated that he had "answered each of the letters sent to me," and the publisher's letter listing the seven doubtful poems specifically requests a response. It seems unlikely that his "curt" note is an expression of angry capitulation, since negotiations over the contents of the book were probably concluded in a missing letter. In any case, Crane had no reason to be annoyed. The radical poems in the published book prove that Copeland and Day failed in their attempt to "cut out all the ethical sense" and "anarchy."

55. "Getting Used to the 'Original Form,' " 37–38.

56. Howard C. Horsford, "He Was a Man," in *New Essays,* 110, 114.

57. "Mr. Stephen Crane: An Appreciation," *The Academy* [London], 55 (1898): 483–84; reprinted in *Stephen Crane's Career: Perspectives and Evaluations,* ed. Thomas A. Gullason (New York: New York University Press, 1972), 139–41.

58. "The American Stephen Crane: The Context of *The Red Badge of Courage,,"* in *New Essays,* 52–53.

INDEX